Texts in Philosophy
Volume 18

Contemporary Problems of Epistemology in the Light of Phenomenology
Temporal Consciousness and the Limits of Formal Theories

Volume 8
Bruno di Finetti: Radical Probabilist
Maria Carla Galavotti, ed.

Volume 9
Language, Knowledge, and Metaphysics. Proceedings of the First SIFA Graduate Conference
Massimiliano Carrara and Vittorio Morato eds.

Volume 10
The Socratic Tradition. Questioning as Philosophy and as Method
Matti Sintonen, ed.

Volume 11
PhiMSAMP. Philosophy of Mathematics: Sociological Aspects and Mathematical Practice
Benedikt Löwe and Thomas Müller, eds.

Volume 12
Philosophical Perspectives on Mathematical Practice
Bart Van Kerkhove, Jonas De Vuyst and Jean Paul Van Bendegem, eds.

Volume 13
Beyond Description: Naturalism and Normativity
Marcin Miłkowski and Konrad Talmont-Kaminski, eds.

Volume 14
Corroborations and Criticisms. Forays with the Philosophy of Karl Popper
Ivor Grattan-Guinness

Volume 15
Knowledge, Value, Evolution.
Tomáš Hříbek and Juraj Hvorecký, eds.

Volume 16
Hao Wang. Logician and Philosopher
Charles Parsons and Montgomery Link, eds.

Volume 17
Mimesis: Metaphysics, Cognition, Pragmatics
Gregory Currie, Petr Koťátko, Martin Pokorný

Volume 18
Contemporary Problems of Epistemology in the Light of Phenomenology. Temporal Consciousness and the Limits of Formal Theories
Stathis Livadas

Texts in Philosophy Series Editors
Vincent F. Hendriks
John Symons
Dov Gabbay

vincent@hum.ku.dk
jsymons@utep.edu
dov.gabbay@kcl.ac.uk

Contemporary Problems of Epistemology in the Light of Phenomenology

Temporal Consciousness and the Limits of Formal Theories

Stathis Livadas

© Individual author and College Publications 2012.
All rights reserved.

ISBN 978-1-84890-082-0

College Publications
Scientific Director: Dov Gabbay
Managing Director: Jane Spurr
Department of Computer Science
King's College London, Strand, London WC2R 2LS, UK

http://www.collegepublications.co.uk

Original cover design by orchid creative   www.orchidcreative.co.uk

Printed by Lightning Source, Milton Keynes, UK

All rights reserved. No part of this publication may be reproduced, stored in a retrieval system or transmitted in any form, or by any means, electronic, mechanical, photocopying, recording or otherwise without prior permission, in writing, from the publisher.

To my sons Haris and Panos
with affection and hope.

Contents

Preface ix

Why Phenomenological Analysis is Relevant with
    Contemporary Epistemological Edifice? 1

Mathematical and Phenomenological
    Continuity-Indiscernibility 15

The Phenomenological Roots of Nonstandard
    Mathematics 29

A Phenomenological Analysis of Observation 51

The Expressional Limits of Formal Language in the
    Notion of Quantum Observation 69

The Transcendence of Time in the Epistemology of
    Observation from a Phenomenological Standpoint 93

Leap from the Ego of Temporal Consciousness to the
    Phenomenology of Mathematical Continuum 115

Impredicativity of Continuum in Phenomenology
    and in non-Cantorian Theories 139

The Continuum Question in Mathematical
    Foundations. A Phenomenological Review 155

Are Mathematical Theories Reducible to Non-analytic
    Foundations? 177

The Notion of Process in Nonstandard Theory and in
    Whiteheadian Metaphysics 205

Is there a Link Between the Continental Ego and the
    Temporality of the Epistemic Domain? 231

Preface

The present work comprises a series of articles most of which have already appeared in numerous journals or (in the case of the first chapter) presented as a thematic lecture in a philosophy seminar. Some have been substantially reedited and updated for this book, while two other articles appear for the first time. These are the book chapters *The Notion of Process in Nonstandard Theory and in Whiteheadian Metaphysics* and *Is There a Link between the Continental Ego and the Temporality of the Epistemic Domain?*; the latter one has been especially written for the present book. A more or less sufficient bibliography will be found in the end of each chapter.

The main topic presented here is, roughly spoken, the relevance of phenomenological analysis, as mainly presented in original Husserlian texts, with fundamental questions of contemporary epistemology meant as a philosophy of science. In this respect, certain developments of current research in the fields of logic and the foundations of mathematics and also of theoretical quantum mechanics are taken into account, while giving also due attention to recent research work standing, for instance, in the interface of phenomenology and the philosophy of mathematics. It must be noted that, in the opinion of the author, the overall non-conventional theoretical approach does not loose any of the vigor of its argumentation in view of the latest news of the discovery of a Higgs-like particle, something that obviously has deep theoretical repercussions, announced by CERN scientists on July 4, 2012. Rather, a phenomenologically motivated approach towards key epistemological issues, in clear distinction to the conventional "static" ontological approach, seems to be more apt in apprehending the inaccessible "residuum" left over in the process of objectification of the world of phenomena originally presented to an embodied time-constituting consciousness. This said, the present work could better be described as a phenomenologically based interpretation of certain objects/state-of-affairs of the epistemic domain, than a vindication of one or the other scholarly position on what Husserl really believed concerning the relation of phenomenology with the other, mainly positive, sciences.

The author wishes to express here his gratitude to the College Publications for their lofty goal of providing an alternative way of publishing original research and especially to the managing editor M. Jane Spurr for her helpful contribution in the preparation of the book. Also thanks are due to Dr. Claire Ortiz-Hill for her suggestion and encouraging attitude.

St. Livadas

Why Phenomenological Analysis is Relevant with Contemporary Epistemological Edifice?[0]

STATHIS LIVADAS

1 Introduction

As it is generally accepted, phenomenological philosophy is on the one hand a continuation, in a certain sense, of classical continental philosophy, mainly in relation to the various nuances of subjective idealism starting from the German idealist tradition of 18th-19th century (Kant, Hegel, Fichte, Schelling) and on the other hand, a philosophy (in the sense of a descriptive *a priori* science as Husserl wanted it) open to developments in the broader epistemological edifice of 19th and 20th centuries, for instance, regarding F. Brentano's and H. Lotze's theories pointing to a psychologistic reductionism or yet G. Frege's logical reductionism concerning mathematical foundations. In view of the influence of the epistemological evolution, going as far back as the Galilean tradition, one may easily refer to Husserl's late well-known work on the crisis of European sciences and the role of phenomenology (*Die Krisis der Europäischen Wissenschaften und die Transzendentale Phänomenologie*, [4]). Given that the knowledge field of phenomenology is associated with that of epistemology, in the sense that the objects of the latter taken as by-products of a constitutional process referring to the perceptual mechanisms of a subject, can be taken as phenomenological objects, this review will attempt to present in a concise manner a phenomenologically oriented interpretation of certain key epistemological questions.

It is broadly accepted that main parts of Husserl's philosophical work are the phenomenological studies of experience, judgement and logical apophantics (e.g., in *Logische Untersuchungen* and *Erfahrung und Urteil*), as well as the descriptive *a priori* analysis of temporal consciousness in his treatise *Zur Phänomenologie des inneren Zeitbewusseins*, ([5]). The phenomenological interpretation in a broad sense, distinguishes itself from psychologistic interpretations of logical laws in that accepting as a foundation the (intentional) experience grounding the knowledge *in rem*, it introduces, however, concerning the logical part a special *a priori* relation that we bear with things themselves,

---

[0]The main body of this article was presented as a lecture on June 2, 2011, in the Cultural Center of the Municipality of Athens, Greece, in the annual cycle of seminars organized by the Greek Philosophical Society.

which is not a physical interaction though our sensitive organs. More on this special kind relation that we bear with the objects of our physical or mental experience, I will more thoroughly develop in the next.

It is remarkable that E. Husserl completed his doctorate thesis in mathematics at the University of Berlin under the guidance of the great mathematician Karl Weierstrass, continued to do research in mathematics for several years and had ample knowledge of the developments in the mathematical foundations and set theory through his exchanges with G. Cantor, G. Frege and D. Hilbert. He had also the opportunity to indulge in fruitful discussions with the founder of the intuitionistic theory in mathematics L.E.J. Brouwer, during his visit to Amsterdam in 1912. It is indicative that in the earlier phase of Husserl's philosophical work belong the Philosophy of Arithmetic (*Philosophie der Arithmetik*, [6]) and his Studies on Arithmetic and Geometry (*Studien zur Arithmetik und Geometrie*, [8]), something that clearly demonstrates the firm mathematical background of the founder of phenomenology. Of course, Husserl's strong mathematical qualifications are not by themselves a vindication of the relevance of phenomenological philosophy with pure logic, the foundations of mathematics and epistemology in general. What is then, that which makes phenomenological analysis relevant with fundamental open questions of contemporary epistemology?

Before dealing with these questions, I do not find pointless to note that the relation between phenomenological philosophy and epistemology is, in the last decades at least, object of a growing and fruitful research generating a growing number number of research papers, books, proceedings of conferences, etc.

Here are some indicative titles: R. Tieszen, ' Phenomenology, Logic and the Philosophy of Mathematics' [19], R. Tragesser, 'Phenomenology and Logic' [20], R. Tragesser, 'Husserl and Realism in Logic and Mathematics' [21], M. van Atten *et al*, ' The Phenomenology and Mathematics of the Intuitive Continuum' [22], F. Lurcat, ' Understanding Quantum Mechanics with Bohr and Husserl' [15], S. French, ' A phenomenological solution to the measurement problem? Husserl and the foundations of quantum mechanics' [1], and S. Livadas, ' Impredicativity of Continuum in Phenomenology and in non-Cantorian theories' [13].

In view of a more thorough treatment of phenomenological analysis as a systematic interpretational tool of contemporary epistemology, I start with a review of some key epistemological questions of our time taking especially into account some current developments of epistemology.

2   A review of the evolution of the epistemological edifice

We have already passed over the first decade of the 21st century and the question of an interpretation of scientific 'truth' and of its limits is ever opportune given the galloping pace of the development of digital and optic technologies, of nanotechnology, of physical and cosmological cutting-edge theories, etc. Yet, certain questions of 'depth' are still pending, if they are not posited already in a quite vague epistemological context: is there a need of a metaphysical entity, creator of at least the conceivable universe? If there is a meaningful answer to this supposedly meaningful question, it can be a negative one if we cling, for example, to the views of S. Hawking and L. Mlodinow as exposed in their book *The Grand Design*, ([3]).

Why should there be something instead of nothing? Is there a sufficient reason to search for the verification of existence of the elusive Higgs particle, which is expected, through the Higgs field, to give an epistemic foundation to the incompatibility of observations between the macroscopic and the quantum level of reality? Is it reasonable to expect that the pharaonic experimental installation of the Large Hadronic Collider of CERN in Geneva will indeed trace this elusive subatomic particle? Is the Bing Bang theory a complete theory for the universe, in the sense that it can theoretically withstand any new results (taken that it is already strongly doubted as interpretationally sufficient), or is it just a theoretical model describing successfully up to a certain point the current empirical-epistemological paradigm? What are the bounds of human observational capacity with regard to the microcosm and how they are defined within the context of the preparation and performance of a quantum measurement? Are quantum objects ontologically self-standing, that is, are they self-hypostasized entities or are they co-constituted in actuality within an observer's temporal consciousness in the sense that consciousness constitutes a quantum object or state-of-affairs by constituting itself?

All these questions have been brought about in a prevalent way for over a century ago, when the positive sciences in a striking advance motivated by the evolution of science and technique after the first industrial revolution of the 19th century - a typical case of crisis of the epistemological paradigm in the sense of T. Kuhn - were led through a process of theoretical questioning to new radical orientations. It was the age of the shaping of quantum theory through the description of black body radiation by M. Planck, in the beginning of 20th century, the age of introduction of special relativity and a decade later of general relativity by A. Einstein. It was the age of uncertainties over established truths in experimental science concerning e.g. the the experimental refutation by Michelson & Morley of the belief in the existence of ether as a standard physical medium, or over established truths in logic and the foundations of mathematics, concerning in particular the so-called crisis of the foundations of mathematics and the initial attempt at their systematic and consistent foundation through the system of *Principia Mathematica* of B. Russell and A.N. Whitehead ([18]).

These radical shake-ups in the classical epistemological edifice which had given, however, theories of such breadth as the Newtonian mechanics, the electromagnetic theory of R. Maxwell, the classical mathematical analysis and the variation calculus of Cauchy-Lagrange, etc., could not but give a new content to the historically charged relation of science with philosophy and analytic logic. All the more so, as the emancipation of western philosophy from older idealistic prejudices had gradually evolved, concerning at least the dialectical materialism of K. Marx - F.Engels and the positivism of A. Compte, into adopting an orientation towards a co-determined naturalism, which was taking into account the laws of Hegelian dialectics in the former case and the empirical-scientific evolution in the latter. Consequently, there was a pretty fertile ground for the development of new philosophical approaches that would take into account the new epistemological edifice, inasmuch as it set forth a context of discussion that covered the ontological-gnoseological field of classical philosophy almost in its entirety, starting from the subatomic realm, the birth and evolution of universe, the placement of universe as an observational-empirical field up to the psychic automatisms and the constitution of the conscious self. Such philosophical trends associated to one or the other degree, in terms of motivation or otherwise, with the aforesaid epistemological developments were the Husserlian phenomenology and its offshoots in the existentialist versions of J.P. Sartre, M. Merleau-Ponty and E. Levinas, the deconstruction theory of J. Derrida, the alternative analytic approach of W.V.O. Quine and others.

In the immediately following, I will try to make clear that among the main 20th century philosophical trends, phenomenological analysis crucially transposes the discussion on the open questions of positive science - primarily referring to quantum mechanics, astrophysics-cosmology, mathematical logic and the foundations of mathematics - to a discussion on the constitution of the objects of experience as well-meant objects within objective spatiotemporality. Regarding the epistemological edifice, with a special reference to the positive science of the end of 19th century and beyond, there is a clear tendency towards the formation of two distinct cognitive contexts: that one of empirical science as a field of 'observation' and physical interaction (e.g. in quantum theory through the triangle embodied consciousness-measuring device-measured object), and that of mathematical science as a formal metatheory of empirical science and also as a formal theory in itself. This distinction seems to generate a two-fold question of an epistemological character: up to what level accede the 'observational' capabilities of an embodied consciousness endowed, in M. Merleau-Ponty's view, with a reciprocal relation of a special 'architecture' with the physical world, and at the same time, up to which point accede the expressional capabilities of a formal language by which are codified on the level of theory the registered empirical observations-measurements? Is there a common underlying foundation in the quest of the limits of physical 'observation' on the one hand and the limits of formal language as a suitable expressional tool on the other? And if, indeed, there is such a common foundation where it should be found? Within a subject's empirical field? That means, within his objective spatiotemporal field, resulting in consequence to an induced circularity inasmuch as the observational-cognitive limits of reality cannot be (at least) co-determined by this same reality, for in that case they would form part of it. We are led then to the paradoxical conclusion that the limits, which are de facto imposed to us through our reciprocal relation with the universe of objective reality, by the same measure to be set to transcend it, to the extent that they cannot be self-referring notions inasmuch as they are comprised in it. Therefore, in final count, there is posed the question of a pre-objective (or hyper-objective) 'reality'. And, if such a transcendental type question can in-

2. A REVIEW OF THE EVOLUTION ...

deed be well-posed, can it be a meaningful one in the absence of at least one consciousness embodied within a physical body-bearer?

These queries will stand as a motivation, after dealing more extensively with certain pivotal questions in quantum theory and the foundations of mathematics, in a way that will make more vivid the contribution of phenomenological analysis to a deeper understanding of certain questions of a conventionally epistemological content.

One might rightfully wonder at this point, why, in the following, I choose quantum theory as a main empirical-epistemological reference context and not, let's say, the general theory of relativity. Actually, this is done, because the time parameter in quantum-mechanical processes is considered as 'external' to the system and in a certain way as co-determining the objective existence of quantum objects, whereas time in macroscopic physical systems irrespective of whether they are Newtonian or relativistic, is considered as an internal parameter of the system susceptible of description through certain continuous mathematical transformations. It is already a predominant conviction within the community of physicists, that quantum 'observation' is associated with a subjectivity of a certain kind that objectifies an entangled quantum state by objectifying time in the transition towards the disentangled quantum state. This subjectivity, which in phenomenological view is ultimately the ever-in-act ego of each one's temporal consciousness, is mediated on the classical level by means of the measuring apparatus and in a formal-mathematical context is represented in the non-isomorphic projection of the holistic non-Boolean field of entangled quantum correlations into a meta-contextual Boolean field that 'disrupts' the physical unity by introducing the self-evident presence of an intentional conscious subject within the physical world. As A.A. Grib has suggested in [2], the jump of truth-values in the process of measurement, which on a formal level are due to the absence of an isomorphism between Boolean and non-Boolean structures (in accepting the latter structure for the description of the 'inner' state of a quantum object/state), puts upon a Boolean 'observer' the constraint of the existence of an objective, continuous time in terms of which he must 'move'.

Moreover, to the extent that the objectification of an entangled quantum state implies its constitution as a temporal object within the homogenous flux of an observer's consciousness, by the same measure it is annulled the possibility of a complete description of the 'inherent temporality' of an entangled state prior to its objectification by an intentional-type consciousness,[1] whence it is posed a de facto limit in the complete knowledge of a quantum state in the absence of its 'observation'. This seems, by all accounts, to be the reason for which there appears to be an impossibility of a physicalistic description, that is, of a description in a physical level, in terms of the 'language' of a measuring apparatus, of what takes place in-between the time of the performance of a

---

[1]The term intentional here is meant in its phenomenological connotation, that is roughly, as referring to the *a priori* orientation of a subject's consciousness towards its object which is, in turn, meant as the content of the corresponding intentional act.

quantum interaction through an experimental arrangement (e.g. in the case of an entangled state $S \otimes Q$, where S is the state of the quantum observable and Q the state of a measuring apparatus at the time of the experimental performance) and the time of the registration of measurement. In the words of H. Margenau and E. Wigner, the reduction of the wave packet " ...when properly understood, takes place when the observer interacts with the measurement apparatus and somehow obtains cognizance of its state. The impossibility of describing this part of the measurement process by means of the equations of quantum mechanics was clearly recognized already by von Neumann as well as London and Bauer" ([16], pp. 7-8).

3 Towards a holistic approach of epistemic objects

The argumentation above reduces, on a fundamental level, the question of the ontification in the quantum level of reality to a question of temporality or more precisely to a question of the constitution of temporal objectivity which is, by essential necessity, associated with a constituting subjectivity. On this account, the epistemological question can be, on the level of evidence, reduced to the phenomenological analysis of the temporal consciousness of a subject and the search for a no further reducible subjectivity which cannot but always 'be' the time-constituting factor and never the time-constituted objectivity. This quest ultimately led the founder of phenomenology, well beyond the description of specific *a priori* intentional structures of temporal consciousness (e.g. the transversal and longitudinal intentionality), to a rather obscure description of the absolute (a-temporal) ego of consciousness which is meant as the absolute constituting factor of the objective flux of temporal consciousness, yet not accessible to reflection but through its temporal objectification.

This supplemental reduction, as it came to be called, to the absolute subjectivity of temporal consciousness remained a vague and abstruse notion to the last Husserlian writings about time constitution, starting from his lessons on the phenomenology of of inner-time consciousness [5], to his Bernau manuscripts [10] and to the recently published late texts on time constitution, [11].

My position is that this absolute subjectivity of temporal consciousness inaccessible to any kind of objectification except through its own ontic reflexion, introducing the transcendence within the immanence of a subject's consciousness inasmuch as it cannot be described in terms of ontological being,[2] underlies as a common transcendental-type root both the constitution of quantum objects on the fundamental level of intentional experience and the constitution of mathematical objects in a sense to be further described. Concerning quantum objects/state of affairs it underlies their constitution as well-defined temporal

---

[2] J. Patočka referred to the notion of the absolute ego of consciousness, which was characterized by Husserl also as *nunc stans* (always in present now), in this way: "As it is by no way within time but always only in the state of passing over, and as time is the condition of every individuality as also of every existence, such as it is known to us not only in the world, but moreover in any first-degree transcendental reflection, we cannot attribute to the *nunc stans* as predicates neither existence nor individuality", ([17], *transl. of the author*, p. 168).

3. TOWARDS A HOLISTIC APPROACH OF EPISTEMIC OBJECTS

objects, whereas its underlying role in the constitution of objects of mathematical theories becomes more evident in those objects incorporating a notion of actual infinity (e.g., those of cardinality greater that $\aleph_0$) or those incorporating that of actual infinitesimality (e.g., the hyperreal numbers).

This approach should obviously consider mathematical objects as a special class of perceptual objects, which was in any case Husserl's view of the matter as he took them in the sense of objects of a pure logic as universal knowledge, as completed mental abstractions through a particular kind of intuition (categorial intuition), independently of any material content or form by which they might be instantiated. To the extent moreover, that mathematical objects are, even in the sense of syntactical objects of a formal theory, objects of the intentionality of consciousness are by this token temporal objects constituted as such within the homogenous flux of the temporal consciousness of a subject. It follows that the constitution of the temporal flux in its own right inherently determines the character of mathematical objects as well-meant temporal objects; it determines, for instance, the essential character of a convergent sequence of natural numbers in the sense of a complete mathematical object, in spite of the fact that it is a re-iterative, finitary process of a discrete character ideally extensible *ad infinitum*. Moreover, the invariant, omnitemporal, and ultimately 'transcendent' character of mathematical objects can be founded, in the context of a phenomenological interpretation, in a radically different way than in classical or naive platonism. In this respect, mathematical objects are meant and grounded as invariants of phenomena, that is, as invariants of our objective temporal experience and yet taken as objects that could exist even in the absence of subjects. For instance, the predicate formula $x \in P$ or $x \notin P$ is omnitemporal, in the sense that it is a syntactical form referring to a certain content that idealizes a cognitive act which can be in principle realized any time by any subject, in a way that it is always intersubjectively the same. For the meaning of the term intersubjectivity, I only intend to explain here, that it is a phenomenological term that founds, among others, the identical, invariant and omnitemporal character of an object, irrespectively of whether it is a physical or an abstract formal one, on the possibility of its definition as the common denominator of the corresponding phenomenological noematic constitutions of potentially all knowing subjects. If this was not the case, then it would be not feasible, for example, to define the mathematical notion of a circle or that of the straight line as everyone could have his own unique way of mentally constituting these objects.

In the following, I will draw attention to two constitutional structures of a phenomenological character which are, in my view, critical in the interpretation of certain mathematical conjectures involving a notion of actual infinity and also in the interpretation of quantum objectification. The first, is the one which has already been referred to, that is, the constitution of intentional objects, including the perceptual objects of the physical world and also the mental-abstract objects of our experience, as temporal objects within the homogeneous objectified flux of temporal consciousness, having as a result that their ontological being is reduced to their temporal re-identification within the continuous unity of the flux. As a consequence, the impredicative[3] character of the subjective origin of temporal consciousness induces an underlying impredicativity of infinite mathematical objects meant as well-defined immanent objects within the homogenous objectivity of the temporal flux of consciousness. For instance, talking about mathematical objects, we note that such an infinite object may be considered an open interval of the real line, which is regarded as an impredicative notion inasmuch as it cannot be described but in terms of its parts (basic open intervals) which are of the same genus as the whole. My position is that all mathematical objects or concepts which the are conditioned, on a formal-mathematical level, on the notion of continuity, e.g. the continuum of real numbers, continuous functions, infinite topological spaces, etc. may be fundamentally reduced to the deeper temporal origin of these objects, meant as intentional objects of a radical reduction-performing consciousness and further constituted in objective time.

The other phenomenological-type structure is a pure intentionality, independent in its description from the notion of constituted time, which is *a priori* oriented in the 'lowest' perceptional level to irreducible individual-substrates of our intentional experience. To make it more clear, let us try to imagine something more fundamental in our intuition than an individual-substrate, irrespectively of whether we refer to a quantum interaction and its registration by a classical-level apparatus or refer to a deconstruction of a formal analytic sentence to its last constituent elements. We cannot transcend, in effect, the 'lowest' perceptual level, which is the intuition or rather the intentionality towards individual-substrates themselves meant as original evidences presented to an intentional-type consciousness and at the same time as no further reducible contents of intentionality, which could be taken as close in meaning to the Aristotelian τόδε τι of an object. These no further reducible intentional objects in the broader sense of general state-of-things (*Sachverhalte*), inasmuch as devoid of any objectifiable content associated with a material or generally a 'thingness' substance, were taken in complete abstraction by Husserl as belonging to the class of objects of pure logic and more specifically as belonging to the domain of formal mathematical theories; for instance, as such may be taken the objects of set-theoretical classes, the objects of the domain of functions, the objects of Euclidean or non-Euclidean multiplicities ([7], pp. 33-34).

This specific intentionality which, in this approach, grounds what in mathematics can be associated with the intuition of concrete, finitistic and discrete, seems to determine on the fundamental level together with other intentional structures (e.g., the transversal and longitudinal intentionality), the intuition of concrete, finitistic mathematical objects, for instance, the intuition of natural numbers, or that of recursive sets, etc. This kind of intuition which can be understood as the grasping of the concrete and 'bounded' in mental rep-

---

[3]Generally, an impredicative notion is one that the *definiens* cannot but be defined in terms of the *definiendum*, in the sense that the definition of an entity (object, concept) somehow involves or presupposes a totality including the entity being defined.

3. TOWARDS A HOLISTIC APPROACH OF EPISTEMIC OBJECTS

resentation, is an intuition that is conditioned on the immanentization within consciousness of (hyletic-noetic) intentional moments toward specific (possibly) empty 'somethings' in the sense described above. It is inconceivable, though, in the absence of a process of temporal constitution of objects which is inherently associated with the impredicative and ultimately transcendental character of the self-constituted continuum of the temporal flux of consciousness.

As it has been more thoroughly developed in [12] and [14], my claim is that the incompatibility of the two intentional-constitutional *a priori* structures briefly discussed above and, in particular, the impredicative character of continuum disclosed by the supplemental radical reduction within objective temporality, can be a totally different interpretational approach towards certain so-called undecidable mathematical sentences that incorporate a notion of uncountable infinity, among them the well-known *Continuum Hypothesis* (**CH**).

I consider my views on an underlying phenomenology of the mathematical continuum as close to the interpretation undertaken by R. Tieszen in [19], with regard to Gödel's second incompleteness theorem. I remind, that Gödel's two incompleteness theorems, which, as it well-known, are of a primary importance in mathematical foundations, have raised far-reaching philosophical questions as to the sound foundations of mathematics and logic, in claiming that no formal-mathematical system, be as simple as the system of arithmetic, can prove its logical consistency with its own 'internal' proof-theoretic means. In other more intuitive words, the semantical content of a formal mathematical system transcends the expressional capacity of corresponding linguistic means. In R. Tieszen's words: " ...it follows, by the second incompleteness theorem, that the objects or concepts needed for the proof of CON(PA) (consistency of Peano arithmetic) must not be completely representable in space-time as meaningless finite, discrete, sign-configurations which are amenable to concrete intuition. In other words, [..] it appears that a proof of CON(PA) requires appeal to the meaning of the sign-configurations and to abstract objects or concepts that are in some sense nonfinite. It will also involve a form of intuition that is not restricted to Hilbert's concrete intuition" ([19], p. 133).

My view is that R. Tieszen's position takes as the deeper reason of the proof of the incompleteness of axiomatical theories the non-eliminable, through a finitary combination of symbols, inner meaning of non-finitary concepts; however he does not make any allusion to a possible reduction of the inherently impredicative character of infinity, e.g. generated in certain incompleteness proofs by the construction of universal categorial formulas (see: [14]), to a phenomenology of temporal consciousness concerning the constitution of the continuous unity of its immanent objects.[4]

---

[4]Immanent objects of a subject's consciousness are roughly described as the temporally constituted objects of the intentionality of a consciousness within its homogenous flux.

4 The bounds of objective reality

As it is made clear above, in phenomenological analysis it is of a primary importance the determination of the role of a conscious subject in the constitution of a co-determined objective reality and the interpretational context generated for that reason. This interpretational context presumably gives the breadth of the field within which, a conscious subject may pose well-meant ontological questions so as to expect well-founded answers.

Let us refer, for instance, to the concept of phenomenological horizon taken not in the usual meaning of physical horizon, but in the meaning of a field that is co-determined by the intentional consciousness of a subject in its self-evident presence in the world and also by nature itself as the pre-phenomenological field. The bounds of this horizon are inalienable to the extent that they refer to the intentional structure of a subject's consciousness and its constitutive modes, but they are all the same transposable to the measure that it is transposable a subject's phenomenological perception (*Wahrnehmung*) field. In this approach current cosmological conjectures about a multiplicity of universes or about parallel universes (e.g. R. Penrose's and A. Linde's views), are at least phenomenologically naive, as any hitherto unfathomable 'new' cosmic reality would stand for a human, who is a biological carrier of a consciousness *a priori* appropriating an intentional-constitutional structure, a simple transposition of his phenomenological horizon.

The reference in one or the other way to a conscious interacting, biological subject and the special 'architecture' of its relation with the surrounding physical world, is a significant factor in the contemporary interpretation of the four global (rather than universal) constants of physics, that is, of the gravitational constant G, of the Planck constant $\hbar$, of the velocity of light c and the Boltzmann's constant κ. Namely, these constants represent the inherent limits of human knowledge which are, on the one hand, inescapable and inalienable but on the other hand, are transposable just as the phenomenological horizon referred to above. It follows out of this, that the four constants of physics articulate the existence of those horizon lines that separate us from the infinitesimally small and the infinitely great.

As it is known, to cite an example, the velocity of light c is according to general relativity theory the velocity upper limit in the universe, because its refutation would lead to phenomena of instantaneous interaction at a distance and to certain bizarre results as those in the well-known thought experiment of Einstein-Podolski-Rosen (even though there exist lately certain counterarguments based on experimental evidence). Concerning Planck's constant $\hbar$, it represents a lowest limit or quantum of action within universe, in the sense of the least action that must be generated from a measuring apparatus so that we can have a 'response' of the measured quantum object, that is, $\tau \cdot \Delta E \geq \frac{1}{2}\hbar$ (Heisenberg's first inequality or uncertainty relation for time and energy). Summing up, we can loosely say that the relativity constants G and c are associated with the impossibility of the definition of an absolute space and an absolute

4. THE BOUNDS OF OBJECTIVE REALITY

time in the universe, whereas constants $\hbar$ and κ are associated with the definition of the bounds of subatomic universe in abolishing at the same time a well-meant and deterministic reality. A modern interpretation, in the context of quantum gravity, of the gravitational constant G in relation with the constants $\hbar$ and c, leads to the notions of time and length Planck and to the suspicion that space-time itself has a quantum structure with the consequence of a further non-apprehensible 'indivisibility'.

Equally important is the claim that the mode of constitution of external reality by a subject-carrier of a self-constituting temporal consciousness determines not only the 'depth' of observation within physical world but also the limits of the formal language of corresponding logical-mathematical models. A reduction, in line with this position, of formal-mathematical objects can be based on Husserl's view in, e.g. *Ideen I*, and *Formale und Transzendentale Logik*, namely that the objects of formal logic, taken as a universal knowledge theory, are abstractions based on categorial intuition of perceptual objects, these latter not necessarily identified with objects of a physical, material content. Due to this reduction, 'lowest-level' objects of analytic and consequently of formal-mathematical sentences lead to no further analytically reducible evidences of our intentional experience. Further, to the extent that the objects of a formal mathematical theory, as complete abstractions by categorial intuition,[5] are in any case well-meant objects-correlates of the intentional structure of a subject's temporal consciousness, they can be taken as inherently temporal objects and by virtue of this it can become meaningful an alternative approach to the interpretation of the undecidability of fundamental mathematical assertions about higher-order than ω infinity.

As it is historically known, the turn of the logical positivism of the Vienna Circle towards the validity of logical theories through their scientific verification and the ensuing theory of verifiability ran opposite to the Popperian argument on the futility of decidability attempts of universal sentences of a formal theory through their scientific verification. For instance, how could we be possibly certain for the validity of a universal mathematical sentence, all the more so for a universal empirical sentence of physics, should we not presuppose an *ad hoc* and ideally *ad infinitum* extension of the field of our physical experience, which nevertheless we have no empirical way to prove? The negation, for instance, of such a universal sentence within the set of real numbers (i.e., the Archimedean property) leads to the 'exotic' universe of nonstandard real numbers.

On this account, the Popperian substitution of the principle of verifiability with the criterion of falsifiability, where it suffices one and only empirical refutation of a formal universal sentence to be declared invalid, reflects, in effect,

---

[5]This special kind of intuition is described in Husserlian texts as reaching a purely formal object, e.g. the objects of formal logic, by abstracting from an intentional content characterized as a 'general something', possibly corresponding to an 'empty form' (*leer-Etwas*). This is not akin to a process of complete abstraction through which we can be led by a modification over content to a common invariant part of the object in question, even one that is left with no traits relative to a material content. See: [9], (pp. 661-665).

the inherent limitations of human knowledge. As it stands out, there is no objective reality independent of its constitutional mode, and if such a reality indeed existed it would not be possible to be described but intermediated and intersubjectively determined by the constituting consciousness of the biological subjects-performers of (phenomenological) reduction that are the human beings. If science is taken, in principle, as the objectification of experience, then experience eludes its scientific description in the 'residuum' of its constitution as an objectified-ontological structure within objective spatiotemporality, and its 'subsequent' abstraction in the context of a formal mathematical theory.

An entangled quantum state, to come back to questions of quantum theory, in the performance of a quantum experiment, is broadly regarded as essentially representing the threshold of a physical situation which 'is' still inaccessible to objectification by an observer's consciousness through the triangle quantum observable-measuring apparatus-conscious subject. On essentially the same grounds, in the modeling of Big Bang theory, the Planck time (10^{-44}) and the Planck length (10^{-33}) represent the threshold beyond which 'collapses' our common physical intuition about gravity and the space-time continuum. I just note here that, in another context, it is still an open question to the mathematical community today whether statements referring to the mathematical continuum or generally to any level of uncountable infinity are ultimately of a non-analytic character and as such can be dealt with.

5 Conclusion

If the great theoretical questions on the incompleteness of mathematical theories having at least the degree of complexity of the theory of arithmetic and also on the undecidability of critical conjectures on the mathematical (actual)[6] infinity (e.g. the well-known *Continuum Hypothesis*, and the *Axiom of Choice*), have a common underlying root with the great open questions of contemporary subatomic physics-quantum mechanics, this might be the reduction of their context of reference to its fundamental constitutive origin. This origin is further reducible to its subjective source, which is the self-constituting subjectivity of temporal consciousness within a surrounding world susceptible of a sense attribution. The special 'architecture' of the reciprocal relation between a biological subject-bearer of a consciousness and the surrounding physical world which are mutually penetrable and at the same time mutually elusive, and the concept of a transposable yet inalterable cosmic horizon that is induced by this kind of 'architecture', determine the limits of scientific knowledge and the breadth of well-posed questions in reference to this physical world. In this sense and taking account of the discussion in the above, one may not accept as well-posed questions those questions that are commonly qualified as metaphysical or teleological, for instance, concerning the soundness of the presupposition of

---

[6] Actual infinity can be taken to be a kind of infinity freely generated through our mental faculties in the sense of the unity of a whole in actual presence. Consequently, it should not be identified with physical spatiotemporal infinity conditioned on the laws of causality, whereas on the formal level could be taken as representing any form of uncountable infinity.

5. CONCLUSION

a sublime entity assumed to 'be' the creator of the universe. It seems that in such cases, we should remain silent in the Wittgensteinian sense of the word.

BIBLIOGRAPHY

[1] French, S.: (2002), A Phenomenological Solution to the Measurement Problem? Husserl and the Foundations of Quantum Mechanics, *Studies in History and Philosophy of Modern Physics*, 33, pp. 467-491.
[2] Grib, A.A.: (1993), Quantum Logical Interpretation of Quantum Mechanics: The Role of Time, *Int. Jour. of Theoretical Physics*, 32, 12, pp. 2389-2400.
[3] Hawking, S., Mlodinow, L.: (2010), *The Grand Design*, New York: Bantau Books.
[4] Husserl, E.: (1962), *Die Krisis der Europäischen Wissenschaften und die Transzendentale Phänomenologie*, Hua Band VI, hsgb. W. Biemel, Den Haag: M. Nijhoff.
[5] Husserl, E.: (1966), *Zur Phänomenologie des Inneren Zeibewusstseins*, Hua Band X, hsgb. R. Boehm, Den Haag: M. Nijhoff.
[6] Husserl, E.: (1970), *Philosophie der Arithmetik. Mit erganzenden Texten (1890-1901)*, Hua Band XII, hsgb. L. Eley, Den Haag: M. Nijhoff.
[7] Husserl, E.: (1976), *Ideen zu einer reinen Phänomenologie und phänomenologischen Philosophie*, Erstes Buch, Hua Band III/I, hsgb. K. Schuhmann, Den Haag: M. Nijhoff.
[8] Husserl, E.: (1983), *Studien zur Arithmetik und Geometrie. Texte aus dem Nachlass (1886-1901)*, Hua Band XXI, hsgb. I. Strohmeyer, Den Haag: M. Nijhoff.
[9] Husserl, E.: (1984), *Logische Untersuchungen*, Hua Band XIX1, (zweiter Band, erster Teil), hsgb. U. Panzer, Den Haag: M. Nijhoff.
[10] Husserl, E.: (2001), *Die Bernauer Manusckripte über das Zeitbewusstsein (1917/18)*, hsgb. R. Bernet & D. Lohmar, Dordrecht: Kluwer Acad. Pub.
[11] Husserl, E.: (2001), *Späte Texte über Zeitkonstitution, Die C-Manuscripte*, Hua Materialien Band VIII, hsgb. D. Lohmar, Dordrecht: Springer.
[12] Livadas, S.: (2009), The Leap from the Ego of Temporal Consciousness to the Phenomenology of Mathematical Continuum, *Manuscrito (Revista Internacional de Filosofia)*, 32, 2, pp. 321-356.
[13] Livadas, S.: (2010), Impredicativity of Continuum in Phenomenology and in Non-Cantorian Theories, in: *Causality, Meaningful Complexity and Embodied Cognition*, (ed. A. Carsetti), pp. 185-199, Springer, 2010.
[14] Livadas, S.: (2012), Are mathematical theories reducible to non-analytic foundations? *Axiomathes Online*, DOI 10.1007/s10516-012-9182-3, Springer.
[15] Lurcat, F.: (2007), Understanding Quantum Mechanics with Bohr and Husserl. In L. Boi, P. Krezberg & F. Patras (eds.), *Rediscovering Phenomenology*, pp. 229-258, Dordrect: Springer.
[16] Margenau, H. & Wigner, E.: (1964), Discussion: Reply to Professor Putnam, *Philosophy of Science*, 31, 7-9.
[17] Patočka, J.: (1992), *Introduction à la phénoménologie de Husserl*, Grenoble: Ed. Millon.
[18] Russell, B. & Whitehead N.A.: (1980), *Principia Mathematica*, New York: Cambridge University Press.
[19] Tieszen, R.: (2005), *Phenomenology, Logic, and the Philosophy of Mathematics*, Cambridge: Cambridge University Press.
[20] Tragesser, R.: (1977), *Phenomenology and Logic*, Ithaca: Cornell University Press.
[21] Tragesser, R.: (1984), *Husserl and Realism in Logic and Mathematics*, Cambridge: Cambridge University Press.
[22] van Atten, M., Van Dalen, D., & Tieszen, R.: (2002), Brouwer and Weyl: The Phenomenology and Mathematics of the Intuitive Continuum, *Philosophia Mathematica*, 10, 3, pp. 203-226.

Mathematical and Phenomenological Continuity-Indiscernibility [0]

STATHIS LIVADAS

1 Introduction

Attempts to provide an alternative conceptual basis to fundamental mathematical ideas like those of countable infinity, uncountability and continuity are known to have come almost shortly after the Cantor-Dedekind construction of infinite cardinalities and the real number system. Mathematicians of the stature of Kurt Gödel and Hermann Weyl are referred to by R. Tieszen, [19], D. Føllesdal, [6], and S. Feferman, [4] & [5], as being influenced by Husserlian thought, regarding in particular the notion of continuum. More specifically, in his review of S. Feferman's paper, 'Weyl vindicated: Das Kontinuum 70 years later' [4], G. Longo stressed that: "What really interests H. Weyl is the understanding of mathematics as part of our human endeavour towards knowledge, in particular of the physical world. Weyl stresses the inadequacies of the mathematical formalization with respect to a crucial aspect of our physical experience: our intuition of the continuity of space and time (Weyl, in fact, contributed greatly to the mathematics of general relativity). In his view, the phenomenal experience of time, as past, present and future, is unrelated to the mathematical treatment of the real numbers. Time cannot be decomposed in points. Present lasts continuously, it is something ever new which endures and changes in consciousness. In our perception of time, an individual point is non-independent [..] it exists only as a point of transition [..] it cannot be exhibited in any way [..] only an approximate, never an exact determination of it is possible. Even the use of limit points or ideal constructions, the essence of mathematics according to Weyl, do not help us sufficiently in grasping the irreducible perception of the continuum (reference are made for this to Husserl and Bergson)." ([11], p. 34).

It should be further noted that Weyl's view of intuitive continuum in Das Kontinuum (Ch. 2, sec. 6), back in 1918, was largely based on the Husserlian descriptions of the consciousness of internal time. This was also true for L.E.J. Brouwer to the extent that his early ideas about the primordial intuition of

---

[0]This article has been published in original form in the journal *Noesis*, (Travaux du Comité Roumain d'Histoire et de la Philosophie des Sciences), Ed. Acad. Rom., (2004), V. XXIX, pp. 51-64.

Mathematics are readily understood in connection with Husserl's phenomenological description of internal time (see, Van Atten et al. in [20], pp. 203-205).

In what follows I am primarily interested in the non-Cantorian approach of the Alternative Set Theory (Vopěnka, Sochor, Pudlak, et al., of the Prague School) and also that of the Internal Set Theory (E. Nelson), towards countable and uncountable infinity. This involves the reduction of the classical continuity and openness of sets to a 'shift of the 'horizon' of countability in Alternative Set Theory (AST), or the presence of an, external to Cantorian Set theory, undefined predicate *standard*, in Internal Set Theory (IST). It should be reminded that in Cantorian set theory uncountable infinity is basically introduced by the power-set axiom and is inherently associated with an infinity statement proved to be independent of the other axioms of **ZFC** theory[1], that is, with the well-known Continuum Hypothesis, (**CH**).

By reviewing the respective approaches in sections 2 and 3, I'll try to show that their approach of continuum stands essentially in the reduction of the idealized (ε,δ) continuity of real numbers and the relevant notions of analysis and topology, to a hereditary finiteness of multiplicities of 'appearances' towards the 'horizon of observability' and the assumption of certain extension principles in AST, or the assumption in IST, of the *ad hoc* nonlogical predicate *standard* and its associated axioms, beyond the fixedness of standard set-theoretic structures in **ZFC** system.

I further claim that these approaches above may be thought, in a sense to be further described, to reflect in mathematical axiomatization the impredicative unity of the absolute flux of consciousness in the constitution of spatiotemporal phenomena. This ultimate impredicativity is put into evidence in the radical reduction to the self-constituting flux of consciousness in Husserlian sense ([16], p. 168). We should keep in mind Husserl's fundamental notion of the genetic-kinetic constitution as the mode in which objects appear within the temporal flow of our experience, this temporal approach being crucial to our understanding of human beings and cultural objects ([13], p. 166). In this way the naturally intuited continuity of physical processes/state-of-affairs is essentially immanentized in the unity of the flow of their multiplicities in the constituting flux of consciousness.[2]

The aforementioned nonstandard axiomatical theories establish an 'observer's' approach to the constituted continuum of our experience, the AST theory in a more closely phenomenological fashion in adopting the 'shift of the horizon' (which is essentially the prolongation axiom) to reach the vagueness of infinity beyond the naturally intuited hereditary finiteness of the horizon of countability. This phenomenological horizon, according to P. Vopěnka, limits our

---

[1]This abbreviation, refers to the standard set theory, namely the Zermelo-Fraenkel set theory with the addition of the Axiom of Choice (**AC**).

[2]In the comments of D. Tiffeneau to the French translation (*La phénoménologie et les fondements des sciences*) of Husserl's *Ideen zu einer reinen Phänomenologie und phanomenologischen Philosophie, Drittes Buch*, "the real being is not given but as a unity of multiplicities; the kinetic method studies how these unities are constituted progressively by restituting them in the flux of multiplicities" (*transl. of the author*, ([9], p. 211).

capacity for observation and distinction in all directions, of course not only in the optical sense, but in the Husserlian sense as understood in E. Husserl's *Krisis der europäischen Wissenschaften und die transzendentale Phänomenologie*, [7].

Moreover in the subsection 2.1, I point to a circularity in the notion of continuity as it was applied by Husserl himself in the description of the flux of appearances (*Erscheinungen*) within consciousness, whereas in subsection 2.2 I note that the notion of the double intentionality, (*Längstintentionalität*), of the flux of consciousness can be satisfactorily modeled by the gluing operators in the mathematical example provided by J. Petitot, [17].

In conclusion, I assess the potential depth of these alternative theories to provide a fertile interpretational ground to a phenomenologically motivated mathematical 'naturalization'.

2 The phenomenology of the continuum

2.1 Irreducibility of the radical phenomenological reduction

It is worth noting, at first, that the phenomenological analysis is of a kinetic (*kinetisch*) and not of a catastematic (*katastematisch*) character.[3] Moreover the conviction to an objective reality in an absolute sense is put in suspense - the corresponding Husserlian term is *Epochë* - by a constituted reality approach which is of a fundamental character in phenomenological analysis. The constituted objects are immanent[4] to the constituting flux of conscience in which they are immanentized in a certain mode, that is, in terms of certain retentional forms of the constituting flux; for instance, in the *vor-zugleich* (anterior-simultaneous) mode of retention which generates a continuous sequence of retained phases trailing behind an original impression, each of which is a retentional consciousness of the preceding one, and this way for each new original impression ([10], pp. 43-48).

The temporal consciousness of immanences is the unity of a whole, an all encompassing unity of retentions of original impressions apprehended in present actuality, that modifies continuously the multiplicities of original impressions into a trailing sequence of just-passed-by retentions together with the retentions of these retentions just-passed-by and so on, in a way that we can talk about a double or longitudinal intentionality (*Längstintentionalität*) of the constituting flux of conscience. By this specific intentional form, Husserl meant first, the

---

[3]The meaning of the term catastematic should be taken here as identical to ontologically hypostasized. The following Husserlian quotation helps to better comprehend the difference between these aforementioned terms: "The mode of ontological consideration is, so to say, catastematic. It takes the unities in their identity and in regard to their identity as something fixed. The phenomenological and constitutive consideration takes such a unity in the flux, which means in terms of the unity of a constituting flux; it is attached on the movements, on the flows in which such a unity and every component, aspect or real property of this unity is correlate of the identity." (*transl. of the author*), [9], App. I, p. 158.

[4]This is a phenomenological term attributed to an object which is no more transcendent to an intentional consciousness, i.e. an object of 'external' reality, but has been modified to a noematic correlate of the constituting flux of consciousness.

retention of an immanent object as such in consciousness, e.g. a sonorous effect in the present now, and the consciousness of the retention of this sonorous effect as such, constituting by this token its immanent unity with the sequence of all former phases preceding this effect in terms of a continuous whole within the homogenous flow of the flux ([10], pp. 106-107).[5]

Therefore, by appealing to the double intentionality of the absolute flux of conscience, Husserl posited the immediate retention of an immanent object in the flux of conscience (the sonorous effect of a sound, for example) on the one hand, and the intentional constitution of the 'descending' sequence of retentions of the original impression of this effect, as a continuous unity always in the anterior-simultaneous mode of the flow. "Thus, the flux is traversed by a longitudinal intentionality which, in the course of flux, overlapps continuously with itself." ([10], *transl. of the author*, pp. 106-107).[6]

However, in the retentional-protentional[7] mode of the self-constitution of the flux lacks a clear definition of the term continuity as it is described in a somehow circular sense in terms of the constituted by the intentional modes unity of the flux; moreover, this self-constitution of the flux as a phenomenon in itself is not but an objectification of what is the ultimate subjectivity, the absolute ego, in other words, the absolute subjectivity of the flux of consciousness. This is the ultimate and most radical phenomenological reduction, probably the key to comprehend the inherent vagueness of the notion of continuity, even in the kinetic terms of the constituted reality in a Husserlian sense. For, Husserl himself claimed that it is impossible to extend the phases of the absolute subjectivity of the flux in a continuous succession, to transform it mentally in a way that each phase 'extends' identically on itself, a certain phase of it belonging to a present that constitutes or to a past that also constitutes (not constituted), to the degree that it is an absolute subjectivity beyond any predication and whose retentional continuity in the constituting flux is not but its objectification, its ontification by its 'mirror' reflexion ([10], pp. 98-99).

It is clear that what is being intuited as a continuous flow in the temporal constitution of a group of simultaneities and corresponding retentions is irre-

---

[5] "The totality of the group of original impressions is bound to this law: It transforms itself into a constant continuum (*in ein stetiges Kontinuum*) of modes of consciousness, of modes of being-in the flow and in the same constance, an incessantly new group of original impressions taking originally its point of depart, to pass constantly (*stetig*) in its turn in the being-in the flow. What is a group in the sense of a group of original impressions, remains in the modality of being-in-the flow." (*transl. of the author*, [10], p. 102).

[6] "If we consider an arbitrary phase in the flux of consciousness (in which phase appears a sonorous present and a fragment of the sound duration in the mode of just-passed by) we see that it comprises a continuity of retentions which possesses a unity in the *vor-zugleich*." ([10], *transl. of the author*, p. 106).

[7] The retention (or primary memory) and the protention are phenomenological terms which are meant as specific intentional modes of consciousness, that is respectively, as an *a priori* in character immediate conservation in memory of the immanence of an original impression and the a-thematic attendance towards a not-yet-perceived impression. These are described by Husserl by means of the transversal intentionality (*Querintentionalität*), in the scheme original impression-protention-retention. For details the reader may consult the Husserlian texts in [10], resp. pp. 43-48 and pp. 71-72.

2. THE PHENOMENOLOGY OF THE CONTINUUM

ducible in terms of an ontological deconstruction to constituent non-durating parts, being essentially the objectification of an inherently elusive process which is always 'on going', where every attempt to simply reflect on it produces its 'mirror' objectification. The underlying role of this ultimate irreducibility in the flux of temporal consciousness which is objectively reflected in the inherent impredicativity of intuitive continuity, I'll try to put in evidence in the axiomatical foundation of Alternative and Internal Set theories as non-Cantorian versions of nonstandard theories in sections 3 and 4.

From the unfolding of the arguments in these sections, it will also become clear how these theories offer a more natural mathematical approach to real processes in life, as at least P. Vopěnka claims that AST theory does. In general, AST tries to imitate real processes in a witnessed and mutually interacting universe by following the unfolding of hereditarily finite multiplicities of phenomena to the horizon of 'observability' and by expressing by *ad hoc* axiomatization vagueness beyond the horizon of 'observability'. Let us keep also in mind what H. Weyl stated in *Das Kontinuum* ([23]), namely that it is an 'act of violence' to assume the perfect coincidence of the analytical construction of the continuum with that of phenomenal space and time, "....the continuity given to us immediately by intuition (in the flow of time and motion) has yet to be grasped mathematically".

It is along the line of this aphorism that non-Cantorian theories as well as intuitionistic ones follow an alternative approach to the notion of continuum.

2.2 Vagueness in phenomenological kinesthesia

Before dealing with the question of continuity in Jean Petitot's modelization of the kinesthetic control of perception with regard to constituted reality, I refer to what Husserl regarded as parallel problems, that is, on the one hand, the constitution of the universal and unique space which is co-perceived in each specific perception to the extent that everything perceived appears as residing in it corporeally and, on the other hand, the constitution of a unique time in which it is inserted the temporality of all things, their duration and the duration of their processes, as well as every corporeal ego together with its 'psychic experiences' ([10], suppl. X, p. 161). Further, the problem of kinesthetic control of perception belongs to "the great question [..] of penetrating as deeply as possible into three-dimensional phenomenological 'creation', or, in other words, into the phenomenological constitution of the identity of the 'body' of a thing through the multiplicity of its appearances" ([8], *transl. of the author*, p. 154).

The kinesthetic control of perception is not only a presupposition for the effective identity of an appearing object, thus founding logical identity upon continuous variability and consequently synthetic *a priori* laws to a continuous synthesis (that is, in fact, a kinetic synthesis): it also "rules phenomenologically, temporal series corresponding to three classes of movements, namely, those of the eyes, the body and objects" ([17], p. 354). Kinesthetic control is essential too, in interpreting phenomenologically the source of each movement as something 'internal' to these Husserlian kinesthetic sensations. As I will proceed now

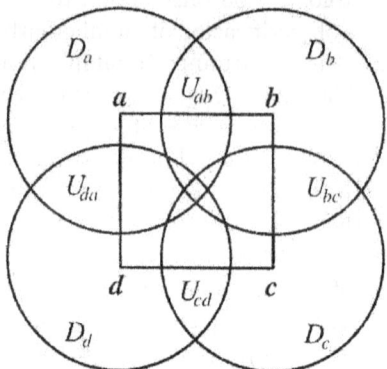

Figure 1.1. *This figure has originally appeared in J. Petitot's 'Morphological Eidetics for a Phenomenology of Perception', see [17].*

with the kinesthesiological analysis of the simplest situation, which is that of a body (subject) being fixed and the objects remaining at rest, it will become evident, at least on the formal level, that continuous 'vagueness' inherently underlies the unity of the constituted movements, even though it is based on the temporal discreteness of the correlations $k_1 \leftrightarrow i_1,.., k_n \leftrightarrow i_n,...$ The particular situation reduces to the purely ocular kinesthetic sensation schematized by the correspondence $k \leftrightarrow i$ between the space of kinesthetic controls K and the space of visual images F, by applying a temporal parametrization through reciprocally corresponding paths k_t, i_t.

In [17], J. Petitot applied the mathematical model below, to inquire into the nature of the association between k_t and i_t (the temporal paths of kinesthetic sensations and those of image variations) and also that of the 'fixed association' of the space of kinesthetic controls K with the visual field M, the latter modelized by a domain D (a two-dimensional disk).

To each point $p = a, b, c, d$ of the square S in Fig. 1 above, corresponds a token Dp of the field D as a way of 'interpreting' the focusing on each such point.

Quoting from Jean Petitot: "If the figure i_a filling in D_a can 'refer' to the figure i_b filling in D_b, it is because D_a and D_b overlap and are glued together through their intersection $U_{ab} = D_a \cap D_b$. This means that there exists a local gluing isomorphism $\varphi_{ab} : U_{ab} \subset D_a \longrightarrow U_{ab} \subset D_b$ identifying the intersection U_{ab} viewed as a subdomain of D_a with the same U_{ab} viewed as a subdomain of D_b. In the continuous limit, there exists a temporal series D_t with gluing operators $\varphi_{tt'}$ for t and t' sufficiently near. This spatiotemporal series is filled in by the image series i_t. To say that the 'pointing' of each i_t to another $i_{t'}$ is intentional, or that intentions 'go through' the series i_b, is to say that intentionality corresponds to gluing operators identifying different points of the visual flow as the same[...]More precisely, intentionality corresponds to the realization in consciousness of the gluing operators. Once again, it is essential here not to confuse, as the natural attitude does, the constituting level and the constituted one[...] This is the main role of kinesthetic controls: the k_t are gluing protocols." ([17], pp. 356-357).

This formalization reducing the kinesthetic constitution of movement, purely ocular in our instance, to gluing operators k_t realized in conscience for t, t' sufficiently near, is a 'transformation' in a mathematically meaningful fashion of the idea of longitudinal intentionality of the flux of conscience. As it was the case in the retentional mode of the constituting flux, here it is also clear that in the phenomenology of movement through kinesthetic controls one cannot avoid the circular introduction of the notion of continuity in the constituted unity of the multiplicity of appearances. In the present case, this continuity factor is represented by the local gluing isomorphisms $\varphi_{t,t'}$ for t and t' sufficiently near, that 'glue' together the temporal series D_t filled in by the image series i_t in the continuous whole of constituted reality. On this account I draw attention, in the phenomenological perspective of the constituted spatiotemporality, to a sequence of immanences of original impressions in the flux of consciousness with a vagueness of a descending tail of retentions in-between, constituted as a continuous unity by the longitudinal intentionality of the retentional (*vor-zugleich*) flux, which is implemented, on the formal level, by the gluing isomorphisms $\varphi_{t,t'}$ in the model-example of J. Petitot.

Before dealing with indiscernibility or vagueness from the standpoint of Alternative and Internal Set theories in sections 2 and 3, I find it purposeful to refer to the Husserlian idea of scale invariance, as evident generic similarity, which can lead to minima visibilia as point-like ultimate minimalities bearing the same eidetic relationships 'discovered' in the macroscopic universe, ([8], p. 166).This idea seems to have a profound effect on the shift of the horizon principle embodied in AST theory.[8]

3 The phenomenological relevance of AST approach

I have already referred in previous sections to the inherent vagueness (or indiscernibility) characterizing, the constituted in terms of the flux of consciousness, phenomenological continuum. As a matter of fact, I sought to present a formal treatment 'interweaving' the discreteness of immanent multiplicities with a vagueness of 'indiscernibilities' filling-in between. At this point it seems purposeful to quote from C. Zeeman's *The topology of the brain and visual perception*, ([24]), that "nothing in physics suggests the existence of so sophisticated a mathematical construction as the real numbers system[..]Nothing in physics suggests even non-countability. Surely we would have a more natural approach to the foundation of physics by postulating only the existence of discrete fundamental parts (which are otherwise undefined) without embedding them in any so-called ether. We should

---

[8]This generic similarity justifies the transposition of the eidetic relationships 'discovered' in the universe of common intuition to that beyond this 'horizon'. It is remarkable, though, that P. Vopěnka seems to deny this principle in [22], (p. 123), where he insists that all ideas held hitherto could collapse beyond some genuinely qualitative shift of the horizon.

then postulate certain combinatorial laws describing which particles are permitted to be within tolerance.".[9]

Now I call attention on how AST reduces the classical sense continuum of topological shapes and motions to the extension, by the application of the axiom of prolongation of classes, of finite segments of natural numbers to class infinities transcending the 'horizon of observation'. In this sense a topology can be defined relying basically on the notion of countable classes in the extended universe of sets and on the principle of prolongation; therefore, one need not adopt the traditional approach of topological openness, connectedness, etc. fundamentally based on the continuity of the real numbers system.

The Alternative Set Theory, as exposed in its fundamentals by P. Vopěnka in [21], assumes a universe of sets formed by sets constructed iteratively from the empty set together with some axioms subjecting the sets of this universe to laws valid in Cantorian set theory for finite sets, excluding 'abnormal' circularities like the set of all sets. This universe is extended by the inclusion of classes of the form $\{x; \varphi(x)\}$ where $\varphi(x)$ is a property of sets from the universe of sets. Classes that are not sets are called proper classes such as the universal class $\prod$. It is remarkable that countability in the sense of hereditary finiteness is closely related to the notion of 'observation' towards a 'horizon'.[10] In giving a formal definition of AST-countability below, we need only know in advance that segment of a class is called a subclass with respect to a linear ordering which contains with each of its elements all its predecessors.

Formally one has two definitions:

– A pair $(A, \leq)$ of classes is called an ordering of type ω iff:

1. (1) $\leq$ linearly orders A

2. (2) A is infinite and

3. (3) for each $x \in A$, the segment $\{y \in A; y \leq x \}$ is finite.

– A class X is called countable iff there is a relation R such that (X, R) is an ordering of type ω. A class is uncountable iff it is neither countable nor finite.

In case one goes beyond the horizon of countability, that is, the 'horizon of observability' in a sense close to that of the phenomenological notion of horizon in Husserl's *Krisis*, one has to adopt the following Prolongation (or Shift of the Horizon) Axiom:

For each countable function F there is a set function f such that $F \subseteq f$.

---

[9]Tolerance is taken in [24] as a formal relation and it is defined as an indiscernibility-like, binary relation on a set X that is reflexive and symmetric.

[10]By the words of P. Vopěnka "if a large set x is observed then the class of all elements of x that lie before the horizon need not be infinite but may converge toward the horizon. The phenomenon of infinity associated with the observation of such a class is called countability" ([21], p. 39).

It is important to point out that P. Vopěnka makes a fundamental distinction between the class of all finite natural numbers FN proved to be a countable class and the set-theoretically definable proper class N of all natural numbers which is uncountable. In a witnessed universe, i.e., one that adopts the viewpoint of an observer of an extensible 'horizon' incorporated in it (thus essentially an intersubjective universe in a phenomenological sense) "The classical natural numbers correspond to the elements of N, whereas FN forms a canonical representative of the way to the horizon." ([21], p. 63)

In this formal-axiomatical context, one can define a topology by the Kuratowski closure operations which are not taken as primitive as it is the case in general topology, but are defined instead in terms of indiscernibility equivalences $\doteq$, which underlie every topological definition and are fundamentally based on the 'shift' of countability, that is, on the prolongation axiom in the AST sense. The underlying idea in the definition of an indiscernibility equivalence is that in each infinite set of 'observed' objects there must be at least one pair (x, y) of mutually indiscernible elements, formally $x \doteq y$.

Further, by defining a class X to be a figure iff X contains with each of its elements x, all y such that $x \doteq y$, then two classes X, Y to be separable, (Sep(X, Y)), iff there is a set-theoretically definable class Z such that Fig$(X) \subseteq Z$ and Fig$(Y) \cap Z = \emptyset$, and also the closure of a class A, $\overline{A}$, to be $\overline{A} = \{x;\ \neg\text{Sep}(\{x\}, A)\}$, P. Vopěnka defines a topology in the extended AST Universe with the notion of indiscernibility as a conceptual and formal foundation for all subsequent topological constructions, including the definition of a formal notion of motion ([21], pp. 87-88 and 98-108).

It seems worthwhile to mention the approach of A. Sochor and A. Vencovská in *Indiscernibles in the Alternative Set theory* ([18]), defining the class of indiscernibles as a class of natural numbers such that there are no two finite increasing sequences of its elements that can be distinguished using a set formula without parameters and proving that there exists a class of indiscernibles which is a Π-class and not a semiset.[11] A class is defined as real iff there is an indiscernibility equivalence such that the class in question is a figure in this equivalence. Further, it is proved that if X is a real class, then there is either a set U with $U \subseteq X$ and $U \approx a$ (U is numerically equivalent to an $\alpha \in N$) or for each $\gamma \in N - FN$ there is a set $U \supseteq X$ such that $U \approx a\gamma$ ([18], pp. 789-790). Evidently the classical real continuity is reduced to the 'uncountability' of the set-theoretically definable proper class of natural numbers N in the AST sense.

In conclusion, indiscernibility relations in the AST sense formalize vagueness or 'blurring of the vision' in topological structures, occurring as we transcend the horizon of countability of finite natural numbers to the uncountability of the infinite proper class of natural numbers. Moreover, we can possibly state that indiscernibility equivalences in the AST approach, can be put in paral-

---

[11]The notion of proper semisets is fundamental to AST theory. They are proper classes inside very large sets whose existence is guaranteed by an axiom 'external' to the AST extended universe of sets. They can be roughly said, to bear the traits of 'fuzziness' or 'non surveyability', ([21], pp. 33-36.

lel with the gluing operators in [17], in the sense that they 'glue' points of classes beyond the horizon of AST countability (or 'observability' in Vopěnka's phenomenologically motivated attitude).

4 The IST approach to continuity-vagueness

I start this section in outlining the main conceptual and axiomatical characteristics of the Internal Set theory's approach to the key ideas of continuity and vagueness, in view of its adoption of an (external to **ZFC** Set theory) undefined unary predicate *standard*, involving indirectly the presence of an observer within classical Cantorian universe. As a matter of fact, the intensional development of a large part of nonstandard analysis essentially coincides with Nelson's Internal Set Theory (IST) appropriately interpreted, where we should keep in mind that in the intensional development of nonstandard analysis, infinitesimals and infinitely large numbers do not exist in an objective way as in the extensional case (e.g. A. Robinson's nonstandard theory), but their existence has a rather subjective meaning and is related to the observational limitations of an interacting 'observer'. In fact, the introduction of the undefined predicate *standard* in E. Nelson's theory is metatheoretically associated with a factor of vagueness with regard to a series of 'observations' carried out in a discrete mode. It is suggested, for instance, that: 'finiteness' + 'vagueness' = 'unlimited', where 'unlimited' is a non-Cantorian equivalent to infinity.

In general, we define a vague predicate R with regard to a series of 'observations' $O_0, O_1, ...O_n$ as following:

1. (i) $R(O_0)$

2. (ii) $R(O_i) \Leftrightarrow R(O_{i+1})$, $i = 0, 1, ..., n-1$, that is, O_i and O_{i+1} are indistinguishable with respect to R, and,

3. (iii) $\neg R(On)$

By applying the Transfer Principle of IST and appropriate theorems within the IST extended axiomatical context we can prove that the predicate *standard* - abbreviated as st - is a vague predicate in the set N of natural numbers:

1. (i) st(0)

2. (ii) st(n) $\Leftrightarrow$ st(n + 1)

3. (iii) There exists a nonstandard $n \in N$

(see: [3], p. 295).

In the proof of this theorem a straightforward result of the IST Idealization Principle is used, namely that every infinite set contains a nonstandard element. In particular, there exists a nonstandard natural number ([14], pp. 5-6).

It is not without importance to refer to the intuition behind the Idealization Principle, which alongside the Transfer and Standardization Principles (respectively, I, T and S principles) are the three extra axiomatical pillars of Internal

4. THE IST APPROACH TO CONTINUITY-VAGUENESS

Set theory: "The intuition behind the idealization principle is that we can only fix a finite number of objects at a time. To say that there is a y such that for all fixed x we have A, is the same as saying that for any fixed finite set of x's there is a y such that A holds for all of them", where A is an internal predicate formula, that is, one that does not involve the 'unknown' predicate *standard* even indirectly

$$\forall^{stfin} x' \; \exists y \; \forall x \in x' \; A \longleftrightarrow \exists y \forall^{st} x \; A$$

[14], p. 5).

As it stands out, we can deduce vagueness along infinity, in terms of the predicate *standard*, with respect to the set N of natural numbers by relying on the idealization principle. Thus we can point to a common conceptual underlying basis between the idealization and the transfer principles which induce, in effect, nonstandard elements[12] and the prolongation principle of AST, in the sense of an axiomatic means to 'shift' the horizon of phenomenological observability to the vagueness of continuum. It is to be noted here that although E. Nelson insists that the predicate *standard* has a syntactical rather than a semantic role in the theory, it is implicitly taken as having a semantic content by the adoption of the three extra axioms. The convergence in the conceptual foundation is all the more evident, to the extent that while in AST theory one may define topological notions with indiscernibility equivalences taken as primitive, in IST theory infinitesimality and unlimitedness (and hence continuity and openness) are defined by taking as primitive the predicate *standard* together with the I,T and S axioms. This means that continuity and topological openness are not necessarily associated to the real number system, as standardness and nonstandardness are not describable solely within the real model R. We should keep in mind that the predicate *standard* may be loosely thought of as close to the notion of fixed (concretely grasped) in informal mathematical discourse, any object that can be uniquely described within internal mathematics assumed to be standard as, for instance, the set of real numbers R, the null-element 0, the transcendental number π, the first uncountable ordinal ω, etc. ([14], pp. 4-17).

The novelty in the IST approach in what concerns classical topological continuity and openness, stands in that it treats these fundamental ideas of mathematical analysis and topology by enriching the existing **ZFC** axiomatical system with the undefined, and implicitly related to the local horizon of an 'observer', external predicate *standard* alongside an appropriate axiomatical equipment with no reference, by necessity, to any particular mathematical model.

In conclusion, there exists a common ground in the foundation of AST and IST theories, consisting in the 'shift' of the bounds of hereditarily finite countability (AST) or of standard fixedness (IST), to the vagueness of infinity by

---

[12]The Transfer Principle essentially states that if something is true for a fixed, but arbitrary x, then it is true for all x, $\forall^{st} t_1 \ldots \forall^{st} t_n \forall^{st}$ **x A** $\leftrightarrow \forall$**x A**] where A is an internal formula whose only free variables are $x, t_1, t_2, \ldots, t_n$.

the adoption of certain *ad hoc* axioms or predicates which are thought of as external to their restricted first-order language axiomatical system. This is essentially the case in the intuitionistic approach, too. In both L.E.J. Brower's and H. Weyl's approach, intuitive continuum is formally described by axiomatizing the shift to an indefinite horizon in terms of *ad hoc* extension principles beyond the natural bounds of the finite and discrete, which in the case of choice sequences is represented by their initial segments.. This axiomatization is primarily expressed by the intuitionistic continuity principles, such as L.E.J. Brower's *Continuity Principle for Universal Spreads* and H. Weyl's *Principle of Open data* ([20], pp. 220-224).

Lastly, we should take into account that the impredicativity of vague infinity manifests itself in classical Cantorian system in the independence, with respect to the other axioms of **ZF**, of the *Continuum Hypothesis* (**CH**) and of the Axiom of Choice (**AC**), which is still a topic of hot debate among set theorists. Referring further to the introduction of nonstandard elements in superstructures that represent the extensional aspect of nonstandard analysis, I point, without intending to enter into deeper and more detailed analysis, to the fundamental role of the Axiom of Choice and its logical equivalent Zorn's lemma, or yet to its stronger form known as the Global Choice, (see: [1], p. 68), in the ultrapower construction (guaranteeing the existence of free ultrafilters in Los' theorem and in the Mostowski collapsing function). To the exposition of an intuitive meaning of the (uncountable) Axiom of Choice, which in the case of nonstandard superstructures reflects in a sense the 'shift' from countability to uncountable infinity, I refer to the ideas of A. Connes *et al*, in ([2], pp. 17-23).

5 Conclusion

In this article, I tried to establish an underlying foundation based, on the one hand, on the Husserlian notion of the transposition of multiplicities of appearances in the self-constituting unity of the flux of consciousness and on the other, on the Husserlian notion of an indefinitely extensible phenomenological horizon, with respect to the mathematical axiomatization of the 'shift' from the discretely intuited as multiplicities in succession to the vagueness and indiscernibility of the continuum. This axiomatization, stands essentially in the adoption of certain *ad hoc* 'external' axioms or predicates in nonstandard and non-Cantorian theories.

Both AST and IST theories enrich but do not replace the existing **ZFC** theory. Nonstandard analysis - quoting E. Nelson - supplements but does not replace internal (i.e. classical) mathematics. As a matter of fact, it is proved that Internal Set theory is a conservative extension of **ZFC** theory, in the sense that every internal theorem of IST is a theorem of **ZFC**, and also that the Alternative Set theory is a conservative extension of **ZF**$_{Fin}$ (i.e., the Zermelo-Fraenkel set-theory with the axiom of infinity substituted by its negation).[13]

Each of the two theories above, with Alternative Set Theory in a more

---

[13] For further details, see respectively [15] and [18].

5. CONCLUSION

manifest way, tries to formalize mathematically a vagueness inherent in the constitution of the external to the consciousness of a subject reality, by adopting a more phenomenologically oriented attitude in the description of the horizon towards vague continuum and its underlying indiscernibility. As it turns out, they are enriched - and in that they resemble less to Husserl's early view of classical mathematics as an exact science of pure idealities in *Ideen I* - with a measure of vagueness reflected in the ultimate irreducibility inherent in the intuition of these fundamental concepts, in the field in which they become meaningful, that is, the field of our intersubjective Life-World (*Lebenswelt*) in its ever shifting horizon. This is about a vagueness, that reflects our inability to describe continuity in an ontological sense and handle it mathematically in the same first-order language (without adding extra *ad hoc* axioms or undefined predicates) as that describing a hereditarily finite countability in our witnessed universe. As G. Longo put it in [12]: "as for geometry, and following Riemann, Poincaré, Weyl, we referred to symmetries, isotropy, continuity and connectivity of space, regularities of action and movement, as 'meaningful properties'. They are meaningful as they are embedded in our main intentional experience as hinted above: life."

BIBLIOGRAPHY

[1] Ballard, D.: (1994), Foundational aspects of "non" standard Mathematics, *Contemporary Mathematics 176*, Amer. Math. Society, Providence, RI.
[2] Connes, A., Lichnerowicz, A., Schützenberger, P.: (2000), *Triangle of thoughts*, trans. J. Gage, Paris: Ed. Oedile Jacob.
[3] Drossos, A. C.: (1989), Foundations of fuzzy sets: A nonstandard approach, *Fuzzy Sets and Systems*, 37, pp. 287-307.
[4] Feferman, S.: (1988), Weyl vindicated: Das Kontinuum 70 years later, in: *Temi e prospettive della logica e della scienza contemporanee*, V. I, CLUEB, Bologna, pp. 59-93.
[5] Feferman, S.: (2009), Conceptions of the continuum, textit*Intellectica*, 51, pp. 169-189.
[6] Føllesdal, D.: (1999), Gödel and Husserl, in: *Naturalizing Phenomenology*, (eds., J. Petitot et al.), pp. 385-400, Stanford: Stanford Univ. Press.
[7] Husserl, E.: (1970), *The Crisis of European Sciences and Transcendental Phenomenology*, Evanston: Northwestern University Press.
[8] Husserl, E.: (1973), *Ding und Raum: Vorlesungen*, Hua Band XVI, hsg. U. Claesges, The Hague: M. Nijhoff.
[9] Husserl, E.: (1993), *La phénoménologie et les fondements des sciences*, Paris: Ed. PUF.
[10] Husserl, E.: 1996, *Leçons pour une phénoménologie de la conscience intime du temps*, transl. H. Dussort, Paris: Ed. PUF.
[11] Longo, G: 1993, Solomon Feferman: 'Weyl vindicated: Das Kontinuum 70 years later', App. *Journal of Symbolic Logic*, 53, 3, pp. 31-35.
[12] Longo, G.: (2001), The Constructed Objectivity of Mathematics and the Cognitive Subject, *Epistemology of Physics and of Mathematics*, Dordrecht: Ed. Kluwer.
[13] Moran, D.: (2000), *Introduction to Phenomenology*, New York: Routledge.
[14] Nelson, E.: (1986), *Predicative Arithmetic*, Mathem. notes, Princeton: Princeton Univ. Press.
[15] Nelson, E.: (1977), Internal Set Theory: A new approach to nonstandard analysis, *Bull. of the American Mathematical Society*, 83, 6, pp. 1165-1298.
[16] Patočka, J.: (1992), *Introduction à la Phénoménologie de Husserl*, Grenoble: Ed. Millon.
[17] Petitot, J.: (1999), Morphological Eidetics for a Phenomenology of Perception, in: *Naturalizing Phenomenology*, (eds. J. Petitot et al.), pp. 330-372, Stanford: Stanford University Press.

[18] Sochor, A., Vencovskà, A.: (1981), Indiscernibles in the Alternative Set theory, *Commentationes Mathematicae Univ. Carolinae Prague*, 22, 4, pp. 785-798.
[19] Tieszen, R.: (1998), Gödel's Path from the Incompleteness Theorems (1931) to Phenomenology (1961), *The Bulletin of Symbolic Logic*, 4, 2, pp. 181-203.
[20] Van Atten, M., van Dalen, D. and Tieszen, R.: (2002), Brower and Weyl: The Phenomenology and Mathematics of the Intuitive Continuum, *Philosophophia Mathematica*, 10, 3, pp. 203-226.
[21] Vopěnka, P.: (1979), *Mathematics in the Alternative Set theory*, Teubner-Texte zur Mathematik, Leipzig: Teubner Verlag.
[22] Vopěnka, P.: 1991, The philosophical foundations of Altenative Set Theory, *Int. J. General Systems*, 20, pp. 115-126.
[23] Weyl, H.: 1977, *Das Kontinuum* (Italian Edition, care of B. Veit), Bibliopolis, Napoli.
[24] Zeeman, C.: (1962), The Topology of the Brain and visual perception, in: *Topology of 3-manifolds and related topics*, pp. 240-256, N.J.: Prentice Hall.

The Phenomenological Roots of Nonstandard Mathematics [0]

STATHIS LIVADAS

1 Introduction

As it is known a more systematic axiomatical approach to the mathematical foundations was motivated out of the foundational crisis of mathematics in the beginning of last century with the consolidation of the Zermelo-Fraenkel plus the Axiom of Choice (**ZFC**) theory, which is generally accepted as the axiomatical theory of standard mathematics. This is essentially a theory born out of the Cantorian construction of the class of ordinal numbers with some additional axiomatical tools so as to avoid circular pitfalls or conceptual confusion brought upon e.g. by Frege's cumbersome definition of sets as classes of objects generated by predicative formulas.

It should be reminded here that the original Cantorian axioms at the time of *Grundlagen* in 1883, involved a definition of sets as 'anything that can be counted' (a set is the range of a one-to-one function with domain a proper initial segment of the ordinal numbers) but it was by the application of a form of the commonly used today Power-Set Axiom that Cantor was able to prove for the first time that the real numbers form a set. He was also able to show that the power of the set of real numbers (that is, the power of the continuum) was that of the set of functions from the natural numbers to a pair, otherwise that $c = 2^{\aleph_0}$ ([13], pp. 95-98). The application of the Power-Set Axiom meant that a conception of sets was introduced in a way that they could not be counted in principle or well ordered in a definable way.

This has its own special meaning with regard to the scope of this article, as the underlying conceptual base of A. Robinson's nonstandard approach is the 'refutation' of the actual infinity[1] concept on which the Cantorian and

---

[0]This article has been published in original form in the *Romanian Journal of Information Science and Technology*, (2005), V. 8, 2, pp. 115-136.

[1]The content of the notion of actual (or Cantorian) infinity within a formal theory, can be thought of as pre-establishing an indefinitely extensible substratum in which one may perform mathematical cognitive acts of a discrete character ideally ad infinitum. In this sense, the Axiom of Choice (AC) may be regarded as an actual infinity axiom to the extent that it presupposes the existence of an infinite substratum in presentational immediacy on which to perform unique cognitive acts of choice.

subsequently the **ZFC** system is founded and the adoption of ideal elements in an enlarged domain of discourse, corresponding to a model theorist's principles of elementary extension and saturation in an enlarged domain ([2], p. 29). It is true that even though, by the words of A. Robinson, non-standard analysis, syntactically viewed, introduces new deductive procedures rather than new mathematical entities, it undertakes, in effect, to recalibrate the platonistic claims associated with the formal results of Zermelo-Fraenkel Set Theory which formalizes the concept of actual infinity in the form of the Infinity and Power-Set axioms.[2]

As a matter of fact, though, the Axiom of Choice (AC) and Zorn's lemma which have a significant position in the proof of Compactness Theorem and the construction of ultraproducts in [19] and [20], presuppose a concept of actual infinity and it is moreover proved by Z. Szczepaniak that the well-ordering principle (which is logically equivalent to the Axiom of Choice) does not follow from **ZFC** minus the Power-Set Axiom (**ZFC**$^-$) if **ZFC**$^-$ is consistent ([29], p. 339).

It is true that Robinson's nonstandard theory is generally considered as a key part of the extensional nonstandard analysis in which nonstandard entities e.g. infinitely large or infinitely small entities are thought of as possessing an objective 'existence' in extensional terms, whereas the so-called nonstandard and non-Cantorian theories, considered as the intensional part of nonstandard analysis, are generally interpreted inside an 'observer's' witnessed universe where nonstandard entities are constrained to his observational modes and inherent limitations.

In these non-Cantorian theories, that is, in the Internal Set Theory, (IST) of E. Nelson (properly interpreted), the Alternative Set Theory (AST) of the Prague School (Vopěnka, Sochor et al) and its offspring, nonstandard entities do not have an objective 'existence', rather they are introduced axiomatically by means of *ad hoc* prolongation axioms or by means of external formulas that implicate the new undefined predicate *standard*.

In the next, the claim I will support is a twofold one: First, that the notion of consistent enlargements of standard systems and the quest of ideal elements in the saturated extensions of their domains, was fundamentally introduced by E. Husserl in the notions of completeness and relative definiteness of axiomatical systems developed in his Göttingen lectures, [7]. This is mainly done in subsections 2.1 and 2.3.

Second, that the nonstandard 'ontological' approach to infinities or infinitesimalities has a close conceptual ground with the phenomenological approach to irreducible individuals in the process of constitution of phenomenological perceptions (*Wahrnehmungen*) (this is done mainly, in subsections 2.2 and 2.4).

---

[2]In A. Robinson's view, actual infinity could be substituted by the introduction of infinitely large or infinitely small numbers whose existence is " neither more nor less real than, for example, the standard irrational numbers. This is obvious if we introduce such numbers axiomatically; while in the genetic approach both standard irrational numbers and nonstandard numbers are introduced by certain infinitary processes" ([19], p. 282).

1. INTRODUCTION

This sort of account is mainly based on Husserl's reduction, in *Transzendentale und reale Logik*, [8], of the laws of analytic logic to their subjective evidences associated with the intentional directedness towards distinct unities/individuals in the lowest degree of evidence in the impredicative (or rather pre-predicative) continuous unity of experience as such.

It should be also stressed the influence that the phenomenology of temporal consciousness, developed mainly in *Vorlesungen zur Phänomenologie des inneren Zeitbewusstseins* ('Lessons for the phenomenology of inner time-conscience'), [9], held on the notions of intuitive continuum and the noetic-noematic constitution of perceptual objects in the works of H. Weyl and L.E.J Brouwer. Taking into account the Husserlian idea that perceptual intuitions as intentional ones are analogous to mathematical intuitions concerning the intuition, for instance, of sequences of natural numbers as sequences of immanent noematic objects in consciousness constituted out of phenomenological perceptions towards 'empty-somethings',[3] one may proceed to a modelization of the continuum of real numbers by means of choice sequences of natural numbers. In this approach we can generate, at any given stage, a real number defined in terms of the species of the generating terms of a choice sequence in their (temporal) extension and not as an outcome of a limiting procedure in the classical sense.

This generating process may be interpretationally connected with the phenomenological constitution of the continuous unity of the flux of time consciousness as such, that temporally 'integrates' the concrete and distinct multiplicities of immanences of perceptual objects within it, along the lines of the original impression-retention-protention scheme ([26], pp. 206-208). I choose not to deal further with the influence that phenomenological analysis bore on the intuitionistic approach of mathematics, for this might might be entirely the subject-matter of another article.

I close this introductory section by noting that insofar as nonstandard objects are taken as novel, ideal elements in consistently enlarged domains of Cantorian axiomatical systems, one may view them as objects beyond the horizon of countable infinity in a sense related to the notion of the horizon of our intersubjective Life-World, described in [10]. This has to do mainly with the AST approach to the natural infinity as explicitly stated by P. Vopěnka in [27], and it is developed in section 3.

---

[3] Husserl claimed that the mathematical objects given in intuition are founded on a specific kind of perception (categorial intuition), yet they are not perceptual objects. In the words of R. Tieszen: *"The intuition of mathematical objects is said to be 'founded' on perception because perceptual acts provide the concrete, immediate and non-reflective basis of all our experience and any intuition of abstract objects must be 'constituted' from this basis. [...] What I have taken to be essential to perceptual intuition is of course the possibility of having sequences of mental acts directed to individual perceptual objects, so this feature should be viewed as playing a crucial role in the founding of the intuition of mathematical objects. On the construal of the intuition of natural numbers I have given, this feature does play a crucial role since the structure or form of sequences in perception (which one gets by abstracting from qualitative differences in perceptual acts) may be viewed as a necessary condition for the intuition of natural numbers"*, ([24], p. 414).

2 A phenomenological interpretation of nonstandard analysis

2.1 Husserl's notion of consistent enlargement in logical-deductive systems

In his Göottingen lectures of 1901 to the German Mathematical Society, E. Husserl presented his views on a matter that had preoccupied him for at least a decade, namely the problem of imaginary objects in mathematics, this latter discipline conceived as a logical-deductive system. His main preoccupations about them were three:

1) Under what conditions can one freely use within a formally defined deductive system, concepts that make no sense according to the definition of the system and can thus be characterized as imaginary?

2) How can one be sure of the validity of the reasoning when one has also made appeal to imaginary entities in reaching a conclusion which otherwise uses the language and the rules of deduction of the formal system? and

3) Under what conditions is it permissible to extend a well-defined deductive system and create a new one in relation to which the older one stands as its formal restriction?

We should remark that the matter of these lectures may be seen in the context of an ongoing discussion that time, regarding the place of imaginary entities in mathematics, whereupon G. Frege banned from his logic any combination of signs and rules that did not designate an object, arguing that " unless an equation contained only positive numbers, it no more had a meaning than the position of chess pieces expressed a truth", and condemning the theory by which one might set down rules by which one passed from given equations to new ones in the way one moved chess pieces ([17], p. 89).

In his critique of the Fregean approach, Husserl maintained that constraints in formal theories banning reference to imaginary or non-existent objects (Husserl regarded as imaginary numbers in arithmetic negative, rational, irrational and complex numbers) only restrict the scope of logical-deductive theories and have nothing to do with the nature of the logical-deductive structure as such. His view was that the theory of complete manifolds (*vollständige Mannigfaltigkeiten*) was the key to the question as to how non-existent concepts could be dealt with as real ones within the realm of non-imaginary numbers. In this sense each syntactically well-constructed proposition exclusively expressed in the language of the domain of a complete manifold and coming out of a purely analytical procedure of a finite number of concepts and propositions drawn from the essential nature of the domain under consideration, could operate freely with imaginary concepts and be true or false in virtue of the axioms of the domain.

In such complete manifolds, he regarded that the notions: true and formal implication of the axioms are equivalent, in a statement akin to Gödel's completenesss theorem for first-order predicate calculus ([17], p. 92).

As a matter of fact, in Husserl's view any system of arithmetic is absolutely

2. A PHENOMENOLOGICAL INTERPRETATION

definite[4] and the reason for this is that " the formulas of the language of arithmetic can always be reduced to systems of equations and inequalities which are decidable" ([5], pp. 433-434). In support of this, he held that any numerical equation is decidable since it can be reduced according to the axioms by means of forms of operations (which are quantifier-free formulas), to an identity (true) or not (false) and any algebraic formula is decidable too because it is decidable for any numerical instance ([7], p. 443). The weak points of this argument are two:

First, it is questionable whether you can call an arithmetical system complete judging by its operation forms only and second, it is questionable whether you can call a general statement (an algebraic formula) decidable whenever its instances are decidable ([5], p. 434). Of course, Husserl's argument about the completeness of arithmetical systems stands in obvious contradiction with Gödel's incompleteness theorem proved in the following years but this contradiction can be easily explained in terms of the difference between them in the interpretation of the term decidability.

As it concerns Husserl's conditions for the possibility of the introduction of imaginary elements in enlargements of formal domains, the key to it is his idea of the relative definiteness of a manifold. With respect to this notion:

" If P is a proposition that says: P holds for the manifold whose existence is proved by the (axiomatical system) A, then this proposition is, for this manifold, either true or false by virtue of the axioms. The manifold contains all the objects proved as existent by virtue of A, which does not exclude, that the same axioms hold for a larger manifold, but in such a way that the extra objects are not defined to exist or proved to exist by means of the axioms without the addition of new ones." ([7], p. 454).

In other words, an axiomatical system is relatively definite (*relativ definit*) whenever a proposition that makes sense according to it can be decided within its ontological domain so that any theorem deducible in its enlargement must contain exclusively concepts that are valid in the narrower one and thus not imaginary or must contain imaginary concepts (new axioms and new elements in the extended ontological domain determined by the new axioms).

Moreover, supposing that A and B are two consistent systems of axioms and B extends A so that the ontological domain of B includes properly that of A thus containing imaginary elements from the perspective of A, then:

If B proves any proposition P in the language $L(A)$ of A, P must be necessarily proved inside A on the condition that the variables of P are restricted to the domain D of A. In that case, imaginary elements of the domain of B are not necessary in proving assertions involving exclusively objects of the domain of A ([5], p. 429).

Absolute or even relative definiteness of an axiomatical system ensures that its domain is complete in Hilbert's sense, namely that no object can be adjoined to the domain and the enlarged structure be still a model of this axiomatical

---

[4]Roughly speaking, a system of axioms is defined by Husserl as absolutely definite (*absolut definit*) in case any proposition that has a sense according to it, can be decided in general.

system. In an 'upward' directed approach, Husserl's imaginary numbers (or elements) are adjoined in consistent extensions of relatively definite systems and cannot by themselves introduce new elements into the extended formal domain to which they belong nor describe in any way this domain inside the structure of which they are essentially imaginary or 'external'. We should note, in addition, that Husserl's view of imaginary numbers is that of pure symbols inaccessible to intuition rather than of 'huge' natural numbers generated by abstraction from given collections of objects ([5], p. 434).

It seems remarkable, though, that later in *Formale und Transzendentale Logik* (1929), he reduced the laws of analytic logic to subjective evidences of experience putting consequently the concepts of definiteness and saturation inside a formal-deductive system under a new purely phenomenological perspective. In relation to the meaning of the (absolute or relative) definiteness of a manifold, developed pretty earlier in the double lecture at Göttingen in the winter of 1901-1902 but not further pursued along this line in subsequent *Logische Untersuchungen*, he asked:

" How can one know *a priori* that a domain is a nomological one and if one takes as an example of such a domain the space in its spatial forms, does the set of immediately evident axioms that is posed 'grasp' completely the essence of the space, that is, does it suffice to determine a nomology? And then, *a fortiori*, in pure formalisation or in the free construction of forms of manifolds: how can one know, how can one prove that a system of axioms is a 'definite' system, a 'saturated' system?" ([8], *transl. of the author*, pp. 131-132).

The critical turn in Husserl's view of a universal manifold in the sense of a Leibnizian *mathesis universalis* is its reduction to a problem of phenomenological interpretation of a global analytical logic. A doctrine of a universal manifold has to define, by virtue of its axiomatical forms, every other manifold which has to include its own fundamental propositional forms with their relevant logical categories that are systematically involved in the construction of judgements. In other words, it has to be constructed upon a prior discipline, that of the sound built-up of judgements (as categorial significations in the apophantic attitude) which can yet be ultimately reduced to primary evidences of experience in phenomenological attitude ([8], p. 136).

In this context, a phenomenological reduction of apophantic sentences in formal-deductive systems can be associated, on a formal-ontological level and to the extent that we talk about the introduction of new 'external' elements to the restricted domain of an axiomatical system, with the quest of ideal elements as new irreducible individualities beyond 'the horizon' of an ever extendible intentional experience, even though any ontological concerns about the status of the concepts of infinity would leave, by the words of A. Robinson, a logical positivist indifferent.

2.2 Reduction of analytic-logical principles of deductive systems to primary evidences of experience

Husserl stated in *Formale und Transzendentale Logik* that a pure analytics has to lead to a phenomenological analysis of vast amplitude and depth if it is to be really a theory of science and indeed found the possibility of an authentic science that makes available the principles of the justification of its authenticity.

As a concrete example of his position he gave the fundamental form (which he considered as one of the idealisations that play a universal role in analytic logic) of *this way in infinitum* which produces an infinity by iteration and has as its subjective correlate the form *one can always do*. It is evident that this constitutes an idealisation as nobody can always perform de facto something anew. All the same though, this kind of idealisation is evidently instrumental in the assumption of analytical principles concerning infinity axioms or in the construction of number systems by iteration e. g. given any set, one can always have a new set to which the former is disjoint and, in addition, adjoin this new set to the first one. Or, given any number a, one can always form a new number $a + 1$ and in this way starting from 1 form the infinite sequence of (natural) numbers.

In this approach, in which he sought to lay bare the subjective, constitutive origins of analytical principles lying 'hidden' behind infinite constructions by iteration or ideal existences in formal mathematics, Husserl referred also to the analytical principles of contradiction, of the excluded middle and the laws of modus ponens and modus tollens:

" In a purely objective perspective the analytical principle of contradiction is a principle on the mathematically ideal 'existence' (and co-existence) that is, on the co-possibility of judgements at the stage of distinction. But it is on the subjective side that it is to be found the *a priori* structure of evidence and the effectuations that usually come out of this structure, structure whose uncovering puts in evidence the essential subjective situations that correspond to its objective sense. and All judgements must be put in contact with 'things themselves' to which they refer, and they have to conform to them whether in a positive or negative completion" ([8], *transl. of the author*, resp. pp. 257, 261).

Positive completion is to be meant in the sense that a judgement is evidently true in the verification and sufficiency brought out out of the coincidence of the categorial objectivity 'viewed' in the presumed judgement with that same objectivity taken as a givenness (*Gegebenheit*) 'in-itself'; whereas, in the reverse case a judgement is evidently false to the extent that in the partial completion of the judgement in question, there is manifested as a givenness 'in-itself' a categorial objectivity opposed to that one apprehended in the intentionality of the original judgement, which becomes, therefore, by necessity invalid.[5]

---

[5](i) The reader may compare, in relation to the Husserlian notions of positive and negative completion, with C. Popper's principle of *Falsifizierbarkeit* in his *Logik der Forschung* (Springer, Wien 1934), concerning the scientific status of universal theories, in contrast to the *Verifizierbarkeit* principle of logical positivists.

In a yet deeper reduction of the principles of analytic logic (and therefore of formal-axiomatical mathematics) to subjective evidences, Husserl held the view that on a purely analytic level every judgement and thus every sentence in apophantic logic can be reduced by syntactical 'deconstruction' to its ultimate object-substrates so that the propositions reached at the final stage can be no longer held to be 'analytic'. These 'lowest level-nuclei' have to be objects of intentionality in the sense that they are irreducible individual-substrates of analytic propositions corresponding to absolute and individual "some-things" for the possibility and essential inner structure of which nothing can be said in analytic terms, even that they by necessity appropriate a temporal form ([8], p. 276).

These individual-substrates reached in the most fundamental level of any syntactical and correspondingly semantical reduction have no further syntactical structure and their existence can be only 'grasped' by intentional experience prior to any analytical form of judgement. Each most original judgement, being the subjective form of the effectuation of an original directedness towards things in general, must be *a priori* directed to individuals as presented in 'lowest-level' experience in its most primary and strongest sense. Moreover, taking into account his doctrine of the universal genesis of consciousness, Husserl thought of judgements[6] not only as complete outcomes of a 'constitution' or 'genesis' bearing a kind of historicity with respect to their original sense but also in their most original and primitive forms as leading to a genetic reduction of predicative evidences to the non-predicative evidence which is experience itself. Consequently, the givenness of 'last things in-themselves' and also of any modalities relative to them in an essential way (proprieties, relations etc.), as well as the subsequent construction of analytic forms of judgements of a higher level do not exclusively belong to the predicative 'universe' but also to the unity of any possible experience that is intentionally directed to these irreducible elements (whether material or formal individuals). This makes possible the cohesion of the content of any original judgement as it is based on the synthetic unity of experience transposed in the flux of consciousness of a subject who forms judgements of any degree of evidence ([8], pp. 295-296).

The Husserlian reduction of the principles of analytic logic to subjective primary evidences of experience in the construction of apophantic sentences (and therefore of formal-mathematical propositions), leads to the following three

---

(ii) Referring further to the analytic principle of the excluded middle, Husserl noted that since it decrees that all judgements can be led, in principle, to a completion, it implies an ideality to which there is no corresponding evidence, something that holds also for many other non-evident judgements, whereas referring to the universal character of analytic principles (or of universal-quantifier logical formulas), he stressed their intersubjective character in the sense of formation of ideal forms out of a multiplicity of subjective experiences that hold for every being.

[6]It should be noted that the term judgement (*Urteil*) in *Formale und Transzendentale Logik* is associated with a sense of formal logic which in Husserl's view bears the double character of apophantic logic and formal ontology, the latter discipline taken as conditioning the former, in the sense that it takes the objects of its domain as registered-in intentional ones ([8], p. 151 & pp. 107-108).

2. A PHENOMENOLOGICAL INTERPRETATION

important remarks in relation to the aim of this article:

First, the reduction of the laws of analytic logic to subjective evidences of intentional experience may well be associated with the underlying metatheoretical content of nonstandard mathematics. The latter stands essentially in the discarding of the platonic nature of the existing Zermelo-Fraenkel with Choice axiomatical system that incorporates the notion of actual infinity, and its substitution by a witnessed universe correlated to the presence of a potential 'observer' in which even though infinities and infinitesimalities are defined axiomatically, they nevertheless refer to his subjective 'observations'.[7]

Second, the fundamental reduction to constituent, indecomposable individuals as primary evidences of experience bearing no further inner structure points to a hierarchy of infinitesimals of various orders in which the infinitesimals of a given order appear to be points without structure to the immediately lower order until we unravel their own structure in a kind of a Russian doll game and reveal a class of infinitesimals of a still higher order playing provisionally the role of points. In nonstandard analysis this relates, for instance, to the definition of points in the nonstandard extension R^* of the standard set of real numbers R, that have an inner structure as equivalence classes of infinite sequences of standard real numbers modulo an ultrafilter F over the set of natural numbers (see, [20]). In such a case the standard real numbers in the classical sense are the irreducible individuals of R^*. In this context, we should also take into account the role of urelements, which are generally considered as elements of a cumulative-type hierarchy of sets with no inner structure themselves, in the definition of internal and external sets in nonstandard structures e.g. by means of an injective mapping $* : S \longrightarrow S^*$, where to every element $s \in S$ in a classical (standard) sense corresponds an inner set (which is a higher-order urelement) $(s)^* \in S^*$, but not conversely since the copy s^* in the nonstandard structure S^* may also contain nonstandard elements ([15], pp. 44-45). It is to be noted too their *ad hoc* introduction in certain nonstandard theories (e.g. the ZFBC theory) that deny the Regularity (Foundation) Axiom and thus allow for the existence of infinite $\in$-chains of sets $x_1 \ni x_2 \ni .... \ni x_n \ni ....$[8]

Third, it gives in phenomenological perspective the dialectical opposition between discreteness and continuity and moreover motivates a nonstandard approach to the notion of continuity as a non-predicative unity of naturally intuited individualities, which is formalized in certain versions of nonstandard mathematics by means of *ad hoc* prolongation axioms in saturated enlargements of the domains of standard axiomatical systems.

---

[7]This can be made clear in the semantical interpretation of the Alternative and Internal Set Theories, as will be seen in next subsections.

[8]The Foundation (Well-Foundedness) Axiom of Zermelo-Fraenkel (**ZF**) Theory, stands in conformity with the natural intuition that if sets are conceived of as collections of objects which in their turn could be collections of other objects and so on *in infinitum* , there must be ultimately a collection of 'things' which are themselves not collections of anything else, i.e. they are urelements.

2.3 Nonstandard models as conservative extensions of models of classical mathematics

Generally, extension in an intuitive mathematical sense means that an object occupies a definite place in 'space' and it is related with concepts like set, class, elements, etc. Thus if a set-theoretical formula $P(x)$ expresses a metatheoretical property p then $A = \{x;\ x \in V \wedge P(x)\}$ is the extension of property p inside the universal set V. In the case of a mathematical object, e.g. of an abstract set A, then any function $f : T \longrightarrow A$ represents an extensional aspect of A (a list of elements $\{f(t) :\ t \in T\}$ of A) which is an approach used in A. Robinson's definition of a higher order structure M.

In this sense the extensional part of nonstandard analysis, whose most significant versions are considered Robinson's nonstandard analysis ([19]) and Zakon's nonstandard ultrapower constructions ([20]), can be thought of as fundamentally based on extensions of the classical Cantorian objects of mathematics, whereas the intensional part of nonstandard analysis is considered as based on the subjective 'observations' of a potential 'observer' realized in a local and non-Cantorian way inside an intersubjective 'universe'. The notions of intersubjectivity as well as those of the locality and extendibility of the observational horizon are closely enough meant, at least by P. Vopěnka [27], in the broad sense of Husserl's *Lebenswelt* described in *Krisis der Europäischen Wissenschaften und die transzendentale Phänomenologie*, [10].

Robinson's quest of ideal elements, in a model theorist's saturation approach, is implemented inside the domain of consistent enlargements of (standard) axiomatical structures in a way that is conceptually close with both Leibniz's idea of an extended mathematical universe in the sense of preservation of 'standard' qualities in the extended one and Husserl's idea of consistent enlargements of (relatively) definite formal-deductive systems developed in subsection 0.2.1. With respect to Husserl's Göttingen approach, the nonstandard elements are 'imaginary' with respect to any sentence within the domain of a standard system and cannot by themselves decide any assertion inside the standard domain. Further, if A and B are two consistent systems of axioms and B extends A, then B cannot prove any proposition P in the language of A that, when restricted to the domain of A, A itself cannot decide (prove or disprove).

In Robinson's nonstandard language this means that no proposition can be proved inside a B-model of the B-enlargement $H_B = K \cup K_B$ of a stratified set of sentences K, which when restricted in all its variables to the domain of K cannot be decided in the model M of K ([19], pp. 33-34). Generally, the Extension and Transfer principles with respect to a standard set S and its nonstandard extension S^* can now be seen from a certain point of view to be proper formalizations in a nonstandard context of the Husserlian views on the extendibility of relatively definite manifolds.[9]

---

[9]If a standard infinite set S and also the superstructure $V(S)$ on S are given, then a nonstandard model for $V(S)$ consists of:

- A superstructure $V(S^*)$ on a nonstandard extension S^* of S and

2. A PHENOMENOLOGICAL INTERPRETATION

It is to be noted, that while Husserl was regarding imaginary elements as rather inaccessible to intuition, Robinson's nonstandard numbers are 'byproducts' of theoretical constructions involving universal quantifiers with regard to an *ad infinitum* extensible horizon of a finite set of constants occuring within a stratified set of sentences K, and are correspondingly intuited as exceeding any standard entity of common intuition ([19], p. 33-34).

In any way, even if A. Robinson stated that on an ontological level nonstandard numbers are no less real than standard irrationals, the new deductive procedures introduced stand in contrast with the platonism of the actual infinity notion embodied in Cantorian mathematics and further introduce implicitly a kind of shift of the 'horizon' of natural intuition. There exists, though, a critical detail in most nonstandard constructions that we should not overlook. Concerning Robinson's introduction of nonstandard elements by the construction of B-enlargements of standard models or Zakon's set-theoretical, non-constructive version of equivalence classes of infinite sequences modulo an ultrafilter over the set of natural numbers, there is an application of the Axiom of Choice and its logically equivalent Zorn's lemma. In Zakon's approach, Zorn's lemma is applied to guarantee the existence of an ultrafilter extending the Fréchet filters of all cofinal subsets of natural numbers, whereas in Robinson's nonstandard version Zorn's lemma (that is, equivalently, the Axiom of Choice) is applied in the construction of an ultraproduct as a model for a set K of sentences, in the proof of the finiteness principle ([19], pp. 13-19). The finiteness principle (or compactness theorem) for the first-order predicate calculus to which the corresponding principle for higher order structures is also reduced is, in fact, instrumental in proving the consistency of B-enlargements ([19], pp. 27-34).[10]

In view of my preceding arguments one might rightfully wonder what it means at least on the level of formal theory the application of the Axiom of Choice or of its logical equivalents in the context of enlarged nonstandard theories. On a formal-deductive level almost nothing, for A. Robinson already admits that nonstandard models are constructed within the framework of con-

---

- An embedding $*: V(S) \hookrightarrow V(S^*)$

that satisfy the following axioms:

- Extension Principle: S is a proper subset of S^* and $(\forall s \in S)\, [s^* = s]$
- Transfer Principle: A proposition φ in the language $\mathcal{L}(V, S)$ holds in $V(S)$ iff its $*$-transfer holds in $V(S^*)$, that is, $V(S) \vDash \varphi$ iff $V(S^*) \vDash \varphi^*$

See, [23].

[10] The generally considered as an actual infinity axiom, that is, the Axiom of Choice or its logical equivalent Zorn's lemma, is also applied in the construction of proper ultraproducts to prove a strong extension principle that leads to a κ-saturated enlargement of the standard universe U in nonstandard ZFBC theory (Zermelo-Fraenkel-Boffa set theory with choice), where again as in the theory of hypersets the well-foundedness axiom is invalid and substituted by global choice and superuniversality axioms.

A universe W is κ-saturated, if for every system $\{A_i;\ i \in I\}$, $A_i \in W$, $|I| < \kappa$, such that $\cap_{i \in J} A_i \neq \emptyset$ for every finite $J \subseteq I$, we have that $\cap_{i \in I} A_i \neq \emptyset$ for any $i \in I$ ([3], pp. 747-748). Loosely speaking, Ballard and Hrbacek have proved the existence of an extended nonstandard universe in ZFBC theory which preserves a large enough supply of urelements even in the absence of a well-foundedness axiom.

temporary (classical) mathematics and " thus affirm the existence of all sorts of infinitary entities" ([19], p. 282). To a greater or lesser measure this is true for all nonstandard extensional models and generally conforms on a formal-deductive level with Husserl's Göttingen view of the consistent extensions of relatively definite manifolds. But on a formal-ontological level it leaves an open question: No matter how explicitly professed is the scope of at least some nonstandard theories of extensional type to circumvent or to outright reject the platonic nature of Cantorian mathematics embodied in the actual infinity axioms, they cannot help introducing actual infinity indirectly in the extended axiomatical system by adjoining new actual infinity axioms as it is the case, e.g., with the introduction of the stronger than AC Global Axiom of Choice (GAC) in Zermelo-Fraenkel-Boffa set theory with choice (ZFBC), or introduce it implicitly within the proofs of fundamental theorems, mostly in the form of the Axiom of Choice (or its logical equivalents), in the construction of ultra-products or ultrapowers in general.[11]

This discussion also concerns those theories of the so-called intensional part of nonstandard analysis which are characterized as non-Cantorian (AST, IST, THS theories, etc.) to the extent that they reduce the notion of an inherently uncountable infinity to *ad hoc* prolongation principles from countable classes to the vagueness of continuum (mainly Alternative Set Theory) and the *ad hoc* axiomatization of the effect of a new undefined, non-logical predicate in the language of **ZFC** theory (Internal Set Theory). This is something that will be dealt with in the following section, along with a more general assessment of the dialectical opposition between discreteness of cognitive acts and continuity of infinity in section 3.

2.4 A phenomenological approach of urelements and prolongation principles in nonstandard theories

In subsection 2.2 we dealt to some extent with Husserl's reduction of the laws of analytic logic, and more generally of the structure of analytic judgements, to primary and direct evidences of experience. This led to an ultimate reduction of analytic sentences in their most fundamental form to their constituents-substrates apprehended by intentionality as irreducible individuals bearing no further inner structure. Further, these individuals as hyletic-noetic moments of intentionality are immanentized within a synthetic unity which is that of the constituting homogenous flux of consciousness of a subject.

In the next, I'll try to show that urelements in the axiomatical structure of nonstandard theories can be phenomenologically interpreted through analytically irreducible individuals - substrates and further that prolongation principles in nonstandard extensions of standard domains retain the essential indi-

---

[11]An attempt has been made to introduce pseudo-ultrapowers in models of **ZF** theory without the Axiom of Choice where, nevertheless, the fundamental theorem of ultrapowers holds. This is done, though, by means of constraints that considerably weaken the mathematical strength of construction, as it concerns countable models of **ZF** and other weakening conditions ([22], pp. 1209-1212).

2. A PHENOMENOLOGICAL INTERPRETATION

vidual and relational character of those individuals - substrates in the induced vagueness of continuum. Intuitively, the urelements are defined to be those mathematical objects which are not sets, therefore we could formally define a set x to be an urelement if $x = \{x\}$.

If a theory $\mathbf{ZFC}^\sigma$ is constructed as an extension of $\mathbf{ZFC}$ by adding a new constant U to $\mathbf{ZFC}$ together with the axiom $(\exists x)\,[x \in U]$, where we choose U to be the set of urelements, then there are two kinds of sets; the sets of $\mathbf{ZFC}$ and the sets of the extension $\mathbf{ZFC}^\sigma$. The elements of U (the urelements) are called inner sets, whereas anything else (the sets of a set theory with urelements) outer sets. If x is an inner set, then the outer set x^* is defined:

$$x^* = \{y \in U;\ y \in x\}$$

An outer set of this form is called an internal set and any subset of U which is not of this form is called external set ([15], pp. 39-45).

If we consider, for example, a natural number $n \in N$ in classical sense then by induction there is a unique inner set $x \in N^*$, where the corresponding outer set x^* has cardinality n (N^* is the nonstandard copy of N). This is implemented by means of an injective mapping $i : N \longrightarrow N^*$ which is generally not a surjection (ibid. p. 45). This means that for each (standard) natural n a unique inner set (urelement) $i(n)$ is defined in N^* by means of i, where the inverse uniqueness does not in general hold. There may be infinitely many numbers $x^* \in N^*$ which are not images by i of any $x \in N$.

In the general case, if S and S^* are respectively a standard and a nonstandard superstructure, it has been proved (by Lŏs theorem and Mostowski's collapsing function) that there is an elementary isomorphic embedding $* : S \longrightarrow S^*$ which is not a surjection (see, [23]), in the sense that there are $s^* \in S^*$ for which there are not $s \in S$ such that $(s)^* = s^*$. If s is a finite number of S then $(s)^* = \{y^*;\ y \in s\} = s^*$ but if s is infinite then $(s)^* = \{y^*;\ y \in s\} \subset s^*$, since s^* can also contain nonstandard elements.

In attempting to give a phenomenologically motivated interpretation to urelements in nonstandard theories we can claim at this point: the urelements are irreducible individuals (atoms) of standard (classical) mathematical structures which, in the context of nonstandard theories, preserve their invariance by isomorphic embeddings into nonstandard structures with regard to their individuality as such (Extension Principle) and their relational properties (Transfer Principle). In this sense they could be interpreted as irreducible individuals-substrates, in the sense of evidences of 'lowest-level' intentionality in Husserlian sense, which are objects-substrates of analytic propositions of a most fundamental level.

It should be stressed here the fundamental importance of the existence of a sufficient number of urelements in the domain of classical axiomatical theories on the way to their nonstandard extensions. This is evident in Robinson's nonstandard analysis in the definition of an extended B-model M of a (stratified) set of sentences K, as long as a sufficient number of constants (urelements) α is presupposed in the language of the theory so that: For every element b (understood as a binary relation) of a subset B of the set of constants occurring in the set of sentences K, there is a constant α of the language of the theory which does not occur in the set K, such that the set of sentences $X_{bg} = \Phi_\tau(b, g, \alpha)$ holds in M, where b, g belong to the set of constants occurring in the stratified set of sentences K ([19], p. 34). The existence of a sufficient number of urelements is also *sine qua non* with regard to nonstandard theories that deny the Foundation Axiom in their axiomatical structure and thus allow for the existence of infinite $\in$-chains of sets.

In ZFBC theory, for instance, the existence of a sufficient number of urelements in a proper class $U_r = \{x;\ x = \{x\}\}$ is guaranteed by the Superuniversality Axiom (BA) ([3], pp. 742-743), and it is preserved in extended nonstandard universe W by means of a strong extension principle to which I have already made reference in footnote [11]. In Hyperset Theory which also rejects the Foundation Axiom, the structural representation of a set is nevertheless made possible by AFA (anti-Foundation axiom), which essentially ignores the cumulative hierarchy of the formation of sets of standard theories and reduces to the fundamental notions of points-nodes as atoms with no inner structure and to arrows between pairs of nodes (edges).

Now, I will try to show that nonstandard entities are fundamentally defined in nonstandard extensions as irreducible individuals too, retaining by *ad hoc* axiomatization their individuality as such and their essential relational properties too. If we take, for example, Robinson's definition of the elementary nonstandard model of analysis R^*, then the nonstandard number $\alpha \in R^*$, which is greater than all (standard) numbers of R, exists by the axiomatical construction of R^* as a B-model of a set of sentences K, where the set $B = \{q\}$. That is, the sentence

$$(\exists q \in B)\ (\forall g \in \Delta_b)\ (\exists \alpha)\ \Phi_{(0,0)}(q, g, \alpha)$$

holds in R^*, where the (concurrent) constant q is interpreted as the well-known order of the reals (the formula $\Phi_{(0,0)}(q, x, y)$ means $x < y$). We must note that the nonstandard number α belongs to the set of constants of the language but does not belong to the set Γ of constants which occur in the set of sentences K that hold in the standard model R. Consequently, we may assume the nonstandard number α to be an irreducible individual-as such 'viewed' from the standard model R which preserves in the nonstandard domain of R^* the same relational properties as 'viewed' from the 'optical' field of R. In a formal sense, for any $a, b \in R$ the formula $[\Phi_{(0,0)}(q, a, b)]$ holds in R^* iff it holds in R. Generally, the irreducible character of the atoms of a standard structure and their relational properties are preserved in elementary isomorphic embeddings into nonstandard superstructures by the axiomatically postulated transfer and extension properties (footnote [10]).

In certain alternative nonstandard theories (e.g. the AST theory) the preservation of the individuality as atoms of the standard elements of the theory and also of their essential relational properties, is ensured by the prolongation principle which roughly axiomatizes the transfer between two kinds of indices, the finite naturals and the infinitely large 'supernaturals'. The very denomination as a prolongation principle reflects precisely the fact that properties concerning the first category of indices are extended or prolonged to the second one. In the next subsection 3.1, I will refer specifically to the role of the prolongation principle, in the context of Alternative Set Theory, as an axiomatical means to preserve in an essential way, the nature and the properties of elements of countable classes in the path towards an ever shifting 'horizon' and well beyond it to the vagueness of continuum. Moreover, in subsection 3.2, I'll provide a similar interpretation to certain extra axiomatical principles attached to a new nonlogical predicate *standard* added to the classical **ZFC** theory.

In summary, we may claim that the semantical content of urelements, in the conceptual framework of nonstandard structures, can be captured by the meaning that Husserl gave, in *Formale und Transzendentale Logik*, to the individuals-substrates of analytic sentences in the most fundamental level of evidence, as irreducible individuals that preserve their essential character within the impredicative synthetic unity of experience. On the formal-mathematical level, the essential character of the syntactical atoms-substrates of mathematical propositions is preserved by *ad hoc* prolongation axioms or by elementary isomorphic embeddings in the extension from standard to nonstandard structures. Moreover, nonstandard elements can be only 'viewed' as individuals themselves through the 'observational' frame of the standard system, while they can be also thought of as the new individuals for a still higher-order nonstandard system. We should emphasize here Husserl's view, in *Ding und Raum* ([11], p. 166), concerning the concept of a thing-like (*sachhaltiges*) 'point' as a 'visual atom' in a process of fragmentation that ultimately leads to *minima visibilia*. He noted there the essential similarity of the visual field to itself, on a large and small scale and explained that " it is obviously this immanent similarity which, as evident generic similarity, justifies the transposition of the eidetic relationships discovered, so to speak, in the macroscopic universe, to the microscopic 'atoms' situated beyond divisibility" ([18], p. 351).

3 Revisiting the intensional part of nonstandard analysis

3.1 Husserl's notion of the horizon and its axiomatization in the language of AST theory

In the Introduction (p. 2), I made a brief reference to the fact that in the intensional version of nonstandard analysis the existence of infinitesimals and of infinities has a subjective 'observational' character possibly linked to the modes of intentionality of an 'observer's' consciousness, who is placed with regard to the absolute **ZFC** framework in a local and non-Cantorian way. By virtue of this, the Alternative Set Theory (AST) and Internal Set Theory (IST) properly interpreted, along with some ultrafinitist ramifications (e.g. concerning the work of J. Hjelmslev, S. Lavine, A. S. Yessenin-Volpin) and lately Nonstandard Class Theory (NCT) and the Theory of Hyperfinite Sets (THS, [1]), are generally considered as the main pillars of this alternative nonstandard approach.

It should be made clear that by a local and non-Cantorian way of 'observing', it is meant that the notion of actual infinity, incorporated in Cantorian **ZFC** theory, is refuted and substituted in AST by a notion of natural infinity which manifests itself in the 'observation' of phenomena present in very large sets, e.g. in relation to the intuition of the topological continuum in 'observing' a concrete physical surface. As 'very large set' is considered a set which from the classical point of view is finite but which, nevertheless, " is not located as a whole and along with each of its elements, in front of the horizon currently limiting the view of the given set. Here we understand 'view' in much more than a visual sense, that is, essentially as a grasping and holding of some field of phenomena." ([28], p. 116).

On a formal-syntactical level, AST theory deals with sets and classes as objects. Sets are definite, (may be very large), sharply defined and finite from the classical point of view, taking into account that in the universe of sets, AST accepts the axioms of Zermelo-Fraenkel theory with the exception of the axiom of infinity; as a matter of fact, it is proved by A. Sochor to be a conservative extension of **ZF**$_\text{fin}$ ([21], p. 145). Classes, on the other hand, represent indefinite clusters of objects such as the class N of natural numbers in the classical sense. Thus the extended universe of sets of this theory includes some extra axioms, in addition to those of the well-known universe of sets V, that are not set-theoretical formulas:

- The axiom of existence of classes:

  For any property $\varphi(x)$ of sets in the universe of sets the extended universe contains the class $\{x;\ \varphi(x)\}$

- The axiom of existence of proper semisets:

  There is a proper semiset. In the AST language,

  $$(\exists x)\ (\text{Sms}(X)\ \wedge\ \neg\text{Set}(X))$$

  In AST theory an important role is played by proper semisets which are classes inside sets and, roughly, represent blurriness and non-surveyability in the 'observation' inside very large sets.

- The Prolongation principle:

  For each countable function F there is a set function f such that $F \subseteq f$.

  It is important here to have in mind that countability of a function is, in fact, countability of a class of ordered pairs of elements and that a set function should be regarded as an (uncountable) set of ordered pairs of elements, see [27], (Ch. I).

3. REVISITING INTENSIONAL NONSTANDARD ANALYSIS

As I have stated above, infinity in AST sense is not beyond but already present in very large sets, e.g. in the application to certain macro or microscale phenomena that appear in very large sets and it is precisely in this sense that it is characterized as natural infinity in contrast to the classical infinity of Cantorian set theory; classical infinity, according to Vopěnka's view, becomes relevant in relation to real world phenomena when it applies its classical infinity results to natural infinity. Natural infinity in its most basic form should be understood as a countable natural infinity, in the sense of an initial grasp of a local finiteness and the subsequent constant shift of the horizon of 'sharpness' and 'discernibility' until it stabilizes to something constantly unchangeable and definite in the sense of classical countability ([28], pp. 116-118).

It is important to emphasize that P. Vopěnka states explicitly that the term horizon above, is understood in the sense of E. Husserl's horizon of Life-World (*Lebenswelt*) reducing, in effect, the AST definition of a countable class of elements to this phenomenological notion: " If a large set x is observed then the class of all elements of x that lie before the horizon need not be infinite but may converge toward the horizon. The phenomenon of infinity associated with the observation of such a class is called countability" ([27], p. 39).

In a purely phenomenological sense a notion of the world as exceeding the perception of things is already found in the first book of *Ideen* under the term of 'halo' (*Hof*) or, more frequently, 'Horizon'. In this context, horizon takes its intentional meaning from what Husserl called *Horizontintentionalität* (horizontal intentionality), originally characterized by the preoccupations of a psychology of 'attention' in the most broad sense.[12] Much later, the term horizon was meant in an *a priori* sense and incorporated in the notion of Life-World[13] as an ever shifting 'bound' of the noematic field of a subject existing in terms of its constituting ego with regard to the Life-World.

In this approach, the countable class FN of natural numbers is considered in AST as representative of the path towards the horizon, in the formal sense of hereditary finiteness of each of its segments. The formal definition of a countable class in AST is the following:

A pair $< A, \leq >$ of classes is called an ordering of type ω iff:

1. 1. $\leq$ linearly orders A

---

[12] " This horizontal intentionality has multiple and diverse modes: retentional and protentional horizon that encompasses the present 'grasp' of an object, active and passive motivation in my accomplishment of various acts, in the realization of the possibility of a certain experience over another, in the enlargement or retraction of my field of view, etc. The horizontal intentionality is thus responsible for the continuity of the life of the subject [...] and (is) the principle that integrates all acts in the continuous unity of life, in the flux of consciousness of the subject" ([4], *transl. of the author*, p. 99).

[13] " To be sure, everyday induction grew into induction according to scientific method, but that changes nothing of the essential meaning of the pregiven world as the horizon of all meaningful induction. It is this world that we find to be the world of all known and unknown realities. To it, the world of actually experiencing intuition, belongs the form of space-time together with all the bodily shapes incorporated in it; it is in this world that we ourselves live, in accord with our bodily, personal way of being." ([10], p. 50).

2. 2. A is infinite and

3. 3. for each $x \in A$ the segment $\{y \in A;\ y \leq x\}$ is finite

A class X is countable iff there is a relation R such that $< X, R >$ is an ordering of type ω. A class is uncountable if it is neither countable nor finite. It may be noted that it is a theorem of AST that each countable class is a proper semiset, thus providing an intuitive approach to semisets as classes with hereditarily finite segments ([27], pp. 39-42).

A drastic and qualitative shift of the horizon leading to the vagueness of intuitive continuum is induced axiomatically by the Prolongation Principle which is, in fact, a saturation principle on a nonstandard model of Peano arithmetic. In a phenomenologically motivated interpretation of AST, a remarkable consequence of the Prolongation Principle is that: If a perceived (i.e. definable inside a intersubjective universe including at least one 'observer') state of affairs φ holds of every element of a sequence (x_n), $n \in \omega$, (where ω is the cardinality of countable infinity in AST) progressing towards the horizon, then (x_n), $n \in \omega$, is extensible to a sequence (x_β), $\beta \leq \alpha$ which crosses the horizon and its members also satisfy φ.

Put in a somewhat less formal language, any collection of elements, these latter perceived in a phenomenological sense (that is, as individuals-substrates of intentional 'observation'), 'in front of the horizon' of AST countability can extend beyond the horizon preserving the essential characteristics of its elements (e.g. individuality, ordering) ([25], p. 394). This is a saturated nonstandard enlargement in the sense of nonstandard theories already discussed, only that P. Vopěnka puts the emphasis on the original and straightforward way that countable infinity is interpreted within AST, i.e., as hereditary finiteness towards a phenomenological horizon which axiomatically motivates nonstandardness.

3.2 The interpretation of IST nonstandard approach

In relation to the Internal Set Theory, described by E. Nelson as a variant on the syntactical level of A. Robinson's nonstandard analysis "without enlarging the world of mathematical objects in any way" ([15], p. 1), there is a tendency to see it as part of intensional nonstandard mathematics. In reaching this conclusion it helps to refer to Nelson's introduction of a new nonlogical predicate *standard* in the language of **ZFC** theory, which by its axiomatical tools can be interpreted as indirectly inducing the presence of an 'observer' within an intersubjective universe.

The axiomatical tools of the new undefined predicate *standard*, even though it purportedly plays a rather syntactical role within the new theory while being loosely associated semantically with a vague notion of fixedness, are the following three axioms, where by the term internal formula it is meant a formula of ordinary mathematics that does not involve the predicate *standard* even indirectly.

- The Transfer Principle (T):

$\forall^{st}t_1...\forall^{st}t_n \ [\forall^{st}x \ A \leftrightarrow \forall x \ A]$, where A is an internal formula whose only free variables are $x, t_1, t_2, ..., t_n$

The intuition behind (T) is that if something is true for a fixed, but arbitrary x, then it is true for all x.

- The Idealization Principle (I):

  $\forall^{stfin}x' \ \exists y \ \forall x \in x' \ A \leftrightarrow \exists y \ \forall^{st}x \ A$ where A is again an internal formula.

  To say that there is a y such that for all fixed x we have A, is the same as saying that for any fixed finite set of x's there is a y such that A holds for all of them. Put more naively, we can only fix a finite number of objects at a time.

- The Standardization Principle (S):

  $\forall^{st}X \ \exists^{st}Y \ \forall^{st}z \ [z \in Y \leftrightarrow z \in X \ \& \ A]$ where A is any formula internal or external.

  Intuitively, we can say that if we have a fixed set, then we can specify a fixed subset of it by giving a membership criterion for each of its fixed elements. See ([15], pp. 3-11).

In line with the phenomenological approach of urelements and prolongation axioms in nonstandard theories, proposed in subsection 2.4, we could interpret the Idealization Principle as prolonging the 'horizon' of finiteness of a collection of standard elements by preserving their standard ('fixed') character, whereas the Transfer Principle could be interpreted as prolonging indefinitely the 'horizon' of standard elements with respect to their individual and relational character expressed in terms of the language of the classical (standard) system **ZFC**. Evidently, in spite of their syntactical role in the the IST theory, these three axioms generate a nonstandard extension in the domain of 'fixed' elements, where in informal mathematical discourse the term 'fixed' can be taken as an intuition of the new predicate *standard*. By the axiomatical machinery above, specifically by the idealization principle (I), it is easily proved that there exists a nonstandard number in any infinite set, including the set of natural numbers, and moreover, continuity and topological properties involving the new nonstandard definitions of infinitesimal and unlimited numbers are straightforward generated by the enriched IST language ([15], Ch. I). Lastly, in accordance with earlier arguments on the possibility of consistently extending relatively definite manifolds in subsection 2.1, this theory is proved to be a conservative extension of **ZFC** theory, in the sense that every internal statement (a statement expressed strictly in the language of **ZFC**) which can be proved in IST can be also proved in **ZFC** ([16], pp. 1192-1197).

Though it is not in the scope of the present article to deal in depth with the theoretical question of the dialectical or complementary opposition of discreteness and continuity on a philosophical level it happened, as a matter of fact, to point out that there exists a notion of actual infinity as an 'underlying substratum' in any approach introducing new nonstandard entities by consistent enlargements of classical axiomatical systems. This was manifest in most nonstandard theories - retaining as valid the Foundation Axiom or not - in the application of the Axiom of Choice and Zorn's lemma in the construction of proofs of fundamental enlargement theorems. In the intensional nonstandard case, the countable infinity horizon was shifted to the vagueness of (uncountable) continuum by *ad hoc* axiomatical principles (e.g., the prolongation principle in AST) or by the introduction of the new nonlogical predicate *standard* along with *ad hoc* generated axiomatization in IST theory.

In view of the overall argumentation developed in this article, it seems that there exists an inherent factor of impredicativity in the notion of intuitive and, formally, of mathematical continuum, which is reflected in its indescribability in any first-order language. This impredicativity might be further radically reduced phenomenologically to the origin of a synthetic unity self-constituted in the homogeneity of the flux of the temporal consciousness of a subject, in the Husserlian approach as developed in his earlier texts in the *Phänomenologie des inneren Zeibewusstseins* and later in his Bernau manuscripts on the phenomenology of time (resp.: [9], [12]); see also, [14]. If phenomenological analysis is to prove of any further significance relative to the core of the matter, we should inquire into how one is led to the self-constituting continuous unity of the flux of temporal consciousness out of discrete multiplicities of appearances (*Erscheinungen*) of immanent objects within it.[14]

4 Conclusion

As the scope of this paper was to interpret the formal-axiomatical structure of nonstandard mathematical theories in terms of a phenomenological motivation, I attempted to do this on two levels: The formal-deductive and the ontological one.

In relation to the first one, I pointed to the convergence on a fundamental level between the Husserlian view of imaginary elements as new elements in the domain of consistent enlargements of relatively definite manifolds and the introduction of nonstandard elements in conservative enlargements of classical axiomatical systems. My review was focused also into how analytical principles are reduced to direct evidences in the lowest level of intentional experience in a phenomenological approach. In so doing, I dealt under this perspective with nonstandard methods that introduce new objects which stand beyond the horizon from the scope of the domains of classical systems to which they are imaginary in the formal sense of Husserl's Göttingen views.

On a formal-ontological level, these new objects can be interpreted as irreducible individuals in a new level of reality that would be an intentional correlate of most primary intentional experience in the sense described in subsection 2.2. They are elements of extended domains of standard systems retaining standard essential characteristics by means of *ad hoc* axiomatical principles, but

---

[14]On the circularity of the notion of continuity generated in a mathematical modelization of the intentionalities of the flux of consciousness, see J. Petitot's *Morphological Eidetics for a Phenomenology of Perception*, [18].

4. CONCLUSION

existing in a horizon beyond common mathematical (and perceptual) intuition. In Alternative Set Theory this was defined to be the horizon of natural infinity, put in formal terms as the horizon of a countable class infinity and motivated by the phenomenological notion of the horizon of the Life-World. In a structuralist approach, based largely on category-theoretical notions, talk is even made about the introduction of new levels of reality by nonstandard extensions (see [6]).

Irrespectively of whether one accepts that phenomenological analysis can be an appropriate interpretational tool of nonstandard analysis, either of an extensional or an intensional specification, it can be certainly argued that it may yet provide a radical theoretical tool to a new evolving, more 'natural' and thus non-Cantorian approach of mathematics.

BIBLIOGRAPHY

[1] Andreev, P., Gordon, E.: (2006), A Theory of Hyperfinite Sets, *Annals of Pure and Applied Logic*, 143, 1-3, pp. 3-19.
[2] Ballard, D.: (1994), *Foundational aspects of 'Non'-standard Mathematics*, Providence: Amer. Mathematical Society.
[3] Ballard, D., Hrbacek, K.: (1992), Standard foundations for nonstandard analysis, *The Journal of Symbolic Logic*, 57, 2, pp. 741-748.
[4] Bernet, R.: (1994), *La vie du sujet*, Paris: ed. PUF.
[5] Da Silva, J. J.: (2000), Husserl's two notions of completeness, *Synthese*, 125, pp. 417-438.
[6] Drossos, C.: (2005), Structure, Points and Levels of Reality, in: *Essays on the Foundations of Mathematics and Logic*, (ed. G. Sica), Polimetrica Inter. Scient. Pub., pp. 83-114.
[7] Husserl, E.: (1970), *Philosophie der Arithmetik*, Husserliana XII, ed. Lothar Eley, Den Haag: M. Nijhof.
[8] Husserl, E.: (1984), *Logique formelle et logique transcendantale*, transl. S. Bachelard, Paris: Ed. PUF.
[9] Husserl E.: (1996), *Leçons pour une phénoménologie de la conscience intime du temps*, transl. H. Dussort, Paris: Ed. PUF.
[10] Husserl, E.: (1970), *The crisis of European sciences and transcendental phenomenology*, transl. D. Carr, Evanston: Northwestern Univ. Press.
[11] Husserl, E.: (1973), *Ding und Raum*, Hua XVI, Ed. U. Claesges, The Hague: M. Nijhoff.
[12] Husserl, E.: (2001), *Die Bernauer Manuskripte über das Zeitbewußtsein (1917/18)*, herausg. R. Bernet & D. Lohmar, Dordrecht: Kluwer Acad. Pub.
[13] Lavine, S.: (1994), *Understanding the infinite*, Harvard Univ. Press.
[14] Livadas, S.: (2009), The Leap from the Ego of Temporal Consciousness to the Phenomenology of Mathematical Continuum, *Manuscrito* (Revista Internacional de Filosofia), 32, 2, pp. 321-356.
[15] Nelson, E.: (1986), *Predicative arithmetic. Mathematical notes*, Princeton: Princeton Univ. Press.
[16] Nelson, E.: (1977), Internal Set Theory: A new approach to nonstandard analysis, *Bulletin of the American Mathematical Society*, 83, 6, pp. 1165-1198.
[17] Ortiz Hill, C., (2002), Tackling three of Frege's problems: Edmund Husserl on sets and manifolds, *Axiomathes*, 13, pp. 79-104.
[18] Petitot, J.: (1999), Morphological Eidetics for a Phenomenology of Perception, in: *Naturalizing Phenomenology*, pp. 330-372, Stanford: Stanford University Press.
[19] Robinson, A.: (1966), *Non-standard Analysis*, Amsterdam: North-Holland Pub. Company.
[20] Robinson, A., & Zakon, E.: (1969), A set-theoretical characterisation of enlargements, in: *Applications of model theory to algebra, analysis and probability*, (ed. W. A. J. Luxembourg), pp. 109-122, New York: Holt, Rinehart & Winston.

[21] Sochor, A.: (1983), Metamathematics of the Alternative Set Theory III, *Commentationes Mathematicae Universitatis Carolinae*, 24, pp. 137-154.
[22] Spector, M.: (1988) Ultrapowers without the axiom of choice, *The Journal of Symbolic Logic*, 53, 4, 1208-1219.
[23] Stroyan, K.D., Luxembourg, W.A.J.: (1976), *Introduction to the Theory of Infinitesimals*, New York: Academic Press.
[24] Tieszen R.: (1984), Mathematical Intuition and Husserl's Phenomenology, *Noŭs*, 18, 3, pp. 395-421.
[25] Tzouvaras, A.: (1998), Modeling vagueness by nonstandardness, *Fuzzy sets and systems*, 94, pp. 385-396.
[26] Van Atten M., Van Dalen D., Tieszen R.: 2002, Brouwer and Weyl: The Phenomenology and Mathematics of the Intuitive Continuum, *Philosophia Mathematica*, 10, 3, pp. 203-226.
[27] Vopěnka, P.: (1979) *Mathematics in the Alternative Set Theory*, Leipzig: Teubner.
[28] Vopěnka, P., *The philosophical foundations of Alternative Set theor y*, Int. J. General Systems, vol. 20, pp. 115–126, 1991.
[29] Zarach, A.: (1982), Unions of ZF^- models which are themselves ZF^-, in: (*Logic Colloquium '80*, 108), *Studies in Logic and the foundations of Mathematics*, pp. 315-342, Amsterdam: North-Holland Pub. Company.

A Phenomenological Analysis of Observation [0]

STATHIS LIVADAS

1 Introduction

In the following I will deal with the question of interpreting, in a phenomenological motivation, the notion of observation as such and several notions associated with it, in an epistemological context. Within the limits of this article, I find it purposeful to focus on particular aspects of the notion of observation pointing mainly to the semantical content of certain relevant parts of formal-axiomatical theories of mathematics and to a certain elaboration of physical reality in quantum physics.

In pursuing the goals of this article, I largely relied on Husserl's original texts, mostly those in [5], [6], [10], [11], that is, those relative respectively to the concepts of the genetic-kinetic constitition of reality, of the constituting flux of temporal consciousness, of the impredicative subjectivity of the flux, of the radical reduction of analytic laws to primary evidences of experience, of the notion of the horizon of Life-World, etc., as presented in section 2. I am also based, in connection with the epistemic sense of the notion of observation, on the mathematical-theoretical work of P. Vopěnka and E. Nelson in section 3 and lastly on the interpretational context proposed by E. Scrödinger in his undulatory image of physical reality, in section 4.

In this last section, I consider motivating to briefly deal with A. N. Whitehead's ontological-categorial scheme in his philosophy of organism, to the extent that it raises the question of continuity in terms of an irreducible concept of process, from both an epistemological and phenomenological vantage point.

2 Observation in terms of a phenomenological constitution

In this section, I will try to present a core of questions originating from the phenomenological analysis of the constitution of a real being and generally of physical reality as a self-donated presense in front of the intentionality of consciousness, to the extent that they will be given a proper epistemic reformulation in the following sections. These questions have been put under a

---

[0]This article has been published in original form in *Phenomenological Inquiry*, (2005), V. XXIX, pp. 29-53.

new perspective in epistemology in the light of a phenomenological approach although in an ontological sense they have been dealt with to one or the other degree by classical Greek and subsequent Occidental philosophy[1].

In the order of presentation these questions are related to:

(i) The genetic-kinetic constitution of beings of 'objective' reality as unities of multiplicities in the constituting flux of temporal consciousness (ii) The ensuing problematic of the continuous unity of constitution in contrast to the sequential character of immanent multiplicities in the flux (iii) The reduction to an impredicative[2] subjectivity as a transcendental source of the unity of time consciousness called by Husserl the pure ego of cogito (iv) The reduction of the principles of analytic logic and consequently of the axiomatical character of logical-deductive systems to primary evidences of intentional experience (v) The intersubjective character of the definition of the objects of intentionality inside an all-incorporating and ever shifting Life-World (*Lebenswelt*).

It would be worthwhile, at first, to refer to E. Husserl's firm statement that " ontology is not phenomenology" in connection with his exposition of the genetic-kinetic character of phenomenological constitution, in the first part of the manuscript preceding *Ideen III* ([5], App. I: pp. 138, 152, 158).

In this respect, " the mode of ontological consideration is catastematic (*katastematisch*), in that it regards unities in their identity and in relation to their identity as something fixed, (whereas) the phenomenological constitutive consideration takes unity in the flux, which is to say as a unity of a constituting flux; it is attached to the motions, to the flows in which such a unity and each component, aspect or real property of this unity is a correlate of the identity. This mode of consideration is, in a certain way, kinetic or 'genetic': a 'genesis' which refers to a 'transcendental' world totally different of that of natural genesis and of that one of natural sciences. [....] In the phenomenological method of *kinesis*, what is one precisely separates into two: the essential directions of intentionality and of its intentional correlates and the essential determinations of the identical being which in the intentional evidences is conscious of its being identical and which represents itself as identical by the order of its correlates." ([5], *transl. of the author*, p. 158).

In view of the multiple aspects of reality entangled in our environment, the kinetic character of phenomenology tries to seize the unities that constitute those species of reality in all their moments; in this sense the real being is

---

[1] One might refer, for instance, to the notion of spatiotemporal continuity of mouvement in Plato's *Parmenides* (156D, E, The Loeb Class. Library), and to the definition of material points or lines as limits in Aristotle's *Coming to be and passing away* (316b 15 and 320b 15, The Loeb Class. Library); also to R. Descarte's notion of *res extensa* in *Discours de la Méthode* and G. Leibniz's monadology in the *Fifth letter to Clark*.

[2] The term impredicativity which is an essentially ontological term is commonly conceived in the sense of impredicative mathematical theories in which there is no stratification of the mathematical universe and, informally speaking, one cannot comprehend (or describe) the elements or the parts but in terms of the whole, or at least of a part of it of the same genus as the whole. It should be noted in addition that in Platonic tradition impredicativity of an object is the impossibility to assign to it any predicates at all, defined identically, therefore, as the non-being (Plato's Parmenides, 163D, The Loeb Class. Library).

2. OBSERVATION

not given but as a unity of multiplicities and the kinetic method studies how these unities are progressively constituted by restituting them in the immanent homogenous flux of multiplicities ([5], p. 211). The genetic-kinetic structure of phenomenological analysis consists thus in the constitution of reality, whose ontological objectivity is bracketed by *Epochë*, as a unity of multiplicities by means of *a priori* intentional forms of consciousness towards a unity of the given profiles of re-identifying objects in the constituting flux, the latter one meant as a phenomenon in itself. In the flux of consciousness, immanent unities (e.g. the immanent sonorous effects of a sound) are constituted within the unity of the flux by a certain mode with regard to the intentional forms of the constituting flux of consciousness. This has to do with the constitution of the unity of a sequence of original impressions together with their protentions, retentions and the descending continuous sequence of their retentions, by means of the double intentionality of the constituting flux of consciousness, as developed in *Vorlesungen zu einer Phänomenologie des inneren Zeitbewusstseins*.[3]

I must point out here that the genetic-kinetic constitution of reality is essentially reducible to the time constitution and that the constituting flux of consciousness is, in Husserlian view, a temporal consciousness constantly generating time in a kind of transcendental, egological genesis to the meaning of which I will refer next. In *Ding und Raum* which came out of his 1907 Göttingen summer lectures, Husserl stated that " In phenomenological perception (*Wahrnehmung*), a thing appears not as a bare content-of-thing, which is evidently pure abstraction, it rather appears as temporal and temporally extended, in this way as a time-fulfilled thing. A thing is in a full sense a temporal extension, a temporality in a fulfilled thingness-content concreteness" ([7], *transl. of the author*, p. 63).

In terms of the genetic-kinetic constitution one has a twofold description of the unity of the constituting flux of consciousness. On the one hand, the continuous association of the immanences of the multiplicities of original impressions with their intentional correlates (i.e. retentions-protentions) within the constituting flux and on the other the self-constituting unity of the flux in itself as an absolute subjectivity. Concerning the latter, we have to note that this is an obscure and ambivalent culmination of the Husserlian supplementary reduction of the objectified flux of consciousness to an absolute subjectivity which in a kind of transcendental, egological genesis constantly generates time. This was termed by Husserl the absolute ego of consciousness and it was conceived as a transcendental subjectivity having no duration or extension, in other words a transcendental and therefore impredicative unifying factor of the constituting flux of time consciousness ([6], p. 99).

I claim that the radical reduction to this impredicative subjectivity[4] not

---

[3]Cf. with J. Petitot's mathematical modelization of the intentional forms of consciousness by means of gluing local isomorphisms $\varphi_{tt'}$ in the continuous limit, where t's are time parameters in the temporal flow which in the particular model entail a correspondence $\kappa_t \leftrightarrow i_t$ between purely ocular kinesthetic sensations κ and visual images i ([21], pp. 355-358).

[4]Husserl described the unity of the pure ego as a temporal being of a totally different

only leads to a back-door re-emergence - although of a totally different type - of the transcendence of 'objective' reality, already banished by *Epochë*, but can be taken moreover as underlying the impredicative character of continuous unity in a formal sense, as opposed to the discreteness of an indefinite collection of formal individuals, both in an analytic-mathematical context and in the observational-interpretational context of quantum mechanics. Regarding the nature of temporal continuity, Husserl had stated already in *Philosophie der Arithmetik* that although we can represent objects in instantaneity, certain particular reflections are needed to be aware of every instantaneity in the representation of an object, which is something that leads to (the nature of) inner experience. " We see in this way, that a collective aggregate ought not be described as a temporal instantaneity" ([8], *transl. of the author*, p. 24).

Husserl came later in *Formale und Transzendentale Logik* (published in 1929) to link his research on the structure and the modes of subjective experience with the analytic-logical principles of formal-deductive systems such as those of axiomatical mathematical systems. By a purely phenomenological analysis he reduced, in effect, analytic principles like those, for instance, of identity, non-contradiction and the excluded middle to fulfillments of primary evidences of experience ([11], pp. 254-258 & pp. 260-264). Going further with the reduction of analytic judgements to their most fundamental constituents, one is led to the ultimate object-substrates of apophantic sentences that can be only thought of as evidences of intentional experience and moreover as no further reducible individuals themselves, for the inner structure of which, even for the fact that they appropriate a temporal form nothing can be said in analytic terms. Any conceivable apophantic sentence has, in final count, its ground meaning based on reference to objects of a formal-ontological domain and " by reductionist elaboration any conceivable judgement has consequently a relation to a real universe, a world or a region of the world for which it is valid" ([11], *transl. of*

---

character of the temporal unity of cogito taken as a phenomenon. This pure ego has no extension nor duration, it stands as an indivisible and inextensible unity for the cogito and identically so for any other cogito but as identical subject of any intentional act it is susceptible to realization in a mode similar to the unity of a sound and in this way enters in what is being realized and adopts the real, empirical character of the objectified consciousness in its psychic states ([5], p. 138). With respect to the impredicative character of the pure ego of consciousness, Jan Patočka proposed that a kind of retention is interposed between the pure ego-in-act and the ego-in-reflection without which the pure or transcendental ego of consciousness would be inaccessible. But this kind of retention, as a presupposition of every possible reflection on the transcendental ego manifests itself as a circularity of terms, since it has been already taken to 'be', in Husserlian description, an intentional form of the objectified flux of consciousness, therefore utterly belonging to what is already an objectified state-of-affairs.

Patočka inferred, in any case, that the 'being' of the transcendental ego independently of its autoalienation, from which it is inseparable, is inaccessible to us without objectification. It follows that as any objectification points to something already objectified, one can ground the presupposition of an absolute subjectivity making possible the unity of the temporal flux as an objective whole, which moreover transcends temporality in objective sense. As, in turn, temporality is the necessary condition of every individuality and every existence in the world as well as of every first degree transcendental reflection, one evidently cannot attribute to the transcendental ego the predicates of existence and individuality ([18], pp. 163-168).

2. OBSERVATION

the author, pp. 276-278).

I need not close this section without reference to two fundamental Husserlian notions, the notion of intersubjectivity and that of the horizon of our incorporating Life-World (*Lebenswelt*), viewed in connection to the interpretational context of quantum mechanics, in particular, with respect to the interaction between an observing subject, the measuring device and a quantum object in proper sense and also to that of certain non-Cantorian versions of nonstandard mathematical theories.

Regarding the notion of intersubjectivity, Husserl made a distinction in the attitude towards the world of physical experience, which is relevant to the orientation to one or the other of two structures of natural reality. On the one hand there is the material, causal and spatiotemporal structure, in which our bodies are inserted as physical-material bodies, possessing certain properties and proper modes of 'appearance'. On the other, there is a somatological structure of nature, that of living (or animated) bodies as fields of localisation of different sensations but integrated in their kinesthesiological function as freely moving bodies, resulting in a reciprocal and essential in character relation between these bodies and nature, the latter meant as *Lebenswelt*.

In this view, material things are in causal relation only to material things and are offered as the most extreme inferior limits of the pre-phenomenal world, which are only to a certain degree accessible to us (see: [9], p. 379), in the sense that we must make abstraction from our substratum as animated bodies to make the most of accessibility towards them.[5] The somatological structure refers, therefore, to the order of animated bodies inside nature, to the structure of their intentional experience and further to their eidetic intuition with respect to the evident givennesses of the objects of intentionality.

The (phenomenological) perception and the kinetic constitution of objects of pre-phenomenal reality as multiplicities of their immanences with their correlated moments in the constituting flux of consciousness induces their objectification in terms of a mutual comprehension (*Wechselverständingung*) between nature in primary sense and the plurality of experimenting empirical egos incorporated in their particular animated bodies which appear to them as they appear to those with whom they mutually 'comprehend', ([5], p. 4). In other words, objectivity in natural reality is founded on intersubjectivity inside an incorporating Life-World meant as an ever extending horizon with which all animated bodies bear a reciprocal relation of co-subordination.[6]

The idea of the horizon of a world-soil was extensively developed by Husserl

---

[5]This is reflected, for instance, in the problematic concerning the physical meaning of the wave function ψ in Schrödinger's time-independent wave equation

$$(-\frac{\hbar^2}{2m}\nabla^2 + V(\vec{r}))\psi(\vec{r}) = E\psi(\vec{r})$$

and its capacity of complete description of a particular state of the quantum system.

[6]Cf. with M.Merleau-Ponty's conception of nature as the grounding soil (*gründenden Boden*) of every possible experience, e. g. in the published notes of his courses in the *Collège de France*, [15].

in *Die Krisis der europäischen Wissenschaften und die transzendentale Phänomenologie*, [10]. Originally it was conceived in terms of what Husserl called *Horizontintentionalität* (horizontal intentionality) which was was characterized by the preoccupations of a psychology of 'attention' in the most broad sense[7] Much later the term horizon was put in a more general context and incorporated in the notion of Life-World[8] as an ever shifting 'bound' of the noematic field of a subject existing in terms of correlation with Life-World. In the immediately following section, I'll look into how this phenomenological notion of an ever shifting horizon, as the bound of a 'witnessed' universe in which a potential observer makes his observations in a local and intersubjective fashion, is axiomatized in certain non-Cantorian and nonstandard theories.

3 The sense of observation in the intensional part of nonstandard analysis

3.1 Husserl's idea of the horizon and its formalization in the language of AST

In the intensional part of nonstandard analysis - in contrast to the extensional part (e.g. Robinson's analysis) in which nonstandard objects are considered to have an 'objective' existence - the existence of infinitesimals and of infinities has a subjective 'observational' character linked to the intentional modes of an 'observer's' consciousness who 'sees' the absolute **ZFC** framework (the Zermelo-Fraenkel plus the Axiom of Choice system of axioms of classical or Cantorian mathematics) in a local and non-Cantorian way.

By virtue of this, Alternative Set Theory (AST) and Internal Set Theory (IST), properly interpreted, along with ultrafinitist theories (e.g. those associated with J. Hjelmslev, S. Lavine, A. S. Yessenin-Volpin) and recently Nonstandard Class Theory (NCT) ([12]) and the Theory of Hyperfinite Sets (THS) ([1]) are the main representatives of this alternative nonstandard approach. I will deal with the first two theories (AST and IST) as they are generally considered as the main pillars of the non-Cantorian mathematical approach, especially in view of the fact that NCT and THS, for instance, are quite close to IST and AST respectively and can be thus taken as their ramifications.

It must be made clear that by local and non-Cantorian way of 'observing' it

---

[7] " This intentionality has multiple and diverse modes: retentional and protentional horizon that determine the 'grasp' of an object, active and passive motivation in the accomplishment of various acts, in the realization of the possibility of an experience over another, in the enlargement or retraction of my field of view. The horizontal intentionality is thus responsible for the continuity of the life of the subject [..] and the principle that integrates all acts in the continuous unity of life, in the flux of consciousness of the subject." ([2], *transl. of the author*, p. 99).

[8] " To be sure, everyday induction grew into induction according to scientific method, but that changes nothing of the essential meaning of the pre-given world as the horizon of all meaningful induction. It is this world that we find to be the world of all known and unknown realities. To it, the world of actually experiencing intuition, belongs the form of space-time together with all the bodily shapes incorporated in it; it is in this world that we ourselves live, in accord with our bodily, personal way of being." ([10], p. 50).

3. THE SENSE OF OBSERVATION

is meant that the classical idea of actual infinity incorporated in Cantor's Set Theory (and axiomatically in the **ZFC** system) is refuted, and substituted in AST, to start with, by a notion of natural infinity which manifests itself in the 'observation' of phenomena present in very large sets, e.g. in the intuition of topological continuum in 'observing' a concrete physical surface. A 'large set' is considered the set which from the classical point of view is finite but which, nevertheless, " is not located as a whole and along with each of its elements, in front of the horizon currently limiting the view of the given set. Here we understand 'view' in much more than a visual sense, that is, essentially as a grasping and holding of some field of phenomena." ([25], p. 116). As a result, infinity phenomena can be encountered in 'large sets' which are nevertheless in Cantorian view finite, therefore making certain axioms of **ZFC** invalid (e.g. the infinity and separation axioms).

In the context of AST, P. Vopěnka stated explicitly that the term horizon is understood in the sense of E. Husserl's horizon of the Life-World as it was developed mainly in *Krisis*, linking, in effect, this notion and the AST definition of a countable class of elements,

" If a large set x is observed then the class of all elements of x that lie before the horizon need not be infinite but may converge toward the horizon. The phenomenon of infinity associated with the observation of such a class is called countability" ([24], p. 39).

As I have already remarked, infinity in an AST sense is not beyond but already present in large sets, e.g. in the application to certain macro or micro scale phenomena which show themselves in large sets and in this sense it is characterized as natural infinity in contrast to classical infinity of Cantorian Set Theory. The latter becomes relevant in relation to real world phenomena when it applies its classical infinity results to the natural infinity. Natural infinity in its most fundamental form should be understood as a countable natural infinity in the sense of an initial grasp of a local finiteness and the subsequent constant shift of the horizon of 'sharpness' and 'discernibility' until it stabilizes to something constantly unchangeable and definite in the sense of classical countability ([25], pp. 116-118).

Therefore, the countable class FN of natural numbers is considered in AST as representative of the path towards the horizon in the formal sense of hereditary finiteness of each of its segments ([24], p. 42). A drastic and qualitative shift of the horizon leading to the vagueness of continuum is induced by an axiomatical principle, which is the prolongation principle[9]. This vagueness of continuum can be reasonably interpreted as the formal reflexion of a deeper temporally constituted intuitive continuum whose origin should be subjective taking into account the theoretical foundation of AST theory in accepting the

---

[9]If F and G stand for functions, which in the AST extended universe are sets or classes, the prolongation axiom states that: For each countable function F, there is a set function f such that $F \subseteq f$. It is important here to have in mind that countability of a function is, in fact, countability of a class of ordered pairs of elements and that a set function can be an uncountable (i.e., a very large) set of ordered pairs of elements.

constituting and participating activity of an 'observing' subject within the world of phenomena, in which he has his specific, local and *a priori* defined ways of 'observing'.

The prolongation principle is, in effect, a saturation principle generating new nonstandard elements over the horizon. In the semantical context of AST[10] a remarkable consequence of the prolongation principle is the following:

If a perceived (i.e. definable inside a intersubjective universe including the 'observer') " state of affairs ϕ holds of every element of a sequence (x_n), $n \in \omega$, (where ω is the cardinality of countable infinity in AST) progressing towards the horizon, then (x_n), $n \in \omega$, is extendible to a sequence (x_β), $\beta \leq \alpha$, that crosses the horizon and its members also satisfy ϕ. Put in a somewhat naive language, any totality perceived in a phenomenological sense in front of the horizon of AST countability can extend beyond the horizon preserving its prior characteristics" ([23], p. 394).[11]

The possibility of an, in principle, indefinite extension of a totality of intentionally perceived objects which is moreover conservative in character, in a formal-mathematical sense, is de facto axiomatized by the prolongation principle, although Vopěnka seemed to refute it in a subsequent paper on the philosophical foundations of the Alternative Set Theory, where he talked about the possibility of a complete collapse of our intuitions beyond a genuinely qualitative shift of the horizon to the *apeiron* ([25], p. 123). However, this position contradicts with both the Husserlian notion of scale invariance and the core content of the meaning of Life-World as the grounding soil (*gründenden Boden*) of an ever shifting horizon.

Evidently, this prolongation induced enlargement is a saturated nonstandard one, in the sense of an extension of the domain of elements of natural infinity to new elements beyond the intersubjective horizon of natural infinity, where these new elements retain their former essential characteristics. That means that these new elements, possibly considered as imaginary in the sense of Husserl's 1901 Göttingen lectures, retain with respect to the original domain of natural infinity their essential characteristics to be individuals-in-themselves and preserve moreover, in the radical shift beyond the horizon of natural infinity, their relational character (e.g. the notion of order or inclusion) that was

---

[10] On a formal-syntactical level, AST works with sets and classes as objects. Sets are definite, (may be very large, but) sharply defined and finite from the classical point of view in the sense that in its universe of sets, AST accepts the axioms of Zermelo - Fraenkel system with the exception of the axiom of infinity (ZF_{fin}) - AST is proved in fact, by A. Sochor, to be a conservative extension of ZF_{fin}, ([22], p. 145). Classes represent indefinite clusters of objects such as the class N of natural numbers in the classical sense. In AST, an important role is played by semisets which are classes inside sets and represent, roughly, blurriness and non-surveyability in the observation inside a very large set ([24], Ch. I).

[11] Husserl held the notion of scale invariance in the phenomenological perception, which can be roughly described as evident generic similarity that can lead to minima visibilia as point-like ultimate minimalities bearing the same eidetic relationships as those 'discovered' in the macroscopic universe ([7], p. 166); cf. with individuals-in-themselves as irreducible evidences of intentional experience and ultimate contents-substrates of analytic judgements in [11], (pp. 273-277).

valid with respect to the original domain. In a phenomenological perspective these new nonstandard entities[12] can be clearly seen as bearing certain eidetic similarities to the irreducible individuals-substrates, as original evidences, in the lowest-level reduction of the content of analytic judgements within the continuous unity of experience ([11], pp. 107-110).

3.2 An implicit sense of IST nonstandard approach

In relation to Internal Set Theory (IST), which is described by E. Nelson as a variant of A. Robinson's nonstandard analysis on the syntactical level " without enlarging the world of mathematical objects in any way" ([16], p. 1), there is a tendency to see it under proper interpretation as part of intensional nonstandard mathematics. In reaching this conclusion it helps to refer to Nelson's introduction of a new unary undefined predicate termed *standard* in ordinary mathematics which along with its axiomatical tools[13] acquires an implicit semantical role in defining nonstandardness as, loosely speaking, generated by the vagueness of continuum beyond 'clearly grasped' (standard) mathematical objects.

By this axiomatical means, it is easily proved that there exists at least a nonstandard number in any infinite set, including the set of natural numbers N ([16], p. 5). This result shows in part that continuity, may be generated in the level of theory, due to the axiomatical-formal structure of the enlarged IST axiomatical system and the implicit semantical content of the predicate symbol *standard* in inducing vagueness inside standard sets.

Moreover, by the introduction of *standard* as a new non-logical predicate, IST adopts in a certain sense the AST natural infinity approach, since it is not allowed to construct subsets by the separation axiom of **ZFC**, in applying the ordinary syntax symbol $\in$ and predicate formulas that include in their syntax the predicate *standard*. In this way, even if IST accepts uniquely defined objects of classical mathematics (e.g., the usual sets N and R of natural and real numbers respectively) as standard, it is not guaranteed that we will not encounter nonstandard elements inside these standard sets. It follows that as it is the case with Alternative Set Theory and its offspring THS, standard sets may contain subclasses which are not themselves sets. In an observational frame sense, this means that a potential 'observer' can encounter blurring phenomena of continuity inside standard sets, the latter taken informally as probably very large but fixed when 'viewed from outside' sets.

The IST theory is proved to be a conservative extension of **ZFC** theory, in the sense that every internal statement (i.e., a statement expressed in the standard language of **ZFC**) proved in IST can be also proved in **ZFC**, ([17], pp. 1192-1197). Moreover, in the sense described above, IST can be possibly

---

[12]Take, for instance, the elements $\alpha \in N - FN$ induced by the prolongation of the class of finite natural numbers FN to the uncountable proper class N of natural numbers which from a classical point view coincides with the ordinary set of natural numbers N.

[13]For more details on the three extra (to **ZFC**) axioms shaping the semantical content of the syntactical predicate standard, see [16] (pp. 5-14) and [13].

susceptible to a phenomenologically motivated interpretation related to the notion of the horizon of Life-World and the observational frame shaped within it.

In conclusion, concerning the intensional part of nonstandard mathematics, it is primarily by *ad hoc* axiomatical means, that is, essentially by the prolongation principle in AST and by the new undefined predicate *standard* (with its *ad hoc* axiomatical tools) in IST, that the natural infinity horizon, meant as as indefinitely extensible horizon of hereditarily finite 'appearances', is shifted to the continuous vagueness of infinity.

4 A phenomenological interpretation of observation in a quantum-mechanical context

4.1 Schrödinger's undulatory view of the world - The problematic of continuity

I shall orient my approach mainly to Schrödinger's interpretation of the nature of the wave function ψ, describing the state of a particle p, and generally to his undulatory image of reality; also to the question of taking quantum particles as constituted individuals in quantum observation as well as to the intersubjective character of measurement.

It is true that Schrödinger initially adopted, among others, the 'orthodox' view of complementarity (the dual corpuscular and wave-like nature of particles) of Niels Bohr and the School of Copenhagen until he later offered an undulatory image of reality going as far as to suggest for a substitute to the realism of material content the realism of pure image[14]. In the light of EPR critique and the antinomies of entanglement states which reduce to the 'metaphysics' of the principle of superposition of states, Schrödinger attempted a re-interpretation of the epistemological questions of quantum theory and a re-examination of the question of the individuality of quantum particles. It is noteworthy that in connection with the assumption of an individuality of quantum particles, French philosopher M. Merlau-Ponty emphasized the generic and not individual character of particles, referring mainly to F. London's & E. Bauer's work in [14] and also to that of P. Destouches-Février's in [3], in which they describe

---

[14] As a matter of fact, Einstein accepted initially all relations of quantum mechanics and by 1931 the universality of the relations of indeterminacy. However, he was not accepting the Copenhagen credo and was closer to Max Born's statistical interpretation, viewing the wave function ψ as a description of aggregates of systems and not of individual systems. It was, in fact, in 1935 that the Copenhagen interpretation was put under a severe test by the well-known EPR article, where Einstein, Podolski and Rosen remark inexplicable correlations if the function ψ represents the individual case, pointing therefore to an incompleteness of the theory if by completeness is meant that any element of the physical reality which can be predicted with certainty can be put in correspondence with an element of the physical theory. The EPR argument served in putting in evidence the local non-separability property of quantum systems and later, thanks to Bell's theorem, the factual and not only formal character of this argument. Einstein strongly opposed anyway local non-separability - which, eventually, recent developments have verified in experimental context (he was talking about spooky action at a distance) - as a requirement for interaction-independent elements of physical reality, (see: [19], [20]).

4. A PHENOMENOLOGICAL INTERPRETATION 61

quantum mechanics as a theory of species and put in doubt the belief that each object of the quantum mechanical world has an individual existence in the sense that the wave function $\psi(x, y, z)$ represents a maximal description of the 'composite' object, consisting in the object in proper sense x, the device y and the observer z, which nevertheless due to its probabilistic nature does not precisely describe the actual state of the object x. It only gives probabilities but only on the condition of an eventual measurement in which case a subject's observation makes the statistical probabilities collapse and emerge an individual existence in-act. Observation in wave mechanics is an act of 'engagement' on the part of the 'observing' subject, which is, in fact, a process of this world and has nothing metaphysical ([15], pp. 128-132). The object assimilated to a physical system in a classical mechanical sense is a wave of probabilities transforming itself into individualities only in case of potential acts of observation, these individualities existing only in-act (ενεργείᾳ, in aristotelian terminology). This means that they cannot be ontologically defined in a catastematic philosophical attitude. It seems that this approach is interpretationally close to Schrödinger's undulatory view as explained below.

As a matter of fact, it was E. Schrödinger's attempt to interpret the formal results of the Bose-Einstein statistics, which implied an indiscernibility of monoatomic gaz molecules, that led him to abandon the corpuscular interpretation and adopt the undulatory view in terms of which the gaz as a physical system should be considered as a system of stationary waves in which molecules are just states of excitation energy deprived of any individuality. Later he gave a physical interpretation in electromagnetic sense to the wave function ψ as solution of his general equation[15] but the underlying intepretation was again that of a wave configuration consisting in the superposition of all kinematically possible point-configurations of the system, each one intervening by its special 'weight' in the physically intepreted formula $\int \psi\psi^*$ (current density). Moreover, his wave image proved more satisfactory in representing atomic transitions by an energy exchange between different vibrations, rather than by a quantum leap between different states in which case one cannot possibly describe this kind of transition in time and space, ([19], pp. 168-169).

I propose to phenomenologically interprete Schrödinger's undulatory view in the following way:

(i) In terms of the kinetic character of constitution of the objects of experience.

On this account, we should have in mind his interpretation of the wave function ψ as a wave configuration consisting in the superposition of all kinematically possible point-configurations of the physical system as stated above. The quantum-mechanical system can be considered as a configuration of the

---

[15]The wave function ψ is defined as time-dependent in the form: $\psi(q,t) = \psi(q) exp^{(-i(\frac{E}{\hbar})t)}$. This time dependence most possibly had interpretationally to do with Schrödinger's idea of continuum as a substratum of his wave configuration pointing to a spatiotemporal geometrization of the properties of matter and indicating a continuous distribution of material properties in classical sense.

modes of probability 'flux' (probability waves of statistical nature) in which individualities (particles) can only be apprehended in-act (ενεργείᾳ) by an act of 'observation' (which is an engaging process) of a potential subject. Moreover ontologically these individualities are considered as illusions inasmuch as they are apprehended only in-act, as excited states of energy or as crests of waves against a continuous substratum in Schrödinger's wave configuration.

In Husserl's notion of genetic-kinetic constitution, the real being is constituted in the flux in a certain mode, as described in section 2, and is constituted as a unity of multiplicities of appearances (*Erscheinungen*) which are modified into discrete immanences of consciousness together with their intentional correlates (protentions and retentions). Moreover, they are bound within a homogeneous temporal unity which is meant to be the inner temporality of consciousness, that is essentially, the objectified form of the self-constituting absolute flux. In this phenomenological view, we can plausibly interpret the wave image of Scrödinger, in the sense that any intuition of individuality transforms into a corresponding immanence of an individual in the constituting flux of consciousness the origin of which is traced in the intentional 'observation' of the subject with regard to the pre-phenomenal reality. This immanence can only be intuited in the mode of unity (partly by means of transversal and longitudinal intentionality) of the constituting flux, indistinguishable from its intentional correlates and thus intuited only as an in-act state. In this interpretation, the wave configuration of spatiotemporal reality on the quantum level can be interpreted in terms of the continuous unity of the flux of consciousness in the kinetic constitution of reality and the individualities of particles in terms of immanent individuals-substrates within the flux taken as noematically modified objects of phenomenological perception (*Wahrnehmung*).

(ii) In terms of the reduction of quantum particles to irreducible individuals within the continuous undulatory unity by means of observations meant as primary evidences of experience.

As stated already, the multiplicities of the immanences of intentional perceptions are bound within continuous unity in terms of the intentional forms and ultimately the self-constituting unity of the constituting flux that makes possible the unity of appearances of an object that changes or remains unchanged in temporal duration. Therefore, the phenomenological constitution of the contents of original impressions as immanent temporal unities with their intentional correlates within the flux of consciousness, appear as identical forms of real objects ([6], pp. 119-120). On this account, particles as individuals-in-themselves can be characterized as the irreducible 'contents' of original intentional perceptions (that is, quantum observations in the present context) generated in the most fundamental level of intentional experience, e.g. in reference to a quantum state-of-affairs. I remind what was said in section 2 (p. 4), namely that nothing can be said of the essential inner structure of these individuals-in-themselves in analytical terms even that they appropriate a temporal form. Moreover, they were also defined to be individuals-in-themselves

4. A PHENOMENOLOGICAL INTERPRETATION

conceivable only within the unity of synthetic impredicative experience genetically constituted in the constituting flux of each one's temporal consciousness. This comes close to Schrödinger's view of particle individualities as excitation states in the macroscopic physical context of an undulatory continuum which are apprehended only distinctly as excitation states inside an ever on-going continuous process. We should note that in physical terms this undulatory continuum meant that Schrödinger could not explain phenomena like the diffraction of X-rays or of material waves without accepting that wave functions 'describe something real', real meaning here that 'the wave acts simultaneously all over the region that covers and not here and there' ([19], p. 184).

Well after his 1935 intepretation undertaking, Scrödinger was led to an even more radical interpretation of the meaning of identity or individuality of particles coming, in my view, even closer to a phenomenological interpretation of individuality as irreducible constitution in consciousness of the permanence of a configuration (*Gestalt*) in its structural form and not of its material content inasmuch as, for instance, we can never prove in a particle trajectory that it is the same particle observed in different instants and regions.[16]

Concerning the notion of undulatory continuity, Schrödinger was relying as late as in 1952, on the principle of superposition in contrast to the notion of quantum leaps which leaves, in effect, completely out of the context of discussion the spatiotemporal reality in-between. In that respect, he thought of the function ψ not in terms of a classical system of material points but in terms of " something that continuously fills space [..] and whose instantaneous photograph would be obtained by leaving open a diaphragm, then letting pass the classical system in all its configurations and the image hold in the (configuration) space q each element of volume $d\tau$ for a time interval proportional to the instantaneous value of $\psi\psi^*$. The charge of each of these points is distributed in continuous fashion throughout the space, etc", ([19], *transl. of the author*, p. 174).

Evidently, the background macroscopic continuity implied by Schrödinger's reference to the classical system in all its configurations can, in the same descriptive context, come to terms with the notion of instantaneity (which is of an ambivalent ontological content) by applying the notion of mathematical infinitesimals which are, in turn, susceptible of a nonstandard formal treatment.

I claim that the deficiency of first-order linguistic means in the description of Schrödinger's undulatory continuum as such and also with respect to microscopic level experimental observations, is due to the fact that, in the level of phenomenological evidence, it is ultimately rooted on the continuous unity of the temporal consciousness of an 'observing' subject, where it is genetically constituted his pre-predicative experience. The essential character of this objective unity is that it 'is' always in-act (ενεργεία) and cannot be conceived but as a kinetic situation being always in the process. The underlying impredica-

---

[16]Schrödinger insisted to the end to a wave image of the world, even though he later ascribed to the wave function ψ a less direct meaning than in his first interpretations insisting in the real character of ψ and the subjective character of its physical content ([19], p. 181).

tivity of spatiotemporal continuum, in one or the other form, is being made apparent in every attempt to conceive or describe a quantum state, as an objective whole, by means of distinct observational states on the quantum scale, whereas in an analytic-logical context this kind of impredicativity is conspicuous in the acceptance of *ad hoc* axiomatical principles 'extending' indefinitely the horizon of distinguishable mathematical objects.[17]

It seems worthwhile here to refer briefly to A. N. Whitehead's approach to the notion of 'extensive' continuum in his ontological-categorial scheme in [26], which, in my view, bears some underlying conceptual analogies with the phenomenological approach.[18] Without intending to enter into the details of the ontological-categorial scheme of his philosophy of organism, I call attention to what he regards as the most fundamental elements of his system, that is, the *actual entities* which are defined as the irreducibly fundamental 'units' constitutive of the world of actuality, the *prehensions* defined as essential relational properties co-constitutive of the process of evolution (or concrescence) of actual entities towards their unique actualization, which point, moreover, to a universe of subjective observations and the *nexus* defined to be an ensemble of actual entities in the process of their unity generated by their mutual prehensions. It is fundamental too, to have in mind Whitehead's ontological concept of the world of actuality as a process, this process being meant as an 'advancing progress' of actual entities which acquire their potential unity through a plurality of actual and non-actual entities in disjunctive diversity. There is a transcendental factor in Whitehead's scheme too, that consists in the essential character of every 'being' to be the potentiality (cf. with δυνάμει in aristotelian sense) of a unique actualisation in a real coalescence of actual entities, ([26], pp. 68-79).

Dealing with the notion of extensive continuum, A.N. Whitehead regarded the contemporary world, to the extent that it is perceived by the senses, as a given 'substratum' susceptible of contemporary actualisations of multiplicities of definite actual or non-actual entities. In that sense it is divisible but not divided. These actual entities, in the sense of real objectifications, are original presentations (cf. with the Husserlian *Gegenwärtigung*) to the experience of a subject in which case " they do not concern directly the subject but to the degree that they appropriate the characteristic of emerging out of a given ('substratum') which is the extensive continuum" ([26], *transl of the author*, p. 132). The extensive continuum (which is regarded as the spatiotemporal continuum underlying universally the world as past, present and future) is,

---

[17] Although Einstein in the EPR argument rejected local non-separability as inducing in physical reality bizarre interactions at a distance (and thus indirectly a certain notion of a non-classically continuous background of entanglements), he was always concerned with incorporating quantum physics in a unified field theory that would naturally involve the notion of a classical continuity of the field. However, he never mixed in his scientific considerations quantum theory and the continuous field ([20], pp. 186-187 & pp. 191-192).

[18] For a more detailed presentation of Whitehead's ontological-categorial scheme in [26], especially in relation to nonstandard theories, see the chapter '*The notion of process in nonstandard theory and in Whiteheadian metaphysics*' included in this book.

4. A PHENOMENOLOGICAL INTERPRETATION 65

in this respect, a unique relational complex, in the ontological field of which all potential objectifications find their actualisations and in which there are always actual entities beyond actual entities as non-entities necessarily imply absence of relations (prehensions). Whitehead considered this continuum in its proper generality as independent of any historicity and thus as not including any forms, dimensions or measurability (ibid., p. 138).

As a matter of fact, the analogies we can draw between the Whiteheadian and the phenomenological-constitutional approach regarding the notion of constitution within the real world stand essentially in:

(i) The subjective role of a potential observer in the emergence and objectification of multiplicities of actual entities, which are meant as the most fundamental 'things'-in-themselves and therefore as irreducible individuals apprehended within extensive continuum. In this sense, objectification of actualities presupposes a kind of immanentisation within an 'observing' subjectivity.

(ii) The extensive continuum defined as an all inclusive universal form of potentialities and actualities of entities, the terrain in which all actual and potentially actual entities, as individuals, acquire their unity in the advancing process. On account of this, the extensive continuum encompasses a transcendental character primarily due to the metaphysical nature of potentiality in the real concrescence of a plurality of actual entities to their unique actualization (ibid., p. 74). In this respect it can be interpreted as bearing certain conceptual similarities (though it is not identical) with the Husserlian genetically constituted continuum in reference to the impredicative and ultimately transcendental character of the self-constituting absolute flux.

(iii) The ever in-act, irreducible character of actual entities as 'indecomposable' individuals, which is something that points to Husserl's fundamental reduction, in [11] (pp. 276-277), to the lowest-level evidences of subjective experience and to their content which are taken to be individuals-substrates bearing no further inner structure. These individuals-substrates are kinetically constituted as immanent unities within temporal consciousness and, evidently, as in-act states in a passive synthesis which is that of the constituting unity of the flux.

4.2 The intersubjectivity principle in a phenomenological and a quantum-mechanical context

As it is well-known to phenomenologists, the principle of intersubjectivity is associated in Husserlian phenomenology with the Life-World of animated bodies, the world of actually experiencing intuition, the horizon of which is thought of as an ever shifting bound of the noematic field of an observer who stands in terms of a reciprocal relation with it. In this perspective, intersubjectivity is founded on the double condition of animated bodies, in reference to the Life-World, that of physical bodies and also that of living organisms bearers of a soul, in other words bearers of a pure ego of consciousness.

By virtue of this, the presence of another subject is characterized by Husserl as non-subjective which means that it is necessarily a phenomenon linked to the order of my body as object and founded on a primordial stratum, the *appresentazion*. This is a kind of passive association by which the phenomenon of my subjective body as an objectivity, of my proper body that acts and reacts this and that way in that and that situation, automatically is associated in an evident way with the corresponding phenomenon of another being. This *appresentazion* would be impossible if it were not the case that we ourselves are given as bodies existing as objects in relation to our subjectivity ([18], p. 200). In short, intersubjectivity is determined by the double architecture of animated bodies, 'inserted' both as physical bodies in the Life-World and at the same time as domains of personal egos of consciousness.

It is on the basis of this phenomenological foundation of intersubjectivity, that can be safely grounded quantum observation by means of the 'triangle', object in proper sense x, device y and observer z and, further, physical objects be defined as (intersubjectively) the same. This means that the view we would have of the system x, y, z, as object, would be essentially the same as the one we would have if we would have taken the place of observer z. Moreover, an observer z doesn't know the exact state of the object in proper sense x, in a formal sense due to the nature of the function $\psi(x, y, z)$, which evidently points to the limited accessibility of material objects themselves, as pointed out in section 2, (p. 5).

In London and Bauer's description: " [..] For him (the observer) there is only the object x and the device y that belong to the external world, to what he calls 'objective'. On the contrary, he entertains with himself relations of a completely different character: he appropriates a well-known and characteristic faculty that we can call 'the faculty of introspection': he can immediately take account of his proper state. It is by virtue of this 'immanent awareness' that he gives himself the right to create his proper objectivity, that is to break up the statistical chains [..] by declaring: 'I'm in the state W_κ" or more simply: 'I see .. $G = gk$' or directly '$F = fk$'. There is not, therefore, a mysterious interaction between the device and the object that produces a new ψ of the system during measurement. It is only the consciousness of a 'myself' which can be separated from the initial $\psi(x, y, z)$ and constitute by virtue of his observation a new objectivity by attributing from then on to the object a new function $\psi(x) = uk(x)$." ([15], *transl. of the author*, pp. 130-131).

In this essentially intersubjective interpretation of quantum measurement, one may be led to a strong conclusion refuting, in effect, the core of objective realism: we cannot learn anything in atomic and subatomic scale but by means of experience and (intentional) experience is, in a way, a violation of nature in the sense of forcing particles to perform their qualities in the mode of our observational 'architecture'; it moreover makes possible to intersubjectively identify them as unique with all other beings sharing the same 'architecture'.

5 Conclusion

In this article I intended to put under the light of a phenomenological analysis the notion of observation taken in an epistemological context, focusing mainly,

5. CONCLUSION

on a logical-analytical level, on nonstandard mathematical theories and, on a physical level, on a certain interpretational version of quantum theory. I chose, in particular, to orient my analysis, on the one hand, to non-Cantorian and nonstandard theories that refute in principle the central Cantorian notion of actual infinity and, on the other, to Schrödinger's undulatory image of the world which is generally considered along with the Copenhagen School's interpretation (Bohr, Heisenberg et al)[19] of a fundamental importance not only to quantum theory as such but also to the philosophical discussion that is still going on regarding the foundations of quantum mechanics.

In the development of the ideas pertaining to the phenomenological interpretation of the notion of observation in the respective fields above, I also dealt to a limited extent with the question of constituted continuum, in general, in which case I included some cornerstone notions of A. N. Whitehead's ontological-categorial scheme to point out a certain underlying common approach with Husserlian phenomenology concerning the inherent impredicativity of (temporal) continuum.

In achieving the scope of this article, that is, by interpreting observation taken in an epistemological sense in terms of key phenomenological notions, I relied primarily on: the genetic-kinetic constitution of reality in terms of the constituting flux of consciousness, the transcendental character of the absolute subjectivity of the flux that underlies the impredicative unity of temporal consciousness and the irreducible content of 'lowest-level' individuals-substrates in phenomenological perception. Not least, I set also myself the task of interpreting phenomenologically the reciprocal, shaping character of 'observation' in quantum mechanical terms as well as the role of a potential observer performing his 'observations' in the local environment of a 'hereditarily finite' witnessed universe, in a mathematical modelization of the horizon of Life-World.

If the outcome leads to some conclusions concerning the possibility of a reinterpretation of the epistemological notion of observation in a phenomenologically motivated context, the author of this article would stick to that one suggesting a promising alternative to classical ontological attitude with regard to certain fundamental questions of contemporary epistemology.

BIBLIOGRAPHY

[1] Andreev, P., Gordon, E.: (2006), A Theory of Hyperfinite Sets, *Annals of Pure and Applied Logic*, 143, 1-3, pp. 3-19.
[2] Bernet, R.: (1994), *La vie du sujet*, Paris: Ed. PUF.
[3] Destouches-Février, P.: (1951), *La structure des théories physiques*, Paris: Ed. PUF.
[4] Feyerabend, K.P.: (1961), Comments on Hill's "Quantum Physics and Relativity Theory", in: *Current Issues in the Philosophy of Science*, (ed. H. Feigl & G. Maxwell), New York: Holt, Rinehart & Winston.

---

[19] There are also those who, like P. Feyerabend, discard both the complementary particle or wave concept and the approach that retains one of these concepts; Feyerabend insisted that neither procedure " will do and that we shall need even a completely new set of observational terms in order to be able to cope with the facts. Bohm's speculations may well lead to such a new conceptual scheme." (see: [4], p. 442).

[5] Husserl, E.: (1993), *Idées directrices pour une phénoménologie et une philosophie phénoménologique pures, Liv. Troisième: La phénoménologie et les fondements des sciences*, transl. D. Tiffeneau, Paris: Ed. PUF.
[6] Husserl, E.: (1996), *Leçons pour une phénoménologie de la conscience intime du temps*, transl. H. Dussort, Paris: Ed. PUF.
[7] Husserl, E.: (1973), *Ding und Raum Vorlesungen 1907*, hrsg. Ul. Claesges, Hua Band XVI, Den Haag: M. Nijhoff.
[8] Husserl, E.: (1970), *Philosophie der Arithmetik*, Hua Band XII, ed. Lothar Eley, Den Haag: M. Nijhoff.
[9] Husserl, E.: (1952), *Ideen II*, hrsg. M. Biemel, Hua, Band IV, Den Haag: M. Nijhoff.
[10] E. Husserl, *The crisis of European sciences and transcendental phenomenology*, transl. D. Carr, Northwestern Univ. Press, 1970
[11] Husserl, E.: (1984), *Logique formelle et logique transcendantale*, transl. S. Bachelard, Paris: Ed. PUF.
[12] Kanovei, V., Reeken, M.: (1995), Internal approach to external sets and universes. Part 1. Bounded set theory *Studia Logica*, 55, 2, pp. 229-257.
[13] Livadas, S.: (2005), The Phenomenological Roots of Nonstandard Mathematics, *Rom. Jour. of Information Science and Technology*, 8, 2, pp. 115-136.
[14] London, F., Bauer, E.: (1939), *La théorie de l' observation en mécanique quantique*, Paris: Hermann.
[15] Merleau Ponty, M.: (1995), *La Nature*, Paris: Ed. du Seuil.
[16] Nelson, E.: (1986), *Predicative arithmetic. Mathematical notes*, Princeton: Princeton Univ. Press.
[17] Nelson, E.: (1977), Internal Set Theory: A new approach to nonstandard analysis, *Bulletin of the American Mathematical Society*, 83, 6, pp. 1165-1198.
[18] Patočka, J.: (1992), *Introduction à la phénoménologie de Husserl*, trans. E. Abrams, Grenoble: Ed. Millon.
[19] Paty, M.: (1993), Formalisme et interprétation physique chez Schröginger, in: *Erwin Schrödinger Philosophy and the birth of Quantum mechanics*, (ed M. Bitbol and O. Darrigol), Paris: Ed. Frontières.
[20] Paty, M.: (1995), The nature of Einstein's objections to the Copenhagen interpretation of Quantun mechanics, *Foundations of Physics*, 25, 1, pp. 183-204.
[21] Petitot, J.: (1999), Morphological Eidetics for a Phenomenology of Perception, in: *Naturalizing Phenomenology*, pp. 330-372, Stanford: Stanford Univ. Press.
[22] Sochor, A.: (1983), Metamathematics of the Alternative Set Theory III, *Commentationes Mathematicae Universitatis Carolinae*, 24, pp. 137-154.
[23] Tzouvaras, A.: (1998), Modeling vagueness by nonstandardness, *Fuzzy sets and systems*, 94, pp. 385-396.
[24] Vopěnka, P.: (1979), *Mathematics in the Alternative Set Theory*, Leipzig: Teubner.
[25] Vopěnka, P.: (1991), The philosophical foundations of Alternative Set theory, *Int. J. General Systems*, 20, pp. 115-126.
[26] Whitehead, N. A.: (1995), *Procès et réalité*, Paris: Ed. Gallimard.

The Expressional Limits of Formal Language in the Notion of Quantum Observation [0]

STATHIS LIVADAS

1 Introduction

The main scope of this paper could be described, in a broad sense, as a holistic theoretical approach towards a notion of object taken as a registered fact by means of an intentionally oriented consciousness. This could entail its elaboration as a formal-ontological object within the structure of a logical-mathematical theory as such and also within the mathematical theory of quantum mechanics in case it is taken as a quantum object registered via a measuring apparatus.

My main interpretative scheme will be that of a phenomenological constitution of the intentional objects of experience by a knowing subject capable of performing phenomenological reduction within the surrounding Life-World (or World-for us).[1] This seems close to a phenomenologically oriented treatment of the measurement question in quantum mechanics in [14] and, from a certain viewpoint, to the version of Active Scientific Realism described in [36] and in [28], [29].

In my view this interpretation should put a focus on the modification of intentional objects of experience to well-defined objects within the temporal flux of consciousness through noetic-noematic constitution which entails an elaboration of them as re-identifying bearers of predicates across phenomenological time in an object-like organization of the world. In a quantum mechanical context this is indirectly linked with a treatment of well-defined objects[2] by a

---

[0] This article has been originally published in the journal *Axiomathes*, (2012), V. 22, 1, pp. 147-169.

[1] The Life-World in Husserlian terminology can be roughly described to a non-phenomenologist as the physical world in its ever receding horizon including in intersubjective sense all reduction performing subjects in a special kind of presence in the World. More on this in E. Husserl's *The Crisis of European Sciences and Transcendental Phenomenology*, [23].

[2] Regarding as phenomenal objects those given primordially in perception, then objects like atoms, electrons, etc. can be also regarded as given by experience and thus considered as real to the extent that their 'reality' is based upon the interpretation of sensible signs in an experimental situation (see: [19], I, p. 5).

mathematical - probabilistic tool as general anticipative frameworks within a Boolean frame corresponding to each specific experimental preparation.

I refer briefly here to the meaning of a noetic and a noematic object, mainly described in E. Husserl's *Ideas I*, [20], for they will be directly or indirectly involved in my general interpretative scheme. A noematic object manifests itself as a 'giveness' in the unity of the flux of a subject's consciousness and it is constituted by certain modes of being as such e.g., a well-defined object immanent to the temporal flux which can then be taken, in Husserlian terminology, as a formal-ontological object[3] and in complete abstraction as a syntactical object of a formal-logical theory naturally including an axiomatical mathematical theory. It can then be said to be given apodictically in experience as: (1) it can be recognized by a perceiver directly as an evident essence in any perceptual judgement, (2) it can be predicated as existing according to the descriptive norms of a language (e.g. in terms of ontic being) and (3) it can be verified as a re-identifying object in multiple acts more or less at will.

In contrast, noetic objects described in terms of moments of hyletic-noetic perception (*hyletisch-noetische Wahrnehmung*) can be only thought of as *a priori* orientations of intentionality[4] by their sole virtue of being originally given as such 'in person' in front of an intentional consciousness inside the open horizon of the Life-World. They are given within a horizon whose outer 'layer' is the boundary between any of the noetic objects in question and the Life-World; the latter notion, taken here as not being the noetic object or any of its parts, is the 'field' of all possible subsequent phenomenological perceptions. In this view, intentional individuals on the lowest level of intentionality taken as things-substrates (*sachhaltige Substrate*) or even empty-substrates (*Leersubstrate*) independently of the possibility of a material content cannot be reduced to any lower level of phenomenological perception (*Wahrnehmung*). This is seemingly the reason for which as noematic individuals in temporal constitution and then in complete abstraction as formal individuals (atoms) within analytic judgements corresponding to 'states of affairs' (*Sachverhalte*) they bear no inner content, at least not one describable by analytic means.

My interpretational scheme will also consist of a supplementary transcendental reduction of most radical form when it comes to the question of the constitution of temporal consciousness in itself as an objectified homogeneous unity of its immanent objects by means of which it is possible to talk about well-defined objects of 'observation'. This continuous unity in the sense of an underlying,

---

[3] Formal ontology deals with the formal structures of facts as registered (by intentionality of experience) whereas apophantic logic deals with the formal structures of facts or state of affairs as supposed, that is, it deals with categorial meanings associated with judgements, theories, etc. ([39], Append., p. 289).

[4] Intentionality is not to be understood as a relation of a psychological character. By intentionality, which is a phenomenological notion, it is meant something fundamentally deeper and *a priori*. To a non-expert in Phenomenology it can be roughly described as grounding the *a priori* necessity of orientation of a subject's consciousness to the object of its orientation.

1. INTRODUCTION

impredicative substratum[5] making possible to reinstate objects as bearers of predicates within each experimental context in kinematical terms can be further reduced to a transcendental subjectivity 'behind' the self-constitution of each one's flux of consciousness ([21], pp. 194-195). In this respect I draw attention to the indirect way the continuous unity of a fulfilled time consciousness is reflected in the mathematical metatheory of quantum mechanics e.g. in the form of classical continuity assumptions in the description of certain quantum phenomena and also in the definition (by von Neumann's postulate in an entangled quantum state) of the eigenvector that represents the state of a measured quantum object before and immediately after measurement.

What can be fundamentally inferred from the mathematical formulation of quantum phenomena is on the one hand the possibility to refer formally to quantum objects in disentangled states as well-defined syntactical individuals described by operator algebras and on the other hand the possibility of their description across time by means of continuous transformations (e.g. by evolution operators of state vectors) which implies an 'inner' continuity of the parameter time. I reduce these fundamental possibilities in a phenomenologically motivated approach to: (i) The grounding of quantum individuals as irreducible objects of intentionality within an outer and inner horizon of phenomenological perception conditioned on the existence of a relation of intentional character between a knowing subject and the objects of his intentionality and (ii) the impredicativity of the self-constituting unity of the time flux of consciousness which ultimately leads to the transcendence of the pure ego of consciousness (left in relative obscurity in Husserlian writings in [22] and [25]). I try to show, in subsections 3.2 and 3.3, that these two fundamental irreducibilities bear a critical though indirect effect in the mathematical formulation of certain quantum phenomena such as the Bohm-Aharonov effect and generally in the mathematical formulation of quantum non-separability phenomena.

Finally, regarding mathematical objects as founded on perceptual objects by means of a special kind of intuition which is the categorial intuition[6] I have added, mainly in section 4, some concluding remarks on the role of the aforementioned irreducibilities in setting the expressional limits of a formal-mathematical language with respect to the notion of observation. In their view as irreducibilities of a rather phenomenological character they can be regarded, by this measure, as providing a common underlying ground of both quantum-

---

[5]The notion of impredicativity of the objective unity of temporal consciousness should be taken as referring to the impossibility to formally describe the continuous whole in any other way but in terms of parts belonging to the same genus as the whole. Think, in analogy, of the mathematical continuum and the circularities produced in definitions where the *definiens* cannot be defined but in terms of the *definiendum* e.g. in the definition of an open interval of the real line.

[6]In E. Husserl's view, perception by virtue of perceptual acts provides the concrete, immediate and non-reflective basis for all our experiences and thus provides the basis for any intuition of abstract objects. Concerning mathematical acts and contents, in particular, Husserl's view was that they are too founded on immediate perceptual acts and contents which could anyway exist even in the absence of mathematical activity. For details, see resp. R. Tieszen's [40], pp. 412-15 and [41], pp. 54-55.

mechanical observation in the sense of a lowest-degree 'observation' implicating a special kind of relation subject-object and the possibility of reduction of the domain of formal-ontological objects of corresponding theory to phenomenological evidences.

2 A phenomenological approach to quantum individuals

In this section I intend to put the issue of quantum individuality in the light of a phenomenologically motivated approach that points to an underlying role of the intentionality of a knowing subject in shaping the individuality of quantum objects. By this token, my approach is a quite original alternative to various approaches of quantum individuality based mainly on a description of individuality as a 'property' possessed by the quantum object itself and whose existence (or non-existence) is independent from the presence of an intentionally oriented consciousness. Before dealing with certain views on the individuality of quantum particles I choose to offer a broad outline of the phenomenological approach to individuals taken as formal-ontological objects.

In *Formale und Transzendentale Logik*, [21], Husserl inquired into the deeper meaning and also the domain of reference of analytic judgements turning to what is most fundamental, in fact what is irreducible in the build-up of analytic statements of any degree of complexity. Assuming that an analytic statement incorporates registered facts as formal-ontological objects, then these objects taken in the sense of signification objects (*Sinnesobjekte*) and predicate bearers (*Seinssobjekte*) with any doxical modalities reflecting consciousness-based states e.g. doubt, certainty, negation etc. belong to the domain of formal apophantics. Although formal apophantics conditions truth within a formal theory and uses categories referring to meanings such as subject, predicate, proposition and judgement yet it derives its senses from the domain of objects ([39], App., p. 274).

In this view, any attempt at a radical 'deconstruction' of the analytic structure of any sentence will ultimately reduce to statements about intentional object-substrates and to properties related to their character as such. As E. Husserl claimed, these sentences are no more of an analytic character as they lead to evidences of intentional experience. This radical reduction which in addition to substrates-predicate bearers reaches their predicative environment as well should also include what is essential to the 'noematic nucleus' of each intentional act; e.g. in case we talk about syntactical atoms of formal-logical formulas, at least the $\in$ predicate as abstraction of the noematic correlate of the corresponding intentional object taken within a horizon whose outer 'layer' is the boundary between the intentional object in question and Life-World. This kind of formal objects, e.g. syntactical individuals of logical formulas, numerals, sets, classes of sets, functions of Pure Analysis, Euclidean or non-Euclidean domains of such functions etc. were considered by Husserl, in the lowest possible level of reduction, as intentionalities towards an empty 'something' devoid of any material content, in other words as intentionalities towards an 'empty substrate' (*Leersubstrat*) ([20], p. 33).

2. A PHENOMENOLOGICAL APPROACH 73

This type of reduction meant as the result of the elimination of all possible doxical modalities in the construction of analytic sentences of any level of complexity as, for instance, in general statements expressing doubt (S might not be p), corroboration (S is in fact p) or negation (S is not p) and so on, includes also forms uniquely defined by their syntactical structure e.g. when one quantifies over elements satisfying a particular analytic property S ($\forall p\, S$ or $\exists p\, S$). What is ultimately left is a multiplicity of individuals-substrates in the sense of intentionally perceived and temporally constituted noematic objects, re-identifying as uniquely determined and well-defined objects in the progression of temporal flux; moreover they are perceived within a predicative nest put formally as the class of all categorial objectivities appropriate to them. The predicative nests as noematic correlates of intentional individuals were termed by Husserl as *Kernformen* ([21], pp. 270-272) and were supposed to invariably define the categorial nature of individuals - substrates in the construction of analytic statements of any order.

As it will become clear in the next section, the notion of an intentional individual-substrate constituted as a re-identifying noematic object across time and an invariant (under various predicative specifications) predicate bearer can provide a common underlying foundation for both formal-ontological objects of analytic statements and for objects of quantum measurement in the sense of noematically constituted objects taken in abstraction as well-defined syntactical individuals of formal metatheory.

Ultimate individuals-substrates of analytic judgements, in the lowest possible level of analytic reduction, whose evidence can only be seized by intentional experience, were described by Husserl as deprived of any inner structure - even lacking a temporal form - at least not one expressible by analytic means ([21], p. 181).[7] Any such object, irrespective of being a thing -or an empty-substrate, together with its noematic correlates-, can be taken on the formal-logical level as a uniquely defined syntactical individual appropriating *eo ipso* a relational property with respect to any other. This kind of approach may indeed help clarify the place of syntactical individuals within the structure of a formal axiomatical theory as abstractions of irreducible contents of intentional acts.

By all accounts owing to the noetic-noematic constitution and to the retentionality of the constituting flux of consciousness[8], it is possible to re-identify

---

[7]Ultimate substrates are classified in the following two categories: the ultimate material substance or the eidetic material singularity with regard to a content and the eidetic formal singularity with regard to a form; both are considered as pure individual singularities with no syntactical content. The latter singularity, termed 'Dies-da' by Husserl (close to the meaning of Aristotelian τόδε τι), is called an individuum inasmuch as it can be instantiated as bearing a concrete 'thingness' substance (*sachhaltiges Wesen*) ([20], pp. 33-35). To this last category belong, as 'state-of-things', the syntactical individuals of logical formulas within a formal mathematical theory in the sense of 'empty substrates'; on the syntactical level they can be thought of as modifications of an 'empty-something' (*Leeretwas*).

[8]For instance the forms of transversal intentionality, that is, retention and protention, are purely phenomenological notions and can be roughly communicated as respectively a kind of spontaneous conservation of immediate past (retention) and a spontaneous expectation of original impression (protention); they are of an *a priori* character in the process of con-

any intentional individual-substrate x of primary experience as the one and same noematic object-substrate x under varying predicative situations in the progression of time flux. Any attempt to pass from these irreducible individual-substrates apprehended as a self-donated presence in front of the intentionality of consciousness to a constituted objectivity of a higher order can only entail circularities in description or *a priori* terms. For instance, in *Ideas I* Husserl referred to the multi-ray intentionality of synthetic consciousness which 'transforms' the perception of a collection of objectivities into the constitution of a single objective whole by what he termed a monothetical act whose *wesensmässig* (essential) mode evidently points to a creeping transcendence ([20], p. 276).

Yet there is the question of how we could possibly ground the irreducibility of an intentional individual-substrate taken as corresponding, even in the absence of a material content, to an empty-something of intentionality. My claim is that both the irreducibility and uniqueness of a 'lowest-degree' individual are induced precisely by being the content of a unique and otherwise irreducible intentional act (in terms of an hyletic-noetic moment of perception) directed to it so that in objective reflection it can be defined as the unique noematic object corresponding precisely to the meaning of our distinct enactment of intentionality; it should be noted that meaning and content of intentional acts are implying each other in transcendental phenomenology.[9]

As a matter of fact, the issue of the relation between identity and indistinguishability concerning both classical and quantum objects has opened up an ongoing discussion among those who hold to the well-known Leibniz's Postulate on the Identity of Indiscernibles and those who have the view that even in the case of quantum particles there should be some kind of 'hidden' individuality underlying commonly admitted quantum non-individuality. At this point, I make reference to an approach towards a property-independent individuality of objects in general, that draws the line between distinguishability of objects requiring in principle the existence of a universe in which there are at least two such objects, and individuality meant as an ontological issue related to a non-qualitative basis of object individuality. In this sense, one can mention the Lockean substance approach in which properties of objects are taken to be inherent in some way to a metaphysically based substance which is absolutely non-describable in terms of these properties and R. Adams' approach to individuality expressed in terms of a primitive, non-qualitative thisness (or haecceity) of objects which cannot be further analyzed (see resp. [15], [1]).

Concerning in particular R. Adams' exposition of arguments in favor of a primitive thisness of objects, in [1], it seems quite interesting that he refers to several ideas that can be seen to bear an indirect phenomenological connota-

---

stitution of a sequence of original impressions together with their retentions in the flux of consciousness. For more details, see [22].

[9] In Husserl's view the content of an intentional act is thought of as the meaning of the act by virtue of which consciousness refers to an object or state of affairs as its own, (see: [41], p. 53).

2. A PHENOMENOLOGICAL APPROACH

tion; this has mainly to do with a notion of direct reference to objects (ibid. p. 16), the application of the notion of transworld identity which has a certain affinity with the Husserlian notion of primitive soil or *Boden* (ibid. pp. 18-20) and finally a left open question on the primitiveness of transtemporal identity of objects (ibid. pp. 20-21). As it is well-known the transtemporal identity of objects is reduced in phenomenological analysis to a re-identifiability of noematic objects within the homogenous unity of the progressing flux of consciousness; as a matter of fact, the primitiveness of transtemporal identity is ultimately reduced to the sort of subjectivity of the self-constituting flux.

The relevance of the arguments above to certain claims of D. Krause & A. Coelho in [30] on the indistinguishability of formal elements of a relational mathematical structure can be appreciated to the extent that the indistinguishability of the elements of such a structure can be 'lifted' by associating ordinal numbers to any collection of such elements. Taking any finite extension of ordinal numbers as essentially corresponding to an intuition of natural numbers with a sense of well-ordering it has much to do with a sense of counting in discrete temporal steps which (for both Husserl and Poincaré) underlies the irreducibility of the mathematical content of arithmetical propositions ([41], p. 300). I take this particular intuition of natural numbers as a process of formal abstraction based on a retentional succession of unique, original evidences of 'state-of-things' as intentional objects of experience.

Thus urelements (roughly, irreducible elememts) of an extended Zermelo-Fraenkel universe (ZFU, $\in$), taken as not identical yet indistinguishable elements by means of the definition of $\mathcal{A}$-indistinguishability within a relational structure, can be made distinguishable by associating to any collection of them an ordinal number, so that it is possible to talk about a collection σ_0, σ_1, σ_3, ..., σ_{n-1} of such objects. This is a result of the simple proof that any ordinal as a well-ordered structure $\langle A, < \rangle$ is a rigid structure, i.e. the only automorphism in this structure is the identity function ([30], p. 201). In other words in a rigid structure $\mathcal{A}$ the notion of non-identical elements and of $\mathcal{A}$-distinguishable elements coincide. Let us note that the question of the individuality of entities in the context of quantum mechanics has provided for much theoretical discussion on the nature of quantum objects as they are regarded by some physicists (notably by Scrödinger) as non-individual upon which a notion of identity does not make sense, whereas by others as bearing a kind of intrinsic individuality by means of which " they might be qualitatively the same in all aspects representable in quantum mechanical models yet numerically distinct" ([42], p. 376). On this account, I note D. Krause's & A. Coelho's claim in [30] that the mathematical structure of quantum mechanics should have a non-trivial rigid expansion (i.e. not one obtained by trivially adjoining the ordinal structure) whose physical intuition is that quantum objects are somehow 'intrinsically' distinguishable.

Yet, in [31] and in [32], D. Krause has presented Quasi-set Theory, a variant of Zermelo-Fraenkel Set Theory with Urelements (**ZFU**), to accommodate a special kind of atoms (m-atoms), thought of as representing non-individual quantum particles, for which the traditional theory of identity does not apply, in other words for which indistinguishability and identity may not be equivalent. In this sense the axioms of identity of formal theory are substituted with the axioms of indistinguishability and a notion of quasi-cardinality is defined to account for those quasi-sets - named by H. Weyl effective aggregates of individuals - where we can know how many elements there are in each such class but not what elements are there in the sense of a well-ordered enumeration. Consequently in these pure quasi-sets a notion of cardinal may have a meaning but not a notion of ordinal. This seems to provide a set-theoretical model for the description e.g. of a Bose-Einstein condensate where collections of atoms in the same quantum state continue to be many though they are absolutely indistinguishable ([31], p. 4). Nevertheless, one could argue that although the formal notions of quasi-sets (q-sets) and quasi-cardinals (q-cardinals) seem to imply formally the possibility of existence of elements with a peculiar kind of individuality (or rather of non-individuality) there is some ground for raising doubts on the well-foundedness of corresponding definitions from a philosophical-foundational standpoint. For instance, the expression "n indistinguishable elements from q-set x" seems to have an inherent contradiction as the act of counting a finite number of elements presupposes a well-defined individuality on their part, yet this expression is taken as bearing a sense and is applied to define a q-set that has some elements indistinguishable from another q-set x and a q-set that has some, but not all elements indistinguishable from the m-atom x ([32], pp. 405-406). On essentially the same grounds, it is questionable whether one can perform universal quantification in logical formulas over m-atoms, as it is the case within Quasi-Set Theory, unless one also implicitly admits their well-defined individuality. Therefore, there is some reason to suspect an underlying individuality of elements even of (pure) q-sets, a fact that could strengthen my arguments on a non-qualitative individuality of quantum particles associated moreover with an outward directed intentionality of a subject.

I draw attention now to a 'creeping' non-qualitative individuality of the particles of a quantum system, possibly linked with a subjective factor, in classical as well as quantum statistical mechanics mostly based on S. French's work in [16], S. French's and D. Krause's in [17] and S. Saunder's in [38]. On this account, in a field theoretical approach of classical statistical mechanics a permuted complexion of a, say, two particles system can be distinguished from an unpermuted one by conferring individuality upon the particles via changes in the system's continuous space-time trajectory; the trajectory is described in [16] in terms of a spatio-temporal continuous succession of individual stages akin, in a certain sense, to the Husserlian description of the absolute flux of consciousness whereas transtemporal identity of the conferred individuality is very close to the phenomenological description of a re-identifying noematic object within the temporal flux ([16], pp. 434-439).

Concerning, on the other hand, the situation in quantum statistical mechanics the discussion on particle individuality can be summed up as follows.

2. A PHENOMENOLOGICAL APPROACH

There seem to be two main alternative views with regard to quantum individuality: either an option of non-individual particles, following from the claim that particle permutations are not observable,[10] and distinguishable, individuated particle states, or an option of individual particles and state accessibility restrictions ([16], pp. 441-445).

Concerning the first option, place permutation operators instead of particle permutations are regarded as observables in the sense of changing the physical state of the system upon the condition, though, of an assignment of wave functions as distinct entities to the particles and consequently identifying them experimentally as given by state labels and not by particle labels. Insofar as the particles can be distinguished by the states they are in and the latter are represented by corresponding wave functions $\psi(x)$, then a re-identification through time for these functions has to be effected by prior performing a re-identification of the particles in terms of position x as it was the case in classical statistics. In both situations one has to perform a transtemporal identity which entails an 'embedding' of space-time continuity within a quantum mechanical configuration in terms of a homogenous, impenetrable temporal unity of a succession of individual stages.[11] As for the second option, a sense of quantum individuation is introduced by establishing the inaccessibility of certain states through the imposition of an extra-physical requirement such as the Indistinguishability Postulate acting now as a 'super-selection' principle by formally dividing the Hilbert space for an assembly of particles into a number of irreducible subspaces. Such a postulate may be taken in any case as introducing indirectly by its theoretical implications, e.g. that of a kind of 'non-individuality' of particles being something more than a mere indistinguishability of particles in physical terms, a subjective constitutional factor in the physical configuration ([16], pp. 440-41 & 443-446).

In S. Saunders view on the other hand, one can even guarantee a kind of particle individuality, termed a weak indiscernibility, at least for a fermions system in case there is a definition of irreflexive physical relations between the particles concerned, a fact actually implied by the antisymmetry of the state of a many-fermions system. D. Dieks & M. Versteegh have shown, however, in [7] that there is an essential difference between many-fermions systems and classical collections of weakly discernible objects in the sense that the only way quantum relations can serve as name givers, for instance, in designating one-particle state-spaces for the description of single particles in a two-fermions system in the singlet state, is through measurement interactions and the dis-

---

[10]This is a direct implication of the Indistinguishability Postulate which states that there is no way of distinguishing those quantum states differing by a permutation of particles only, ([16], pp. 440-441).

[11]This homogenous space-time continuity must fulfill the three minimal conditions set for the trajectory of re-identifying individuals in [16], p. 434. In short: 1) the trajectory must be spatio-temporally continuous, 2) the trajectory must be qualitatively continuous in the sense that any individual stage on the trajectory must be qualitatively similar to the neighboring one and 3) there is a sortal term S such that the succession is a succession of S-stages or the trajectory underlies such a succession.

turbances caused by them ([7], pp. 6-9). But this may be taken again as an argument for the necessity of the presence of a subjective consciousness in shaping the individuality of objects in general and their quantum counterparts in particular. This will be further elaborated in the next sections.

3 Can a quantum mechanical interpretation be related to a phenomenology of constitution?

3.1 Some remarks on the mathematical language of quantum mechanics

In this section I will argue for the possibility of an interpretation of quantum mechanics along phenomenological lines especially in connection with the notion of an intentional relation subject-object and the constitution of quantum objects in decoherence states as well-defined noematic objects within the self-constituted unity of consciousness. This is a view that seems quite close to S. French's approach to the measurement problem in [14]. In this context, it should be also mentioned F. Lurcat's work, ([35]), on the relevance of a phenomenological approach to quantum mechanics (**QM**) especially in connection with N. Bohr's interpretation; as a matter of fact, there have already been various interpretations of quantum mechanics beyond the mainstream options of realism and instrumentalism, such as M. Bitbol's views in [5] motivated by an attempt at a transcendental deduction of quantum mechanics and the *Many-Worlds Interpretation* (**MWI**) in B. De Witt's approach of H. Everett's 'relative state' formulation of **QM**.[12]

Concerning M. Bitbol's approach I stress his original type transcendental deduction summed up as providing an internal correlation between a unifying mode of appearances of phenomena and certain laws of understanding considered as preconditions of experience. This seems, in quite general terms, to shift the view towards a field where the mental faculties of a subject might actively take part in grounding experience as such and also in shaping up the objects of experience. Also we should keep in mind his sense of lifting the constraint of contextualization (which corresponds a Boolean subframe to each experimental preparation) by applying a unified mathematical tool of probabilistic prediction irrespective of the context associated to the measurement that follows the preparation ([5], p. 11). In such a case, based on the notion of a re-identifying object across time which in my view presupposes the existence of an otherwise irreducible intentional relation subject/object one can ascribe to each experimental preparation a unified, predictive tool whose valuations are associated with a Boolean framework irrespective of the context associated with the measurement.

This seems interesting to the extent that: a) it presupposes an object-like

---

[12]With regard to this consciousness-related orientation I specifically point to its 'psychological' version where the quantum measurement process is reduced to a 'splitting' of a single consciousness before interaction to several afterwards yet retaining by a certain psychological mode its unity through time. See, [8] and [9].

organization of phenomena which are described in the language of a Boolean observer 'attached' to each experimental situation and b) it implies a unifying mathematical tool bridging, in effect, the contextual frames of the preparation of an experiment and its measurement.

The former condition can be understood as leading to the following assumptions. The indirect introduction of a participating 'observer' who has a particular mode of 'observation'; that is, a particular mode of constituting the objects of his 'observations' which is, in fact, a mode of representing them in a predicative universe as well-defined objects within the structure of a formal language. In the case of an experimental preparation and measurement this is linked in my view with an observer's capacity to transform his intentionalities as moments of hyletic-noetic perceptions of the real world to noematic objects in the sense of re-identifying objects across time and thus as well-defined objects of a formal ontology. Then one would be able to talk, in principle, about these constituted objects as syntactical objects under formal predication in the descriptive norms of a formal language.

In view of the above, I propose an interpretation of the presence of a knowing subject who performs quantum measurements via a measuring apparatus in the following sense: The measured property produces a macroscopic effect on an instrument (e.g. a pointer reading or a track in a bubble chamber) which is a material sign. This can be considered as having a double reality; its material one as a pointer sign or a bubble track and an intentional one in the sense of a sign susceptible to be constituted as a formal-ontological object. A sign regardless of its particular material content has the mode of being a sign-as such and in being so it can be thought of as an intentional object of noetic perception by virtue of being merely a certain 'state of affairs' (*Sachverhalt*); in other words, possibly an 'empty something'. A knowing subject performing the experiment should then be apriorically directed to it by means of the measuring device. In any case, it may be assumed that the signs of a measuring apparatus are symbols of certain physical properties (natural symbols) insofar as they are uniquely determined by the interaction with a quantum entity in terms of which they 'translate' the hidden state of the quantum entity into uniquely determined sensible signs ([19], p. 174-175).

Evidently, these signs which are part of the 'physicalistic language' of the measuring apparatus can be considered as intentional objects of a performing subject who can possibly turn them to formal-ontological symbols; the latter is conditioned on his capacity to constitute them as well-defined noematic objects in his flux of consciousness. As syntactical objects then of a linguistic statement they may be taken not just as material reality signs in abstraction but as abstractions generated by intentionality towards specific 'state-of-things' which are moreover bearers of two important properties: 1) They do not determine a unique linguistic statement; they can be object-substrates of equivalent logical-mathematical formulas inasmuch as they are abstractions of a uniquely determined material sign and 2) They are devoid of any inner analytic content as they are linguistic symbols abstracting in each case a unique and irreducible intentional object, e.g. the sign-as such of the bubble track of a particle.

At the stage a knowing subject will be able to represent moments of hyletic-noetic perception as well-defined objects of formal-ontological discourse he should by necessity have constituted them already in a kind of synthetic unity to be able to talk about them together at once; arguably this unity should be a temporal unity. But this may reduce to a constitution of internal time in the form of a continuous unity of temporal consciousness which has almost nothing to do with external (or scientific) time e.g. time as an internal parameter of a macroscopic physical system in newtonian or relativistic mechanics.

In this approach, quantization conditions stemming from appropriate boundary conditions and also the continuity of the time-evolution operator of quantum particle states are regarded as owing to the intrinsic property of quantum objects as outcomes of sufficiently reproducible experiments, to be 'embeddable' in a unified meta-contextual temporal frame of probabilistic description. This is equivalent to embedding reproducible 'observations' in a meta-contextual Boolean substructure associated with a homogenous internal time flux. This possibility involves at once, on a phenomenological level, a relationship subject-object of an intentional character and the noematic constitution of quantum objects as well-defined objects within the unity of consciousness. Independently of the context that follows the preparation of a quantum experiment there should be some intrinsic way by which quantum objects taken as intentional objects become re-identifying immanent objects of a constituting consciousness invariably over homogenous temporal unity. Eliminating then all time-related modes of noematic constitution (e.g., simultaneity, succession, casual relationship) there should be an underlying temporal substratum of the predicative universe of quantum mechanics whose temporality should be something radically different from the ordinary objective time taken as an internal parameter of a classical macroscopic system. In this view the unifying, meta-contextual time of the predictive tool can be seen as ultimately reflecting the objectified unity of the absolute flux of temporal consciousness of some 'observer' which should be in an intersubjective sense the same objectified unity of any other potential 'observer'.

I close this subsection by referring to a well-known quantum effect where the derivation of quantization conditions from classical continuity assumptions as constraints provides a clue to the necessity of assuming an impenetrable temporal substratum to which I have just referred.

It is known that in the case of a potential well the discrete eigenvalues of the energy operator is the formal result of continuity assumptions on the wave function ψ at the boundaries of a potential well and of constraints put on the wave function out of the classically permitted region in the 'observational limit' to infinity.[13]

---

[13] Based on the continuity of the wave function of a free particle at the boundaries $x = \pm\frac{a}{2}$ of a potential well V we get the equations $\psi(\frac{a}{2}) = \psi(-\frac{a}{2})$ and $\psi'(\frac{a}{2}) = \psi'(-\frac{a}{2})$. For $x < -\frac{a}{2}$ or $x > \frac{a}{2}$, in the limit to infinity it holds that: $\lim_{x \to \pm\infty} \psi(x) = 0$ for the wave function ψ of a

3. CAN A QUANTUM MECHANICAL INTERPRETATION... 81

Both constraints underlie an observational capacity linked at least indirectly to a notion of subjective temporal continuum. In this sense, the condition of continuity at $x = \pm\frac{a}{2}$ of the wave function and of its derivative implies the necessity of existence of a continuous domain of valuations of the particle wave function whereas the normalization condition $\lim_{x \to \pm\infty} \psi(x) = 0$, which is in accordance with the natural intuition that the physical state of a free particle should vanish at infinity, is a classical limit equation also presupposing an underlying continuous domain of the wave function ψ. In a phenomenological view, the classical limit equation $\lim_{x \to \pm\infty} \psi(x) = 0$ and the equations of continuity of the wave function ψ at the boundaries $x = \pm\frac{a}{2}$ imply an underlying homogenous spatiotemporal unity which may be taken, in the quantum context, as ultimately presupposing an objectified continuous unity of the temporal consciousness of a potential 'observer' in the sense described above.

To sum up, discrete eigenvalues of bound states of a quantum system are in part formally due to classical limit and continuity assumptions against an underlying continuum of propagation that may be ultimately reduced to the objectified continuum of a temporal consciousness within the triangle knowing subject-quantum object-measuring apparatus. On the same grounds, an objectified fulfilled Continuum (*erfüllte Kontinuum*) must be also presupposed in the phase of second (or field) quantization in the relativistic version of quantum mechanics where single particle wave functions of classical version are transformed into quantum field operators on quantum states defined at any space-time point.

To show the underlying assumption of an impenetrable spatiotemporal substratum in the formal theory of quantum mechanics I make a brief reference, in the following subsection, to the well-known Bohm-Aharonov effect. This effect as well as that of a potential well can be put within the frame of a discussion concerned with the evolution of a quantum system in a configuration space in terms of which the wave function must be described. In this view the implications of quantum interactions may be encoded in the topology of the configuration space by identifying certain points of this space e.g. those corresponding to particle permutations and adopting several irreducible assumptions ensuring, for instance, that no two particles occupy the same point of the space ([15], p. 9). This approach is considered as conceptually connected with the Space-Time Individuality approach which claims that it is the points of space-time that confer individuality and re-identifiability of quantum objects while instantiating their properties. My own view on the matter, though, is that there should be a deeper connection on a phenomenological level between quantum objects as objects of a physicalistic language and their representation as formal-ontological objects embeddable in the domain of a formal structure.

---

free particle of energy E (with $E < V$) which in this region of the plane takes the form of a descending exponential function $\psi(x) = C\exp(k_1 x) + D\exp(-k_1 x)$ (see any **QM** textbook).

3.2 The case of the Bohm-Aharonov effect

In view of my approach, the reference to the Bohm-Aharonov effect serves mainly to indicate the way certain irregularities on the observational-physical level are reflected in mathematical formalization into peculiar topological properties of the configuration space. This particular topic may deserve a more extensive and thorough research but at this point I only touch on the issue to the extent that it connects with my overall view of the question of the limits of 'observation'.

The irregularity in the Bohm-Aharonov effect, roughly put, has to do with the presence of a solenoid that causes a shift in the interference pattern of a double slit in the notable absence of an external magnetic field. As a matter of fact, the physical effect observed which is the change in phase difference of the electron interference pattern $\Delta \delta = \frac{e}{\hbar} \int \text{curl} A \, dS$ depends only on $\text{curl} A$[14] in a way that it could be deduced that an electron is influenced by fields which are only non-zero in regions inaccessible to it. In formal terms, this amounts to a non-locality of the integral $\oint A dr$. In general conclusion, the Bohm-Aharonov effect owes to the non-trivial topology of the vacuum and the fact that electrodynamics is a gauge theory (see, [37]). It has been demonstrated that the vacuum in gauge theories has a rich mathematical structure associated with certain physical consequences and the Bohm-Aharonov effect is a simple illustration of a deeper connection that may exist between certain irregular kinds of physical interaction and the corresponding 'pathologies' in topological modelization ([37], p. 101).

Being a bit more specific without intending to enter into details of the experimental context, the Bohm-Aharonov effect is formally reduced to a certain topological peculiarity of the configuration space of the null-field; this is a plane with a hole in it which is the non-simply connected circle S^1. In mathematical elaboration, this generates a many-valued gauge function x mapping the group space S^1 onto the configuration space of the experiment $S^1 \times R$ such that not all such x are deformable to a constant gauge function ($x = $ const). In that case, it would produce $A_\mu = 0$ and no Bohm-Aharonov effect ([37], p. 105). Mathematically the function x satisfying $A = \nabla x$ turns out to be a many-valued function and this becomes possible since the space on which it is defined is not simply connected. That is, the group space of the gauge group of electromagnetism $U(1)$ is the non-simply connected circle S^1 where, intuitively speaking, a non-simply connected space is one in which not all curves may be continuously shrunk to a point.

If x were single-valued, then $B = \text{curl} A = \text{curl} \nabla x \equiv 0$ everywhere, so there would be no magnetic flux Φ and consequently no physical effect taking into account that $\Delta \delta = \frac{e}{\hbar} \Phi$.[15]

---

[14] The vector potential A is linked to the magnetic induction B by the well-known formula $B = \text{curl} A$.

[15] In their exposition of the experiment in [4], D. Bohm & B.J. Hiley propose an interpretation which implies a physical effect for the vector potential A on the quantum level by means of a mathematical formalism which reduces again to a peculiarity of the mathematical

3. CAN A QUANTUM MECHANICAL INTERPRETATION...

In view of the previous discussion, I point to a 'transposing' of the irregular characteristics of the quantum effect in question to a peculiarity of the topology of the configuration space of experiment which, in the present case, reduces to the non-simple connectedness of the topological structure of group space S^1. But prior to the assumption of topological discontinuities, such as the non-simple connectedness, one must assume the constancy across time of an objective spatiotemporal continuum formally abstracted as mathematical continuum. This can be, in turn, reduced to the constancy of a fulfilled time-consciousness self-constituted as a continuous unity bridging, in effect, the context of an experimental preparation with that of measurement. Arguably this may be taken as providing some clue in placing under the same interpretational context the bounds of quantum 'observation' and the limits of its formal description through mathematical metatheory.

3.3 Interpreting quantum non-separability

In quantum mechanical theory quantum non-separability arises as a result of the principle of superposition of states and, on a purely formal level, from the impossibility to provide, given a compound system S and its corresponding Hilbert space H, a decomposition of it into a tensor product $H = H_1 \otimes H_2 \otimes ... \otimes H_N$ of the subsystem spaces H_i such that an observable A of S can be expressed in the canonical form $A = A_1 \otimes A_2 \otimes ... \otimes A_N$ of suitable observables of the subsystems S_i. Formally this is the result of a particular feature of the tensor product, namely, that it is not a restriction of the topological product $H = H_1 \times H_2 \times ... \times H_N$ but includes it as a proper subset. Given that in quantum mechanical theory there are no reasonable criteria that would guarantee the existence (and uniqueness) of such a tensor product decomposition of the whole system the question is how we could possibly derive it and on what terms on the operational level.[16]

Active Scientific Realism proposes, for instance, to discuss the question of non-separability as presupposing the feasibility of the kinematical independence between a component subsystem of interest and an appropriate measuring system including its environment (see: [28], [29]); it presupposes, in general, the

---

model of the configuration space; this is almost bizarre if one thinks in classical terms as, indeed, the physical effect of A becomes negligible in classical limit. But as they point out, a common mistake is to take the classical idea about the vector potential to hold quantum mechanically ([4], pp. 50-54.)

[16] A prototype of a compound (EPR - correlated) system experimentally confirmed is the compound system S of spin-singlet pairs. It consists of a pair (S_1, S_2) of spin $\frac{1}{2}$ particles in the singlet state

$$W = \frac{1}{\sqrt{2}} \{|\psi_+ > \otimes |\phi_- > - |\psi_- > \otimes |\phi_+ >\},$$

where $\{|\psi_\pm >\}$ and $\{|\phi_\pm >\}$ are orthonormal bases of the two dimensional Hilbert spaces H_1 and H_2 associated with states S_1 and S_2 respectively. In such a situation, it is theoretically predicted and experimentally confirmed that the spin components of S_1 and S_2 have always opposite orientations. As a matter of fact, this set-up may be a compound two-fermions system used to illustrate S. Saunders' position concerning the weak discernibility and, for that reason, the particular kind of individuality of quantum objects; see relevant discussion on p. 77.

separation between the observer and the observed. In such a view, taking the physical world as an unbroken whole we have to separate it, to perform a breakdown of the entanglement of subsystems. In what is called a Heisenberg cut, we have to decompose the compound entangled system into interacting but disentangled components that is, into measured objects on the one hand and measuring systems (uncorrelated observers in a broad sense) on the other with no (or insignificantly so) holistic correlations among them. By means of the Heisenberg cut, well-defined separate objects can be generated in their contextual environments in terms of a process projecting the holistic non-Boolean domain of entangled quantum correlations into a meta-contextual Boolean frame that breaks the wholeness of nature by means of an effective participation of a knowing/intentional subject in the physical world ([28], pp. 300, 303). Moreover, the notion of an effective participation of a knowing/intentional subject in the physical world seems to imply the Aristotelian idea of *potentia* since, for any effective observer there should be two categories of entities on a quantum level; those posterior to his knowing/intentional acts which, as already pointed out, he has some inherent mode to recognize as well-defined objects and those prior to his purely intentional acts which should by necessity be for him mere potentialities; in that sense, " a quantum object exists, independently of any operational procedures, only in the sense of 'potentiality', namely, as being characterized by a set of potentially possible values for its various physical quantities that are actualized when the object is interacting with its environment or a pertinent experimental context" ([29], p. 290).

In view of the description of a relation between a knowing-intentional subject and the object of his intentionality, referred to in subsection 3.1, we may argue that there exists a certain convergence of the interpretational content of phenomenological analysis with the positions of Active Scientific Realism[17] inasmuch as:

The implementation of the Heisenberg cut can be taken as presupposing a notion of co-existence and also of separation in the domain of intentional 'observation' between a consciousness intentionally directed to its object and the object in-itself as a direct and unambiguous presence in front of the intentionality of consciousness. A knowing subject by applying his intentionality creates a particular context to inquire e.g. into the 'hidden status' of an entangled quantum state in the following two stages: 1) on the hyletic-noetic level by apprehending any sensible sign as such (by means of the measuring apparatus) irrespectively of its material content in the sense of a unique sign as such in original giveness distinguishable from any other possible sign in the protention of his intentionality (see: [24], p. 8); at this stage he has already lost his claim on acceding to the inner reality of the entangled state for he noetically

---

[17]In a certain sense this approach is formally related to H. Everett's 'Relative State Interpretation' of Quantum Theory with regard to a decoupling to world components $\psi^{(R)}$, $\psi^{(L)}$ of a certain superposition state $\psi(t) = e^{iHt}\phi(\varphi_R \pm \varphi_L)$ corresponding to a localization of consciousness not only in space and time but also along certain Hilbert space components (see: [43], pp. 73-74).

apprehends what he apprehends in the 'physicalistic language' of the apparatus and 2) he 'thereafter' constitutes it as a noematic object immanent to his consciousness in the modes already referred to and can possibly transform it to a formal-ontological object of a formal metatheory.

Moreover, the notion of the effective presence of a knowing/intentional subject inside the Life-World can put under an alternative perspective the Aristotelian notion of potentialities (believed by some people to have its place in the interpretation of quantum reality) as it seems to somehow weaken its vaguely metaphysical character exactly by the introduction of the intentional/constituting subject as effective part of the Life-world. Thus, from a phenomenological point of view, a World where pre-predicative experience (i.e. an intentional one), linked with the presence of an intentional/constituting subject, determines by 'anticipation' (protention) actual instances may be defined as a domain of real possibility anterior to actuality. This seems partly to eliminate the vague ontological - not to say purely metaphysical - character of the Aristotelian theory of potentialities for it replaces to the principle of a first *entelechy*, reached by regression ad infinitum of all classes of potentialities, the principle of at least one constituting subject in pre-phenomenological World. This means that upon 'enactment' of the intentionalities of a participating subject within a contextual experimental frame certain potentialities of a quantum whole are actualized on the level of hyletic-noetic perception whereas others are not. From a certain viewpoint, this seems relevant to the principle of actualization put up by R. Omnés as an additional external rule not emerging from the internal structure of **QM** to postulate the passing from phenomena to facts and used ' merely as a licence to use consistent logic to reason from present brute experience' ([12], p. 1335).

At this point we should face the question of the underlying role of time in the measurement process of an entangled quantum state. As the knowing/intentional subject, acting as a constituting factor, transposes the 'unity' of real-world experience to the a-thematic, impredicative unity of his self-constituted flux of consciousness ([21], pp. 186, 195) we can possibly claim that this inner subjective temporality as constitutionally posterior to the apprehension of the undissectable wholeness of a quantum non-separable state sets a *de facto* limit to a complete scientific cognizance of a contextual physical reality. A primary reason for this limitation might lie in the fact that we lack any possible means 'to go beyond' intentionality and consequently lack the means to fully describe the 'inner' time of an entangled state prior to its subjective temporal constitution; generally, it seems that we lack the means to unconditionally approach the temporality of the pre-phenomenological World (the World before the phenomenological reduction of a constituting *Ich*) which in Husserl's writings is presupposed as the constant synthetic unity of every possible experience and also the common denominator in terms of substance of all beings in the World.

On this account, even if a contradiction produced in the theory of **QM** can be overcome on the purely logical grounds[18] that ' any apparatus which realizes the reduction of the wave function is necessarily only a metatheoretical object' ([6], p. 338) the question, in the first place, of providing a physicalistic description as to what 'takes place' in-between the time of experimental preparation of a compound quantum system $s \otimes \mathcal{Q}$ and the time of its measurement remains open; in this case, s is the state of a quantum object at time t and $\mathcal{Q}$ a measuring apparatus identified with a Boolean-minded observer assigning truth values to non-Boolean quantum substructures. The jump of truth values in the process of measurement which is formally the result of the absence of an isomorphism between Boolean and non-Boolean structures - assuming that a quantum object, considered as an objective existence, is the non-distributive lattice of its properties - forces for a Boolean observer the need of the existence of an objective time in which he must 'move' ([18], p. 2396).

This question is also linked with J. von Neumann's Projection Postulate (or 'the reduction of the wave function' postulate) as it introduces indirectly the need for a self-constituting time flux by assigning to the mathematical translation $\tau((s)(t))$ of the physical state $s(t)$ of a quantum quantity Q_i upon a first-kind measurement at time t the same eigenvector ψ_κ as to the translation of the state $s(t_1)$ of the quantity Q_i at time t_1 soon after the measurement.[19] As a matter of fact, even if we assume Von Neumann's Projection Postulate or Van Fraassen's modal interpretation of quantum mechanics as 'external' metatheoretical conditions in a purely logical way we cannot be led by any analytic linguistic means to a complete description of the 'change of states' that takes place during the measurement process in the compound system 'system + apparatus'.

The issue had been brought up by F. London & E. Bauer who noted the critical role played by the consciousness of an observer in the transition from an entangled to the pure case by forging a global wave function $\Psi(x,y,z)$ corresponding to the composed system [object(x)- apparatus(y)- observer(z)]. Furthermore, they claimed that it is not due to some kind of interaction between the apparatus and the object that produces a new ψ for the system

---

[18] In this connection, I refer to M.L. dalla Chiara's view of the measurement problem of quantum mechanics as a characteristic question of the semantical closure of a theory, in other words as to 'what extent a consistent theory (in this case **QM**) can be closed with respect to the objects and the concepts which are described and expressed in its metatheory'. According to dalla Chiara, quantum mechanical theory as a consistent theory satisfying some standard formal requirements, turns out to be the subject of some limitations due to purely logical reasons concerning its capacity to completely describe and express certain physical objects and concepts.

[19] A form of J. von Neumann's Projection Postulate is the following: Let the mathematical translation τ of the physical system s at time t be: $\tau((s)(t)) = \sum c_j \psi_j$ where ψ_j are eigenvectors of $\rho(Q_i)$, $\rho(Q_i)$ being the mathematical interpretation of operationally defined quantity Q_i. Suppose someone carries out a first-kind measurement (i.e. one in which the measured system described by s is taken to interact with the measuring apparatus described by quantum state ϕ, so that the total wave function before the interaction is $s \cdot \phi$) for the quantity Q_i in state $s(t)$ getting as a result the interval $r_\kappa \pm \epsilon_{Q_i}$ where r_κ is an eigenvalue of $\rho(Q_i)$ with corresponding eigenvector ψ_κ. Then, soon after the measurement (at $t_1 > t$) the translation of $s(t_1)$ will still be ψ_κ, that is, $\tau((s)(t_1)) = \psi_\kappa$. See, ([6], p. 334).

during measurement but rather the consciousness of an 'I' cutting the statistical correlations built in the global function $\Psi(x,y,z) = \sum_k \psi_k u_k(x) v_k(y) w_k(z)$ and setting up a new objectivity by attributing to the object a new function $\psi(x) = u_k(x)$ [34]. This raises again the prospect of a phenomenological approach towards a homogenous self-constituting temporal consciousness and the constitution of objects within it as noematic correlates of moments of an outward directed intentionality.

S. French in [14], largely motivated by London & Bauer's view of the role of the consciousness of an observer in quantum measurement, proposes a phenomenological reading of the 'action' of a very special character of the 'I', or ego in Husserlian terms, which is very close to my own view inasmuch as: he sets, at first, the domain of a potential observer within that of quantum mechanics and, second, he applies the Husserlian notion of a characteristic act of reflection by means of which the phenomenological ego can reflect on its act of 'observation' and ultimately on itself. By this act of reflection the ego can on the one hand separate itself from the superposition and on the other hand set up a new objectivity thought not in terms of a collapse of wave function but rather as a mutual separation of an Ego-pole and an object-pole establishing a relation subject-object of intentional character through this very act ([14], pp. 484-85).

By intentionality the Ego-pole cannot but constantly 'be' engaged in an 'empty looking' at any potential object, its act of objectification being meant in quantum context as an attribution of a definite state to a quantum object among the different components predicted by the theory. My point, however, is that although S. French refers to the Ego-pole as something not substantial, an absolute subjectivity over and above its act of reflection (making reference mainly to Husserl's *Ideas*) he has not taken into consideration the temporal character of the phenomenological ego in establishing new objectivities upon 'observation'. For one thing, considering the constituting role of the absolute ego of consciousness, we must concede that it 'forces' its unidimensional temporality upon seizing the objects of phenomenological perception within the homogenous immanent flux. But what about its own temporality? Any original act of reflection on itself will produce its objectified version and consequently will be constituted in the same objective continuous temporality as all temporal objects. In my view, this is a deep enough question that has ultimately to do with the origins of temporality and may be indirectly related on an epistemological level with the external to the system time parameter in quantum mechanical processes. Yet, it may provide ground for further research on a yet unexplored field and it is a problem that according to Husserl's own confession presented him with grave difficulties to the end. I just note that later in the *Bernauer Manuskripte* he described the absolute ego in terms of an unknown primordial process (*unbewusster Urprozess*) even beyond temporality whose reflection upon itself cannot but produce its own objectification (which is obviously not itself) in continuous temporal unity ([25], pp. 203-207).

Closing this section, I turn to the fundamental irreducibilities which in my view shape our 'observational' frame in an intersubjective world of an unbounded horizon of events and underlie its (incomplete by Gödel's incompleteness theorems) description by a formal-mathematical metatheory: On the one hand we have intentionalities of an *a priori* character directed on the lowest level of experience to individuals-substrates 'transposed' thereafter with their noematic correlates as immanences of the flux within each subject's consciousness. On the other hand, we have the intuition of continuous unity[20] as a substratum divested of any quality on which to formally describe and deliver a meaning to well-defined noematic objects. This continuous unity can be phenomenologically viewed as subjective, self-constituting unity of temporal consciousness which leads ultimately to the transcendental ego of consciousness (see: [22], pp. 73-75).

Saying it in other words, as much it is impossible to reduce the mental process by which we abstract from an original impression in immediate awareness, evidently distinct from any other within temporal flow, to anything more fundamental in noetic-noematic constitution it is just as impossible to capture what is constituting the unity of a whole in consciousness by means of the former activity.

4 Observation in the language of formal systems. Where is the irreducibility and where the transcendence?

As the main purpose of this article was to discuss the limits of observation as such and those of a formal language, in particular that of quantum mechanics, I sought to reach the most fundamental level of observation beyond the limits of the common intuition of this notion. In doing so, I took into account the Husserlian view that mathematical objects are complete abstractions of perceptual objects[21] by means of a special kind of intuition termed as categorial intuition, leaving aside any counter-arguments of a rather artificial nature, e.g. as to whether the mathematical object $\{\emptyset\}$ should be also considered as a perceptual object.

My theoretical standpoint, linking quantum observation with a phenomenology of constitution puts under the same perspective the formation of objects of mathematical logic as syntactical elements in a formal-ontological environment corresponding to 'states of affairs' (*Sachverhalte*) and the formation of

---

[20] The implicit assumption of an underlying continuous unity may be also noted in the bid for a properly defined probability density (at detection time) in the continuum limit within the frame of a consistent histories approach to quantum mechanics; see C. J. Isham, C. Anastopoulos, papers in, respectively, [26], [27], [2], [3].

[21] This kind of abstraction is not meant as a free variation in content leaving common traits as invariants but as a complete evacuation of all traits relative to a content. This abstraction leads to the form of a mathematical object in general, an eidetic form whose specific instances bearing a content are just a fulfillment within temporality. This is, moreover, related with the meaning of empty-substrates, as abstract forms lacking any material content, which are taken as intentionalities towards certain 'states of affairs' (mentioned on p. 72). These empty eidetic forms are considered to be the class of objects of Mathematical Logic, see [20], §14, p. 33.

4. OBSERVATION IN THE LANGUAGE OF FORMAL SYSTEMS

quantum entities as well-defined noematic objects in consciousness 'generated' by the moments of intentional perception in the physical world. It is obvious that in such an approach we should consider mathematics as divested of any platonist hue and possibly revisited against the inconveniences of Cantorian-type actual infinity. In this connection, mathematical theories of an alternative non-standard character especially those which incorporate a notion of natural infinity as an open-ended shift of classes of hereditarily finite 'observations' (for instance, Alternative Set Theory and Hyperfinite Set Theory) seem more adapted to my view of mathematical activity as a special kind of abstraction in an intersubjective and interactive field of events of a local but ever receding horizon. It is of a certain importance to know that there exists already a research activity in providing non-standard mathematical models of quantum mechanics (see, e.g. [10], [11]).

In my view, dealing with an irreducible individual in formal discourse, which is moreover a predicate-bearer, lies in a certain underlying sense on the same ground irrespectively of whether it is a syntactical atom of a stratified mathematical formula corresponding to a unique 'state of affairs' or it is a formal-ontological object abstracted from an intentionally perceived quantum individual by a knowing/intentional subject using a measuring apparatus as an extension of his consciousness. As long as they can be apprehended as distinct to any other possible hyletic-noetic perception on the lowest level of intentionality and as they are, moreover, constituted as bearers of an otherwise undefined sense of 'order', they can be taken as syntactical individual-substrates bearers of appropriate to them categorial objectivities, characterized by Husserl as nuclei-forms (*Kernformen*). Is there a way to penetrate even more deeply, to open and 'read' the inner content of those individuals, in a word, to reach a deeper level of perception? The answer seems to be negative and moreover not as a contingent but as a generic state of affairs. The strongest evidence is our own intuition through the direct original giveness of the intentional individuals-substrates of our experience; in fact, the lowest-level intentionality is described as precisely an intentionality towards irreducible individuals as such. I would call it a most fundamental irreducibility of human perception and it is at the same time rather 'friendly' and easy to co-operate with our other mental faculties. It is thanks to this fundamental intuition that we can comprehend and handle almost anything from sequences of natural numbers to the capacity to reflect on images of distinct particle trajectories in a bubble chamber.

On the contrary, there is another irreducibility which, though it is almost our most common intuition, it proves most difficult to comprehend let alone describe by formal first-order linguistic means. This is the intuition of continuum including everything from the common intuition of our existence as a continuous flow of events to the intuition of a curve on a piece of paper as a continuous set of black points, to the intuition of subatomic events as taking place against a fulfilled temporal background. What is it that makes possible this coherent unity in constitution reflected as a formalized continuity within mathematical theories irrespectively of the domain of reference?

E. Husserl made a clear distinction between phenomenological time, the homogenous form of all living experiences within the flux of consciousness and the objective or scientific time. By necessity every real experience is a durating experience which is a fact extracted by pure intuition of its enactment and it is constituted by a certain *a priori* mode as an infinitely fulfilled continuum of durations. Going deeper into the 'ontology' of phenomenological continuum Husserl was led to the transcendental pure ego of consciousness. This ego as an absolute subjectivity is only accessible by its objectification as a 'mirror image' of itself and it is only in this way possible to reflect on the continuum as an objective whole and also on the notion of an unbounded infinity in a Kantian sense ([20], p. 331).

The matter in last count is, independently of whether one should accept in principle a 'built-in' transcendence of intuitive and formally of the mathematical continuum by means of a phenomenological reduction, the hard fact that any attempt to describe formal continuum by first-order linguistic means inevitably leads to circularities in definitions or entails some form of *ad hoc* axiomatization[22], for instance, the introduction of the *ad hoc* extension or prolongation principles axiomatizing the embedding of standard structures into saturated nonstandard domains (see: [33]).

Using a metaphor we can think of a pendulum with the aforementioned irreducibilities taken as its extreme points; the intentionality towards individual-substrates on the one hand and the intuition of a subjective, impredicative Continuum on the other. In a quantum context, as I tried to show in Section 3, these irreducibilities seem to underlie among other things the incompatibility on a formal level between sequences of observations as described by operator algebras on the one hand and the continuously changing wave function on the other.

But these might be in principle elusive and beyond any complete formal description on the grounds of the circular question: On what terms can the mind capture the mind?

BIBLIOGRAPHY

[1] Adams, R. (1979). Primitive Thisness and Primitive Identity, *Journal of Philosophy*, 76, 1, 5-26.
[2] Anastopoulos, C. (2001). Continuous-time Histories: Observables, Probabilities, Phase Space Structure and the Classical Limit, *Journal of Mathem. Physics*, 42, 8, 3225-3259.
[3] Anastopoulos, C., Savvidou, D. (2006). Time-of-Arrival Probabilities and Quantum Measurements, *Journal of Mathem. Physics*, 47, 122106-1 - 122106-29.

---

[22]This is in part reflected in the proof of the independence of actual infinity principles such as the *Continuum Hypothesis* and the *Axiom of Choice* from the other axioms of the Zermelo-Fraenkel Set Theory. As a matter of fact, there is an ongoing theoretical discussion on the possibility of a non-analytic character of the *Continuum Hypothesis* question in the foundations of mathematics; on this account, I refer to S. Feferman's claim in [13] that 'the *Continuum Hypothesis* is an inherently vague problem that no new axiom will settle in a convincingly definite way'. A more thorough analysis of mathematical objects as objects of intentional observation will be given in a forthcoming paper.

4. OBSERVATION IN THE LANGUAGE OF FORMAL SYSTEMS 91

[4] Bohm, D., Hiley, B.J. (1993). *The Undivided Universe*, London & New York: Routledge.

[5] Bitbol, M. (1998). Some Steps towards a Transcendental Deduction of Quantum Mechanics, *Philosophia Naturalis*, 35, 253-280.

[6] dalla Chiara, M.L. (1977). Logical Self Reference, Set Theoretical Paradoxes and the Measurement Problem in Quantum Mechanics, *Journal of Philosophical Logic*, 6, 331-347.

[7] Dieks, D., Versteegh, M. (2007). Identical Quantum Particles and Weak Discernibility, *arXiv: quant-ph/0703021v1*, 1-11.

[8] Everett, H.D. (1957). 'Relative State' Formulation of Quantum Mechanics, *Reviews of Modern Physics*, 29, 454-462.

[9] Everett, H.D. (1957). *The Theory of the Universal Wave Function*, Ph.D. thesis, Princeton. Reprinted in De Witt B.S. and Graham N. *The Many-Worlds Interpretation of Quantum Mechanics.*, Princeton University Press, 1973.

[10] Farrukh, M.O. (1975). Application of Nonstandard Analysis to Quantum Mechanics, *Jour. of Mathematical Physics*, 16, 2, 177-200.

[11] Francis, C.E. (1981). Applications of Non-standard Analysis to Relativistic Quantum Mechanics, *J. Phys. A: Math. Gen.*, 14, 2539-2551.

[12] Faris, W. (1996). Review of Roland Omnés, The Interpretation of Quantum Mechanics, *Notices of the AMS*, 43, 11, 1328-1339.

[13] Feferman, S. (1999). Does mathematics need New Axioms?, *American Mathematical Monthly*, 106, 99-111.

[14] French, S. (2002). A Phenomenological Solution to the Measurement Problem? Husserl and the Foundations of Quantum Mechanics, *Studies in History and Philosophy of Modern Physics*, 33, 467-491.

[15] French, S. (2006). Identity and Individuality in Quantum Theory, *The Stanford Encyclopedia Of Philosophy*, (Spring 2006 Edition), Ed. N. Zalta (ed.), http://plato.stanford.edu/archives/spr2006/entries/qt-idind, 1-18.

[16] French, S. (1989). Identity and Individuality in Classical and Quantum Physics, *Australasian Journal of Philosophy*, 67, 4, 432-446.

[17] French S. & Krause D. (2006). *Identity in Physics: A Historical, Philosophical and Formal Analysis*, New York: Oxford University Press.

[18] Grib, A.A. (1993). Quantum Logical Interpretation of Quantum Mechanics: The Role of Time, *Int. Jour. of Theoretical Physics*, 32, 12, 2389-2400.

[19] Heelan, P. (1988). *Space-Perception and the Philosophy of Science*, University of California Press.

[20] Husserl, E. (1995). *Ideen zu einer Reinen Phänomenologie und Phänomenologischen Philosophie, Erstes Buch*, Hua III/I, Dordrecht: Kluwer Acad. Pub.

[21] Husserl, E. (1974). *Formale und Transzendentale Logik*, Hua XVII, hgb. Paul Janssen, Den Haag: M. Nijhoff.

[22] Husserl, E. (1966). *Zur Phänomenologie des Inneren Zeibewusstseins*, Hua X, hgb. Rudolf Boehm, Den Haag: M. Nijhoff.

[23] Husserl, E. (1962). *Die Krisis der Europäischen Wissenschaften und die Transzendentale Phanomenologie*, Hua VI, hgb. Walter Biemel, Den Haag: M. Nijhoff.

[24] Husserl, E. (1966). *Analysen zur Passiven Synthesis*, Hua XI, hgb. M. Fleischer, Den Haag: M. Nijhoff.

[25] Husserl, E. (2001). *Die Bernauer Manusckripte über das Zeitbewusstsein (1917/18)*, herausg. R. Bernet & D. Lohmar, Dordrecht: Kluwer Acad. Pub.

[26] Isham, C. J. (1994). Quantum Logic and the Histories Approach to Quantum Theory, *J. Mathematical Physics*, 35, 2157-2185.

[27] Isham, C. J. & Linden, N. (1994). Quantum Temporal Logic and Decoherence Functionals in the Histories Approach to Generalised Quantum Theory, *J. Mathematical Physics*, 35, 5452-5476.

[28] Karakostas, V. (2004). Forms of Quantum Nonseparability and Related Philosophical Consquences, *Journal for General Philosophy of Science*, 35, 283-312.

[29] Karakostas, V. (2007). Nonseparability, Potentiality, and the Context-Dependence of Quantum Objects, *J. of Gen. Philos. of Science*, 38, 279-297.

[30] Krause, D., Coelho, A.M.N. (2005). Identity, Indiscernibility, and Philosophical Claims, *Axiomathes*, 15, 191-210.

[31] Krause, D., Da Costa, N.C.A. (2007). Logical and Philosophical Remarks on Quasi-Set Theory, *Logic Journal of IGPL*, (online version), 1-11.
[32] Krause, D. (1992). On a Quasi-Set Theory, *Notre Dame Journal of Formal Logic*, 33, 3, 402-411.
[33] Livadas, S. (2005). The Phenomenological Roots of Nonstandard Mathematics, *Romanian Jour. of Infor. Science and Technology*, 8, 2, 115-136.
[34] London, F., Bauer, E. (1983). The theory of Observation in Quantum Mechanics. In J.A. Wheeler & W.H. Zurek (Eds.), *Quantum Theory and Measurement*, (pp. 217-259). Princeton: Princeton University Press.
[35] Lurcat, F. (2007). Understanding Quantum Mechanics with Bohr and Husserl. In Luciano Boi, Pierre Krezberg & Frederic Patras (Eds.), *Rediscovering Phenomenology*, (pp. 229-258). Dordrect: Springer.
[36] Primas, H. (1993). The Cartesian Cut, the Heisenberg Cut, and Disentangled Observers. In K.V. Laurikainen & C. Montonen (Eds.), *Symposia on the Foundations of Modern Physics*, (pp. 245-269). Singapore: World Scientific.
[37] Ryder, L. (1996). *Quantum Field Theory*, Cambridge: Cambridge University Press.
[38] Saunders, S. (2006). Are Quantum Particles Objects? , *Analysis*, 66, pp. 52-63.
[39] Sokolowski, R.: 1974, *Husserlian Meditations*, Evanston: Northwestern University Press.
[40] Tieszen, R. (1984). Mathematical Intuition and Husserl's Phenomenology, *Nous*, 18, 3, 395-421.
[41] Tieszen, R. (2005). *Phenomenology, Logic, and the Philosophy of Mathematics*, Cambridge: Cambridge University Press.
[42] van Fraasen, B. (1991). *Quantum Mechanics: An Empiricist View*, Oxford: Clarendon Press.
[43] Zeh, H.D. (1970), On the Interpretation of Measurement in Quantum Theory, *Foundations of Physics*, 1, 1, 69-76.

The Transcendence of Time in the Epistemology of Observation from a Phenomenological Standpoint [0]

STATHIS LIVADAS

1 Introduction

As it is implied by the title, this article is an attempt to provide within an epistemological context a strong evidence towards a transcendental factor of temporality mostly as it is manifested in physical phenomena associated with interactions on the quantum level; the latter can be justified on the grounds that, generally, in a quantum system time is regarded as an external parameter partly because it can be taken as a co-constitutive factor in shaping the objective existence of quantum objects e.g. in quantum decoherence phenomena (see, [9]). In view of my overall approach I chose to deal with a particular offspring of quantum measurement theory, the (consistent) time-histories theory, for the main reason that it is more focused than canonical quantum theory, both formally and interpretationally, on the role of time parameter in the context of quantum measurements.[1] On this account it purportedly claims to a more rational comprehension of time in both its discrete and continuous aspects in the process of quantum measurements and a more consistent formal elaboration of it so as to provide an appropriate framework for ongoing theoretical activity on the subject.

There is a further epistemological dimension to the question of the transcendence of temporal consciousness engendered mainly by the works of J. Eccles in [5] and S. Dehaene in [2] and also the works in [13] and [4]. The first is a quantum mechanical interpretation of the 'choice' between possible exocytosis states in the neuronal net of synapses which leads to the assumption of a mental subjectivity which reaches by means of psychons (or mental unities) the quantum exocytosis states in a unity-to-unity connection and it also demonstrates the reality of this effect as a lived-in experience schematized by the interconnection between World 1 and World 2.[2]

---

[0] This article has been published in original form in the journal *Manuscrito*, (2011), V. 34, 2, pp. 435-469.

[1] In this view, canonical quantum theory is considered as conceding too much on the interpretational level to paradoxical credos such as the Copenhagen School's wavefunction collapse or to interpretationally evasive decoherence assumptions as von Neumann's projection postulate.

[2] In [5], J. Eccles schematically describes World 1 as the part of the brain that serves as

Moreover Eccles' views can be seen as a sum up of corroborative evidences based in part on experimental data that lead to a notion of a subjective factor, termed by him spirit, acting as a unifying pole of lived experiences through a non-material field analogous to the probability fields of quantum mechanics ([5], p. 253). In this respect his self-conscious spirit can be linked to the phenomenological notion of ego as an ever-in-act subjective factor making possible by its very objectification the unity of lived experiences as an unbreakable whole within the temporal flux of consciousness.

Concerning the work of S. Dehaene I mainly emphasize his results in [2] that present, as I will argue in a later section, a strong experimentally grounded claim for the relevance of a phenomenological approach towards a constitution of intentionally perceived objects as immanent objects of consciousness within a self-constituting temporal substratum that can be, in fact, an object of reflective attitude solely by its own objectification. In the specific phenomenon of attentional blink, Dehaene presents some results that point to a difference between conscious and unconscious processing, on the one hand in the sense of a response triggered by events taken as primary correlates of conscious perception and on the other by an underlying unconscious process manifested in the detection of brain potentials which are not evoked by some kind of conscious activity.

The difficulties encountered in finding a linguistically meaningful way to deal with the absolute subjectivity behind objective temporality are brought up in Section 5 where a brief reference is made to Husserl's late work on temporality in *Bernauer Manuskripte*. There, as well as in his recently published last writings on temporality in [21], he constantly moves from the Scylla of getting trapped into objective temporality to the Charybdis of generating a predicative discourse for what is by nature non-predicative. This is meant as a concluding section, inasmuch as it focuses on the core problematic of inner time consciousness coming out of a phenomenologically motivated review of the question of time in an epistemological context, as it was elaborated in the preceding sections.

2 The subjective temporal substrate of a formal theory

The main purpose of this section is to put forward certain arguments on the relevance of the phenomenological approach towards objects of formal theories, e.g. of quantum theory, which are abstracted from registered facts of physical reality through some kind (quantum mechanical in this case) observation. At the same time, the question of time and the source of temporality as inherently linked to the notion of constitution of well-defined objects of intentional observation will be thoroughly considered. In this respect, my approach is a phenomenologically motivated one in regarding, first, formal sciences within a context of intentionalities and second in regarding the apophantic domain

---

an intermediary to World 2, which is referred to as comprising those mental components representing interior and exterior perceptions and also self-conscious mind; see, [5], pp. 272-273.

of theoretical forms such as those introduced in *Formale und Transcendentale Logik* (**FTL**), [18], as receiving their senses from the objective domain yet interpreting them as supposed ([28], pp. 286-288). This point of view may generally lead to a new approach beyond that of pure logic and mathematics taken as diverse disciplines in classical tradition or may yet lead beyond an extensional approach producing paradoxes of the kind of Russell's antinomy.

This approach would seek a common ground underlying the objective and apophantic domain of a mathematical theory respectively shaped by the following principal fields: the field of formal ontology using categories referring to objects and the field of formal apophantics using categories referring to meanings, as they were mainly developed in **FTL**. As it will be elaborated in the following, both fields are reduced on a still deeper level to a notion of object as an intentional object whose meaning is ultimately grounded on being the content of an intentional act in temporal fulfillment and also to the notion of an internal phenomenologically constituted time.

The aforementioned fields shape a judgement in clear and distinct existence in terms of the following: **a)** Once a judgement is brought out in full existence in distinction to any other it already refers to objects as noematic correlates of registered facts bestowed with the meanings which is all that is expressible about them[3] e.g., the relations subject-predicates attached to it or subject of an act-object of an act in the synthetic unity of the three temporal states of judgement, (1) before, (2) during and (3) after registration ([28], p. 240) and **b)** Any judgement at the level of distinction should be inevitably reduced, no matter how syntactically complex, to ultimate object-substrates ([18], pp. 210-213) which are deprived of any analytical character being only capable of a sole qualification as phenomenological evidences.

The second condition is the core matter of formal ontology which deals with objects as registered intentionalities of a living subject, bearer moreover of a consciousness, with all categorial objectivities associated with them irrespective of being taken as irreducible 'thingness' substrates (*sachhaltige Substrate*) or 'empty' substrates in complete abstraction. These latter objects (or aggregates of them) are referred to in *Ideas I* as (last) empty substrates (*Leersubstrate*). Empty substrates as states of affairs (*Sachverhalte*) in complete abstraction deprived of any trait of material content (since they are not considered to be variations over common content) can be thought of as objects of mathematical logic in the form of numbers, or of elements of sets, of classes of sets, of domains of functions, etc ([14], p. 33). Taken that apophantic sentences receive the sense of their objects from the domain of experience, albeit they interpret them as supposed, and that these objects are ultimately reduced to last object-substrates registered by hyletic-noetic moments of intentionality, we can put up the following claims based on the fact that these moments are not of a psychological character but rather something *a priori* grounded on the idea of

---

[3]In Husserl's view in *Ideas I* (pp. 297-298) the content of an intentional act is thought of as the 'meaning' of the act by virtue of which consciousness refers to an object or state of affairs as its own.

knowledge as such and associated with some form of intentionality ([20], p. 240).

One can soundly raise the possibility of forming an object of knowledge roughly based on the following conditions referred to in *Logical Investigations*: a) the *a priori* character of the noetic form of intentionality independently of any concrete empirical act conditioned on psychological constraints and b) the purely logical character of the ideal conditions of an object's knowledge grounded on the 'content' of the act of knowledge. On account of the first condition a thinking subject should be, in principle, capable of implementing all sorts of acts to ground theoretically his knowledge and on account of the second condition we should consider theoretical meaning, associated with truthfulness of judgements in descending order and with logical laws reducible to fundamental logical principles, as expressions of conditions grounded on the 'content' of acts of knowledge. Though these laws as *a priori* conditions of knowledge can be taken as such independently of a possible relation to a subjectivity, yet they were considered by Husserl as somehow 'susceptible to a reversal' by means of which they acquire as expressive experiences (*ausdrückliche Erlebnisse*) a relation towards a knowing subject.

This is also claimed in the supplementary volume to *Logical Investigations* completed in 1913, ([19]), where the expressibility of lived experiences is explicitly conditioned on the acts of judgement of a subject who, irrespective of whether an object of judgement is transcendental or immanent to his consciousness, he can form an expression referring, for instance, to an experienced feeling of desire, in fact any lived-in experience non-expressible as such, by a judgemental act that: directs to it a reflective phenomenological perception (*Wahrnehmung*), puts it under the general meaning of 'desire' and through this meaning and the particularity of the content of the specific desire gives it its definite meaning ([19], p. 63). Husserl indirectly introduced at this stage an intentional subjectivity, associated with his well-known thematic from *Ideas I* and the *Phenomenology of Inner Time-Consciousness* on intentionally constituted objects of consciousness, by referring to the meaning of a word-object, taken as supposed within a linguistic form, as the reflective expression of the 'empty significative intention' corresponding to it ([19], p. 74).

The matter is further clarified pertaining to the meaning of a theory (also of a truth) in view of their standing as the ideal contents of a possible knowledge. By this token, a single truth corresponds to the same content of a multiplicity of individual knowing acts put up then as their ideal and identical content. Inversely, to a multiplicity of individual knowing acts, by means of which each time and for any individual subject the same meaning becomes the content of a knowing act, corresponds the same meaning as their ideal identical content. Although Husserl claimed that in this way meaning is built up not on acts but on ideal elements such as truths and principles, e.g. the ideal form of premiss and implication, it is nevertheless conditioned on the capability of performing acts reducible to *a priori* noetic ones on the part of an (intentionally) oriented subject ([20], pp. 240-242). This last claim constitutes, in fact, Husserl's turning point in *Logical Investigations* at least with regard to his previous psychologistic description of objects of arithmetic and algebraic theory in his *Philosophy of Arithmetic*. Furthermore, a common foundation of object and meaning was envisaged as the double-sided content of knowing acts in terms of which the possibility of a theoretical knowledge can have no other sense than the meaningfully thought objects; in reverse, as we can turn back from objects to meanings the possibility of a theory can ' mean nothing else than the "validity" or better the substantivity (*Wesenhaftigkeit*) of the related meaning.' (ibid. p. 242).

In this sense, talking about the meaning of an object and the fulfillment of a meaning-oriented intention essentially express the same thing inasmuch as objects are thought of as contents of intentional acts and their intuiting (*Anschauung*) as fulfilled through a meaning-oriented intention in a dynamical relation unfolded within phenomenological temporality ([19], pp. 39-40). In what proves to be a fundamental difference between the constituting and the constituted level, Husserl considered the temporally constituted objects of an intentional act of cognition to be in a statical relation, whereas he considered the realization of any intentional act towards its content, inasmuch it is a fulfillment within temporal consciousness, to 'be' in a dynamical relation.

Overall, the solid foundation of meaningfully thought objects irrespective of whether they are taken as fundamentally registered by intentionality (formal-ontological objects) or as supposed (objects of an apophantic domain) is traced back to their possibility of existence as fulfillments of the intentionality of a temporal consciousness. It provides, in effect, a common view of registered-in, lowest-level intentional objects and their formal-ontological representations (including in abstraction objects of logical-mathematical theories) as being constituted as re-identifying immanences within temporal flux, which is, in turn, ultimately conditioned on the transcendental root of the unity of temporal consciousness. As I will try to show in the next sections this kind of transcendence within immanent temporality (referred to by Husserl as the absolute ego of consciousness or absolute subjectivity of the flux in [15], p. 75) stands as a metaphysical 'vacuum' in the epistemological foundations of formally representable physical theories such as Quantum Mechanics. This might be relevant too, concerning abstract formal theories in the context of mathematical foundations and could be the field of further research.

3 Temporality in the histories approach to quantum theory

My main purpose in the following will be to show, taking into account that time enters in quantum theory as an external parameter,[4] that there is not a

---

[4]The main motivation in dealing with the question of temporality on the quantum level is the fact that the time parameter in quantum mechanical processes is regarded as external to the system thus susceptible to a phenomenologically motivated interpretation in evident difference with the notion of time as an internal parameter of macroscopic physical systems in newtonian or relativistic mechanics.

formally definable way to capture the transition from a proposition referring to a 'sharp' moment of time to a proposition referring to the time-history of a quantum event. In other terms, that there is no way to 'capture the residuum' between a measurement at a 'sharp' moment of time and the subsequent spontaneous reflection on the particular measurement (in terms of the triangle: quantum object-measuring apparatus-conscious observer), without applying quantum principles such as the von Neumann-Lüders reduction postulate (applied also in the form of von Neumann's projection postulate in canonical quantum theory) or without formally assuming standard continuity and infinity in applying integral and differential calculus; or yet, alternatively, by applying the principles of non-standard mathematics which may be viewed as a non-conventional way to incorporate classical infinities and infinitesimalities within formal discourse.

I note in passing, that the application of nonstandard mathematical notions to quantum mechanical formulation can be seen as a way to capture, for instance, 'instantaneous' transition of states of dynamical observables in a way that no distinction is made between the continuous and discrete spectra of observables. Specifically, by defining an ultra eigenvector f to be a unit vector ($\| f \| = 1$) corresponding to a unique eigenvalue λ that belongs to the spectrum of an operator A (irrespectively of whether it is discrete or continuous) such that $\| Af - \lambda f \|$ is infinitesimal, one can formulate the axiom of measurement of a non-standard version of quantum mechanics like this: ' The result of any measurement of an observable can only be one of the standard spectral values of the corresponding operator. As a result of the measurement, the physical system finds itself in a state represented by an ultra eigenvector of the operator representing the measured observable, corresponding to the measured spectral value.' ([7]), pp. 178-179 & p. 191). This is particularly relevant in the case of transition to states $\{g_i; i \in I\}$ corresponding to the same ultra eigenvalue λ as to that of the ultra eigenstate representing the operator A after measurement by means of the relations: **(i)** $\| Ag_i - \lambda g_i \| \approx 0 \; \forall i \in I$ (i.e. $\| Ag_i - \lambda g_i \|$ infinitesimal) and **(ii)** (the non-standard form of the orthogonality condition) st $< g_i, g_j > = \delta_i^j \; \forall i, j \in I$ where δ_i^j is the well-known symbol defined by: $\delta_i^j = 1$ for $i = j$ and $\delta_i^j = 0$ for $i \neq j$ ([7]), p. 191). But this non-standard reformulation of quantum mechanics may finally reduce to ambiguities associated with the set-theoretical foundations of non-standard mathematics themselves, e.g. concerning the axiomatical treatment of non-standard magnitudes (see, [25]).

Further we may note, regarding a view of quantum individuality (the Space-Time Individuality, **S-T.I.**) in which it is the points of space-time that confer both individuality and re-identifiability to quantum objects in the sense that there is nothing but the properties and the points of space-time at which they are instantiated ([8], p. 439), that a significant underlying factor in the description of a sequential quantum measurement lies in the texture of the topology of configuration space; e.g. in the construction of a space of history propositions in Lorentzian manifolds with a non-globally hyperbolic metric as it will

3. TEMPORALITY IN THE HISTORIES

be described in some detail later. However, this modelisation can be regarded, independently of the particular context, as a formal structure rooted ultimately in an idea of a 'pre-existing' subjective continuum.

In this context, I am rather inclined in the quantum histories approach to the notion of quantum measurement initiated by Gell-Mann & Hartle (see, [10], [11], [12]) and subsequently by C. J. Isham as an alternative way to capture temporal transition in terms of sequential propositions corresponding to measurements, by applying a quantum version of temporal logic rather than the single-time logic of the single-time propositions approach of canonical quantum theory (see, [22] & [23]). A key supposition, motivated by 'the problem of time' in a quantum gravity context, is that the familiar concepts of space-time 'emerge' well above the Planck scale as also the Hilbert space mathematical formalism of canonical quantum theory tied to the standard picture of space and time. As a matter of fact, a histories-based interpretation of quantum theory inasmuch as it is associated with this particular non-standard version of the single-time propositions approach can be seen as moving from observables to 'beables' something that is particularly attractive in any theory attempting to address issues of quantum cosmology ([23], p. 2).

On this account, I point to the claims, (e.g. [27]), that the formalism of a (consistent) histories approach to quantum propositions that involve the time parameter, mathematically distinguishes between two qualities of time: ' its partial ordering properties (the notion of before and after) and its status as a dynamical parameter in the equations of motion' ([1], p. 3227). In this sense the consistent histories approach deals with sequences of values of quantities and not with results of measurements of quantities thus surpassing the dubious theoretical assumption of the 'collapse' of the state vector whenever a measurement is made in the standard interpretation of quantum theory. However, there are still problems arising from the definition of a locally defined notion of 'internal' time in quantum gravity and the ensuing physical repercussions associated with the particular choice of internal time. Under these assumptions the distinction on the formal level between the two forms of time ('being' in quantum temporal logic and 'becoming' in dynamical equations) looks questionable ([24], pp. 23-24).

In general, it seems that the key to understanding the formal representation of time in theoretical physics may lie in a deeper comprehension of the double role of real numbers in labelling (ordering in strict mathematical sense) the points of 'being' and also pertaining to the 'becoming' in the application of the dynamical differential equations, e.g. Scrödinger's equation, which is mixing up in its standard form the two concepts of time (the discrete, stepwise and the continuous one). My point is that even in the consistent histories theory one may still get 'trapped' in the impredicativity of a kind of internal temporality reflected in the mathematical structure of temporal supports associated with consistent histories of propositions; i.e., reflected in the adoption of topological structures such as the basic regions (open sets) as nuclear temporal supports of a quasi-temporal situation ([22], pp. 29-30), a supposition that will be shown to presuppose the implicit assumption of the impredicative mathematical continuum.

In particular, the formal distinction between the two qualities of time in the consistent histories approach mentioned above is seen, for instance, in the definition of the probability assignment:

$$\text{Prob}(\alpha_{t_1} = 1 \text{ at } t_1 \text{ and } \alpha_{t_2} = 1 \text{ at } t_2 \text{ and.... } \alpha_{t_n} = 1 \text{ at } t_n; \rho(t_0)) =$$

$$\text{tr}(\alpha_{t_n}(t_n)...\alpha_{t_1}(t_1)\,\rho(t_0)\,\alpha_{t_1}(t_1)...\alpha_{t_n}(t_n)) \quad \textbf{(I)}$$

which is the joint probability of finding all the properties corresponding to a sequence of measurements corresponding to propositions $\alpha_{t_1}, \alpha_{t_2}, \ldots, \alpha_{t_n}$ at times $t_1, t_2, \ldots, t_n$, and in the definition of the decoherence functional $d(\alpha, \beta) = \text{tr}(\widehat{C}_\alpha^+ \widehat{\rho}_0 \widehat{C}_\beta)$ whose properties determine the satisfaction of conditions rendering the probability assignment **(I)** meaningful even for a closed system ([22], p. 7); that is, even in the absence of of an external 'observer' with associated measurement-induced state vector reductions.[5] The remarks below concern the class operator

$$\widehat{C}_\alpha = \widehat{U}^+(t_1)\,\widehat{\alpha}_{t_1}\,\widehat{U}(t_1)...\widehat{U}^+(t_n)\,\widehat{\alpha}_{t_n}\,\widehat{U}(t_n), \quad \textbf{(II)}$$

($\widehat{U}(s) = \exp(-i\widehat{H}s)$ is the unitary time-evolution operator) that represents a history α in a discrete-step causal evolution corresponding to a string of projection operators $\widehat{\alpha}_{t_1}, \widehat{\alpha}_{t_2}, \ldots \widehat{\alpha}_{t_n}$, and also the projection operators corresponding to a homogenous history α^6 in probability assignment **(I)**; they are also relevant in the general case of HPO (History Projector Operator) theory, referring to a complete space $\mathcal{UP}$ of history propositions, where a quasi-temporal type of dynamical evolution together with an associated Heisenberg picture can be implemented ([22], pp. 23-24).

Thus in Def. **(II)** we have in the same formula two completely different aspects of time parameter, the discrete part linked to a sequential order of temporal steps and the continuous part incorporated as an argument of the exponential form of time-evolution operator $\widehat{U}(s)$, in the sense that the operator $\widehat{C}_\alpha$ depends also explicitly on the dynamics of the system as it uses the Heisenberg-picture operators $\widehat{\alpha}_{t_n}(t_n)$. This means that the aspect of temporal order represented by the string $\widehat{\alpha}_{t_1}, \widehat{\alpha}_{t_2}, \ldots, \widehat{\alpha}_{t_n}$ of projection operators that represent history α (formally defined in [22] as a history filter α to provide a formalization of it as a sequential conjunction defined as 'active' over a finite set of temporal points) is conditioned on the assumption of a continuous function $\widehat{U}(s) = \exp(-i\widehat{H}s)$ representing the dynamical evolution of the system with definite values $\widehat{U}(t_1), \widehat{U}(t_2), \ldots, \widehat{U}(t_n)$ at corresponding time steps

---

[5]The decoherence functional $d(\alpha, \beta)$ is a complex-valued function of a pair of histories α, β that measures their mutual quantum interference (being indirectly a probability measure) such that a set of exclusive and exhaustive histories is called consistent if for all pairs of different histories α, β in this set the equation $d(\alpha, \beta) = 0$ holds.

[6]A homogenous history is defined as any time-ordered sequence $(\widehat{\alpha}_{t_1}, \widehat{\alpha}_{t_2}, \ldots, \widehat{\alpha}_{t_n})$ of projection operators.

3. TEMPORALITY IN THE HISTORIES

$t_1, t_2, \ldots, t_n$. The dynamical part of the class operator $\widehat{C}_\alpha$ generates moreover the transformations $\widehat{\alpha}_{t_1} \to \widehat{\alpha}_{t_2}$ in the continuum limit.

Thus, in the histories formalism the sequential conjunction of properties in finitely many ordered time steps cannot be effected but on the underlying assumption of time as the parameter of a Heisenberg-type evolution which means that one is left with a residuum of a continuous time-flux formalized in terms of the continuous argument of unitary time-evolution operator.

In fact, as it will be made clear next, my overall argument is also indirectly connected with the construction of a new Hilbert space $\otimes_{t \in T}^{\Omega} H_T$ associated with an infinite tensor product $\otimes_{t \in T}^{\Omega} B(H)_T$ of operator algebras $B(H)$ to accommodate arbitrary temporal supports. The tensor product $\otimes_{t \in T}^{\Omega} B(H)_T$ is defined to be the weak closure (in the weak operator topology) of the set of all functions from T to $B(H)$ which are equal to the unit operator for all but a finite set of t-values ([22], p. 23). This topological property ensures, in fact, that any history, even one corresponding to an infinite set of projection operators, can be formally treated as the weak limit of a convergent sequence of homogenous histories with finite (temporal) support.[7] Indeed, the overall formal structure of $\otimes_{t \in T}^{\Omega} H_T$ is such that it is fundamentally connected with a notion of temporal support defined as the finite set of time-points $t \in T$ for which a history proposition $\alpha_t \neq 1$; that is, it is associated with the set of time-points for which the history filter α is the non-trivial proposition, in other words, it is associated with the finite set of time-points for which α is active ([22], p. 23).

The intrinsic need to refer to a finitistic temporal support on which to implement a sequential conjunction of the type 'α_{t_1} is true at time t_1, and then α_{t_2} is true at time t_2, and then ....and then α_{t_n} is true at time t_n' corresponding to a history filter $\alpha = (\alpha_{t_1}, \alpha_{t_2}, \ldots, \alpha_{t_n})$ in the language of temporal logic can be noted, also, in the general situation where the HPO theory is applied to the quasi-temporal situation of a four-dimensional manifold $\mathcal{M}$ with a non-globally hyperbolic Lorentzian metric γ. In the particular case, the temporal support of the test function f_i on $\mathcal{M}$ of each member $P(f_i, I_i)$, $I_i \subset R$, $i = 1, 2, \ldots, n$, of a class of propositions corresponding to a history filter, is a finite collection of open subsets O_i of $\mathcal{M}$ (termed basic regions O_i) which are topologically connected and have compact closure so that each proposition is localized in the space-time $\mathcal{M}$ and they are moreover associated in such a way that any two O_i's either follow one another or they are space-like separated in alternative case

---

[7]The temporal support of a history filter α may be described as the finite set of time points $t \in T$ for which α is active, i.e. those points $t \in T$ such that $\alpha_t \neq 1$. Its underlying role is associated with the semi-group homomorphism $\sigma : \mathcal{U} \to S$ that assigns a temporal support $s \in S$ to each history filter $\alpha \in \mathcal{U}$ in such a way that a history filter $\beta = (\beta_{t'_1}, \beta_{t'_2}, \ldots, \beta_{t'_m})$ is said to follow a history filter $\alpha = (\alpha_{t_1}, \alpha_{t_2}, \ldots, \alpha_{t_n})$ if $t_n < t_{1'}$ and the combined history $\alpha \circ \beta$ is defined as $\alpha \circ \beta = (\alpha_{t_1}, \alpha_{t_2}, \ldots, \alpha_{t_n}, \beta_{t'_1}, \beta_{t'_2}, \ldots, \beta_{t'_m})$. This means that, by virtue of the homomorphism equality $\sigma(\alpha \circ \beta) = \sigma(\alpha) \circ \sigma(\beta)$ any sequential conjunction of projection operators corresponding to a history proposition is 'tied' to a (causally evolving) ordered temporal conjunction.

([22], p. 30). This assumption which underlies the definition of a 'time point' as a finite collection of disjoint basic regions space-like separated from each other leads to the following argument: the individuality of each time-point, inasmuch as it is associated with the realization of a proposition $P(f_i, I_i)$, is grounded on its definition as a nuclear support s under semi-group composition law $\circ$, i.e., it cannot be written in the form $s = s_1 \circ s_2$ where both constituent nuclear supports s_1, s_2 are different from the unit (temporal) support $*$; in other words, individuality of each 'time-point' is associated with a unique and irreducible intentional act in the sense of 'performance' of an act of quantum measurement inherently irreducible to any class of causally related acts. In this sense, in general history theory, a nuclear support is meant as analogous to a time-point abstracted as an extensionless point of the real continuum (think of a natural number within real continuum) in terms of irreducibility to any further temporal subdivisions.

However, the 'finitistic' character of an act of reflection upon a particular intentional act of measurement carried out in the present now of the flux of consciousness is represented by the topological properties of compactness and connectedness assigned to each of the finitely many basic regions O_i of a nuclear support s while letting slip a 'creeping' continuity factor by the topological definition of each basic region O_i. Thus in the quasi-temporal logic associated with a non-globally defined temporality the impossibility to associate a single-time proposition with a physical measurement enacted in a fictitious 'dimensionless' time-point is reflected in the formal definition of the nuclear support s as set-theoretically non-point-like while underscoring, at the same time, on the formal level the deficiencies engendered by the definition of time-points as atemporal abstractions in formal representation. Moreover from a certain viewpoint, the aforementioned definition of a nuclear support may be associated with the Husserlian notion of specious present as a non-point-like present now of original impression *a priori* (in objective temporal continuity) connected with a-thematic protention (a kind of expectation) and fulfilled retention (a kind of memoration) while retaining the 'finitistic' character of an instantaneity in objective reflection (see, [15], pp. 29-31 & pp. 52-53). Of course such an assertion would imply, in the first place, a view of mathematical points, taken here as finite classes of space-like, separated open sets equipped with a compact and connected topological structure, as complete abstractions by categorial intuition of empty forms of thingness-substrates on the lowest level of phenomenological perception (p. 3); second, it would condition their status as formal-ontological objects on their prior phenomenological foundation as re-identifying temporal individual-substrates.

On the other hand, there is an acceptance of a version of the von Neumann projection postulate in deriving the sequential conjunction of propositions of the form 'α_{t_1} is true at time t_1 *and then* α_{t_2} is true at time t_2 *and then*....α_{t_n} is true at time t_n' contained in the definitions of joint probability and the decoherence functional of histories. In definition (**I**), for instance, the following formula for the density operator state, retained for further calculations, is valid

3. TEMPORALITY IN THE HISTORIES

by von Neumann-Lüders reduction:

$$\rho_{\text{red}}(t_1) := \frac{P(t_1)\rho(t_0)P(t_1)}{\text{tr}(P(t_1)\rho(t_0))}$$

where $\rho(t_0)$ is the density operator state at time t_0.

In my view, the implicit application of the above version of von Neumann's projection postulate in the histories formalism, conditions the derivation of the joint probability P and the decoherence functional $d(\alpha,\beta)$ on the possibility of a joint assignment of values for history propositions on singleton-set temporal supports $\{t_i\}$ upon an underlying subjective temporal continuity; this can be further associated with an assumption of existence of a subjective continuous temporal unity on which to constitute objects of phenomenological perception and then apply a reflective regard on these constituted objects at once, as immanent objects within the homogenous flux. On this account, J. von Neumann's projection postulate can be seen as introducing indirectly the necessity for a self-constituting time flux by assigning to the (mathematical translation of) state $s(t)$ of a quantum quantity Q_i upon a first-kind measurement[8] that yields an eigenvalue r_κ (within an interval $r_\kappa \pm \epsilon_{Q_i}$), the same eigenvector ψ_κ as to the state $s(t_1)$ of the quantity Q_i at time $t_1 > t$ soon after the measurement. Even in the insertion of the trivial unit-proposition as the limit $\alpha_{t_i} \to 1$ within a homogenous history $(\alpha_1, \alpha_2, \ldots, \alpha_{t_{i-1}}, \alpha_{t_i}, \alpha_{t_{i+1}}, \ldots \alpha_{t_n})$, in the application of K-operators for which the evolution property

$$K(t_{i-1}, t_i)K(t_i, t_{i+1}) = K(t_{i-1}, t_{i+1}) \quad \textbf{(III)}$$

holds, a sort of retention of temporal values of transition operators must be assumed analogous to the conditions set by von-Neumann's projection postulate. As a matter of fact, assumptions of this type 'are incorporated' in the continuity of decoherence functionals on the set of all history propositions $\mathcal{UP}$ as dynamical information encoded in non-standard decoherence functionals via evolution operators K of the above form. These operators act on Hilbert spaces H associated with single-time propositions, within systems of a quasi-temporal structure ([23], pp. 33-34).

In the bottom line, definitions of a decoherence functional for continuous-time histories fail to provide a satisfactory definition of it as the inductive limit of the decoherence functional defined on $H^I \times H^{I'}$ for all choices of finite partitions I and I' of the time interval T (taken as a subset of real line) for the formal reason that one cannot continuously embed the lattice of single-time propositions to the lattice of history ones. This problem is essentially due to the 'undefinability' of a sharp moment of time, abstracted as a point on the

---

[8]This is one in which the measured system described by quantum state s needs to interact with the measuring apparatus described by quantum state ϕ, so that the total wave function before the interaction is $s \cdot \phi$ and by unitary evolution the final total wave function gets: $s \cdot \phi \to \sum_n c_n s_n \phi_n$ where s_n are eigenstates of the operator to be measured and ϕ_n the orthonormal states of the measuring apparatus.

real axis of zero measure, since at this time-point an observable can be well-defined only if we take the function $f : T \to R$, ($T \subseteq R$, R the set of reals) in the definition of time-averaged operators A_f, to be a delta function. But this is unacceptable in a consistent histories construction due to the fact that we have to define a decoherence functional for continuous-time histories as the inductive limit of a discrete-time expression defined on $H^I \times H^{I'}$ for all choices of time-discretizations I and I', whereas a delta function is known to run wildly at 'sharp' points.

Taking into account that attempts to properly define a continuous-time decoherence functional encounter various difficulties fundamentally associated with the incompatibility of the notion of temporal continuum on the one hand and that of a sharp moment in time on the other, the discussion about a decoherence functional associated in final count with a properly defined probability measure in a consistent histories approach may reduce to the following assertion: no matter the particular mathematical techniques employed to circumvent the problem[9] the deeper issue is that we cannot, in fact, continuously embed the lattice of single-time propositions to the lattice of history ones. This is a question that seems to run deeper into the character and inner modes of temporal constitution as a self-constituting continuous objectivity (in phenomenological terms) and may be reasonably taken to be reflected in formal metatheory in this kind of incongruity.

Before closing this section it seems worthwhile to consider for a moment the role of the aforementioned delta function $\delta(x)$ within quantum formalism. The essential reason for employing the concept of delta function is to provide a proper mathematical tool for treating certain kinds of infinities arising in mathematical formalism e.g. in P. Dirac's definition of the non-vanishing product $<X|Y>$ of two kets expressed as an integral of eigenkets of an observable ξ: $<X|Y> = \int \int <\xi'x|\xi''y> d\xi' d\xi''$ (see, [3], p. 39 & pp. 58-62). It is well-known then, that the function $\delta(x)$ such that $\int_{-\infty}^{\infty} \delta(x)dx = 1$ and $\delta(x) = 0$ for $x \neq 0$ is, in fact, not a function of the variable x in the usual definition of a function, that is, as having a definite and unique value for each point in its domain but rather a mathematical convenience to ensure well-defined integrals in case wild variations of quantum variables bordering to infinity are involved. For that reason, it looks pointless to treat the delicate question of properly defining an observable at a 'sharp' moment of time by applying the delta function.

Maybe the whole issue of assigning a well-defined meaning to quantum properties and eventually to quantum probabilities in sequential time-measurements without getting trapped in the constraints of contextuality, as Bell's, Wigner's and Kochen-Specker's theorems demonstrate, reduces, to a significant extent,

---

[9]Certain alternative approaches such as incorporating the information about initial condition in an object that is extended in time or defining the decoherence functional with respect to a structure of propositions about phase-space histories that involve the mathematical notion of measurability, cannot be implemented without some unwelcome effects such as sacrificing the quantum logic structure of history propositions (see, [1], p. 3256).

to a deeper understanding of time as a subjective constituting factor in shaping propositions about quantum properties.

4   Towards an epistemological corroboration of the ego of absolute consciousness

My main scope in this section is to put up some epistemologically motivated claims on the possibility of a transcendental root of the homogenous unity of temporal consciousness. As it was mentioned in section 1, I mostly rely on J. Eccles' and S. Dehaene's approaches in [5] and [2] to point out the relevance of the phenomenological analysis of temporal constitution, (see, [15] & [16]), taking into account their respective attempts to provide an epistemological context to the clues of an underlying presence of a subjective unifying ego of consciousness and, on the basis of experimental data, to point to a creeping unconscious level of 'awareness' even in the absence of any event-provoked activation of consciousness.

Concerning Eccles' view with regard to the notion of a unifying subjectivity termed as ego or spirit in [5], I regard some of his claims not only susceptible of a phenomenological reading but moreover better formulated within a context incorporating an intentionally oriented subject who is also a bearer of a self-constituting temporal consciousness in terms of which he can 'transpose' the non-predicative evidence of his experience. In view of this, it is remarkable that Eccles, gives a temporal dimension to the underlying 'factor' of mental unity by pointing to a subjective apprehension of everyone's mental unity as manifested in the continuity of most distant memories; in fact, this dimension is proclaimed as the base of ego, in the sense that it provides at each moment the unity of experience in reflection by integrating an almost infinite number of neuronal activities taking place in the brain at the same moment. In view of this kind of subjectivity Eccles makes reference to W.R. Uttal [29], who has arrived on operational terms at a 'metaphysical' description of spirit as being of a holistic and non-divisible nature which is a problem utterly unresolved by psychology; or yet to K. Lorenz in [26], who alludes ' to the mysterious barrier which is in the center of what constitutes the unity of our personality and separates the objective physiological events taking part in our body from the subjective experience we have of them.' ([5], p. 272).

Moreover, he is inclined to assert that a self-conscious spirit is not only a 'passive onlooker' of the neuronal activities of the brain taking place all at once in front of its 'regard' but it is enacting its intentional regard to choose among an infinite plurality of such activities at any instant in any zone of the brain ([5], pp. 273-274). This way the self-conscious spirit unifies the living experience in a way close to the act of phenomenological ego which constitutes the immanent flux of events by constituting itself. But in attempting to describe this unifying activity of spirit in terms of a type of quantum mechanical interaction with the brain he falls, as I will try to show next, in the closed loop of producing new transcendences in the place of those associated with the holistic, non-material nature of self-conscious spirit. This may be taken as corroborating my main claim in this paper, namely, that there is indeed a hidden immanent transcendence in the constitution of each one's temporal consciousness which is, in fact, the subjective ever-in-act constituting factor of temporal unity; this is utterly not possible to be predicated as existing according to the descriptive norms of the language of a formal metatheory but only 'after' its own objectification as an impredicative, continuous substratum.

As a matter of fact, J. Eccles proposed an epistemologically based interpretation of the interaction spirit/brain by assuming that this interaction is analogous to a field of probability in quantum mechanical theory which does not possess mass or energy but can nevertheless cause tangible effects in a micro-site. By this assumption a reflection on an intentional act can provoke neuronal effects in a way parallel to the probability fields of quantum mechanics ([5], p. 253). Accordingly, one may adopt a model based on the transmission of cellular activities, that is, the structure of neuronal synapses associated with transmission by exocytosis of presynaptic vesicles[10] which are indeed of an order of magnitude susceptible to the application of Heisenberg's Principle of Uncertainty[11]. In this model the phenomenon of exocytosis of a vesicle through the synaptic membrane can be effected by an intentional act acting in the sense of a field of quantum probability.

To produce macro-effects capable of a modification of neuronal activity, Eccles proposes to consider as neuronal unity a structure called dendron, composed of a bundle of dendrites and comprising tens of thousands of presynaptic vesicular nets susceptible to be 'chosen' for exocytosis; each dendron can be penetrated by a mental unity termed psychon on a unity-to-unity, non-local relation. These mental unities (psychons) are taken to serve as intermediaries in the bidirectional relation spirit/brain representing in particular and uniquely on the physiological level the dendron on which they are 'attached'; nonetheless they are left with no further specification as to their epistemological or even ontological status and no less with a dubious temporality. This remark can be drawn by their presumed role in channeling non-locally a mental intention to tens of thousands of activated presynaptic vesicular nets through each dendron and in reverse order in registering the effect of each vesicular exocytosis and transmitting it to the mental World 2 which in Eccles's classification comprises internal and external perceptions and also the interacting self-conscious spirit ([5], p. 273). The acts of psychons should take effect, though, in objective time for it could be otherwise impossible to conceive them as a physical interaction and consequently even if we would take them as some kind of non-material unities they should be necessarily temporal objectivities susceptible, in principle, to the eventuality of non-homogeneities of the spatio-temporality of the physical world. For that reason they can be hardly taken as a kind of 'atempo-

---

[10]Roughly speaking, presynaptic vesicles are molecular agglomerates in the vicinity of neuronal synapses.

[11]See, [5], p. 255 and p. 249 for schematic diagrams of neuronal synaptic activity in the stages of interaction spirit/brain.

4. TOWARDS AN EPISTEMOLOGICAL CORROBORATION   107

ral messengers' of a constituting homogenous temporality. In such a case they should be regarded themselves as the self-conscious spirit and the constituting factor of temporality but then a circularity would be engendered as they should be by necessity assigned another interposing temporal objectivity to transmit mental intention as a physical world effect.

In view of my general approach, we should take into account, considering Eccles' description of the kind of transcendental subjectivity, termed a self-conscious spirit, the aforementioned circularity concerning the role of psychons in 'instantaneously' transmitting mental intentions to the extent that: it can be plausibly claimed that it provides us with clues to the transcendental source of subjective temporality inasmuch as it engenders a possibly endless regression of transcendences reached by making use of a physicalistic language (a quantum mechanical in the particular case) to describe its temporal objectification.

On the other hand, I find of a particular relevance with regard to a phenomenological approach, Eccle's claim in [6] that a number of indications point to a relation of unity-to-unity concerning the act of each psychon upon its particular dendron as each unique, registered-in-actuality experience may be associated with a particular psychon. Inasmuch as this bidirectional 'interaction' is uniquely constituted by the presence of self-conscious ego and its intentional-like orientation towards a (possibly abstract) something it can be rightfully taken close to phenomenological perception meant as as uniquely founded on lowest-level intentionality towards individuals. To the extent that 'lowest-level' individuals are themselves irreducible as original givennesses, they ground by this very token the uniqueness of each phenomenological perception towards a state-of-things (*Sachverhalt*) ([18], pp. 212-214).

We may also establish a connection with a temporal unity constituting ego and also consider certain intentionality associated neuronal mechanisms in view of recent experimental evidence in the work of S. Dehaene et al ([2]), T.C. Handy's *et al* ([13]) and J.J. McDonald's *et al* ([4]) among others. Concerning, in particular, S. Dehaene's presentation in [2] a phenomenological interpretation can be relevant inasmuch as: it establishes a difference between conscious and unconscious processing by detecting early intact potentials (P1 and N1) evoked by unseen words, which is a fact suggesting that these brain events are not primary correlates of conscious perception something that could be taken as grounded on a pre-existing immanent process of consciousness prior to the 'enactment' of an intentional relation subject-object. In this sense the detection of 'pre-activation' potentials of the brain may indeed point towards the evidence of an existing, ever-in act, self-constituting temporal flux.

On the other hand, the detection of a rapid divergence around 270 ms after which brain events were evoked solely by seen words[12] can serve in corroborat-

---

[12]In a repeated trials experiment, subjects were asked to respond to two visual targets T_1 and T_2 depicting number words during the attentional blink caused by the attentional demands of one, let's say T_1, of the tasks. In the dual task of responding to words on both T_1 and T_2 for short stimulus onset asynchrony (SOA), identification of the first target T_1 hinders the detection of the second target T_2, although T_2 is easily seen when no task on T_1

ing the claim that the 'enactment' of phenomenological perception towards a particular object standing as an unambiguous and original givenness in front of the intentionality of consciousness together with the possibility of reflection upon this 'enactment' are *a priori* capacities of a bodily consciousness radically different from the (transcendental) root of its self-constituting objective unity. Moreover, by virtue of the hyletic-noetic character of phenomenological perception one should expect an evidence of its 'enactment' in spatiotemporal terms which is, in fact, detected in present case by the triggering of a late wave of activation that is distributed through a network of cortical association areas. Moreover, the divergence between seen and unseen T_2's at 270 − 300 ms was detected as coinciding with the end of the late P_{3b} waveforms evoked by the T_1 task; a fact that, taken into account that the T_1 task affects components of event-related potentials (ERP) similar to those correlating with conscious access to T_2, lends support to the idea that these components of ERP index a capacity-limited stage capable of processing only one task at a time ([2], pp. 1393, 1396). There is yet a question here, analogous to the question of 'temporal residuum' discussed in Section 3, concerning a lingering temporality bridging in effect the detection of activation potentials evoked solely by seen words and the 'enactment' of conscious perception whose primary correlates are precisely these words. In other words, the temporal factor bridging the subjective awareness ratings concerning targets T_1 and T_2, taken in the sense of purely intentional objects, and the objective identification and 'naming' of corresponding target-words in the sense of a reflection upon intentionalities. This empirical evidence might be again interpreted by the evidence of an objectified absolute flux of consciousness in whose temporal homogeneity are 'embedded' by certain noematic modes the objects of phenomenological perception (*Wahrnehmung*).

In connection with T.C. Handy's *et al* experimental data in [13], I point to the detection of certain visuomotor transformations by event-related potentials and by event-related *fMRI* techniques facilitated by the presence of objects automatically grabbing visual-spatial attention. It must be noted that visually guided grasping movements are conditioned on a rapid transformation of visual representations into object-directed motor programs. On this account, visual-spatial attention to event-related object locations was automatically activating cortex areas associated with visually guided actions and their planning. This activity might be associated with a notion of intentionally 'triggered' kinesthetical sensations in the sense described in the Husserlian texts of *Ideas III* ([17], pp. 120-123).

Lastly, in connection with J.J.Mc Donald's *et al* work in [4], I point to the

---

is required. Although no significant difference was observed in the early visual P_1 and N_1 waves (96 and 180 ms) evoked by seen and unseen T_2's either in amplitude or in topography, a first difference was observed around 170 ms with a slightly stronger positivity for seen T_2's. A larger divergence was observed around 270 ms when seen T_2's evoked a stronger left-lateralized posterior negativity N_2 followed by a more anterior negativity (N_3, 300 ms) that was absent for unseen T_2's. Two subsequent waveforms (P_{3a}, 436ms, P_{3b}, 576ms) were also detected only when T_2 was seen; see, [2], p. 1392.

evidence of an intentionally based visual time-ordered perception by means of the detection of attentional shifts provoked by a sudden sound stimulus in terms of enhancement of the amplitude of neural activity in visual cortex rather than in terms of processing speed in the earlier visual-cortical pathways.

5 A deeper phenomenological view of the character of temporality

In the *Bernauer Manuskripte*, Husserl attempted to clarify the notion of the absolute ego of consciousness which was left rather vague and unrefined in the *Phenomenology of Inner Time-Consciousness*, ([15]). As a matter of fact, in spite of the brave intellectual quest to elucidate the origins of temporality within the immanence of consciousness he was further led to the intricacies of the deeply transcendental character of the source of temporality.

In these later texts, instead of the transcendental (or absolute) ego of consciousness of earlier texts he used various other terms essentially designating the same notion such as Substrate (*Hintergrund*), Original Process (*Urprozess*), Original-Living (*Urleben*) or yet Original Living-Self (*ursprüngliches Ichleben*), while, nevertheless, not reaching an unambiguous elucidation of the deeper meaning of this notion meant as the constituting subjectivity of temporal unity. At one point he reached the conclusion that *Urleben* can neither be temporal itself nor can it make temporal objectivities within it perceived as such ([16], p. 196). For, in case *Urleben* would be temporal we could then turn our 'reflective regard' towards the givenness of its phases which would be a temporal continuum in the scheme original impression in the present now - descending sequence into the past and thus the experience of these phases as givennesses themselves would be also a temporal sequence upon which to turn anew our reflection, which would become again givennesses upon which to turn our reflection and this way in infinitum. In such a case we would end up in an endless regression of reflections meant as consciousness-of something in the sense of temporal acts extended in an infinite series of successive terms. What we should derive, in any case, is that evidently what becomes an object of reflection has to be in a temporal form and should be also taken to be identically the same in the flux of multiplicities of its givennesses.

In that case, how could we possibly take Original Process (or -Living) (*Urprozess*) to 'be' an objectivity-preceding reflection? Husserl suggested that in this case we would be led to a 'primary current' (*Urstrom*), perceived as a temporal current but which nevertheless cannot be consciousness of a temporal current nor a phenomenological perception of it ([16], p. 197). This is meant in the sense that as Original Process steadily constitutes first-degree phenomenological time, it 'is' ever a consciousness process, a process of intentional experiences. For in the alternative case, it would be a process of original hyletic data sufficient for the constitution of hyletic unities of experience which imply, in turn, a constitution of durating immanent apprehensions (*Auffassungen*), assumed though not to be necessary in that case. It turns out that we know about Original Process through phenomenological perception and that it is plainly given as a process by means of a self-constituting consciousness that constitutes temporal objectivity. Put in other words: taking the evidence of an immanent event, we can accomplish a reflection upon its phenomenological perception, as well as we can reflect upon the flux of the parts and phases of its immanent temporal objectivity, upon the flux of 'experiences' which are themselves 'consciousness-of' of certain other experiences and upon all that pertains to them ([16], p. 204).

In attempting to thoroughly comprehend the nature of Original Process, Husserl proposed to consider phenomenological time and events taking place within it as given by phenomenological perception. In this view, an event takes place within the unity of phenomenological time without its particular unity having by necessity the 'privilege' of being brought to reflection by means of phenomenological perception ([16], p. 198). This remark motivates a view of Original Process as associated with a phenomenological perception of events prior to their immanent seizure (*Erfassung*) in the constituting temporality, thus avoiding the assumption of an endless regression of reflecting subjectivities. In this connection, he wondered whether the field of constituted temporality is the all-inclusive field of Original Living-Self, that is, whether Original Living-Self is a perception in the sense of an apprehensive (*aufmerkendes*) or properly apprehensive (*sonderbemerkendes*) seizure or rather a perception in broadest sense that is directed towards an intentional object without the object in question being taken as identical with the 'act', that is, with the intentional experience as consciousness of it ([16], p. 199).

Further, in taking account that a known process would be itself an immanent event, how could it be that such a process might constitute another immanent event? In the last count, genetically talking (Husserl gets here deeper entrenched in a problematic bordering to metaphysics), would it be thinkable that all temporality for a conscious subject is there by means of a genetically emerging apperception (*Apperzeption*), where the unknown processes passing throughout are not temporality-constituting and are themselves in no way temporally constituted? ([16], p. 200). Nevertheless, as Husserl followed by grounding each hyletic-noetic act, each seizure in immanence manifested through the consciousness of their succeeding and durating objectivities, to unknown processes possible on the grounds of their apperception, he seems to get already trapped in the circularity induced at least by the linguistic connotation attributed to the term apperception. For how can we perceive a sequence even of genetically emerging apperceptions without reflecting on them in succession within temporality, something that presupposes the occurrence of unknown processes prior to these apperceptions and not as a joint 'consequence' of them?

Either in taking Original Process as a constant constituted-from-within temporality bearing time-fulfilled immanent objects upon which we can always draw a reflective glance or taking it as a 'current' with no temporally constituted perceptions within it but rather as a potentiality enacting temporal constitution and immanentisation through reflection, a delicate question to reorient the discussion is this: Can a transcendental event such as a time-constituting process be perceived by any other means except by (temporal) reflection? Isn't it necessarily a givenness in reflection? And what meaning can we bestow to the term reflection? Moreover, how could a non-temporally constituted process be given otherwise than by reflection? How could it draw phenomenological perception in the sense of a fulfillment of intentional experience without being the content of a consciousness intentionally directed upon it? Its phenomenological perception would then be inaccessible to reflection except by being in the form of a time-constituting process whose object would be the Original Process. In Husserl's view though, this kind of process not only can be given in reflection in temporal form but there also exists evidence that this process is constituted as a process prior to any reflection, which means that being and being-in constituting within it are inseparable ([16], p. 206).

Undoubtedly, the recourse to this transcendence within the immanence of consciousness in attempting to ground a temporal unity-constituting subjectivity and at the same time to avoid an endless regression of reflective regards 'out of it' and 'towards it', being meant as consciousness-of something, bears in mind the description of the absolute ego of consciousness in Husserl's *Phenomenology of Inner Time-Consciousness* as an essentially a-temporal subjectivity, root of the self-constituting unity of the absolute flux of consciousness ([15], § 36).

As a matter of fact, Husserl would not come closer even in his latest texts to elucidating the inherently vague concept of absolute ego of consciousness (or of any term used as close in meaning to it). In my view, this is a manifestation of the transcendental and therefore impredicative root of all temporally constituted continuous unity of the Life-World, of all physical and mental processes within it (involving the special presence of a bodily consciousness), which is reflected in their formal-ontological representation in formal-axiomatical structures.

As a concluding remark to this article, the question of a continuous residuum of time in quantum-mechanical 'observation' (reflected also in corresponding mathematical metatheory) taken as most closely associated with phenomenological lowest-level intentional 'observation', as well as relevant clues drawn from an empirical-experimental context, seem to lead to a deeper subjective root of the continuous unity of the broadly conceived epistemological edifice of the physical world. Even in abolishing any phenomenological motivation, it is hard to argue that such a root would not be time-constituting.

BIBLIOGRAPHY

[1] Anastopoulos, C.: 2001, Continuous-time histories: Observables, probabilities, phase space structure and the classical limit, *Jour. of Mathematical Physics*, 42, 8, pp. 3225-3259.
[2] Dehaene, S., Sergent, C., & Baillet, S.: 2005, Timing of the brain events underlying access to consciousness during the attentional blink, *Nature Neuroscience*, 8, pp. 1391-1400.
[3] Dirac, P.: 1981, *The Principles of Quantum Mechanics*, Oxford University Press.

[4] Di Russo, F., Mc Donald, J., Teder-Sälerjärvi, W., , Hillyard, S.: 2005, Neural basis of auditory-induced shifts in visual time-order perception, *Nature Neuroscience*, 8, pp. 1197-1202.
[5] Eccles, J.: 1992, *Évolution du cerveau et création de la conscience*, transl. Jean-Mathieu Luccioni, Paris: A. Fayard.
[6] Eccles, J.: 1989, The mind-brain problem revisited: the microsite hypothesis, in J.C. Eccles & O.D. Creutzfeldt (eds) *The Principles of Design and Operation of the Brain*, Vatican City: Pontificiae Academiae Scientiarum Scripta Varia.
[7] Farrukh, O.M.: 1975, Application of nonstandard analysis to quantum mechanics, *Journal of Mathematical Physics*, 16, 2, pp. 177-200.
[8] French, S.: 1989, Identity and Individuality in Classical and Quantum Physics, *Australasian Journal of Philosophy*, 67, 4, pp. 432-446.
[9] French, S.: 2002, A phenomenological solution to the measurement problem? Husserl and the foundations of quantum mechanics, *Studies in History and Philosophy of Modern Physics*, 33, pp. 467-491.
[10] Gell-Mann, M. & Hartle, J.: 1990, Alternative decohering histories in quantum mechanics. In K.K. Phua and Y. Yamaguchi, editors, *Proceedings of the 25th International Conference on High Energy physics, Singapore, August, 2-8, 1990*, Singapore, World Scientific.
[11] Gell-Mann, M. & Hartle, J.: 1990, Quantum mechanics in the light of quantum cosmology. In S. Kobayashi, H. Ezawa, Y. Murayama, and S. Nomura, editors, *Proceedings of the Third International Symposium on the Foundations of Quantum Mechanics in the Light of New Technology*, pages 321-343. Physical Society of Japan, Tokio.
[12] Hartle, J.: 1993, Spacetime quantum mechanics and the quantum mechanics of spacetime. In *Proceedings on the 1992 Les Houches School, Gravitation and Quantisation*.
[13] Handy, T., Grafton, S., Schroff, N., Ketay, S., Gazzaniga, M.: 2003, Graspable objects grab attention when the potential for action is recognized, *Nature Neuroscience*, 6, pp. 421-427.
[14] Husserl, E.: 1995, *Ideen zu einer reinen Phänomenologie und phänomenologischen Philosophie. Erstes Buch*, Husserliana, Band III/I, herausg. K. Schuhmann, Kluwer Acad. Pub., Dordrecht: The Netherlands.
[15] Husserl, E. 1966, *Zur Phänomenologie des Inneren Zeitbewusstseins*, herausg. R Boehm, Husserliana Band X, M. Nijhoff, Haag: The Netherlands.
[16] Husserl, E. 2001, *Die Bernauer Manuskripte über das Zeitbewusstsein (1917/18)*, Husserliana Band XXXIII, herausg. R. Bernet & D. Lohmar, Kluwer Acad. Pub., Dordrecht: The Netherlands.
[17] Husserl, E.: 1997, *Ideen zu einer reinen Phänomenologie und phänomenologischen Philosophie. Drittes Buch*, Husserliana Band V, herausg. M. Biemel, Kluwer Acad. Pub., Dordrecht: The Netherlands.
[18] Husserl, E.: 1974, *Formale und Transzendentale Logik*, Husserliana Band XVII, herausg. P. Janssen, M. Nijhoff, Den Haag: The Netherlands.
[19] Husserl, E.: 2002, *Logische Untersuchungen, Ergänzungsband, Erster Teil, [Entwürfe zur Ummarbeitung der VI. Untersuchung und zur Vorrede für die Neuauflage der Logischen Untesuchungen (Sommer 1913)]*, Husserliana Band XX/I, herausg. Ul. Melle, Kluwer Acad. Pub., Dordrecht: The Netherlands.
[20] Husserl, E.: 1975, *Logische Untersuchungen*, (Erster Band: Prolegomena zur Reinen Logik), Husserliana Band XVIII, herausgb. E. Holenstein, M. Nijhoff, Den Haag: The Netherlands.
[21] Husserl, E.: 2006, *Späte Texte uber Zeitkonstitution (1929-1934): die C-Manuskripte*, Husserliana: Materialienband VIII, herausgb. D. Lohmar, Springer, Dordrecht: The Netherlands.
[22] Isham, J.C.: 1993, Quantum Logic and the Histories Approach to Quantum Theory, *arXiv:gr-qc/9308006v1 9 Aug 1993*.
[23] Isham, J.C. & Linden, N.: 1994, Quantum Temporal Logic and Decoherence Funcionals in the Histories Approach to Generalized Quantum Theory, *arXiv:gr-qc/9405029v1 11 May 1994*.
[24] Isham, J.C. & Savvidou, N.K.: 2002, Time and Modern Physics. In K. Ridderbos (Ed.), *Time*, pp. 6-26. Cambridge: Cambridge University Press.
[25] Livadas, S. (2005). The Phenomenological Roots of Nonstandard Mathematics, *Romanian Jour. of Infor. Science and Technology*, 8, 2, 115-136.

[26] Lorenz, K.: 1977, *Behind the Mirror*, London: Methuen.
[27] Savvidou, N.: 1999, The action operator for continuous-time histories, *Jour. of Mathematical Physics*, 42, 11, pp. 5657-5674.
[28] Sokolowski, R.: 1974, *Husserlian Meditations*, Evanston: Northwestern University Press.
[29] Uttal, W.R.: 1978, *The Psychobiology of Mind*, Hillsdale, NJ: Lawrence Erlbaum.

The Leap from the Ego of Temporal Consciousness to the Phenomenology of Mathematical Continuum [0]

STATHIS LIVADAS

1 Introduction

In what follows, my approach to the question of mathematical continuum might indeed make sense for someone finding that mathematics fundamentally involve some particular functions and properties of human consciousness, while it might seem almost irrelevant to someone regarding mathematical objects as ideal objects preexisting in some kind of platonic realm or yet on the other extreme to someone else regarding mathematics as reducible to a consistent set of axioms and rules presiding a game of otherwise meaningless symbols.

My general view is to a significant extent based on the Husserlian idea of mathematical objects as intentional objects within the real world of phenomena, formed in complete abstraction by means of categorial intuition,[1] thus leading to the theoretical possibility of reducing mathematical continuum (**MC**), taken as a purely formal notion, to the intuitive continuum of perceptual experience. In turn, intuitive continuum may be described after the notion of phenomenological continuum by following a phenomenological analysis of the constitutive flux of consciousness which on a yet deeper level can lead to the necessity of introducing a transcendental factor (the absolute ego of consciousness) to en-

---

[0] This article has been published in original form in the journal *Manuscrito*, (2009), V. 32, 2, pp. 321-356.

[1] As a matter of fact, Husserl used the close concept of essential insight (*Wesenschau*) well before his notion of categorial intuition which is specifically related to the constitution and meaning attribution with regard to mathematical objects as abstract objects originating from a formal-ontological domain. The essential insight is not to be understood as the creation of concepts by isolating, through some kind of variation, certain common characteristics from a multiplicity of objects that possibly bear a material content. Instead, it is meant as a species-building intuition arising from a single act of meaning, e.g. in acquiring the essence of red by looking to a red object appearing before us, as the single identical 'red' possibly becoming an object of reflection even in the absence of the original object bearing this particular color ([12], p. 106). In a parallel way, categorial intuition is not about the construction of mathematical essences as a common 'content' form built through free variation over individual cases. It is primarily related to the constitution of objects-substrates of logical-mathematical theories as contents of intentional acts towards 'something in general', together with the essential to those 'somethings' categorial objectivities which are possibly not instantiated in any material form. For further details, see [9], (pp. 80-82) & [17].

sure the continuous unity of the self-constituting flux, see: [13]. This reduction to a phenomenological continuum was largely L.E.J. Brouwer's, and with some variations H. Weyl's approach, to the notion of intuitive continuum in their attempt to provide an intuitionistically oriented foundation of mathematical analysis (see: [23]).

In this respect I draw a parallel, on the one hand, between L.E.J. Brouwer's 'two-ity' intuition introducing elements of any infinite choice sequence as 'durationless' points and E. Husserl's notion of intentional acts of a subject constituted as noematic objects[2] in the unity of his temporal flux of consciousness; on the other hand, I draw a parallel between Brouwer's assuption of the existence of an intuitive continuum as an underlying continuous substratum divested of any predicative character (termed the primordial intuition of Mathematics) on which to 'embed' objects of the 'two-ity' intuition, and Husserl's description of the transcendental character of the self-constituting absolute flux of consciousness.

To ground my claims on the possibility of a phenomenology of mathematical continuum (**MC**) tracing its subjective origin in the transcendental (and thus formally impredicative) character of the temporal ego of continental tradition, I will be primarily based on Husserlian phenomenology. This seems to provide a well-articulated descriptive context in which to describe the objects of analytic formulas and consequently those of pure and mathematical logic as formal-ontological objects[3] formed in complete 'evacuating' abstraction from objects that correspond to intentionalities and are constituted in a kind of homogenous synthesis within the unique flux of temporal consciousness.

I note, in passing, that there seems to be a common base between the existentialist approaches of M. Heidegger and J.P. Sartre[4] and the Husserlian

---

[2] It seems purposeful here to be a bit more specific about the meaning of the phenomenological terms noetic and noematic described primarily in E. Husserl's *Ideen I*, [11]. A noematic object manifests itself as an immanence in the flux of a subject's consciousness, constituted by certain modes as a well-defined object immanent to the temporal flux, which can then be taken in the sense of a formal-ontological object as a syntactical object of a formal-analytic theory naturally including a formal mathematical theory. It can then be said to be given apodictically in experience inasmuch as: (1) it can be recognized by a perceiver directly as a manifested essence in any perceptual judgement (2) it can be predicated as existing according to the descriptive norms of a language and (3) it can be verified as such (a reidentifying object) in multiple acts more or less at will. In contrast, a noetic object by hyletic-noetic perception (*Wahrnehmung*) can be only thought of in terms of real 'moments' of an intentionally directed consciousness by its sole virtue of being given as such 'in person' in front of it, inside the open horizon of Life-World.

[3] Formal-ontological objects in Husserlian sense can be roughly characterized in the context of formal ontology, as those objects registered-in by intentional experience and further temporally constituted and possibly modified within the immanence of each one's temporal consciousness, (see: [21], p. 46 & pp. 274-277).

[4] I refer, in particular, to the Sartrean idea of the temporal ego, dealt with in *L'être et le néant*, [19], where one is led to the impredicative character of moments of actuality and, most important, to the necessity to turn to some kind of non-temporal subjectivity of the Being-for-itself (*être-pour-soi*). By all accounts, one may also deduce a transcendence in Heidegger's description of the form of temporality of Being-in-the-World (*Dasein*), precisely by the description of its ecstatic temporality which cannot be characterized in terms of ontic

1. INTRODUCTION

phenomenology with regard to the subjective character of temporal consciousness to the extent that they make a reduction to a kind of absolute subjectivity of the temporal ego which is non-describable in terms of being in temporal objectivity without alienating itself from its mode of 'being' as a subjectivity. In this point of view, the phenomenological analysis of temporal consciousness and the temporality of existentialist ego can possibly lend themselves to a deeper understanding of the impredicative character of the constituted continuous unity in each one's mental reflection inasmuch as they both lead to the inherent impossibility of an ontological definition of the absolute subjectivity of consciousness except by its 'auto-alienation' in objective reflection. In fact, the Husserlian analysis of temporal consciousness can be seen to lead indirectly, by the notion of longitudinal intentionality (*Längstintentionalität*)[5] of the flux, to a yet deeper self-constituting level, termed the absolute ego of consciousness, which is essentially a pre-reflective, non-objectifiable and thus impredicative subjectivity, the ever in-act subjectivity of the continuous unity of temporality.

My scope in the following, will be to seek an interpretational approach to questions pertaining to the nature and properties of **MC** and, in a broader sense, to those pertaining to the notion of uncountable infinity, that ultimately reduce to the continuous unity of the flux of temporal consciousness taken as an objectivity and yet deeper to the transcendental character of the flux in itself taken as an absolute subjectivity. As these phenomenologically grounded reductions of purely mathematical questions might seem at first sight as far-fetched, I would offer as a corroborative argument at this stage the need to generally assume some kind of pre-given infinite continuous substratum in explicit or implicit fashion in proving mathematical statements of a higher order than those involving at most a countable infinity. The reason this kind of assumption on the analytic-mathematical level can be taken as a reflexion of constitutional processes of a phenomenological character as those mentioned above, will be made clearer in the development of my arguments in later sections.

There, I will inquire into the reasons the impossibility to capture phenomenological continuum ontologically may be reflected in the impredicative character of **MC**. I will also point to the necessity of an underlying assumption of actual infinity[6] in trying to decide a well-known continuum statement, as it is the

---

being as it is rather an *élan vital*, an impetus alienating any 'being-in-itself' from its substance and transforming it into a ceaseless motion.

[5]Intentionality, in phenomenological terms, should not be understood as a relation of a psychological content, since it is meant something fundamentally deeper and *a priori*. To a non-expert in Phenomenology it can be described as grounding the *a priori* necessity of orientation of a subject's consciousness to its object of orientation. Intentional forms of the transversal intentionality of the constituting (absolute) flux of consciousness can be regarded the retention and protention which are 'attached' to any original impression in temporal actuality, while by longitudinal intentionality we can roughly understand the constitution of the descending sequence of retentions of each original impression as a continuous whole, (see: [13], § 12 & § 39.

[6]In the present context actual infinity is taken as a Cantorian-type infinity, i.e. a pre-existing, indefinitely extending, uncountable infinity.

Continuum Hypothesis (**CH**) proved to be independent from the other axioms of commonly acceptable Zermelo-Fraenkel & **AC** Set Theory (see: [16]). I will review the metatheoretical reason, the so-called actual infinity assumption, i.e. the *Axiom of Choice* (**AC**) - proved also to be independent from **ZF** - is applied to prove the consistency of both *Continuum Hypothesis* and its negation with the other axioms of **ZFC** theory.

In Subsection 0.3.2, I try to interpret the undecidability of **CH** and **AC** within **ZF** theory as a consequence of Gödel's First Incompleteness Theorem by taking into account, on the metatheoretical level, of an elusive notion of actual infinity 'creeping' in the proof of the non-recursiveness of the set of theorems deduced from a consistent and recursive set of axioms extending **ZF**. In fact, the incompleteness of formal systems with at least the expressive power of formal arithmetic is interpreted as fundamentally due to the non-rigorously finitistic character of metatheoretical objects taken as formal objects, for instance, in an extension by definitions with regard to a consistent formal theory S.

My general conclusion is that there is no way to define mathematical continuum (**MC**) by first-order means without generating evident circularities in definition. Also, there is no way to settle questions dealing with the cardinality or properties of **MC** without some form of *ad hoc* actual infinity assumption applied in the process owing, in my view, to the fundamentally non-analytic character of **MC**, which may be reduced on the level of phenomenological constitution to the inherently impredicative (and even deeper transcendental) nature of each subject's continuous unity of temporal consciousness whose 'reflexion' on the logical-mathematical level is the formal impredicativity of mathematical continuity.

2 Can Mathematical Continuum be reduced to a Phenomenological Continuum?

At this point the reader might rightfully wonder what all this stuff about the ego of phenomenological analysis taken as an ever in-act subjectivity of temporal consciousness has to do with the notion of continuum in formal mathematical theory or anyway with any sort of mathematical activity. My answer, in the first place, to this reasonable objection is again the claim put forth in the beginning of Introduction; the acceptance of an argumentation of this kind depends, in principle, on the general philosophical attitude of someone doing mathematics and specifically foundational mathematics. If he finds mathematics as basically a formal abstraction of certain functions of the human mind, then he might be willing to accept my discussion as meaningful and my clues as making some headway towards a deeper understanding of mathematical continuum.

As already mentioned in the Introduction, E. Husserl gave a common conceptual ground underlying perceptual objects on the one hand and mathematical objects on the other by means of categorial intuition; the latter objects together with their *a priori* 'attached' categorial objectivities are obtained from

2. CAN MATHEMATICAL CONTINUUM BE REDUCED?   119

perceptual evidences by categorial intuition and abstracted to the formal status of mathematical entities. As it will be noted below, purely formal objects of mathematical theories as eidetic objects are not thought to be obtained by eidetic variation on material essences reducing thus to a possibility of common content; they are, instead, the result of a complete abstraction originating from an intentional orientation towards a 'general something' and therefore eliminating all traits relative to a material content, which is then taken to be a contingent material fulfillment. A counterargument to this Husserlian view is put up by those who insist on a fundamental difference between mathematical and perceptual intuition on the grounds that perceptual objects are determinate and individually identifiable ones, which is what seems to be missing in the case of mathematical objects, e. g. in the intuition of the symbol ∅ standing for the empty set, ([22], pp. 399-400). This counterargument, though, can be easily refuted as it might be taken to refer to the empty set as a convention of formal mathematical language just as the term absolute vacuum refers by all accounts to a conventionality within the theory of standard quantum physics.

But there is more to it and goes deeper into a converging approach of perceptual and mathematical objects on the level of intentionality. In *Ideas I*, Husserl characterized objects-substrates of mathematical theories on the 'lowest' intentional level as empty-substrates (*Leersubstraten*) referring to 'empty somethings' in general, taken with their *a priori* categorial objectivities, which generate, in turn, corresponding syntactical objectivities as modified forms of these 'empty-somethings'. This class of intentional objects as 'states-of-things' (*Sachverhalte*) with all categorial objectivities *a priori* attached to them, constitute the class of objects of pure logic as *mathesis universalis*, e.g. syntactical elements of set-theoretical formulas, sets, classes of sets, numerals, functions defined in Euclidean or non-Euclidean domains, etc. ([11], p. 33).

Taking now, for instance, the reading of a pointer registering the measurement of a quantum experiment as a perceptual sign, that sign regardless of its particular material content has a mode of being a 'sign-as such' and therefore, as an intentional object (of hyletic-noetic perception), it can be taken as a 'state-of-affairs' which in noematic constitution can be, as a well-defined object, assigned a unique mathematical value.[7] This subtle distinction between perceptual objects and objects of formal mathematics can be nevertheless understood on the phenomenological-intentional level as a coherence factor in taking both of them as ultimately intentional objects irrespective of any possible material content. It is noteworthy, that K. Gödel in the supplement to his well-known paper *What is Cantor's Continuum problem?* figured out that there is something more than just through sensations or combinations of sensations that perceptual objects are given to us. He insisted, in particular, on "

---

[7]To come back to the instance of null set ∅, which presumably formalizes 'ontological' nothingness, we can say that since it 'presents itself' in original givenness as an 'empty-something' of the intentionality of consciousness it will be absurd to call it nothingness in phenomenological sense; for, as an original givenness it has already become a concrete fulfillment in time.

the idea of the object itself [...] Evidently, the 'given' underlying mathematics is closely related to the abstract elements contained in our empirical ideas." ([5], p. 398).

Gödel's point was, contrary to Kant's assertions, that if these abstract elements do not follow by some kind of action of things upon our sense organs, they are nevertheless not purely subjective but they must represent some other kind of relation between ourselves and reality. D. Føllesdal takes in [5] these abstract features and primarily Gödel's emphasis on the idea of the object itself as linked to a notion of individuation of objects, leading to the notions of identity and distinctness and consequently to the act of counting which makes them representable as principal mathematical elements, ([5], p. 399). Given my aforementioned interpretation of the syntactical objects of pure and mathematical logic as radically reduced to intentional objects, this kind of individuation can be thought of as rooted in their perception as irreducible individuals of intentionality. Their uniqueness as individuals-substrates is grounded, in turn, on their very 'being' as unique original givennesses of intentionality irreducible to anything more fundamental.

At this stage, based on the intentionality-motivated approach to perceptual and mathematical objects, one can possibly review specific mathematical objects, such as choice sequences[8] and the mathematical continuum itself, by reading again in this new context Brouwer's two-ity intuition and the primordial intuition of intuitionistic mathematics. This seems to be to the point, as the intuitionistic approach to the continuum is not only to a large extent modelized -at least in Brouwer's and Weyl's writings- after the phenomenology of temporal consciousness but also because it is in this approach that can be put under an alternative point of view the fundamental difference between the two-ity intuition and the primordial intuition of mathematics, the latter principle roughly defining intuitive continuum.

As a matter of fact, L.E.J Brouwer in his early formation (Ph.D thesis, 1907) and later made several comments on the intuitive continuum that can be seen to be pretty much based on the description of temporal consciousness by E. Husserl. This is also the case with H. Weyl working independently and elaborating his ideas in the well-known monograph *Das Kontinuum* (1918). I do not intend here to enter into great details in describing Brouwer's or Weyl's foundation of intuitive and eventually mathematical continuum put up in accordance with phenomenological principles (van Atten *et al* offer a fine exposition in [23]); I will rather call attention first to the radical difference between the first act of intuitionism (two-ity intuition) and the primordial intuition of mathematics

---

[8]Choice sequences, in intuitionistic theory, as sequences in time progression were originally taken as a means to represent points of the intuitive continuum and are generally divided to lawlike and lawless ones. What basically distinguishes a lawlike sequence from a lawless one, is that the former even when not given by a prescribed formula, it is a determinate one and thus has a fixed horizon of progression, whereas the latter is fully or partially indeterminate and its horizon is not fixed in advance. In the unfolding of a lawless sequence anything can occur in progression except for the obvious specification of the uniqueness of the value for each term.

2. CAN MATHEMATICAL CONTINUUM BE REDUCED?

(intuitive continuum) and next to a phenomenologically motivated exposition of the graph-extensional version of the *Weak Continuity Principle* presented by van Dalen *et al* in [24].

As it stands out, there exist certain similarities in L.E.J Brouwer's discussion of the intuitive continuum as the primordial intuition of mathematics and the phenomenological description of the absolute flux of consciousness. These similarities can be easily traced in a first reading inasmuch as in Brouwer's description the intuitive continuum is: " The substratum, divested of all quality, of any perception of change, a unity of continuity and discreteness, a possibility of thinking together several entities, connected by a 'between', which is never exhausted by the insertion of new entities" ([23] p. 205). In his view, the intuitive continuum is an impredicative substratum in which continuity and discreteness occur as inseparable complements, where it is impossible to construe one of them as a primitive entity without implicating in some way the other in the same primitive sense.

The intuition of discreteness on the other hand, called two-ity, is the empty form of all intuitions of distinct intentional objects in temporal succession and can ground the discrete aspect of all mathematical constructions; by means of two-ity intuition we can generate natural number sequences and also any finite combinatorial object generated from natural numbers ([23], p. 206). Brouwer's two-ity intuition can be largely interpreted by means of the transversal intentionality of the absolute flux of consciousness (*Querintentionalität*), in the scheme original impression–retention–protention, the two latter terms meant as *a priori* intentionalities respectively towards past and future (see: [13], pp. 44 & 71). In this view natural numbers are taken by two-ity intuition as durationless points in abstraction, whereas cannot be claimed the same about real numbers considered as incomplete objects. Yet, in the flow of inner time we are not aware of any durationless now-point as there is no 'autonomous' present in original impression but rather a specious present *a priori* 'composed' of original impression–retention–protention. We can, however, approach a durationless point of intuitive continuum by an infinite sequence of nested rational intervals the lengths of which converge to 0. This possibility, called the 'second act of intuitionism', allows a modelization of intuitive continuum on the basis of the generation of freely proceeding convergent sequences, where each real number as an ideally durationless point is characterized as the species of such non-lawlike sequences. To be consistent with his view of real numbers as incomplete objects, L.E.J. Brouwer regarded lawless sequences, in the sense of indefinitely proceedable sequences, as better representing intuitive continuum, e.g. a point P (representing a real number) to which a freely proceeding sequence of rational nested λ-intervals $\lambda_{\nu_1}, \lambda_{\nu_2}, .., \lambda_{\nu_n}, ..$ of the general form $[\frac{\alpha}{2^{\nu-1}}, \frac{\alpha+1}{2^{\nu-1}}]$ converges is defined as the sequence itself and not something as a limiting point of the sequence ([23], p. 212).

However, both Brouwer and Weyl handled choice sequences in the bounded formulas of continuity principles as complete and determinate objects in infinite projection so as to provide an intuitionistic foundation for real analysis. In that sense, intuitionistic continuity principles such as the Weak Continuity Principle (**WC-N**) are, in principle, black box principles extending *ad infinitum* the horizon of finitely many intentional acts (essentially by two-ity intuition) of a generating subject towards the vagueness of infinity; the latter notion presupposes the existence of an impredicative, indefinitely extensible substratum in the sense of the primordial intuition of mathematics.

In [24], the main motivation of van Dalen *et al* for providing a graph-extensional version (**GWC-N**) of Brouwer's Weak Continuity Principle (**WC-N**)[9], was to extend the latter principle to all kinds of choice sequences (lawlike and lawless ones), considering any kind of restriction on the free generation of the unfolding terms of the sequence as stemming from a noetic-noematic correlation of the intentional acts of a freely generating subject with the intensional properties of the sequence in question.

Such restrictions, which in any case accept an existing initial segment of the choice sequence could be definitive, '*From now on restriction P_j^i holds and will not be revised any more*' or provisional, '*for an unspecified number of stages restriction P_j^i holds*' ([24], pp. 335-36). Formally, there is no difference except for one with respect to the following continuity principle, (**WC-N**), between Van Dalen *et al* and L.E.J Brouwer.

$$\forall \alpha \, \exists x \, A(\alpha, x) \implies \forall \alpha \, \exists m \exists x \forall \beta \, [\bar{\beta}m = \bar{\alpha}m \longrightarrow A(\beta, x)]$$

where α, β range over sequences of natural numbers, m, x over natural numbers and $\bar{\alpha}m$ stands for $< \alpha(0),....,\alpha(m-1) >$, i.e. the initial segment of the sequence α of length m. The difference, in question, is that in **GWC-N** the predicate $A(\alpha, x)$ is stronger than extensional in the classical definition of the term; it is actually graph-extensional which means that the choice sequence α enters $A(\alpha, x)$ only through its values. Therefore, what is the role of the graph-extensionality of $A(\alpha, x)$ in **GWC-N**, in view of its capacity to cover the widest possible range of choice sequences and what does it mean from a deeper phenomenologically oriented view?

I propose to give the following interpretation in accordance with my general scope. Any two-ity intuition can be linked to a noetic-noematic type generation of a sequence of natural numbers where these numbers are registered only as such, that is, by their distinct values as signs-in themselves. Consequently, the **GWC-N** principle is, by this token, a valid continuity principle since any restrictions on the part of a sequence-generating subject acting by hyletic-noetic perception should be only 'first-order' restrictions. Such restrictions, on a phenomenological level, might be solely considered the retention in consciousness of each original impression in actual present, that is, of each new term of the choice sequence together with the retention of the 'descending' collection of the terms generated thus far as a whole, that is, of the initial segment of the

---

[9]This fundamental continuity principle, (**WC-N**), has as a direct consequence the well-known intuitionistic theorem, namely, that all total functions are continuous and thus the continuum is unsplittable, (see: [8], p. 46).

3. THE REFLEXION OF THE IMPREDICATIVITY

sequence. Evidently, the latter retention refers to what Husserl called longitudinal intentionality (*Längstintentionnalität*), which bears already the creeping transcendence of continuum by forming the continuous unity of a sequence of retentions as a whole.

Consequently in this approach, **GWC-N** eliminates, by the graph-extensionality of predicate $A(\alpha, x)$, any higher order restrictions on the generation of the terms of the sequence. Such restrictions, e.g. a provisional restriction of the type '*from now on, the choice sequence α is constant*' cannot be characterized as being of an intentional character. It is noteworthy that van Dalen *et al* have proved (an alternative proof is given by A. Visser in the same paper) that the original version of the continuity principle **WC-N** does not hold in general for extensional predicates, precisely by producing a higher order restriction in the process of a strictly numerical unfolding of the terms of a choice sequence ([24], pp. 340-41).

3 The reflexion of the impredicativity of phenomenological continuum in formal theory

3.1 The notion of constitution and its role in the independence of CH

In the intuitionistic theory the notion of continuity is basically founded on continuity principles such as those already mentioned or on general versions of them (e.g. Brouwer's Universal Spread Law). In turn, these principles are, as claimed above, conditioned on phenomenologically motivated assumptions such as the primordial intuition of mathematics and the first act of intuitionism.

On the other hand, in Cantorian **ZF** theory the continuum is basically introduced by the application of two axioms: these are, the Replacement Axiom and the Power Set Axiom. There is a fundamental difference between the two: the first one defines a new set by means of a functional predicate, the second is a qualitatively different axiomatical tool generating a richer set $\mathcal{P}(X)$ with cardinality greater than that of its base set X; in case X is a countably infinite set it gives rise to the extremely rich set C whose cardinality is defined to be the cardinality of continuum. As P. Cohen put it, " it is unreasonable to expect that any description of a larger cardinal which attempts to build up that cardinal from ideas deriving from the Replacement Axiom can ever reach C". He was referring of course to the set $\aleph_1$ of all countable ordinals but also to any cardinals such as $\aleph_1, \aleph_\omega, \aleph_\alpha, ...$ where $\alpha = \aleph_\omega$, etc., produced by a piecemeal process of construction starting from $\aleph_0$ and applying at each stage the Replacement Axiom. In this case C would be greater than each of these cardinals and the *Continuum Hypothesis* would be obviously false something left to future generations to decide perhaps by seeing more clearly the problem ([1], p. 151).

In my view, the 'asymmetric' character of the Power Set Axiom with respect to the other axioms of **ZF** owes much to the radical difference between two fundamental intuitions. The process of an enumeration *ad infinitum* which can be thought of as some form of intentional 'act' close to the meaning of the two-ity intuition in intuitionistic theory and the process of forming subsets of infinite enumerations as objective wholes including all their elements at once. The latter seems in a first reading linked to L.E.J. Brouwer's intuition of continuum as an impredicative substratum deprived of any quality (the primordial intuition of mathematics). On a yet deeper level we may reach a condition of mental constitution that should be a rather temporal one, to ground the passing from the level of the noetic perception of zero-level elements of sets, taken as formal individuals-substrates, to subsets forming 'instantly' from them as objectivities in temporal unity. This could lead, on a phenomenological level, to first admitting certain intentionalities of the absolute flux of consciousness conditioning the immediate retention of the original presence of each zero-level element as an 'empty-something' and second the retention of any such aggregate of 'somethings' as an objective whole by means of longitudinal intentionality. At each stage of temporal reduction we have to turn into impredicative, that is, to non-susceptible to a first-order formal description, forms of the flux to ground the objective unity of any indefinite aggregate of intentional objects in consciousness, in the particular case of the power set of an infinite countable set, e.g. of elements of categorial formulas. Ultimately we are led to a pure a-temporal transcendence which 'is' the absolute subjectivity behind the immanent continuous unity, taken in the form of an objective whole in temporal constitution.[10] In a mathematical sense, it should be taken as the subjectivity behind an otherwise impredicative continuous (temporal) substratum through which we can represent well-defined mathematical objects and further collections of such objects, classes of such collections and so on *ad infinitum*, in the form of objective wholes at once in original givenness. Evidently, we cannot describe by analytic means inside any formal system what by its nature is non-analytic and ever 'in-act', for it can be never objectified as it 'is' the absolute ego of any conceivable temporal unity.

In this respect, there are lately quite a few mathematicians mostly working in mathematical foundations who have doubts about the possibility of defining continuum as a set and who admit of an at least non-analytic character of the question of the cardinality of continuum; among them there is S. Feferman who insists that **CH**[11] is an inherently vague statement that cannot be settled by any new axioms added to **ZFC** theory ([4]). As **CH** is generally considered more than any other relevant conjecture linked with the nature of mathematical continuum and as its independence is proved to underlie the independence of

---

[10]The recourse to an absolute subjectivity of a transcendental type to ground the objective unity of temporal consciousness and of its immanent objects is the common denominator of the existentialist trends mentioned in the introduction and the Husserlian view of temporal constitution. Of course the relevance of respective approaches to mathematical objects, including the notion of mathematical continuum, presupposes a view of mathematical objects conditioned on some kind of categorial intuition and based on their constitution as durating, well-defined and immanent objects of temporal consciousness.

[11]The Continuum Hypothesis (**CH**) roughly assumes that the number of subsets of a set of the power of countable infinity $\aleph_0$ has the power of continuum C, i.e. $2^{\aleph_0} = C$.

3. THE REFLEXION OF THE IMPREDICATIVITY

other infinity statements within **ZFC** (e.g., Suslin's Hypothesis, the question of the product of any two **c.c.c.** spaces), I set myself the task to show the need to implicitly assume a notion of (temporal) constitution in the following cases: 1) in the classical proof of the fundamental result $X \prec \mathcal{P}(x)$ for any infinite set X and **2**) in the assumption of the *Axiom of Choice* as an actual infinity axiom in the proof of the consistency of both **CH** and $\neg$ **CH** with the rest of **ZFC**.

It is well-known that the Cantor theorem stating that, generally, for any nonempty set X the cardinality of $\mathcal{P}(X)$ is greater then the cardinality of X ($X \prec \mathcal{P}(x)$, where $\mathcal{P}(x)$ is the power set of X, gives a positive answer to the question whether there are any infinite cardinalities greater than continuum. In the following, in a phenomenologically oriented approach its proof can be reduced, on a fundamental level of evidence, to a condition of temporal constitution irrespective of the order of cardinalities involved. In this point of view any higher order cardinality than that of the countable infinity cardinal $\aleph_0$ can be considered as an idealization of a second level which is not based on possible experience, taken as an idealization of the first level the one based on the intuition of the set of natural numbers **N**, by admitting to the possibility of an indefinitely open horizon of re-iterating intentional acts of the form 'I always *can do*' to produce each time a new $n \cup \{n\}$ (see: [18]).

The classical proof consists in the construction of a 1-1 mapping from X into $\mathcal{P}(x)$ which cannot be onto. Let us assume that there is such a mapping f corresponding each element x of X to the singleton $\{x\}$. Obviously it is 1-1. We then define a subset A of X in terms of $A = \{x;\ x \notin f(x)\}$. Since f is assumed onto $\mathcal{P}(x)$ there must be an $a \in X$ such that $f(a) = A$. Then a has two possibilities: to be either in A or in $X \setminus A$. If it is in A then $a \notin f(a) = A$, so we get $a \in A \rightarrow a \notin A$; this is impossible so a must be in $X \setminus A$. Then $a \notin A$ so $a \in f(a) = A$. Again we get the contradictory $a \notin A \rightarrow a \in A$, so the mapping f cannot be onto.

Although this theorem sets an upward scale of infinite cardinalities by taking each time as the new set X the class of all subsets of the previous set, the underlying mental process in the argumentation of each proof is essentially the same; the element a is successively taken in two fundamentally different levels of phenomenological perception. First, it is taken as an element of the set X, this set conceived of as the general 'environment' of a bearing no influence on the individuality of a. In this sense the element a can be taken as an abstraction of a noetic perception directed intentionally to a as an'empty-something' (i.e., a *Sachverhalt*). In the next stage of the proof the element a is taken as bearing a double nature, that of an individual-in itself and also that of an object-element of an aggregate of other objects-elements of X satisfying a primitive property of inclusion expressible in formal language by the undefined predicate $\in$. At this stage we have to presuppose the constitution of a as a well-defined object and the simultaneous constitution of an indefinite collection of other elements $x \in X$, such that $x \notin f(x)$, at once in continuous temporal unity; this should correspond to a state in which a is noematically constituted in the temporal flux simultaneously with a retentional indefinite aggregate of other noematic objects of the same kind, taken as an objective whole in the present now of consciousness. At the stage we have formed the subset $A = \{x;\ x \notin f(x)\}$ to which the element a may or may not belong, we have to implicitly assume a retentional unity of an indefinite aggregate of elements x formed as a complete whole of immanent objects in the progression of the absolute flux of consciousness. There is an already 'creeping' impredicative continuity here, independently of the order of the infinite cardinality of the set X, owing to the inherently impredicative character of the longitudinal intentionality of the flux and ultimately of the absolute flux itself.[12] In my approach, the retentional forms of the absolute flux of consciousness (longitudinal and transversal intentionality) could partially account on a phenomenological-constitutional level for clinging to P. Cohen's view that " it is unreasonable to expect that any description of a larger cardinal which attempts to build up that cardinal from ideas deriving from the Replacement Axiom can ever reach C".

Now I pass to the implicit assumption of a notion of actual infinity and consequently, on a phenomenological level, of an impredicative temporal substratum in the application of the *Axiom of Choice* (**AC**) in the proof of the independence of **CH** within **ZFC**.

It is well-known that one of the common forms of **AC** states that given a non-empty class of non-empty sets $\{Xi\}$, $i \in I$, we can choose exactly one element from each set in the class to form the non-empty product $\prod_{i \in I} X_i$. It is also known that this axiom, characterized as an actual infinity axiom by certain non-standard set theorists in the sense of being conditioned on a pre-existing actual infinity of a Cantorian type, is applied to produce the independence of *Continuum Hypothesis*. As a matter of fact it is at least indirectly presupposed in Gödel's proof of the consistency of **CH** with the axioms of **ZFC** and also in P. Cohen's proof (by the forcing method) of the consistency of ¬ **CH** with the axioms of **ZFC**. In the rest of this subsection I'll try to sketch a phenomenologically oriented interpretation of **AC** and then show its implicit role in the 'proof' of ¬ **CH** as it gives a strong clue to the assertion that no matter what model we are working in (for instance, a countable transitive base model **M** in forcing theory) we have to assume some actual infinity principle to prove a conjecture about uncountable infinity.

In this approach the basic underlying intuition of **AC** can be summed up as extending, in principle, over an indefinite horizon the right to 'observe' and manipulate individuals as such and in relation to any collection of them. On

---

[12]My phenomenologically motivated argumentation here for Cantor's result $X \prec \mathcal{P}(x)$, seems in a certain sense to be in perfect consonance with D. Lohmar's view of the same question, namely of the fundamentally different character of the concept of an element as a categorial intuition and the act of constituting a collection as the complete series of unifications of its elements, which is then an object of a radically different kind from the elements of this set ([18], p. 238). In this view, it goes as far as questioning the lawfulness of assuming the existence of the set of all sets since such an idealization in the sense of a complete series of unifications in constitution, is taken then as an element of itself.

3. THE REFLEXION OF THE IMPREDICATIVITY 127

a phenomenological-constitutional level, we may say that as any individual-as such is, in original givenness, the object of intentionality at the lowest level of phenomenological (noetic) perception, there exists a notion of ordering by the sole virtue of the intentional 'property' of the individual in question to bear an outer horizon, i.e. that part of the Life-World[13] which is not the object or parts of the object, thereby defining in complementary sense the field of next intentional 'observations'. Consequently a notion of well-ordering is induced by representing intentional individuals as noematic objects possibly belonging to aggregates of other such objects in the constituting flux of consciousness. Now, what is left after discarding all other details of constitution is the possibility to intentionally 'observe' individuals at least as 'general-somethings' (*Etwas-überhaupt*) probably with no material content, and the protentions of intentionality towards them as *a priori* potentialities defining an ever receding complementary domain of 'observations'. In addition, the *Axiom of Choice* should be conditioned on the notion of a pre-existing actual infinity which might be conceived in terms of temporal constitution as an objective and invariably existing temporal substratum on which to 'embed' intentional individuals as noematic objects within immanent continuous unity.

In conclusion, **AC** can be phenomenologically interpreted as founded first on the existence of a subject performing acts of an intentional character ideally *ad infinitum*, and second on the existence of a constituting flux of consciousness of the subject in question, in the continuous unity of which any noetically apprehended object can be constituted as a temporal, well-defined and uniquely determined (in varying predicative situations) noematic object. Any such object in its essential categorial form can be defined both as an object-in-itself and in some kind of categorial relation to any other or to any collection of others. Grounded then as a well-defined noematic object it can be taken as a formal-ontological object provided with proper sense mathematical properties e.g. extensionality, a notion of order in strictly formal sense, etc.

Regarding the implicit role of **AC** in the proof of the consistency of $\neg$ **CH** with the other axioms of **ZFC**, it seems pointless in the present article to offer a detailed exposition of the fundamentals of P. Cohen's theory of forcing as it would be certainly lengthy, possibly difficult to comprehend and at the same time not absolutely necessary in reaching my point.[14] Instead, I'll try to be as explicative as possible in the presentation of my arguments.

Generally, in forcing techniques we rely on global properties forced to objects, such as to a function f_G of a forcing model $\mathbf{M}[G]$, by means of a P-generic set

---

[13] The World-for us or Life-World, (*Lebenswelt*) in Husserlian terminology, can be roughly described to a non-phenomenologist as the physical world with its ever receding horizon including in intersubjective sense all knowing subjects in a special kind of presence in the World. More on this in E. Husserl's *The Crisis of European Sciences and Transcendental Phenomenology*, [10].

[14] For a detailed exposition of forcing theory the reader may consult P. Cohen's original presentation in *Set Theory and the Continuum Hypothesis*, [1], K. Kunen's *Set Theory. An Introduction to Independence Proofs*, [16] and F. Drake's & D. Singh's *Intermediate Set Theory*, [2].

G over a countable transitive base model **M**, where P is a partially ordered set of forcing conditions $(P, \leq)$ in **M**. The P-generic set $\mathbf{G} \in \mathbf{M}[G]$ is defined to have the property of a special filter to force compatible extensions of any condition p over **M** and is moreover very generic in the sense of having non-empty intersection with any dense set of conditions p over **M**; in the strictly formal level, the forcing conditions p are to be understood as merely elements of the partially ordered set P. We are going to see that the generic properties of **G** can lead to contradictions in case the poset $(P, \leq)$ of forcing conditions has not the property **c.c.c**.[15]

The **c.c.c** condition is a necessary constraint to be satisfied by a set of forcing conditions P of **M** in the proof of the consistency of $\neg$ **CH** with **ZFC**, as it preserves cardinalities between the base model **M** and the extended model **M**[G] ([16], p. 207). In the construction of the proof, it is possible based on the Δ-system Lemma,[16] to define an appropriate set of conditions, namely the set of finite partial functions $\text{Fn}(\kappa \times \omega, \mathbf{2})$ from $\kappa \times \omega$ into $\mathbf{2}$ satisfying c.c.c. (κ an uncountable cardinal of M and ω the cardinal number of countable infinity). It turns out, though, that the proof of Δ-system Lemma for $\text{Fn}(\kappa \times \omega, \mathbf{2})$ needs the **AC**.

The necessity of the **c.c.c.** constraint for the poset $P = \text{Fn}(\kappa \times \omega, \mathbf{2})$ may now become clear as it reduces uncountably infinite possibilities in the domain of conditions $p \in \text{Fn}(\kappa \times \omega, \mathbf{2})$ to countably many compatible extensions of these conditions. Let's keep in mind that forcing a compatible extension h for each condition p of P, in the common intuition of extension and this way *ad infinitum*, can be taken as fundamentally rooted on intentional acts, let's say of a higher order than that of the two-ity intuition of natural numbers referred to in section 0.2, to the extent that each time one can consistently enlarge the noematic field of a concrete intentional object; in this sense it can be abstracted as a cognitive act performed by a subject in time progression. In the mathematical context we discuss, these acts should correspond to an open-ended class of countably many compatible extensions. This is, in effect, ensured by the definition of the **c.c.c.** condition, which in the case of the proof of consistency of $\neg$ **CH** with **ZFC**, is dependent on the application of Δ-system Lemma mentioned above and ultimately on **AC**.

I'll spare now some space just to show the key role of the **c.c.c.** condition

---

[15] A partially ordered set (poset) $(P, \leq)$ has the *Countable Chain Condition* (**c.c.c.**) iff every antichain (i.e., every family of pairwise incompatible elements) of the poset P is countable. Letting $P \neq \emptyset$, the elements $p, q \in P$ are defined as compatible if,

$$(\text{for } p,\, q \in P)\ \exists r \in P\ (r \preceq p \land r \preceq q)$$

that is, r extends both p and q in the usual intuition of extension. For example, if p, q are finite partial functions from ω to $\mathbf{2}$ and $p \preceq q$ iff $q \subset p$, then p and q are compatible iff they agree on $\text{dom}(p) \cap \text{dom}(q)$, in which case $p \cup q$ is a common extension of p and q.

[16] A family $\mathcal{K}$ of sets is called a Δ-system iff there is a fixed (finite) set r, called the root of the Δ-system, such that $a \cap b = r$, whenever a, b are distinct members of $\mathcal{K}$. The Δ-system Lemma states that if A is any uncountable family of finite sets, then there is an uncountable $B \subseteq A$ which forms a Δ-system (see: [16], p. 49).

3. THE REFLEXION OF THE IMPREDICATIVITY

in the proof of the consistency of ¬ **CH** by citing an example, (offered in [16], p.55), demonstrating that the non-existence of the **c.c.c.** property of $(P, \leq)$ can lead to inconsistencies. This will also help to better clarify my overall approach to the proof of the above mentioned consistency:

Let $(P, \leq)$ be the set of finite partial functions from ω to **2**, that is, $P = \{p : p \subset \omega \times \mathbf{2}, |p| < \omega\}$ and $p \leq q$ iff $q \subset p$ as functions. If **G** is a filter in P then the elements of **G** are pairwise compatible by its very property of being a filter; therefore, if we define $f_G = \bigcup G$ then f_G is a function with $\operatorname{dom}(f_G) \subset \omega$. How can we conceive of f_G as being truly generic? In such case we have to apply the statement $MA(k)$ which is part of Martin's Axiom **MA** and guarantees a P-generic set **G** for any non-empty **c.c.c.** partial order $(P, \leq)$.[17] Let for $n \in \omega$ $D_n = \{p \in P; n \in \operatorname{dom}(p)\}$. As any $p \in P$ can be extended to a compatible condition with n in its domain, D_n is a dense family and by statement $MA(k)$ $\forall n \in \omega$ $(G \cap D_n \neq \emptyset)$. Then obviously the domain of f_G ia all of ω, that is, $\operatorname{dom}(f_G) = \omega$. Therefore, we can build a fairly generic function $f_G = \bigcup G$, first, by relying on the properties of the filter **G** to define the function f_G and, second, by forming countably many compatible extensions of finite partial functions p by adjoining to any $\operatorname{dom}(p)$ a finite subset of ω so that the class D_n be dense. Then, relying on the **c.c.c.** property of the particular set of forcing conditions $(P, \leq$, we apply $MA(k)$ to get a generic **G** intersecting all such dense sets.

The situation can become complicated, however, in case uncountable cardinals are involved and $(P, \leq)$ does not have the **c.c.c.** property, as it is the case where the set of conditions is $P = \{p : p \subset \omega \times \omega_1 \wedge |p| < \omega\}$ where ω_1 is the first uncountable ordinal. As above we can easily see that there exists a generic function $f_G = \bigcup G$ with $\operatorname{dom}(f_G) \subset \omega$ and $\operatorname{ran}(f_G) \subset \omega_1$. For $\alpha \in \omega_1$ let $D_\alpha = \{p \in P; \alpha \in \operatorname{ran}(p)\}$, then D_α is straightforward checked to be dense as we can always generate a compatible extension of $p \in P$ with $\alpha \in \operatorname{ran}(p)$. If there existed a generic set G intersecting each D_α for all $\alpha \in \omega_1$ we would have that $\operatorname{ran} f_G = \omega_1$ even though $\operatorname{dom} f_G \subset \omega$ which is obviously impossible if f_G is to be a function. But now $(P, \leq)$ lacks the c.c.c. property as it can have an uncountable class of pairwise incompatible conditions $\{< 0, \alpha >\}$ for $\alpha \in \omega_1$. This is, actually, what the **c.c.c.** condition is all about in the present context: it eliminates an uncountable number of incompatible conditions p, meaning that even in the presence of uncountable numbers in the range of such conditions we can nevertheless proceed with countably many compatible extensions of them and this way by applying statement $MA(k)$ define a fairly generic set **G**. In a more intuitive nuance the **c.c.c.** property opens up the possibility to 'suppress' the uncountable infinity factor underlying the 'field' of definition of forcing conditions p_α, in view of an operation of forming (in countably many steps) compatible and consistent extensions of p_α, something that can be linked to the discrete mode of a series of cognitive acts (bearing a 'concrete' content)

---

[17] $MA(k)$ is the statement: Whenever $(P, \leq)$ is a non-empty **c.c.c.** partial order and $\mathcal{D}$ is a family of $\leq_\kappa$ dense subsets of P, then there exists a filter G in P such that $\forall D \in \mathcal{D}$ $(G \cap D \neq \emptyset)$. **MA** is the statement $(\forall \kappa < 2^\omega)$ $MA(k)$.

of an intentionally performing subject.

As the **c.c.c.** condition, satisfied in general by finite partial functions $\mathrm{Fn}(I,J)$ of a countable range J, depends mainly on the Δ-system property of $\mathrm{Fn}(I,J)$ and as, in turn, the Δ-system property depends implicitly on the *Axiom of Choice*, this should be taken as a strong indication of the implicit need to turn to some form of actual infinity principle (here the **AC**) in order to prove in an essentially countable 'operational' context a statement involving uncountable cardinalities, such as the consistency of $\neg$ **CH** within **ZFC**.

3.2 How to interpret the undecidability of infinity statements within ZF theory?

A key step in proving the incompleteness of a recursive consistent extension **T** of theory **ZF**, is to prove that the set of theorems of the extension **T** is not recursive (see: [16], p. 14). On this account the notion of a recursive (or decidable) set plays a major role through the following theorem **3.1** which represents recursive sets e.g. the set of natural numbers or the set of finite sequences, by means of formulas of **ZF**. In a certain sense, a recursive set might be linked, on the level of subjective evidence, to the discrete way an 'observer' applies his intentional 'observation' towards a (recursively) enumerable collection possibly by the intermediary of a digital device. We must have in mind that a recursively enumerable set S is a set of natural numbers defined as that one for which there is an algorithm that enumerates its members.

THEOREM 3.1. *Given any recursive set R of natural numbers there is a formula $\chi_R(x)$ which represents R in the sense that for all n,*

$$n \in R \longrightarrow (\mathbf{ZF} \vdash \chi_R(\ulcorner n \urcorner) \text{ and } n \notin R \, (\mathbf{ZF} \vdash \neg\chi_R(\ulcorner n \urcorner))$$

Recursive sets of finite sequences and recursive predicates in several variables are likewise representable.

([16], p. 40). I note that this theorem is proved in metatheory that is, in a language referring to finitistic metatheoretical objects by means of natural numbers in the place of symbols introduced in an extension of **ZF** by definitions. Now I give a proof that the set of theorems of a consistent and recursive set of axioms **T** is not itself recursive.

THEOREM 3.2. *Let T be any consistent set of axioms extending* **ZF**. *Then the set of theorems $\{y; \, T \vdash y\}$ is not recursive.*

Proof: If it were recursive, then by 3.1 there would be a formula $\chi(x)$ such that for any $y \in \{y; \, T \vdash y\}$:

$$(T \vdash y) \longrightarrow (\mathbf{ZF} \vdash \chi(\ulcorner y \urcorner))$$

and for any $y \notin \{y; \, T \vdash y\}$:

$$(T \nvdash y) \longrightarrow (\mathbf{ZF} \vdash \neg\chi(\ulcorner y \urcorner)).[18]$$

---

[18]The term $\ulcorner y \urcorner$ in W.V.O. Quine's convention corresponds to the symbol by definition in formal theory, representing the 'object' y of metatheory.

3. THE REFLEXION OF THE IMPREDICATIVITY

Now we fix y (by 3.3, p. 18) such that: $\mathbf{ZF} \vdash y \leftrightarrow \neg\chi(\ulcorner y \urcorner)$ **(1)**.

But this means that $T \nvdash y$ **(2)** for obviously y would not belong to the set $\{y; T \vdash y\}$ since it is logically equivalent to $\neg\chi(\ulcorner y \urcorner)$. Also by **(1)**, $\mathbf{ZF} \vdash y$ since $\mathbf{ZF} \vdash \neg\chi(\ulcorner y \urcorner)$. But then $T \vdash y$ **(3)** as T is taken to be a consistent extension of **ZF**.

By **(2)** and **(3)** we have that $T \nvdash y$ and $T \vdash y$ which means that T is inconsistent, a contradiction◇

It is straightforward to see how this result fits in the proof of Gödel's First Incompleteness Theorem, namely that if **T** is a recursive consistent extension of **ZF** then it is incomplete in the sense that there is a sentence φ such that $\mathbf{T} \vdash \varphi$ and $T \nvdash \neg\phi$. The simple proof of K. Kunen in [16] (p. 38) is as follows:

If there were no such φ, then for every φ either $\mathbf{T} \vdash \varphi$ or $\mathbf{T} \vdash \neg\varphi$ and, assuming **T** consistent, these cannot both be valid. Then we could decide whether $\mathbf{T} \vdash \varphi$ by programming a computer to start listing all formal deductions from **T** and stop when a deduction of φ or $\neg\varphi$ has been found. But this is conditioned on the recursiveness of the set $\{\varphi; \mathbf{T} \vdash \varphi\}$ which was proved by Theorem 3.2 not to be recursive.

In case we take **T** to be **ZF**, its incompleteness is in fact explicitly demonstrated by the undecidability of the *Axiom of Choice* (**ZF** $\nvdash$ **AC** and **ZF** $\nvdash$ $\neg$**AC**), whereas in case **T** is extended to **ZFC** its incompleteness is demonstrated by the undecidability of *Continuum Hypothesis* (**CH**) (**ZFC** $\nvdash$ **CH** and **ZFC** $\nvdash$ $\neg$**CH**).[19]

I turn again to the steps leading to the proof of incompleteness of any recursive and consistent extension **T** of **ZF** before going on with my arguments on the possibility of a phenomenological view of the matter.

By 3.1, it is proved by indirectly applying metatheoretical means that any recursive set, essentially any recursively enumerable process, is formally representable within **ZF** by corresponding to any metatheoretical (finitistic) object a **ZF**-formula with a free variable as a constant by definition in the place of the object. But, by Theorem 3.2, it is proved that there can be no recursively enumerable process to check all formal deductions from **ZF** (or from any recursive consistent extension **T**), which is a result partly due to the non-rigorous definition of the notion of finitistic in Level-2 assertions. This is particularly important, from my standpoint, as Level-2 assertions[20] do not involve

---

[19] Generally, no matter that one extends **ZF** to a recursive and consistent **T**, the First Incompleteness Theorem guarantees that there will always be sentences undecidable by **T**.

[20] An example of a Level-2 satisfaction formula within **ZF** is:

$$\mathbf{ZF} \vdash \forall x \in \omega \ (\chi_{\text{odd}}(x) \lor \chi_{\text{odd}}(x + \ulcorner 1 \urcorner)) \ \mathbf{(1)}$$

where there is no strict definition of the finitistic character of objects x, whereas in a Level-1 formula such as $\chi_{\text{odd}}(x) \equiv \exists y \in \omega \ (x = 2\ulcorner y \urcorner + 1)$ **(2)** one should be able to check, for instance, whether $\mathbf{ZF} \vdash \chi_{\text{odd}}(\ulcorner 7 \urcorner)$ or $\mathbf{ZF} \vdash \neg\chi_{\text{odd}}(\ulcorner 12 \urcorner)$.

The 'asymmetry' with respect to the finitistic character of the formal objects-variables of formulas in **(1)** and **(2)**, is evidently due to the 'asymmetric character' between the universal and existential quantifiers of respective formulas. It seems reasonable, on this account, to draw a parallel with the *Verifizierbarkeit* and *Falsifizierbarkeit* principles in the Popperian theory of knowledge (see: *Logik der Forschung*, Wien: Springer, 1934).

rigorously defined finitistic objects and consequently do not fall within the range of strictly acceptable formulas in the sense of 3.1. Such an assertion, i.e. **ZF** $\vdash \forall u\ \exists! w\ x(u,w)$, is a key step in the proof of the following well-known theorem by which it is partly due 3.2; this theorem also stands behind the Second Incompleteness Theorem and Tarski's Undefinability of Truth.

THEOREM 3.3. *If $\varphi(x)$ is any formula in one free variable, x, then there is a sentence ψ such that*

$$\mathbf{ZF} \vdash \psi \leftrightarrow \varphi(\ulcorner \psi \urcorner)$$

(see: [16], pp. 40-41).

It seems there is some underlying effect of the non-rigorously finitistic character of the metatheoretical objects represented at least in the satisfaction formula **ZF** $\vdash \forall u\ \exists! w\ x(u,w)$ in getting the result of the theorem above and consequently of 3.2. In turn, 3.2 is applied to prove the First Incompleteness Theorem, i.e., that there exists a sentence φ within a recursive and consistent extension **T** of **ZF** such that $\mathbf{T} \vdash \varphi$ and $T \nvdash \neg \phi$.

The constraint of finitistic with regard to a formal object U is also evident in S.C. Kleene's approach, in [15], to be able to talk about a decision procedure or, in other words, about a metamathematical effectively decidable predicate $\mathcal{R}(\mathbf{x}, Y)$, where Y is a proof of the formal object $A(\mathbf{x})$, $\mathbf{x}$ being the numeral corresponding to a natural number x. This would make possible by a Gödel numbering of the metamathematical statement 'Y is a proof of $A(\mathbf{x})$' to correlate to the effectively decidable predicate $\mathcal{R}(\mathbf{x}, Y)$ an effectively decidable number-theoretic predicate (function)

$$R(x,y) \equiv \{y \text{ is the natural number correlated to formal object } Y$$

$$\text{such that } \mathcal{R}(x,Y)\}.$$

This way, and also by Church's thesis, mainly based on heuristic evidence, that every effectively calculable function (every effectively decidable predicate) is general recursive, we are led to an equivalence of the notions of a general recursive and an effectively decidable predicate. This leads, though, to an unsolvability of the decision problem within a formal system **S**, that is, to the non-existence of a decision procedure for determining the provability of any formula in **S** ([15], pp. 309 & 313)). It turns out that determining a formula of the system **S** as provable by effectively defining a corresponding formula $B(\mathbf{x})$ for any given natural number x, would implicitly involve a non-rigorous notion of finitistic for the formal objects involved as it was the case in the derivation of 3.2 which resulted in the non-recursiveness of the set of theorems deduced from a recursive and consistent extension **T** of **ZF**.

The vaguely finitistic character of metatheoretical objects in establishing incompleteness results can be also seen in the original form of Gödel's First Incompleteness Theorem, as presented in [15], (p. 208). As it stands, we can generate, relying on Gödel numbering, an undecidable formula $Ap(\mathbf{p})$ by

3. THE REFLEXION OF THE IMPREDICATIVITY

substituting in applying Cantor's diagonal method the numeral **p** for the free variable α in $A_p(\alpha) \equiv \forall \mathbf{b}\ \neg A(\alpha, \mathbf{b})$, where p is the Gödel number of the formula $Ap(\alpha)$, and **b** is the the Gödel number of the proof of this formula. Therefore, the formula $A_p(\mathbf{p}) \equiv \forall \mathbf{b}\ \neg A(\mathbf{p}, \mathbf{b})$ asserts its own unprovability but on the (dubious) implicit assumption that Cantor's diagonal method preserves the finitistic character of metamathematical objects in an *ad infinitum* process of enumeration.[21]

So far undecidable statements of **ZF** have to do in an explicit or implicit sense with some kind of uncountable infinity e.g. **CH**, **AC**, **SH** (*Suslin's Hypothesis*), **KH** (*Kurepa's Hypothesis*), etc., and they are moreover proved to be in one or the other way interconnected; for instance, **Con(ZFC)** $\longrightarrow$ **Con(ZFC+ CH)** and **Con(ZFC)** $\longrightarrow$ **Con(ZFC+¬CH)**; **SH** follows from **MA + ¬CH**[22] but it also holds: $\Diamond \to \neg$**SH** while $\Diamond$ is consistent with **GCH** ([16], Ch. II).

As **CH** is a statement most directly associated with mathematical continuum, it is worth referring to P. Cohen's conclusion in *Set Theory and the Continuum Hypothesis* that " the problem of **CH** is not one which can be avoided by not going up in type to sets of real numbers. A similar undecidable problem can be stated using only the concept of real numbers." ([1], pp. 151-152). Cohen went on to state that even in postulating as a vague article of faith that any statement in arithmetic is decidable in a higher order system such as **ZF** Set Theory by adding perhaps some extra appropriate infinity axiom, there will still remain set-theoretical questions which cannot be expressed as statements about integers alone. Now, keep in mind that on p. 18 I referred to the underlying effect a non-rigorous definition of finitistic, concerning metatheoretical objects, might have on proving the non-recursiveness of the set of theorems deduced from a consistent extension of **ZF**. We may say that a loose notion of finitistic in metatheory (as reflected, e.g. in Level-2 assertions) 'plants a bug' in the structure of the proof of 3.3, whose application thereafter in 3.2 leads to the proof of non-recursiveness of the set of theorems of a consistent extension **T** of **ZF**. The latter result essentially means that the expressional depth of set-theoretical statements exceeds that of any statement involving only integers.

Insofar, the content of the discussion can motivate a two-fold claim: 1) to the extent that finitistic metatheoretical objects are conceived by some form of concrete intuition as unique and well-defined objects in a finite-time apprehension or, in a phenomenological approach, as well-defined, noematic objects

---

[21] There is a certain controversy with respect to Cantor's diagonal method known also as *Diagonalverfahren*, as it is thought to use self-referential or non-predicative concepts like 'the set of all sets'. On account of my approach developed in this article, this may be related with the dubious finitistic character of metamathematical objects in an *ad infinitum* enumeration and the possibility of forming classes of corresponding formal objects as properly meant sets. Lastly, concerning alternative versions of incompleteness proofs presented, for instance, in [3] and [20] they do not vary substantially in content and thus change nothing to my arguments.

[22] **MA** is the well-known Martin's Axiom which is also a statement making claims about uncountable infinity.

of finitely many intentional acts in the open-ended horizon of experience, they may define in abstraction recursive sets such as those of 3.1 and they can be represented by means of set-theoretical formulas as 'lawful' formal objects in any consistent **ZF** extension. 2) in the case, though, that they are not rigorously finitistic but let a shade of inherent vague infinity in their conception, in a sense contrary to the above, their metatheoretical non-finitary content 'slips' through the syntactical structure of corresponding proofs (for instance, that one of 3.3) to finally generate the non-recursiveness of set-theoretical deductions and consequently undecidability results on a formal-theoretical level.

Serious doubts have been expressed concerning the **CH** question, namely, whether any new axioms will settle the matter alluding to an inherent vagueness of this hypothesis that seems to point to some kind of non-analytic character of **CH**. It is noteworthy that in 1947 in *What is Cantor's Continuum Problem?* [6], K. Gödel claimed that if Cantorian theory completely describes some well-defined reality then it should ultimately decide **CH** as either true or false and its eventual undecidability would mean that the difficulties of the problem " are perhaps not purely mathematical". It was well after his views at the time, that P. Cohen (in 1962) proved the independence of **CH** from the rest of the axioms of **ZFC** (along with that of **AC** from **ZF**), thus leaving the discussion open till now as to the fundamental character of these questions within Cantorian theory.

My view is that there should be some inherent reason that these statements have been proved independent from the existing axioms of **ZF** or **ZFC** theory. In one or the other way these or any other sentence making claims about the nature and properties of actual infinity touch on what by its very nature is non-analytic; they touch, as we saw in earlier sections, on what ultimately grounds continuous unity as an objective whole. For instance, they 'touch' on what is making possible to conceive the first m terms of an unfolding choice sequence all at once in actual presence, $< a_{(0)}, a_{(1)}, .., a_{(m-1)} >$, prior to the assumption of a continuity principle in intuitionistic analysis. Or, in yet another case, assuming the power-set axiom, on the possibility to conceive the set $\mathcal{P}(\omega)$ of all finite subsets of a set of the power of first countable limit ordinal ω, as an actually existing collection of finitistic objects.

To come back to the notion of temporal reduction on a phenomenological level, talking about the possibility of an objective continuous whole is a way of introducing an absolute subjectivity on which this objective whole should be rooted and this subjectivity should not be reducible to any other kind of objectivity for it would then belong to the universe of all possible objectivities. In a yet deeper leap of thought this subjectivity should be taken as a 'non-temporal' subjectivity which by its very essence 'constitutes' and cannot be objectively constituted, and on this account it cannot be predicated even by the predicates of existence and individuality for it should then be an objectivity in constituted time. Then we are left with no analytic means to describe it and its only possible ontification is through its objective 'mirror'-reflexion, as an ever-instantiated continuous whole in the progression of temporal consciousness. This transcendental ego of the most radical (or supplementary) reduction of temporal consciousness, which Husserl in his later Bernau Manuscripts (1917/18) [14], identified with the rather obscure notion of primitive process (*Urprozess*) may be taken, as bold an assertion this might sound, to underlie the inherently impredicative character of objective (intuitive) continuum 'reflected' on the formal-mathematical level in the impredicativity of mathematical continuum; for instance, this kind of impredicativity seems to underlie the special inclusion relation part/whole, in which the part belongs to the same genus as the undivided whole or yet the circularities generated in such definitions where the *definiens* cannot be defined but in terms of the *definiendum* (e.g. in the definition of an open interval of the real line).

This way we are led to two fundamentally distinct levels of perception: the constituted one, on which to 'embed' the known predicable universe of any analytic theory, naturally including any formal-mathematical discipline and the constituting one which is founded on the presupposition of a purely transcendental subjectivity. Therefore, inquiring on whether the cardinality of $\mathcal{P}(\omega)$ should be equal or greater to the next cardinal ω_1 (or whether the *Generalized Continuum Hypothesis* (**GCH**) holds for any cardinal α : $2^{\aleph_\alpha} = \aleph_{\alpha+1}$), seems to reduce on a constitutional level, and irrespective of any particular cardinalities on the canonical scale involved, to the fundamentally distinct character between what belongs to the constituted level of reality, that is, what is predicable and analytically expressible by first-order means in a finite or ideally in a countably infinite number of steps and what constitutes this very level, objectified as a continuous whole and where any analytic description necessarily engenders some kind of circularity. For example, producing a sequence of finitistic objects as subsets of ω by some digital device is a recursively enumerable process and it belongs to the constituted level. However, this is done against the backdrop of the constituting level making possible, e.g. to conceive the collection $\mathcal{P}(\omega)$ of all (or of some) subsets of ω, in its totality, as a constituted whole in continuous unity.

Consequently, in the context of this discourse, we can clearly distinguish, e.g. between the level corresponding to recursively enumerable processes and consequently to recursive sets, such as the set of natural numbers, which involves the intuition of strictly finitistic metatheoretical objects and the level corresponding to an intuition of actual infinity associated with non-rigorously finitistic objects in Level-2 assertions or in Cantor's *Diagonalverfahren*.

4 Conclusion

In this article I have tried to articulate a possible relation between the transcendence and consequently the impredicativity on the level of constitution of temporal consciousness and the inherent impredicativity of intuitive continuum within the first-order predicative environment of a formal theory. In doing so, I turned my attention to the subjective ego of the continuous unity of temporal consciousness in Husserlian phenomenology as the possible underlying 'root' of the impredicativity of mathematical continuum. Probably, this is not the kind of approach that would make a professed platonist or an unrepentant formalist eager to applaud.

Yet, there has been an approach nurtured some decades now towards a view of mathematical activity and of mathematical objects, in general, as ultimately linked to specific mental processes and consequently to certain modes of functioning of the brain or even deeper of consciousness. The possibility of establishing a connection of a yet largely unexplored breadth between the modes of constitution of temporal consciousness and of certain formal questions relative to the mathematical continuum seems grounded, in principle at least, on the claim put forth in the Introduction and in Section 2, that objects of formal-mathematical theories are abstractions of perceptual-intentional objects through a certain kind of categorial intuition. Moreover, the fact that we come across the impredicative character of mathematical continuum in everyday mathematical practice, e.g. in terms of an overlapping of the definition of a *definiens* with that of *definiendum* in many formal definitions, is something that no present day mathematician can possibly deny.

It is hard to tell the outcome, in view of the ontological (not kinetic) character of the descriptive tools of any formal theory, that an in-depth review of mathematical continuum might have, as fundamentally related to each subject's modes of constitution of temporal consciousness, but it could possibly offer a whole new approach to the general question of continuum and perhaps an interaction with other disciplines (e.g., quantum mechanics, neurobiology, etc.). The pending question in the core of this discussion could anyway be whether there is something transcendental, almost bordering to the 'mystical', in the self-constitution of temporal consciousness as the ultimate source of the unity of the world and its objects (including formal ones), or whether the impredicativity of intuitive and mathematical continuum rather stems from the fact that we may not be entitled to a consistent and complete description of the objects of a universe - be it a material or a formal one - that contains the universe (and ourselves) as one of its objects.

BIBLIOGRAPHY

[1] Cohen, P.: (1966), *Set Theory and the Continuum Hypothesis*, Mass.: W.A. Benjamin.
[2] Drake, F., Singh, D.: (1996), *Intermediate Set Theory*, Chichester: J. Wiley & Sons.
[3] Enderton, H.: (1972), *A Mathematical Introduction to Logic*, New York: Academic Press.

4. CONCLUSION

[4] Feferman, S.: (1999), Does mathematics need new axioms?, *American Mathematical Monthly*, 106, pp. 99-111.
[5] Føllesdal, D.: (1999), Gödel and Husserl, in: *Naturalizing Phenomenology*, pp. 385-400, Stanford: Stanford Univ. Press.
[6] Gödel, K.: (1947), What is Cantor's Continuum Problem?, *The American Mathematical Monthly*, 54, 9, pp. 515-525.
[7] Heelan, P.: (1988), *Space-Perception and the Philosophy of Science*, University of California Press.
[8] Heyting, A.: (1966), *Intuitionism, An Introduction*, Amsterdam: North-Holland Pub.
[9] Husserl E.: (1974), *Formale und Transzendentale Logik*, Hua, Band XVII, hsgb. P. Janssen, Den Haag: M. Nijhoff.
[10] Husserl, E.: (1970), *The Crisis of European Sciences and Transcendental Phenomenology*, transl. D. Carr, Evanston: Northwestern University Press.
[11] Husserl, E. (1976), *Ideen zu einer reinen Phänomenologie und phänomenologischen Philosophie, Erstes Buch*, Hua, Band III/I, hsgb. Karl Schuhmann, Den Haag: M. Nijhoff.
[12] Husserl, E.: (1984), *Logische Untersuchungen*, Hua, Band XIX/1, Zweit. Band, Erst. Teil, hsgb. U. Panzer, Den Haag: M. Nijhoff.
[13] Husserl, E.: (1966), *Vorlesungen zur Phänomenologie des inneren Zeibewusstseins*, Hua, Band X, hsgb. R. Boehm, Den Haag: M. Nijhoff.
[14] Husserl, E.: (2001), *Die Bernauer Manuskripte über das Zeitbewußtsein (1917/18)*, hsgb. R. Bernet & D. Lohmar, Dordrecht: Kluwer Acad. Pub.
[15] Kleene, S.C.: (1980), *Introduction to Metamathematics*, New-York: North-Holland Pub.
[16] Kunen, K.: (1982), *Set Theory. An Introduction to Independence Proofs*, Amsterdam: Elsevier Sci. Pub.
[17] Livadas, S.: 2012, Are mathematical theories reducible to non-analytic foundations?, *Axiomathes Online*, DOI 10.1007/s10516-012-9182-3.
[18] Lohmar, D.: (2002), Elements of a Phenomenological Justification of Logical Principles, including an Appendix [...] on the Transfiniteness of the Set of Real Numbers, *Philosophia Mathematica*, 10, 3, pp. 227-250.
[19] Sartre, J. P.: (1943), *L'être et le néant*, Paris: Ed.Gallimard.
[20] Shoenfield, J.: (1967), *Mathematical Logic*, Reading, Mass.: Addison Wesley Pub.
[21] Sokolowski, R.: 1974, *Husserlian Meditations*, Evanston: Northwestern University Press.
[22] Tieszen, R.: (1984), Mathematical Intuition and Husserl's Phenomenology, *Noûs*, 18, 3, pp. 395-421.
[23] Van Atten, M. van Dalen, D. Tieszen, R.: Brouwer and Weyl: (2002), The Phenomenology and Mathematics of the Intuitive Continuum, *Philosophia Mathematica*, 10, 3, pp. 203-226.
[24] Van Dalen, D., van Atten, M.: (2002), Arguments for the Continuity Principle, *The Bulletin of Symbolic Logic*, 8, 3, pp. 309-347.

Impredicativity of Continuum in Phenomenology and in non-Cantorian Theories [0]

STATHIS LIVADAS

1 Introduction

Edmund Husserl held the early idea that pure mathematics belongs to the realm of exact sciences dealing with idealities, whereas phenomenology is a descriptive eidetic science of pure mental processes, as taken in the phenomenological attitude. They are fundamentally different in that they use distinct cognitive tools and turn their view to essentially different objects. This is Husserl's prevalent attitude to which he made references especially in *Ideen I* ([11]), where he asserted that even though they can reconcile, nevertheless they cannot take the place of one another.

It is my aim, in this article, to demonstrate how the phenomenological analysis of temporal consciousness cannot only provide a model of the intuitive and ultimately mathematical continuum, something that had already attracted the theoretical interest of prestigious mathematical names as that of H. Weyl and L. E. J. Brouwer, in early twentieth century, but can also motivate a novel approach of the ontology of intuitive continuum and its *ad hoc* axiomatization in the language of non-Cantorian theories. On a phenomenological level, I am mostly based on the analysis of the phenomenological constitution of time as it is developed in Husserl's *Phänomenologie des inneren Zeitbewußtseins* [14] and in the relevant work of J. Patočka in [20], as well as on the more general Husserlian notion of genetic-kinetic constitution. The genetic-kinetic character of constitution in phenomenological analysis is based on the assumption that the world of objects, suspending the question of its objective existence, is not given but as a unity of multiplicities as they are constituted in progression in the homogenous flux of multiplicities within temporal consciousness.

In this outlook, Husserl confronted in *Phänomenologie des inneren Zeitbewußtseins* the issue of a transcendental, non-temporal subjectivity objectified in the self-constituting unity of the flux of consciousness, which in a somehow circular turn is thought of later as constituted genetically in a kind of transcendental 'genesis' constantly generating temporality. Being convinced that the

---

[0]This article has been published as a chapter in: *Causality, Meaningful Complexity and Embodied Cognition*, (ed. A. Carsetti), Springer, (2010), pp. 185-199.

transcendental ego is given in temporal profiles - " time is the universal form of all egological genesis" he professed in the *Fourth Cartesian Meditation* - he was introducing, in effect, an impredicativity rooted in the phenomenology of time to the extent that it was radically reduced to an absolute transcendence.[1]

In any case, the phenomenological constitution of time may provide a model for the intuitive continuum and its associated impredicativity in the form of an objective unity[2] a motivation to reflect on its formal representation as an extension or beyond the 'horizon' factor in certain non-Cantorian mathematical theories that provide an alternative, phenomenologically oriented version of standard mathematics by negating conventional actual infinity and following the ever shifting horizon of our incorporating Life-World (*Lebenswelt*) as it happens, e.g. with the Alternative Set Theory (AST) of the Prague School (see [26]).

In the present article, I claim that the adoption of *ad hoc* extension principles or 'external' undefined predicates to standard Cantorian theories with respect to vagueness or fuzziness (roughly taken as associated with uncountable infinity), reflects on a formal-axiomatical level the impredicativity of the intuitive continuum conceived of as an objectified form of unity rooted in the absolute flux of consciousness and further reducible to the transcendental ego of consciousness in the Husserlian sense; this latter ego meant as the constituting factor of the continuous unity of the flux of inner temporality. As a matter of fact, concerning the intuitionistic approach to continuum which is founded on the notion of choice sequences, strong extension principles are also adopted, e.g. for the elements of the universal spread C ([25], p. 223). It should be noted that intuitionistically oriented H. Weyl had already developed, in *Das Kontinuum* (1918), a view of the intuitive continuum largely based on the phenomenological description of the consciousness of internal time ([25], p. 203).

Finally, as I take a closer look of these alternative approaches to the continuum, I point to its inherent indescribability by means of a first-order formal language[3]. I hold that this 'indescribability' originally manifests itself in the phenomenology of consciousness as the irreducibility of the continuous unity of

---

[1] Husserl did not clarify to the end the meaning of the absolute ego in general, of his *Cartesian Meditations* [7], and has drawn criticism on the part of philosophers such as Th. Adorno, who claims that Husserl did not succeed in getting rid of a grounded Cartesian ego ([1], pp. 227-228).

[2] The term impredicativity is used here in an analytically founded meaning in which the *definiens* cannot but be defined in terms of the *definiendum*, in the sense that the definition of an entity (object, concept) somehow involves or presupposes a totality including the entity being defined. This concerns, for example, the definition of an object by a quantified sentence in which the scope of the quantifiers includes the entity being defined; intuitively speaking, one cannot comprehend (or describe) the elements or parts but in terms of the whole. It should be noted in addition, that in certain Platonic texts, by impredicativity of an object it is meant the impossibility to assign to it any predicates at all, defined therefore as identically the non-being (Plato's *Parmenides*, 163D, Loeb Class. Library).

[3] A first-order formal language $\mathcal{L}$ is one that, roughly speaking, allows quantification over countably many variables of the language and does not allow quantification over higher order objects, e.g. sets or functions.

the constituting flux in itself, in contrast to the discrete mode of appearances of phenomena constituted as immanent unities within it.

In the immediately following section, I examine how the question of continuity in the fundamental level of evidence, arises as a circularity in the phenomenological description of the constitution of time consciousness.

2 Continuity in the Constituting Flux of Consciousness

In phenomenological analysis it is known that the conviction to an objective reality in an absolute sense is suspended by *Epochë* and substituted by a constituted reality approach. The constituted objects are immanent to the constituting flux of consciousness in which they are reflected in a certain mode, that is, for instance, in the *vor-zugleich* (anterior-simultaneous) mode that entails a continuum of phases trailing behind an original impression, each of which is a retentional consciousness of the preceding 'present' ([14], p. 104).

The temporal consciousness of appearances (*Erscheinungen*) is the continuous unity of a whole, that is, an all encompassing unity of the simultaneity and anteriority of the original impressions of actuality, transforming continuously every group of original impressions in the simultaneity, in a way that trails into an immediate posteriority which is a continuity and each of whose points is in the form of a homogeneous flow.[4]

It seems there is still a need to a more radical interpretation, in the phenomenological-kinetic fashion, of the continuous mode of the anterior-simultaneous flow of the original impressions with the tail of their retentions in the flux of consciousness. Husserl responded to this problematic by appealing to what he called the double intentionality of the flux of consciousness, that is, the immediate retention of an immanent object in the flux of consciousness, e.g. the immanence of the sonorous effect of a sound on the one hand, and the retention of the 'descending' sequence of passed-by retentions (in the anterior-simultaneous mode) of each original impression, as a continuous unity within the flux " Therefore, the flux is traversed by a longitudinal intentionality which, in the course of flux, overlaps with itself continuously", ([14], *transl. of the author*, p. 106-107); see also [2].

In this retentional-protentional mode of the constitution of the flux of consciousness - where by the term protention we must understand intentional, a-thematic expectation similar but asymmetrical to retention - there is a deficiency with regard to a definition in ontological terms of the term continuity, in characterizing the mode of constitution of the flux in itself. Husserl used this term as the mode in which retentions are constituted in a 'descending' sequence form, each term of this sequence being a continuous retention of the continuity

---

[4] " The totality of the group of original impressions is bound to this law: It transforms into a constant continuum (*stetiges Kontinuum*) of modes of consciousness, of modes of being-in-the flow and in the same constance, an incessantly new group of original impressions taking originally its point of depart, to pass constantly (*stetig*) in its turn in the being-in-the flow. What is a group in the sense of a group of original impresions remains in the modality of the being-in-the flow", ([14], *transl. of the author*, p. 102).

of preceding phases. This is also the case in the second part of *Phänomenologie des inneren Zeitbewußtseins*. There, referring to the retentional structure of the flux, Husserl talked about the essential nature of every linear continuum that makes possible departing from a point of intensity, to think of every other point as produced continuously from that one, where continuous production is being meant as production in continuous iteration. In this view, the constituted continuum of time, is a flux of continuous production of modifications of the modifications ([14], p. 130).

The term continuity is treated, in this respect, as a modality without any further specification in the description of the double intentionality of consciousness, that makes possible to fix the regard to the flux in itself constituted as a unity in consciousness. This would sooner or later lead to difficulties as, ultimately, one reaches the transcendence in the constitution of the flux in itself. We may note, in passing, that one is left *in vacuum* as to the ontological nature of continuum also in classical philosophy.[5]

In this phenomenological view, impredicativity is inherently associated with the constitution of the continuous unity of the absolute flux in itself and by itself in contrast to the discrete multiplicities of appearances, the latter taken as immanent objects of the flux of consciousness. In referring indirectly to this kind of impredicativity, Husserl claimed that it is impossible to extend the phases of this 'flux' in a continuous succession, to transform it mentally in a way that each phase 'extends' identically on itself, a certain phase of it belonging to a present that constitutes or to a past that also constitutes (not constituted) to the degree that it is an absolute subjectivity beyond any predicate and whose retentional continuity in the constituting flux is solely its objectification, its ontification by its 'mirror' reflexion ([14], p. 98).

We should also take into account that Husserl had already explicitly stated in *Philosophie der Arithmetik* ([8], pp. 24-25) the impossibility of the description of a collection of objects in phenomenological representation as a temporal instantaneity (*zeitliches Zugleich*), something that evidently points to the structure of inner experience.

---

[5]This problematic arises from the difficulty to describe ontologically under the same terms the continuum as a whole and its constituent elements in the sense of indecomposable individuals. In Plato's *Parmenides* the instantaneous change in the state of a physical body is attributed to the effect of a somehow intermediate state between rest and motion, termed ἐξαίφνης, which is not expressible in spatiotemporal terms (*Parmenides*, 156D, E, Loeb Class. Library), whereas in Aristotle's *On Coming to be and Passing away*, material points or lines are defined as limits, ⁀ορια, of material bodies which in turn cannot be composed by points or attachments but by indivisible bodies or magnitudes (*Coming to be and Passing away*, 320b 15 and 316b 15, Loeb Class. Library).

In R. Descartes, physical space in its infinitely divisible parts (up to extentional points) is defined as a primary substance, *Res extensa*, filled up with matter, as spatial extension is a substantial characteristic of matter (*Discours de la Méthode*, pp.168-169, Garnier Flammarion, Paris). These extensional individualities are defined in Leibnizian monadology as incarnations of unique monadic localities representing in particular the body which they 'affect' and whose entelechy realize. Space is thus, what results from those uniquely defined monads taken together (G. Leibniz, *Fifth Letter to Clark*, §47).

The self-constitution of the flux as a phenomenon in itself is not but an objectification of what is the ultimate subjectivity of the flux, put later in the *Cartesian Meditations* in the most general terms as the absolute ego. This phenomenological transcendence, the source of all temporality as Husserl came to believe, will be conceptually linked to the axiomatization of continuum in certain non-Cantorian mathematical theories, as phenomenologically constituted time may be regarded as the basis of the intuition of all continuity phenomena.

3 Impredicativity of the Phenomenological and Mathematical Continuum

3.1 The Phenomenological Reduction to the Absolute Subjectivity

Husserl came gradually to thoroughly examine the idea of the absolute ego in general, and in the Fifth Logical Investigation, around 1913, thought of the phenomenologically reduced ego as a 'residuum' resisting all reduction " identified with the unity of the set of structures which cause the various acts of consciousness to glue together into a single self-related stream" ([10], p. 541). It was not until the 1920s that Husserl began to face squarely the problem of the articulation of the nature and role of the transcendental ego in general, as deeply related to the source of temporal consciousness ([18], p. 173); as a matter of fact, a deeper account of it will emerge at the end of the 1920s in the Cartesian Meditations[6].

This does not mean that the problematic of a transcendental or absolute subjectivity and its relation to time consciousness had not already preoccupied him as it is evident from his lectures of 1904-1905 at Göttingen and his work up to 1910 and later, published in *Phänomenologie des inneren Zeitbewußtseins* under the nominal editorship of Martin Heidegger, and also in the Bernau manuscripts of 1917-1918. Moreover, in *Ding und Raum*, edited out of his 1907 lectures, Husserl talked of the unity - in fact continuous, unbroken unity - that is the primary characteristic of the phenomenological perception (*Wahrnehmung*), regarding the constitution of all spatiotemporal phases in consciousness out of pre-phenomenal experience. The particular abstract phases of this unity cannot be taken as such on their own but only as abstractions out of the continuous unity of the temporal flux. Concerning the spatiotemporality of things, Husserl acknowledged that he had not yet reached deep enough in the constitution of temporality and was conscious of the difficulties posed by the problem. It is very important to stress, at this point, his aporeia as to how the moments of *Wahrnehmung* in temporal constitution, make that appear in it so substantially different a time point and a time interval and (makes also) apprehensible the wondrous difference between any 'now'

---

[6] " The universe of living that composes the 'real' content of the transcendental ego is not co-possible but as the universal form of the flux, a unity in which all particular elements are integrated as flowing by themselves. We can see in them [the forms of the states of living] the formal laws of the universal genesis, according to which, thanks to a certain noetico-noematic structure, are constituted and united continuously the modes of flux: past, present, future." ([7], *transl. of the author*, pp. 63-64).

and 'just-passed-by' ([12], pp. 60-65).

If the double intentionality of the retention is a mode of constitution both of an object as such and of the immanent flux in itself, it is evident that it concerns an objectification of the flux in its extension. This means, if the most radical reduction is to be effectuated, we have to apprehend what is most subjective in the subject refusing to admit whatever is constituted and thus presented in a temporal extension.

What is left after this ultimate reduction is a transcendence that Husserl called also by the term *nunc stans* or eternal present (that is, beyond time) ([20], p. 165). This *nunc stans* which is a name for the transcendental ego of consciousness (or the ego in-act) cannot be brought into reflection but only through its 'mirror' autoreflexion, so there must be something interposed between its subjectivity acting now and its mirror objectification in the reflection.

J. Patočka implied that a kind of retention is interposed between pure ego in-act and reflected ego without which pure or transcendental ego of consciousness would be inaccessible. But retention, as a presupposition of every possible reflection on the transcendental ego is by itself a circularity since it has been previously put as a modal characteristic of the objectified flux of consciousness without any ontological or other designation. Patočka inferred, in any case, that the transcendental ego independently of its 'auto-alienation' in objectification, from which it is inseparable, is inaccessible. It follows that since each objectification points to something objectified one can secure the presupposition of an absolute subjectivity making possible this very objectification of the temporal flux as a whole and which transcends temporality in a phenomenological sense. Since, in turn, temporality is the necessary condition of every individuality and every existence in the world as well as of every first degree transcendental reflection, one cannot attribute to this transcendental ego the predicates of existence and individuality ([20], pp. 163-168). It turns out, that ultimately one is led to an impredicativity of the transcendental ego of consciousness in radical reduction which was, in fact, already implicitly present in the description of the double intentionality mode of the self-constituting flux.

The recourse to an impredicativity is implicit in Husserl's subsequent reduction, in *Formale und Transzendentale Logik*[7], of the laws of analytic logic to subjective laws of evidence. In the structure of analytic judgements that must ultimately refer to the 'things in themselves', one is led to a group of judgements referring directly to individuals for the possibility and essential structure of which nothing can be said in analytic terms, even that they necessarily possess a temporal form, a duration and a qualitative plenitude of duration ([13], p. 276).

Further, as individuals in themselves are given in the 'lowest level' by intentional experience, in the sense of a direct reference to individuals in themselves, it can be inferred that these individuals are the ultimate contents-substrates

---

[7]The original German text under the title '*Formale und Transzendentale Logik. Versuch einer Kritik der logischen Vernunft*', was published in 1929 in the *Jahrbuch für Philosophie und phänomenologische Forschung*, edited by E. Husserl, tome X, pp. 1-298.

of original judgements which are based on the most primary evidence which is that of experience. In view of this, Husserl turned to the phenomenological - transcendental principle of universal genesis of consciousness to provide a theoretical foundation to the passing from predicative evidences (originally given in the 'lowest-level' of evidence as individuals-in-themselves along with their categorial objectivities) to the impredicativity of experience as such, genetically constituted in every being's unity of the flux of consciousness (ibid., pp. 282-286 & pp. 293-296).

I call attention with regard to this phenomenologically generated impredicativity in the flux of time consciousness, to G. Longo's view, in [17], in which he states that the intuitive circularity in phenomenological time is reflected in the apparent paradoxes of mathematical construction where the " impredicativity of analysis permits a possible formalization of this intuitive circularity" ([17], pp. 406-407).[8] It is also significant to remark that the intuitive continuum as conceived by L.E.J. Brouwer and H. Weyl is largely based on the Husserlian description of the consciousness of 'internal' (i.e., phenomenologically constituted) time, while both Brouwer and Weyl distinguished between 'internal' or intuitive time and 'external' or scientific and measurable time. Moreover, Brouwer's idea of the primordial intuition of mathematics is concerned only with 'internal' (intuitive) time ([25], pp. 203-204).

3.2 The Continuum in the Alternative and Internal Set Theories

It seems purposeful, at first, to refer to the Husserlian idea of scale invariance, as evident generic similarity which can lead to minima visibilia as point-like ultimate minimalities bearing the same eidetic relationships 'discovered' in the macroscopic universe, (see [Husserl, 1973], §48, p.166). This idea seems to have an important influence on the 'shift of the horizon' principle in the Alternative Set Theory (AST)[9].

In the *Crisis of European Sciences and Transcendental Phenomenology* [9], Husserl made more broadly known his notion of the Life-World (*Lebenswelt*) as the sense-intuited preidealized world which is the grounding soil for the 'objective-true' world of the sciences of exactness. Out of this sense-intuited world is substructed the classical mathematical world of idealized limit-shapes and the plena to which they belong. This intuitively given world can be intuited as an endlessly and ever shifting horizon in reference to which all particular causalities can be anticipated and are not themselves given. It was this par-

---

[8] Impredicative notions in mathematics are generally considered those in which the *definiens* uses the *definiendum*, e.g. an open set (open interval) of the real line is not defined as a collection of its points but in terms of other basic open sets (bounded open intervals).

[9] This evident generic similarity justifies the transposition of the eidetic relationships 'discovered' in the universe of common intuition to that beyond its 'horizon'. Although P. Vopěnka implicitly assumes this phenomenological principle in his prolongation axiom, he seems to deny it in a later expository article on the philosophical foundations of Alternative Set theory where he allowed for the possibility of a complete collapse of our intuitions beyond a genuinely qualitative shift of the horizon to apeiron ([27]). But this eventuality contradicts with the Husserlian idea of our Life-world as *grndenden Boden* (grounding soil) of an ever shifting horizon.

ticular idea of the shifting horizon of *Lebenswelt* that motivated P. Vopěnka's definition of the countability of a class ([26], p. 39):

" If a large set x is observed then the class of all elements of x that lie before the horizon need not be infinite but may converge toward the horizon. The phenomenon of infinity associated with the observation of such a class is called countability".

Two of the fundamental ideas of Alternative Set Theory, as exposed in [27], are those of natural infinity in contrast to idealized classical infinity and the sharpening of the horizon toward infinity involving by necessity the presence of an observer. In this phenomenologically motivated perspective, natural infinity presents itself to us as a converging series of finite 'appearances' to an ever shifting horizon, the closer to which they are the less definite and sharp they seem. In taking account of such a sequence, natural infinity in its most basic form presents itself as countable natural infinity. Classical countable infinity is derived from this sequence by constantly sharpening our view, that is by moving the horizon further and further so that it stabilizes as 'unchangeable, definite and sharp' ([27], p.118). The most radical and qualitative shift of the horizon, beyond which natural infinity no longer sharpens and becomes vague and uncountable, is axiomatized by the adoption of prolongation principle[10] whose deeper content is reflected, in classical Cantorian mathematics, in the 'incompatible' character of the power-set axiom which refutes, in effect, the original Cantorian conception of a set as anything that can be counted ([16], , p. 95).

The prolongation principle, taken as a conservative extension axiom, together with an *ad hoc* existence axiom (i.e., the axiom of existence of proper semisets), considered as 'external' to a first-order axiomatical system with a built-in predicate for the natural numbers in Weyl's sense, axiomatize the indefiniteness and blurriness of infinity beyond the horizon of countability. In this sense they reflect, in axiomatization, the impredicativity of the intuitive continuum which is irreducible to a countable infinity in advancing to an ever shifting horizon.[11] The conceptual motivation is explicitly stated by P. Vopěnka, as that of extending the 'sense'-intuited AST universe of countable classes to the vagueness of infinity beyond countability, shifting in effect the horizon of Husserlian *Lebenswelt*.

Countability of classes is an ever shifting finiteness, whereas uncountability

---

[10] If F and G stand for functions, which in the AST extended universe are considered as sets or classes, the Prolongation Principle states that: *For each countable function F, there is a set function f such that $F \subseteq f$.* It is important here to have in mind that countability of a function is, in fact, countability of a class of ordered pairs of elements and that a set function can be an uncountable set of ordered pairs of elements.

[11] In the formal level, AST works with sets and classes as objects. Sets are definite, might be very large but sharply defined and finite from the classical point of view. Therefore, in its universe of sets, AST accepts the axioms of Zermelo - Fraenkel system with the exception of the axiom of classical infinity. Classes represent indefinite clusters of objects such as the set N of natural numbers in the classical sense. In this context the notion of a semiset represents, roughly, blurriness and non-surveyability in the 'observation' inside a very large set (see: [26], Ch. I).

3. IMPREDICATIVITY

is essentially identified with the vagueness or indiscernibility beyond the horizon of intuitively based hereditary finiteness. But in formalizing continuous unity beyond the horizon of discreteness, AST has to adopt extension principles that are, in fact, *ad hoc* external principles within a first-order universe of a countable domain. On this account, the prolongation principle is an *ad hoc* axiomatical foundation for the definition of continuity properties in AST theory, by means of indiscernibility equivalences[12] which, even though they are formal-mathematical notions, incorporate in their definition the actual infinity[13] character of this principle.

In my view, the two aforementioned axioms of AST, fundamentally reflect the impredicativity generated by the phenomenology of temporal consciousness, in the sense that these *ad hoc* axioms, axiomatizing the 'passing' to the continuum within the formal theory, 'bridge', in effect, the gap between the naturally intuited discreteness of a countable path to the horizon, and the continuous unity intuited as a hazy vagueness beyond it; think in parallel, the discreteness of the multiplicities of appearances (of original impressions) as immanences within temporal consciousness, held together within the continuous unity of the flux in itself and by itself.

Concerning the Internal Set Theory (IST), which is considered a nonstandard mathematical theory and, moreover, a non-Cantorian version of Robinson's nonstandard analysis, in the sense that it is (indirectly) based on the implicit presence of an interacting 'observer' performing his 'observations' in a local and non-Cantorian way, the axiomatization of continuum is based on the introduction of a (seemingly syntactical) 'external' predicate, termed *standard*. I must remark here that the non-Cantorian designation means generally that the Axiom of Choice (AC)[14] of the Cantorian system does not hold. Moreover, since AC implies the excluded middle principle, the negation of the latter implies the negation of AC, (see: [5]). But to the extent that the negation of actual or Cantorian infinity is a conceptual presupposition of the negation of AC, it follows that any theory that denies actual infinity in its axiomatization can be characterized as non-Cantorian. In this respect as mentioned above,

---

[12]The indiscernibility equivalences $\doteq$ are binary relations which are Π-classes (having the reflexive, symmetric and transitive property among others) and equipped in addition with the property of compactness; that is, for each infinite set U there is at least a pair (x, y) with $x, y \in U$ such that, $x \neq y$ and $x \doteq y$. For further details and AST topological definitions (monads, figures, closures, connected sets, etc.), based on indiscernibility equivalences, see: [26], (pp. 83-96).

[13]Actual infinity, taken in the sense of the continuous unity of a whole in presentational immediacy, should be regarded as a kind of infinity freely generated through our mental faculties, where any possible imaginable bound can be automatically annulled by further extending it through imagination.

[14]In a less strict mathematical formulation the Axiom of Choice states that: *Given a non-empty class of non-empty sets, a set can be formed containing precisely one element taken from each set in the given class.* Although the Axiom of Choice might strike someone as being intuitively obvious, it may prove to be less so if one has to deal with sets or classes of uncountably infinite cardinalities. An intuitive version of AC is produced by AST theorist A. Sochor with respect to countable classes in an AST sense ([15], p. 152).

IST theory is linked to the intensional development of nonstandard analysis in which infinitesimals and infinitely large numbers do not exist in an objective way as in the extensional case (Robinson's nonstandard approach, ultrapower constructions, superstructures)[15], but their existence has a subjective meaning related to the limitations of an 'observer' for whom, within his witnessed universe, the predicate *standard* plays the semantic role of 'fixed' or 'sharp' in informal mathematical discourse.

E. Nelson's Internal Set Theory essentially adopts the axioms of Zermelo-Fraenkel & the Axiom of Choice Theory (**ZFC**), together with three extra axioms 'taking care' of the semantic content of the undefined predicate *standard*. These axioms, i.e. the Idealization Axiom (I), the Standardization Axiom (S) and the Transfer Axiom (T) can be thought of as close in semantic content with the prolongation and the existence of semisets axioms of AST, to the extent that they generate in the syntax of IST a shift of the horizon of 'fixedness' ([19], pp. 2-12). The intuition, for instance, behind the Idealization Axiom is that we can only fix a finite number of objects at a time and the intuition behind the Transfer axiom is that if something is true for all standard (fixed) but arbitrary x's then it is true for all x's.

By direct application of the Idealization Axiom one may prove that there exists at least a nonstandard element in every infinite set. In particular there exists at least a nonstandard natural number, a fact that by itself implies that vagueness or indiscernibility is not necessarily linked to the real number structure in a model-theoretic sense but it is rather the result of the introduction of the 'external' predicate standard along with its *ad hoc* axiomatical equipment in the Cantorian **ZFC** system; it is by this axiomatical means that the horizon of IST standardness is 'shifted'. As it is the case with the AST-indiscernibility, all subsequent definitions involving vagueness along infinity (or infinitesimality) and all relevant topological notions are expressed in terms of external formulas involving the predicate *standard*.[16]

Topological and continuity properties, and more generally vagueness, are ultimately reduced to the 'influence' of the external to the Cantorian mathematics predicate *standard*, which in spite of its rather syntactical role in the context of IST at least as claimed by E. Nelson, acquires by the addition of the three *ad hoc* axioms above, a significant underlying semantic role in axiomatizing

---

[15] Concerning the extensional development of nonstandard analysis, mainly A. Robinson's version, one is led to the introduction of nonstandard elements in endorsing the Axiom of Choice or its logically equivalent Zorn's lemma in the definition of free ultrafilters, both in the construction of nonstandard structures as such and also in the proof of critical theorems (e.g., with respect to Loś theorem and Mostowski's collapsing function). For more details, the reader is referred to [21], [22] and to [4]; the last one for a more intuitive presentation of the Axiom of Choice.

[16] For instance, regarding any object that can be described uniquely within internal mathematics as standard, a real number x is defined as *infinitesimal* in case for all standard $\epsilon > 0$, we have $x \leq \epsilon$. Then, $x \cong y$ (x is *infinitely close* to y) in case $x - y$ is infinitesimal and, further, if $E \subseteq R$ and E is standard, E is *compact* in case for all $x \in E$, there is a standard $x_0 \in E$ with $x \cong x_0$. As far as classical mathematical continuity is concerned, then if f and x are standard, f is continuous at x in case: $y \cong x$ implies $f(y) \cong f(x)$, (see: [19], pp. 14-15).

3. IMPREDICATIVITY

vagueness.[17]

This axiomatically established shift of the horizon of 'fixedness' to the vagueness of continuum inside IST, by means of the adoption of the undefined predicate *standard* along its appropriate axiomatical forms, reflects on a formal-axiomatical level the impredicative character of the intuitive continuum 'generated', in a phenomenologically motivated approach, by the transcendental foundation of inner temporality; keep in mind that, as aforementioned, the impredicativity of continuous infinity in AST, is formally reflected in the adoption of the prolongation and the existence of proper semisets axioms.

The impredicativity of the Husserlian absolute ego of consciousness is essentially reflected in the impossibility to express under the same predicates of existence and individuality the structure of the temporal flux in itself as a self-constituting continuous unity and its 'constituent' immanences of phenomena together with their retentions - protentions. It is, in my view, this phenomenological transcendence that induces an 'indescribability' inside a non-Cantorian theory with regard to the vagueness of continuum generated by, so to say, hereditarily finite classes of 'observations', in making no use of *ad hoc* extension principles.

3.3 The Intuitionistic Approach to Continuum

I have already mentioned that Weyl based largely intuitive Continuum on the Husserlian description of the consciousness of internal time, whereas Brouwer's idea of intuitive Continuum can be readily comprehended in connection with Husserl's analysis of the phenomenology of internal time. In this context, the intuitionistic approach to natural numbers is based on an abstraction from a temporal process in which they are intuited as durationless sensations in discrete succession. Evidently the concept of duration does not apply to natural numbers, however the same cannot be held to be true of real numbers which are viewed, in intuitionism, as 'incomplete' or 'unfinished' objects. It is very important to state that in intuitionistic view " an act of abstraction that would give us a real number as a durationless point is not something of which we would be capable" ([25], p. 207).

Just as we do not experience durationless points in time, we do not experience extensionless points in space, therefore the intuitive continuum, as Brouwer and Weyl thought it, cannot be understood as a set of durationless or extensionless points. As it was the case with the alternative set theories described thus far, one is confronted, sooner or later, with the impredicative character of intuitive continuum. In this respect, both Brouwer and Weyl held that in order to capture the fluidity of intuitive continuum one should replace the element/set relation with a part/whole relation in which parts are of the same lowest genus as the undivided whole.

In view of this, Brouwer 'split' the continuum or interval (a non-denumerable set) into parts (subintervals) homogenous to the whole under the relation of

---

[17] For a thorough development of the notions of general topology based on the predicate and axioms of standardness in IST, I refer to [6], (p. 109).

inclusion (part/whole) in which the order relation between disjoint intervals is the natural order of the continuum abstracted from the progression of time. In this construction, a point P (or a real number P) is an indefinitely proceedable sequence of nested λ-intervals and a main difference with the classical approach lies in the fact that the point P is not something like the limiting point to which these nested intervals converge, in which case it would be defined as the accumulation point of the midpoints of these intervals.[18] The point P is the sequence itself and the λ-intervals are parts of the point P ([25], p. 212).

It may yet be be argued that even in the intuitionistic approach the part-/whole relation could be reduced to an element/set one if one assigns to each of the nested intervals a corresponding natural or rational number. Then the indefinitely proceedable sequence of those intervals could conceptually, in AST terms, stand for the countable class FN of natural numbers which, as aforementioned, represents a path to some vastly remote horizon inaccessible to us, beyond that of hereditarily finite countability.

This particular example is just a case of choice sequences as an intuitive foundation for real analysis. The underlying idea is that these sequences need not be lawlike, in the sense that when given an initial segment of them there need not be a law prescribing in advance any future terms of the sequence except of course for the natural assumption of the assignment of a unique value in each step. Brouwer's rationale was that by the indefinite procession of a choice sequence, irrespective of whether it is a lawlike or a lawless one, we preserve the intuition of continuum in the meaning that it cannot be reduced to a durationless point as it is always in progress; in contrast, Weyl had certain reservations about the status of lawless sequences as genuine and individual mathematical objects something that was also Husserl's point of view.

In any case both had to adopt, as it is the case with the previously reviewed non-Cantorian theories, certain *ad hoc* extension principles in the form, e.g. of the *Weak Continuity for Numbers* or the stronger *Continuity Principle for Universal Spreads* (L. Brouwer) or yet the *the Principle of Open Data* (H. Weyl), so as to formally axiomatize the intuitive continuum.

As a matter of fact, L.E.J Brouwer formulated the continuity principle for a universal spread C by prior defining a spread as a " law on the basis of which, if again and again an arbitrary complex of digits (a natural number)

---

[18]Let the λ-intervals be intervals of the form $[\frac{\alpha}{2^{\nu}-1}, \frac{\alpha+1}{2^{\nu}-1}]$. Then L.E.J Brouwer, in ([3], p. 69), defined real numbers as follows: We consider an indefinitely proceedable sequence of nested λ-intervals $\lambda_{\nu_1}, \lambda_{\nu_2}, .., \lambda_{\nu_n}, ..$ which have the property that every $\lambda_{\nu_{i+1}}$ lies strictly inside its predecessor λ_{ν_i} ($i = 0, 1, 2, ..$). Then, by the definition of λ-intervals, the length of each interval $\lambda_{\nu_{i+1}}$ at most equals half the length of λ_{ν_i} and therefore the lengths of the intervals converge to 0. [...] We call such an indefinitely proceedable sequence of nested-intervals, a point P or a real number P. It should be noted that the point P is thought of to be the sequence $\lambda_{\nu_1}, \lambda_{\nu_2}, .., \lambda_{\nu_n}, ..$ itself and not something as the limiting point (the unique accumulation point of the midpoints of these intervals) to which according to the classical conception these nested λ-intervals converge. Each of these λ_{ν_i} is considered then as part of the point P ([25], p. 212).

4. CONCLUSION

of the sequence ζ (a natural number sequence) is chosen, each of these choices either generates a definite symbol, or nothing, or brings about the inhibition of the process altogether with the definitive annihilation of its result;[...] Every sequence of symbols generated from the spread in this manner (which, therefore, is generally not representable in finished form) is called an element of the spread. We also consider the common mode of formation of the elements of a spread M as, for short, the spread M". Then, the *Continuity Principle for a Universal Spread* C is stated as following:

" A law that assigns to each element g of C an element h of A (the set of natural numbers), must have determined the element h completely, after a certain initial segment α of the sequence of numbers of g has become known. But then to each element of C that has α as an initial segment, the same element h of A will have to be assigned.", (see: [25], pp. 222-224). On the other hand, Weyl's principle of open data in its simplest form can be put formally as follows: $A\alpha \rightarrow \exists n \ (\alpha \in n) \ \& \ \forall \beta \in n \ (A\beta)$ where A stands for a syntactical variable of a predicate formula and α, β stand for lawless sequences. This principle essentially identifies under predication a lawless sequence α with all those lawless sequences of its 'neighborhood' starting with the same initial segment n, ([24], p. 14).

In a stronger than this continuity principle, if one denotes by Cont_{LS} the class of lawlike operations on lawless sequences assigning natural numbers to lawless sequences such that:

$$\text{for } \Gamma \in \mathrm{Cont}_{LS} \ \forall \alpha \ \exists x \ \forall \beta \in <\alpha_0, \alpha_1, .., \alpha_{x-1}> \ (\Gamma\alpha = \Gamma\beta)$$

then:

$$\forall \alpha \ \exists x \ A(\alpha, x) \longrightarrow \exists \Gamma \in \mathrm{Cont}_{LS} \ \& \ \forall \alpha \ A(\alpha, \Gamma\alpha)$$

([24], pp. 14-19). In conclusion, these extension principles, given an initial segment of any choice sequence, treat them as complete, individual objects by means of continuity (lawlike) operations, essentially in an extension to a vague horizon approach. In this way, intuitive continuum is 'grasped' axiomatically by *ad hoc* extension principles shifting the natural bounds of the finite and discrete which is represented, in the case of choice sequences, by their ever extensible initial segments.

4   Conclusion: A Reflection on the Impredicative Character of Continuum

In following Husserl's path to the transcendence of the absolute flux of consciousness and further of the pure ego in general, I came to realize that the content of the notion of intuitive continuum is deeply related to the original source of temporal consciousness as a necessary foundation for the objectified unity of each one's constitution of inner temporality. In view of this, an impredicativity of a constituted continuous whole is inevitably induced, as it is impossible to describe the constitution of the continuous flux of consciousness in itself in terms of the distinct, immanent multiplicities of registered-in objects of experience, without falling into circularities with regard to the notion of continuity, e.g. in the longitudinal retention of immanences. It is the essentially impredicative nature of continuum that is, on account of a reasoning in terms of a transcendental phenomenology with special emphasis on the character of inner temporality, reflected in the axiomatization of continuum in nonstandard and non-Cantorian versions of mathematical theories when they have to shift the hereditarily finite bounds of the local 'environment' of a potential 'observer' to the vagueness of (uncountable) infinity.

Adopting the Husserlian notion of Life-World intuited as an endlessly open and ever shifting horizon in Alternative Set Theory, or inducing vagueness at infinity as nonstandardness in Internal Set Theory, non-Cantorian and also intuitionistic theories, get in final count 'trapped' in the impredicativity of continuum when they shift the boundaries beyond naturally intuited countability within our witnessed universe. They have to adopt extra *ad hoc* extension axioms 'external' to the structure of a first-order mathematical system, something that essentially reflects the impredicativity or rather the impossibility of an ontology of the continuum. As Gödel was refuting Carnap's syntactical program using his second incompleteness theorem, he was proving in effect that " the mathematical essences we intuit could not be linguistic conventions. There are constraints on them that we do not freely invent or create. One might also say that this content or meaning will be 'abstract' relative to the rules of syntax. Mathematical intuition will therefore not be eliminable. In Husserl's language, categorial intuition will not be eliminable. Thus, instead of clarifying the meaning of abstract and non-finitary mathematical concepts by explaining them in terms of syntactical rules, abstract and non-finitary concepts are used to formulate the syntactical rules." ([23], p. 193).

The intuition of continuum as such, as well of objects of formal-mathematical theories bearing the essential possibility of correlation within a synthetic unity can be considered as based on a categorial intuition founded, in turn, on the intentional forms of 'lowest-level' experience genetically constituted within the continuous unity of the temporal flux of consciousness.

The impredicativity of continuum is manifest too in the impossibility to describe topological structures, to the extent that they are ultimately reduced to the notion of openness of sets which is inherently associated with the intuition of continuum, within the expressional means of a first-order formal language. Back in 1918, H. Weyl stated that it is an 'act of violence' to assume the perfect coincidence of the analytical construction of continuum with that of phenomenal space and time " [..]that is, the continuity given to us immediately by intuition (in the flow of time and motion) has yet to be grasped mathematically" ([28]).

It seems very doubtful that it could be ever grasped mathematically in any sense that would reflect the existence of an ontology of the continuum.

4. CONCLUSION

BIBLIOGRAPHY

[1] Adorno, T.: (1982), *Against Epistemology: A Metacritique* trans. W. Domingo, Oxford: Blackwell.
[2] Bernet, R.: (1983), "La présence du passé dans l'analyse husserlienne de la conscience du temps", *Revue de métaphysique et de morale*, 2, pp. 178-198.
[3] Brouwer, L.E.J.: (1992), *Intuitionismus*, (ed. D. van Dalen), Mannheim: Bibliograph. Institut, Wissenschaftsvelag.
[4] Connes, A., Lichnerowicz, A., & Schützenberger, M. P.: (2000), *Triangle of thoughts*, trans. J. Gage, Paris: Ed. Oedile Jacob.
[5] Diaconescu, R.: (1975), Axiom of Choice and complementation, *Proc. AMS*, 51, pp. 175-178.
[6] Diener, Fr. & Diener, M.: (1995), *Nonstandard Analysis in Practice*, Berlin: Springer-Verlag.
[7] Husserl, E.: (1931), *Méditations Cartésiennes*, transl. Emm. Levinas & G. Peiffer, Paris: Librairie A. Colin.
[8] Husserl, E.: (1970), *Philosophie der Arithmetik*, Hua XII, hsgb. Lothar Eley, Den Haag: M. Nijhoff.
[9] Husserl, E.:(1970), *The Crisis of European Sciences and Transcendental Phenomenology*, transl. D. Carr, Evanston: Northwestern University Press.
[10] Husserl, E.: (1970), *Logical Investigations*, transl. J.N. Findlay, New York: Humanities Press.
[11] Husserl, E.: (1982), *Ideas pertaining to a pure phenomenology and to a phenomenological philosophy*, trans. F. Kersten, London: M. Nijhoff Pub.
[12] Husserl, E.: (1973), *Ding und Raum: Vorlesungen*, Hua XVI, hsgb. U. Claesges, Den Haag: M. Nijhoff.
[13] Husserl, E.: (1984), *Logique formelle et logique transcendantale*, transl. S. Bachelard, Paris: Ed. PUF.
[14] Husserl, E.: (1996), *Leçons pour une Phénoménologie de la conscience intime du temps*, transl. H. Dussort, Paris: Ed. PUF.
[15] Lano, K.: (1993), The intuitionistic alternative set theory, *Annals of Pure and Applied Logic*, 59, pp. 141-156.
[16] Lavine S.: (1994), *Understanding the Infinite*, Cambridge Mass.: Harvard Univ. Press.
[17] Longo, G.: (1999), The Mathematical Continuum: From Intuition To Logic, in: *Naturalizing Phenomenology*, Ch. 14, pp. 401-425, Stanford: Stanford Univ. Press.
[18] Moran, D.: (2000), *Introduction to Phenomenology*, New York: Routledge.
[19] Nelson, E.: (1986), *Predicative Arithmetic. Mathematical notes*, Princeton: Princeton Univ. Press.
[20] Patočka, J.:(1992), *Introduction à la Phénoménologie de Husserl*, transl. Er. Abrams, Grenoble: Ed. Millon.
[21] Robinson, A.: (1966), *Non-standard Analysis*, Amsterdam: North-Holland Pub.
[22] Stroyan, K.D., Luxemburg, W.A.J.: (1976), *Introduction to the theory of infinitesimals*, New York: Academic Press.
[23] Tieszen, R.: (1998), Gödel's Path from the Incompleteness Theorems (1931) to Phenomenology (1961), *The Bulletin of Symbolic Logic*, 4, 2, pp. 181-203.
[24] Troelstra, A.: (1977), *Choice sequences. A Chapter of Intuitionistic Mathematics*, Oxford: Clarendon Press.
[25] Van Atten, M., Van Dalen, D., & Tieszen, R.: (2002), Brouwer and Weyl: The Phenomenology and Mathematics of the Intuitive Continuum, *Philosophia Mathematica*, 10, 3, pp. 203-226.
[26] Vopěnka, P.: (1979), *Mathematics in the Alternative Set theory* Teubner-Texte zur Mathematik, Leipzig: Teubner Verlag.
[27] Vopěnka, P.: (1991), The Philosophical foundations of Alternative Set Theory, *Int. J. General Systems*, 20, pp. 115-126.
[28] Weyl, H.: (1977), *Das Kontinuum*, (ed. B. Veit), Napoli: Bibliopolis.

The Continuum Question in Mathematical Foundations. A Phenomenological Review [0]

STATHIS LIVADAS

1 Introduction

The main scope of this article is to give a phenomenological perspective to questions pertaining to the conception and nature of continuum in mathematical foundations. In doing so, I concentrated primarily on the relevant mathematical stuff and on phenomenologically motivated methods of interpretation. This naturally involves the question of the properties and the cardinality of continuum in mathematical foundations, in particular the landmark independence proof of *Continuum Hypothesis* (**CH**)[1] by K. Gödel and P. Cohen.

One might wonder, in the first place, whether the mathematical theory of continuum in the context of Cantorian set theory has anything to do with the phenomenology of intuitive continuum; my answer to this rightful objection is that this depends to a considerable extent on the general philosophical stance of someone doing mathematics and especially foundational mathematics. If he regards mathematical objects as ideal objects preexisting in some kind of platonic mathematical realm or on the other extreme if he regards mathematics as reducible to a consistent set of axioms and rules presiding a game of otherwise meaningless symbols, then he might find the following discussion as rather meaningless. But if he finds mathematics as essentially representing certain functions of human consciousness then he might accept my discussion as meaningful indeed and my conclusions as making some headway towards a novel approach to certain open questions of a formal-analytic character.

A significant part of this work reviews the question of **CH** in a phenomenological context, which is partially focused on the reduction of analytic propositions to non-analytic in content individuals-substrates as irreducible intentional moments of non-reflective consciousness and on their subsequent constitution

---

[0]This article has been published in original form in the journal *La Nuova Critica*, (2009), V. 53-54, pp. 23-50.

[1]In the *Generalized Continuum Hypothesis*, (**GCH**), it is stated that $2^{\aleph_\alpha} = \aleph_{\alpha+1}$ for any ordinal α, which means that the number of subsets of a set of power $\aleph_\alpha$ is $\aleph_{\alpha+1}$. The simpler in form *Continuum Hypothesis* (**CH**) assumes that the number of subsets of a set of power $\aleph_0$ (countable infinity) is the power of continuum c. The nature of the continuum question is such that it is essentially reduced to deciding **CH**.

within the unity of the temporal flux of consciousness. This approach was mainly presented by E. Husserl in *Formale und Transzendentale Logik* ([11]), published in 1929 shortly after his discussions with L. E. J. Brouwer in Amsterdam. My approach is also focused on the ultimate subjectively founded root of the impredicativity of intuitive continuum and further of formal continuum, taken as an objective continuous whole in actual reflection.

It is to be noted that a phenomenologically based reduction of the principles and structure of analytic logic, followed Husserl's earlier ideas on the logical - deductive nature of mathematical systems, presented in the so-called double lecture of Göttingen (1901-02). In this posterior approach he asked:

" How can one know *a priori* that a domain is a nomological[2] one, and if one takes as an example of such a domain the space in its spatial forms, does the set of immediately evident axioms that is posed 'grasp' completely the essence of the space, that is, does it suffice to determine a nomology?

And then, *a fortiori*, in pure formalization or in the free construction of forms of manifolds: how can one know, how can one prove that a system of axioms is a 'definite' system, a 'saturated' system?" ([11], *transl. of the author*, p. 100).

In the specific mathematical part, with respect to the *Continuum Hypothesis*, I mostly relied on the original stuff presented in P. Cohen's *Set Theory and the Continuum Hypothesis* ([2]) and the more or less standard texts of K. Kunen's *Set Theory. An Introduction to Independence Proofs* ([13]) and F. Drake's & D. Singh's *Intermediate Set Theory* ([4]).

Regarding K. Gödel's original presentation of the construction of the class of all constructible sets L as a model of the theory **ZF** [3] and the proof of **CH** in L by applying eight relatively simple functions iterated in turn to get the constructible universe of sets ([6]), I thought the symbolism and the overall structure of the model is quite abstruse for the context and aims of this article.

In my approach to this still hotly debated question of foundations, I try to clarify those details in the texture of the proofs of the consistency of both **CH** and ¬ **CH** that are possibly susceptible of a phenomenological approach in the sense already proposed, and also indicate an explicit or implicit use of other independent or strong infinity principles in the respective constructions. On this account, I stress P. Cohen's view in [2] that **CH** will be eventually accepted as false on the grounds of the inherent inaccessibility of the cardinal c of continuum generated by the *Power Set Axiom* in contrast to a build-up of the sequence of cardinals $\aleph_n, \aleph_\omega, \aleph_\alpha, \ldots$, (where $\alpha = \aleph_\omega$, etc.), by basically applying the *Replacement Axiom*.

My main intention, on questions relating to the nature and properties of continuum, in general, and to the independence of **CH**, in particular, is to make clear the reduction to two fundamental irreducibilities; even if the reader does

---

[2] It seems reasonable to assume that by the term nomological domains, Husserl referred to absolutely definite domains.

[3] The usual abbreviation for the commonly accepted Zermelo-Fraenkel Set Theory is **ZF**, whereas with the inclusion of the *Axiom of Choice* (**AC**), it is **ZFC**.

2. THE PHENOMENOLOGICAL REDUCTION

not adhere to a phenomenological approach towards questions pertaining to the mathematical continuum, he should keep at least in mind, in the following, the non-analytic character of these irreducibilities. These are taken, on the one hand, the irreducible individuals as syntactical substrates of absolute formulas inside transitive classes and on the other, the impredicative continuum[4] intuited as the continuous unity of a whole. This manifest 'incompatibility' may be ultimately associated in the phenomenology of perception, with a transcendence which goes, in terms of living experience, as far back as to the pre-predicative (a-thematic) unity of experience genetically constituted in any subject's flux of consciousness ([11], pp. 295-96).

In support of my claim that the question of the cardinality of continuum has at least a non-analytic dimension (in my view related to a constitution of objects as temporal ones within the self-constituting continuous unity of the temporal flux), I refer to S. Feferman's view in [5] that the *Continuum Hypothesis* is an inherently vague statement which cannot be settled by any new axioms added to **ZF** theory.[5]

Finally, in the Remarks subsection, I give a brief exposition of an intuitionistic approach to the **CH** question in the same interpretative context, and I also refer to the semantic role of atoms - urelements which retain by *ad hoc* axiomatical machinery their individual and relational character in nonstandard extensions of standard axiomatical systems; it is well-known that, precisely, continuity properties are defined in the saturated domains of these nonstandard extensions.

2 The phenomenological reduction of analytic sentences in logical-deductive systems

Husserl stated in *Formale und Transzendentale Logik* that a pure analytics has to lead to a phenomenological analysis of a vast amplitude and depth if it is to be really a theory of science and found the possibility of an authentic science that makes available the principles of the justification of its authenticity.

As a specific example of his position he gave the fundamental form (which he considered as one of the idealisations that play a universal role in analytic logic) of *this way ad infinitum* which produces an infinity by iteration and has as its subjective correlate the form *one can always do*. It is evident that this constitutes an idealisation since nobody can always perform de facto something anew. All the same though, this idealisation is evidently instrumental in the 'morphology' of analytic principles especially concerning infinity axioms or the construction of number systems, for instance, given any set, one can always have a new set to which the former is disjoint and, in addition, adjoin this new set to the first one and so on. Or, given any number a one can always form a

---

[4]The term impredicative continuum, is meant here in the sense that nothing can be asserted with regard to the formal-mathematical continuum in a first order language without producing evident circularities in the definition.

[5]For an exposition of counterarguments to S. Feferman's position, see [9].

new number $a + 1$ and this way starting from 1 form the infinite sequence of (natural) numbers.

In this approach in which he sought to lay bare the subjective, constitutive origins of analytic principles lying 'hidden' behind infinite constructions by iteration or ideal existences in formal mathematics, Husserl referred to the analytic principles of contradiction, of the excluded middle and the laws of modus ponens and modus tollens:

" In a purely objective perspective the analytic principle of contradiction is a principle on the mathematically ideal 'existence' (and co-existence) that is, on the co-possibility of judgements at the stage of distinction. But it is on the subjective side that it is to be found the *a priori* structure of evidence and the effectuations that usually come out of this structure, whose uncovering puts in evidence the essential subjective situations that correspond to its objective sense.[...]All judgements must be put in contact with 'things themselves' to which they refer and they have to conform to them whether in a positive or negative completion" ([11], *transl. of the author*, pp. 198 & 202,).

Further reducing the principles of analytic logic (and therefore of propositional statements of formal mathematics) to subjective evidences, Husserl held the view that on a purely analytic level every judgement and thus every sentence in apophantic logic can be reduced by syntactical 'deconstruction' to its ultimate object-substrates, so that the propositions reached in the final stage can be no longer held to be analytic. These 'final nuclei' have to be objects of intentionality in the sense that they are irreducible individuals-substrates of analytic propositions corresponding to absolute (and devoid of analytically reducible content) 'some-things', for the possibility and essential structure of which nothing can be said in analytic terms, even that they by necessity appropriate a temporal form ([11], p. 211).

The individuals-substrates (*Kernstoffen*) reached in the most fundamental level of a syntactical deconstruction have no inner syntactical structure and their existence as such together with their *a priori* attached categorial objectivities or nuclei-forms (*Kernformen*) can be only 'grasped' by intentional experience prior to any analytic form of judgement. On this account, they invariably retain their syntactical character as nuclei-formations (*Kerngebilde*) in the build-up of analytic sentences of a higher level. Any original judgement being the subjective form of the effectuation of the most original and direct evidence must be *a priori* directed to individuals-substrates originally given by first-degree experience in its most primary and strongest sense, defined precisely as direct reference to individuals. I note that in *Ideen I* ([10], pp. 230-231), Husserl described the objects of such 'lowest-level' phenomenological perception (*Wahrnehmung*) in terms of real hyletic-noetic moments of intentionality 'prior' to their temporal constitution as well-meant noematic objects.

As the objects of mathematical theories (elements, classes of elements, relations, etc.) were regarded by Husserl as specific cases of perceptual objects[6]

---

[6]See: [16], p. 414.

2. THE PHENOMENOLOGICAL REDUCTION

reached by categorial intuition, then any analytic formula of any degree of complexity involving mathematical objects as syntactical elements, can be in principle, and in accordance with Husserl's view, reduced to fundamental formulas which are no longer of analytic character but are instead reducible to direct evidences of nonreflective experience. They should ultimately refer to intentional objects of experience as irreducible individuals-substrates in *a priori* association with their predicative formations.

For instance, the set-theoretical atomic formula, $x \in y$ makes almost no mathematical sense unless we regard it as a stratified one in which (by the *Foundation Axiom* of **ZF**) x is an 'indecomposable' individual, in formal sense an urelement, bearing by its very essence the $\in$-relation with respect to any inclusive object or collection of objects.[7] As a matter of fact, W. v. O. Quine argued in *New Foundations for Mathematical Logic* [15], that all known paradoxes in set theory were being produced by using the *Comprehension Axiom* for unstratified formulas, basically by taking the formula $x \in y$ as unstratified.

As all intentional objects of experience in the most fundamental level are constituted noematically as well-meant temporal objects within the flux of consciousness in a kind of 'parallel' intentionality ([10], p. 241), mathematical objects (elements, sets, geometrical shapes, etc.) as specific noematic objects should be represented, in the first place, in a predicative universe described by a first-order formal language in which the fundamental undefined predicates would be the $\in$ and $=$ predicates.

In his doctrine, though, of the universal genesis of consciousness, Husserl thought of judgements[8] in their most original and primitive forms as leading to a genetic reduction of predicative evidences to the non-predicative evidence which is experience itself.

In this view, the givenness of 'things in-themselves' (considering, in particular, the formal objects of predicate formulas of mathematical logic) and also of any modalities correlative to them (essential properties, relations etc.), and the subsequent construction of analytic forms of judgements of a higher level, do not exclusively belong to the predicative universe but also to the unity of possible experience which 'refers' intentionally to these syntactical elements (whether material or formal individuals-substrates). This makes possible the cohesion of the content of any original judgement as it is based on the syn-

---

[7]The fact that in $x \in y$ the element x remains an individual as such with respect to any including object y in an ascending $\in$-chain, is secured by the transitivity property of the set-theoretical collection to which x belongs, i.e., if $x \in y$ and $y \in z$, then $x \in z$. The transitivity property of a set B (or of a formula $B(x)$), implies that atomic formulas and the bounded quantifier formulas built-up inductively from them are invariably 'carried through' B; for instance, assuming that the transitive formula $B(x)$ denotes '$x \in L_\alpha$' then $B(x)$ & $y \in x \rightarrow B(y)$.

[8]The term judgement, in *Formale und Transzendentale Logik*, is used in the sense of a formal logic which bears the double character of apophantic logic and formal ontology, disciplines which were regarded by Husserl as distinct but closely related taking into account that they are in universal correlation up to the very last details and thus can value as one and the same science ([11], §42).

thetic unity of experience[9] genetically constituted in the flux of consciousness of a subject who forms judgements of any degree of evidence ([11], pp. 226-27).

Husserl's 'embedding' of the predicative universe of intentional objects as ultimate contents of most original judgements to the synthetic impredicative unity of each subject's flux of consciousness, leads in turn to an impredicativity of the flux itself, and further to what Husserl called the absolute ego of consciousness. It is noteworthy, that in a conceptually parallel approach, L.E.J. Brouwer 'embedded' his two-ity intuition of natural numbers in an impredicative continuous substratum, termed the *primordial intuition of mathematics* ([17], p. 205).

In view of the above, assuming that mathematical activity is, in a broad sense, generated by certain modes of consciousness, then an impredicativity factor should lie 'hidden within', for instance, in the form of *ad hoc* infinity or formally independent principles, with regard to any higher-order mathematical statement, in effect to any statement pertaining implicitly or explicitly to the nature of continuum. This should ultimately reflect the impredicative character of a continuous unity immanentized as the objectified form of the self-constituting absolute flux of consciousness, even though it is intentionally directed, in terms of real hyletic-noetic moments, in a 'discrete mode' to its intentional objects and their *a priori* attached categorial objectivities.

In the next, I'll turn my attention to demonstrating the intrinsic need to resort to other actual infinity assumptions in the proof of the independence of **CH** from the other axioms of **ZFC**.

3 Infinity principles and the role of individuals in the independence of Continuum Hypothesis

3.1 The Continuum Hypothesis in Gödel's constructible universe L and the notion of absoluteness

In this section I'll mainly focus on the role of absolute formulas[10] within transitive classes in the proof of the consistency of **CH** with **ZFC** theory in Gödel's Constructible Universe L, mainly motivated by the Husserlian approach to atoms - substrates as invariable bearers of predicates in analytical sentences of a fundamental level. I will also call attention to the intuitive meaning of the

---

[9] All constituted synthetic objectivities, in other words all noematic objects constituted within the temporal flux by means of a kind of universal synthesis can be reflected in reverse order as pure forms in apophantic interpretational forms of formal logic; they make possible a nominalisation (*Nominalisierung*) of constructs of sentences and thus provide the abstract conceptual material of formal ontology including in this way all formal-mathematical disciplines ([10], pp. 274-77).

[10] If φ is a formula of $\mathcal{L}_x$ with free variables $x_1,...., x_k$ and $X \subseteq Y$, then φ is absolute between X and Y if:

$$\forall\, x_1, x_2,..., x_k \; (x_1 \in X \wedge x_2 \in X \wedge .... \wedge x_k \in X \Rightarrow (\varphi^X \Leftrightarrow \varphi^Y))$$

where φ^X and φ^Y are the relativizations of the formula φ to sets or classes X and Y respectively.

3. INFINITY PRINCIPLES

application of the *Axiom of Choice*, as an actual infinity axiom independent from the rest of **ZF**, in the proof of **CH**.

As it is known, Gödel proved the relative consistency result, namely that, if the system **ZF** is consistent then so is **ZF** plus **AC** plus **CH**, by constructing a collection L of all constructible sets which is a proper class, contains all ordinals and it is closed under the ordinary operations of set theory (such as unions, pairing of sets, images of functions, etc.). This minimal proper class L is constituted of sets satisfying formal axioms in a first-order language and it is proved to be a model of all the axioms of **ZFC** plus of **CH**. In fact, by the *Axiom of Constructibility* every set is assumed to be constructible in Gödel's sense so that it holds **V=L**. Some brief expository material below may help the reader to follow easier my arguments in the context of discussion.

It is notable that in the construction and properties of L it is generated a kind of 'parametrization' of the elements of an original set X by the definition of a complete sequence of formulas (FmlSeq) and the application of transfinite induction over these elements in the proof of the transitivity property of any 'stage' L_α inside the hierarchy $L = \bigcup_{\alpha \in On} L_\alpha$.

This way given any transitive set X, a language of set theory $\mathcal{L}_x$ is constructed with constant symbols $\mathring{x}$ added as syntactical individuals to denote each element x of X. The proper class L will be constructed from definable sets $\mathcal{D}_x$ which are projections of sets of satisfying assignments $S(i)$ 'parametrizing' the elements x of X by means of satisfaction relations $\models$ such that $(X, \in) \models$ $\models \varphi_i(\mathring{x})$, where $\varphi_i(\mathring{x})$ is a formula obtained from a set-theoretical one by prefacing it with $\exists u_j$ for each variable u_j which occurs free in φ with $j \neq i$ and substituting $\mathring{x}$ for free occurrences of u_i. I note here that I use the term parametrization between quotation marks not in the conventional sense, to mark the introduction of the elements of definable sets in terms of satisfaction sequences.

In a more detailed picture that leads by necessity to some formalism, a Gödel-set $\ulcorner\varphi\urcorner$ is defined for any formula φ of $\mathcal{L}_x$ belonging to a complete sequence of formulas (denoted by FmlSeq) and constituted in compound form from basic formulas (existence (Efml(x, y)), implication (Ifml(x, y, z)), negation (Nfml(x, y)), etc). These are based in turn on atomic formulas of the form $x = y$ or $x \in y$, where x and y are terms of the language $\mathcal{L}_x$ that is, either variables u_i, $i \in \omega$ (ω is the first limit ordinal) or constants $\mathring{x}$ representing elements $x \in X$.

Assuming that a set X is the formal outcome of a sequence of formulas, a notion of length of X ($Vlength(X)$) can be defined roughly as an ordinal belonging to ω which is defined to be one more than the greatest variable's index that appears in X.

Now we get the elements of a set $\dot{X}$ by defining for each subformula of X a corresponding set of satisfying assignments S consisting of all functions with domain $Vlength(X) = r$ and range the original transitive set X such that, for e.g. an atomic formula $x(i) = \ulcorner u_j \in u_l \urcorner$ we get $S(i) = \{\alpha \in X^r; \alpha(j) \in \alpha(l)\}$. If $y \in X$ then for the formula $x(i) = \ulcorner u_j \in \mathring{y} \urcorner$ we get $S(i) = \{\alpha \in X^r; \alpha(j) \in$

$y\}$.

Therefore, by defining the i-projection of $A \subseteq X^r$, $r \in \omega$ by: $\text{proj}_i(A) = \{a(i);\ a \in A\}$ for $i < r$ and $\text{proj}_i(A) = \emptyset$ for $i \geq r$, we can form a definable power set

$$\mathcal{D}(X) = \{\text{proj}_i(S(j));\ i, j \in \omega \wedge \exists x\ \text{SatSeq}(S, x, X)\}.$$

where $\text{SatSeq}(S, x, X)$ stands for all the satisfaction sequences produced out of all formulas belonging to the complete sequence $\text{FmlSeq}(u, x, n, X)$.[11] In this way the elements of the original set X are 'parametrized' by means of a countable class of formulas expressible in **ZF**, which in turn produce sets of satisfying assignments $S(i)$, where the sequence values $\alpha(i)$ of X^r are assigned to variable-terms of formulas $x(i)$ of $\mathcal{L}_x$ and elements x of the original set X are assigned to constants $\mathring{x}$.[12]

Proceeding this way, a recursive definition of L, the class of all constructible sets, is possible by defining:

$$L_0 = \emptyset$$

$$L_{\alpha+1} = \mathcal{D}(L_\alpha)$$

$$L_\lambda = \bigcup_{\alpha < \lambda} L_\alpha \text{ for limit } \lambda \text{ and}$$

$$L = \bigcup_{\alpha \in On} L_\alpha$$

A first remark to be made is that a nice property of the constructible universe L, that is, the transitivity of the 'stage' L_α for any ordinal α is proved by transfinite induction on the elements of the corresponding definable power set and depends on the transitivity of the sets L_β for all $\beta < \alpha$.

In a closer inspection of the technicalities involved in the process, we may find that a significant part of the proof of **CH**[13] relies on the notion of absoluteness of a class L_α (for any ordinal α) inside L, which is something that is also instrumental in proving that the class L is a model of all **ZF** axioms plus of the *Axiom of Constructibility* (i.e., **V=L**). In the proof construction though, one has also to prove the equality of cardinalities $|L_\alpha| = |\alpha|$ for any infinite ordinal α, which needs at least some form of the *Axiom of Choice* ([13], pp. 168-69).[14] The application of the *Axiom of Choice* in the present discussion is

---

[11] See for details: [4], pp. 128-133.

[12] Another presentation is offered in [13] (pp. 165-169), where the definable power set $\mathcal{D}(A)$, is the set of subsets of A which are definable from a finite number of elements of A by formulas relativized to A. These formulas belong in turn to the set $\bigcup_n \text{Df}(A,n)$ defined recursively as the least set of relations on A containing the fundamental relations $=$ and $\in$ and closed under intersection, complementation and projection ([13], pp. 152-153).

[13] Strictly speaking, the proof of the consistency of **CH** with the other axioms of **ZFC**.

[14] It is suggested by K. Kunen in [13], that the equality $|L_\alpha| = |\alpha|$ can be also proved without **AC**; however this alternative proof must be based on another theorem, namely that there exists a transitive model M for a finite sequence $\varphi_1, \varphi_2, ...\varphi_n$ of axioms of **ZF+V=L** such that $|M| = \omega$ and $\wedge_{i=1}^n \varphi_i^M$, which in turn goes back by yet another theorem to fixing

3. INFINITY PRINCIPLES

not without some phenomenologically motivated remarks, which I'll discuss at the end of this section.

As a matter of fact, absoluteness of formulas $X = L_\alpha$ or $X \in L_\alpha$ within L is pretty much due to the reason that functions defined recursively and involving absolute notions in their construction are themselves absolute, something that partly depends on the transitivity of the corresponding model ([13], p. 129). Also this particular absoluteness involves results which reduce to the absoluteness of atomic $\in$ and $=$ formulas and the absoluteness of certain relations within transitive classes e.g. the relation of ordered pairing $<x,y>$, the union $x \cup y$ and the intersection $x \cap y$ in the subsequent recursive construction of the definable power sets $\mathcal{D}(L_\alpha)$.

The notion of absoluteness within L remains very important in the final stage of the proof of the consistency of **CH**,[15] concerning, in particular, a proposition in which one needs to show that for a finite conjunction $\mathcal{X}$ of axioms of **ZF+V=L** and any transitive proper class M we have that $M = L(o(M))$.[16] Again the trick is to rely on the absoluteness of L_α for any ordinal α inside L and also on the transitivity of a model M of a finite conjunction $\mathcal{X}$ of axioms of **ZF+V=L** ([13], pp. 172-76).

The machinery of the proof of the consistency of **CH** needs also the Skolem-Löwenheim[17] and the Mostowski Collapsing theorems which involve, in their part, several other instrumental notions such as the closure of a set X under the set of Skolem functions H_i and the notion of a well-founded, set-like, extensional relation R on a set A. It is important to note, in connection with my scope, without intending to enter more deeply into mathematical intricacies:

- The Mostowski collapsing function G of a set A which is defined by $G(x) = \{G(y);\ y \in A \ \wedge\ y \in x\}$ and it is proved to be a $1-1$ isomorphism for the $\in$ relation onto a transitive set M, presupposes the extensionality and the well-foundedness of the $\in$ relation on A. The latter assertion is conditioned on the *Foundation Axiom*, which entails a

---

a well-order $\triangleleft$ in a certain class $Z(\beta)$ (where β is a limit ordinal) such that any formulas $\phi_1, ... \phi_n$ are absolute for classes $Z(\beta)$ and Z ([13], pp. 139-40). But fixing a well-order in any class is well-known to be equivalent to **AC**.

[15] Given that the *Axiom of Constructibility* (**V=L**) is proved consistent with **ZFC**, the consistency of **CH** amounts to proving that for all infinite ordinals α the power set of L_α is a subset of the definable power set of the next ordinal α^+ in the canonical scale: $\mathcal{P}(L_\alpha) \subset L_{\alpha^+}$.

[16] By definition, $o(M) = M \cap \mathbf{ON}$ where **ON** is the class of all ordinals. It can be proved that for a transitive set M, $o(M) \in \mathbf{ON}$ and $o(M)$ is the first ordinal not in M ([13], p. 172).

[17] The (downward) Skolem-Löwenheim theorem roughly states that a structure M in a language $\mathcal{L}$ has elementary substructures of all smaller infinite cardinalities than that of M. Actually in the proof of the consistency of **CH**, a slightly different version is used, the one that states for a transitive class Z and set-theoretic formulas $\varphi_1, ..., \varphi_n$:

$$\forall X \subset Z\ [X \text{ is transitive} \longrightarrow \exists M [X \subset M \ \wedge\ \bigwedge_{i=1}^{n}(\varphi_i^M \leftrightarrow \varphi_i^Z) \ \wedge\ M \text{ is transitive} \wedge$$
$$\wedge\ |M| \leq \max(\omega, |X|)]]$$

([13], p. 140).

property known to be held by all sets of the cumulative type structure, in other words by all sets which may contain 'indecomposable' atoms as elements.

- The Skolem-Löwenheim theorem is partly based on the existence of a set A which is the closure of an original set X under the Skolem functions $H_1, ..., H_i$. The definition of each such function H_i on a set $Z(\beta)$, for any ordinal β, is dependent on the fixing of a well-order $\triangleleft$ on $Z(\beta)$ by the application of **AC** ([13], pp. 137-140). Of course, there are also other proofs of the Skolem-Löwenheim theorem (one of them presented in [18], p. 112-113) but in every case the application of the *Axiom of Choice* or of some of its equivalent forms is deemed necessary.

One might rightfully wonder at this stage what all this intricate mathematical stuff has to do with phenomenology, in the first place, even in the context of a discussion associating analytic-mathematical sentences to component fundamental sentences ultimately referring to original evidences of an intentionally directed experience.

I ask the reader to take the pains to rethink for a moment the final stage of the proof of the consistency of **CH** which is the theorem stating that

If **V=L** then for all infinite ordinals α, $\mathcal{P}(L_\alpha) \subset L_{\alpha^+}$

and consider two critical parts of the proof. First, the result that for each ordinal α the class L_α is transitive and second that for any finite conjunction $\mathcal{X}$ of axioms of **ZF+V=L** there is a transitive set M such that $M = L(o(M))$. The former result relates to the transitivity of a recursively built set, whhile the proof of the latter depends in a straightforward way on the transitivity of M and the absoluteness of L_α inside L. The next step is by 'deconstructing', on a yet 'lower' level, parts of the respective proofs to make clear the role of transitivity in establishing absoluteness results and further as a property of a set of elements in its own right. It would then become hopefully clear how it may connect to the Husserlian ideas briefly discussed in section 0.2.

Let's turn, for that reason, our attention to the proposition that for each ordinal α the constructible set L_α is transitive which is proved by transfinite induction over the class of ordinals. At some stage of the induction we need to know that any transitive set B is a subset of its definable power set $\mathcal{D}(B)$. Taking the formula $x \in u$ of the sequence of formulas FmlSeq we have by definition of $\mathcal{D}(B)$ that

$$\forall u \in B \ [\{x \in B;\ x \in u\} \in \mathcal{D}(B)]$$

which taking account of the transitivity of B reduces to $\forall u \in B \ [u \in \mathcal{D}(B)]$ which is obviously $B \subset \mathcal{D}(B)$ ([13], p. 166). But how could it be so, had the elements $x \in B$ that satisfy the formula $x \in u$ not retained their invariably

3. INFINITY PRINCIPLES 165

individual character 'throughout' B to constitute in their collection the element u of $\mathcal{D}(B)$, something that is otherwise the essential character of the transitivity property of B?

I reach now the next part, which is the theorem stating that for any finite conjunction $\mathcal{X}$ of axioms of **ZF+V=L** relativized to a transitive model M, it holds that $M = L(o(M))$. The proof follows in two steps; the first one is the proof of the equation $L^M = L(o(M))$ which depends on the absoluteness of L_α, which we have already discussed, and the second is the proof of $M = L^M$ which depends on the transitivity of M ([13], pp. 172-73). Here once again the transitivity property of M is reflected in the preservation of the invariably individual character of the elements of M and moreover of their $\in$ inclusion relation as an invariable property inherently 'attached' to their individuality. For, taking as the only part of the conjunction $\mathcal{X}$ the axiom **V=L** and then relativizing it to M for any element $x \in M$, we have $(\forall x \ (x \in L))^M$ which implies straightforward that $M = L^M$. But how could it be once again so, had the bounded variable x of the relativized universal quantifier formula above, not invariably retained its irreducible individuality as an element of M?

My view is that the ultimate reduction, within a hierarchy of transitive classes, to the absoluteness of atomic $\in$ and $=$ formulas and to the absoluteness of formulas (which underlie most absoluteness results) of the form $(\exists x \in y) \ \phi$ or $(\forall x \in y) \ \phi$ built inductively from atomic formulas ϕ in which all quantifiers are bounded, admits of a certain phenomenological interpretation in terms of a fundamental reduction to the level of intentionalities towards individuals-substrates (as 'general-somethings') and their categorial objectivities as developed by Husserl in [10] (pp. 33-35) and [11] (pp. 80-82). In connection with my arguments concerning the invariably individual character of the syntactical atoms of absolute formulas φ of any $X \subseteq L_\alpha$, I note that atomic formulas of the form $\mathring{y} \in \mathring{x}$ and $\mathring{y} = \mathring{x}$ (where $\mathring{x}, \mathring{y}$ are treated as syntactical atoms) are not affected by relativization over general hierarchical structures and consequently over L, and are therefore evidently absolute.

Taking account of the fundamental character of these 'general-somethings' as irreducible individuals (guaranteed, e.g. by the *Foundation Axiom*) in formulas expressible in the language of **ZFC** and also of their $\in$-relational character preserved within a hierarchy of transitive classes, these individuals-substrates can be interpreted in the sense of Husserl's reduction of objects of 'lowest-level' analytic sentences to syntactically indecomposable individuals in the most fundamental level of 'observation'.

As the transitivity property of sets consists in the preservation of the individuality as such and of the $\in$-inclusion character of elements of the lowest rank, something that notably helps in proving that bounded quantifier formulas are absolute between transitive sets,[18] these elements together with

---

[18] If a set-theoretic formula φ is absolute between transitive sets (or classes) M and N with $M \subset N$, then so are proved to be the formulas $(\exists x \in y) \ \varphi$ or $(\forall x \in y) \ \varphi$ by treating the relativized syntactical individuals of M as invariably irreducible individuals in themselves:

$$[\exists x (x \in y \land \varphi(y, z_1, .., z_n))]^M \longleftrightarrow \exists x (x \in y \land \varphi^M(y, z_1, .., z_n))$$

their fundamental predicative formations can be reasonably viewed as nuclei-forms (in the sense described in Section 0.2, p. 4) in the subsequent construction of compound formulas and thus of analytic sentences of a higher level within a recursively defined hierarchy of transitive universes which are, in the case under review, the classes of constructible sets L_α within the constructible universe L. There is nothing that can be further said on the analytic level about those lowest rank elements of transitive classes, and therefore I can now claim to be taken as formal representations of 'lowest-level' intentional observation towards 'thingness' or even 'empty' 'somethings' within the real world of experience.

Any attempt to prove absoluteness of formulas of any other form throughout L, such as those of $X = L_\alpha$ or $X \in L_\alpha$, must refer to the transitivity of the hierarchies of L_αs, basically involving transfinite induction over ordinals. Ordinals are absolute almost solely by virtue of their definition as transitive and $\in$-well-ordered sets and they can moreover be thought of as the only means of performing enumeration and transfinite induction processes within any transitive class or within any hierarchical structure of classes in general. This would be, in principle, unthinkable had we not acquired the intuition of irreducible 'zero-level' elements of a class which by their very essence bear an inherent sense of 'order' in relation to any collection of elements of the class and moreover invariably preserve their individual and $\in$-relational character inside the class. As a matter of fact, transitive models have been proved to be defined by their sets of ordinals on the condition though that the *Axiom of Choice* is satisfied in at least one of them ([19]). Moreover, preservation of cardinals is conditioned on that of ordinals as it happens, e.g. in the preservation of cardinals between the ground countable model M and the extended model $M[G]$ in Cohen's proof of consistency of the negation of **CH** with the rest of the axioms of **ZFC**.

As already pointed out in the process of proving the consistency of **CH**, the *Axiom of Choice* which is generally regarded as an actual infinity axiom is called to use. Moreover, it has been already proved that the *Axiom of Constructibility*, an indispensable foundation of Gödel's constructible universe L, implies **AC**: **V=L** → **AC**.

The application of another independent infinity axiom such as **AC** in the proof of the consistency of **CH**, strengthens my arguments concerning the 'ontological' nature of continuum and the role of individuals-substrates in mathematical foundations precisely by the underlying intuition of **AC** extending, in principle, over an indefinite horizon the right to 'observe' and manipulate individuals as such and at least in $\in$-relation with any class of them.

Moreover, and this seemingly is why it is commonly called an actual (or Cantorian) infinity axiom, the **AC** presupposes the mental constitution of an objectively and invariably existing continuous substratum in actual presence[19]

---

[19]This temporal continuous substratum is immanent to the self-constituting consciousness and as such is freely generated in imagination as actually existing in the form of objective

3. INFINITY PRINCIPLES

on which to 'embed' the nonreflective possibility of a unique choice of individuals as such among indefinitely large collections of them. This latter possibility can be interpreted as founded on the existence of a subject performing acts of an intentional character *ad infinitum* and also on the existence of an intentional correlation between a knowing subject and any noetically apprehended object 'subsequently' constituted as a well-defined and unique noematic object in its proper predicative form. Then, as noematically constituted, an object may be defined both as an objectivity in itself and in some kind of relation to others, consequently it can be provided as an object of formal ontology with proper sense mathematical properties, e.g. the extensionality property, a notion of order in strict sense, etc.

In the following section I will take special notice of the implicit ways in which the fundamental actual infinity axiom, that is the **AC**, is assumed to prove the consistency of the negation of **CH** with the rest of the axioms of **ZFC**.

3.2 Revisiting P. Cohen's refutation of Continuum Hypothesis

In the following I will argue that the possibility to interpret forcing as a global notion of 'order' defined on a transitive, countable ground model M to produce sets of any infinite cardinality does not rid us of the need to even implicitly appeal to actual infinity assumptions to prove the falsity of **CH**.[20] As it was the case in the last section, my arguments will be mostly based on a phenomenologically motivated approach to individuals - substrates vs. continuous unity. I'll start by offering a brief and certainly insufficient introduction to the notion of forcing in general.

At first, it should be noted that in proving the existence of a minimal, countable transitive model M of **ZF** (as a result of the application of *Skolem-Löwenheim* Theorem) P. Cohen had to invoke the SM Axiom which postulates the existence of a set M which is naively a model of all of **ZF** (or of **ZFC+V=L**) under the standard $\in$-inclusion taken in the sense of a stratified formula ([2], p. 78).

It is well-known to set-theorists that P. Cohen proved the independence of **CH** and **AC** from the other axioms of **ZF** by adding new subsets to a countable transitive $\in$-model M of **ZF** by the forcing method which roughly defines forcing conditions withi the set M by means of a generic set of forcing conditions G which is usually not in M. This way, the ground model M of **ZF** is extended to a model $M[G]$ of **ZF** such that $M \subseteq M[G]$ and $G \in M[G]$. By the definition of a generic set G we get that every member of G is compatible with any p belonging to a partially ordered set $P \in M$ and this is an information 'enforced' inside the model M.[21]

A forcing relation $p \Vdash \varphi$ in the forcing language $\mathcal{L}_M$ is such that $p \Vdash$

---

continuous whole and freely extensible. Therefore, is not to be confused with the natural spatiotemporal continuum conditioned on the laws of causality and bound to (empirical) physical laws. The former meaning, is obviously the content I give to the term actual infinity in characterizing certain axioms of mathematical theory throughout the text.

[20] Strictly speaking, to prove the consistency of $\neg$**CH** with the other axioms of **ZFC**.

[21] Assuming that M is a countable transitive $\in$-model of **ZFC** and $(P, \preceq)$ is a partial order

$\varphi(\mathring{x}_1, \ldots, \mathring{x}_n)$ iff $M[G] \models \varphi(x_1^G, \ldots, x_n^G)$ inside the extended model $M[G]$ (*Truth Lemma*). It is essential here is to note that for a P-generic set G over M the satisfaction relation in $M[G]$ is equivalent to a forcing relation $\Vdash$ expressible in terms of the language $\mathcal{L}_M$ where the name-terms $\mathring{x}$ are assigned as variables of formulas φ. The names or terms $\mathring{x}$ are 'forced' by $p \in G$ to satisfy $p \Vdash \varphi(\mathring{x}_1, \ldots, \mathring{x}_n)$, while in $M[G]$ they represent sets of the form $x^G = \{<p_i, y_i>; \ i \in I\}$, each y_i inductively corresponding to a name $\mathring{y}_i$. Therefore, to each $x \in M$ corresponds a term $\mathring{x}$ in terms of $\mathcal{L}_M$ which in $M[G]$ represents the set:

$$x^G = \{y^G; \ \exists p \in P \ (<p,y> \in x \land p \in G)\}$$

What is notable in the definition of x^G is that the p_i's 'force' their inherent order as members of the P-generic G to the elements of the set x^G which includes things already in (by means of pairs $<p, y> \in x$) and it is thus possible by the well-foundedness of the $\in$-relation to perform a transfinite induction on the rank of x. Intuitively we could say that the new forcing sets in the extended model $M[G]$ are those whose elements are kept 'under watch' by a complete sequence of forcing conditions $\{P_n\}$ by means of statements $n \in a$ or $\neg n \in a$, for a not necessarily in M, densely enough over the original model M.

As a matter of fact, P. Cohen's construction of the refutation of **CH** within **ZFC** essentially involves the addition by forcing to a countable model M of κ new reals (the reals thought of as subsets of ω), where κ can be any cardinal in M (thanks to the Skolem-Löwenheim Theorem, may be $\geq \aleph_2$). A critical step is to construct for each $\alpha < \kappa$ a total function f_α on ω which is a characteristic function of a real $x_\alpha \subseteq \omega$ that is new to M in the sense that if $y \in M$ is a subset of ω then it must hold $y \neq x_\alpha$.

Passing to the core of the proof of the consistency of $\neg$ **CH**, the main trick is to produce an appropriate P_κ-generic set G of uncountable cardinality κ over M, where P_κ is defined to be the set $\text{Fn}(\kappa \times \omega, 2)$ of all finite partial functions p from $\kappa \times \omega$ into **2** ordered by extension in the usual sense of the extension of functions. We may think of generic G as coding a κ-sequence of functions from ω to 2 in the form $f_\alpha(n) = (\cup G)(\alpha, n)$ for $\alpha < \kappa$, $n < \omega$. Then based on its absoluteness, the κ-sequence $\{f_\alpha : \alpha < \kappa\}$ is in the forcing model $M[G]$

---

with $P \in M$, then letting $P \neq \emptyset$, the elements p, q are defined as compatible $(p||q)$ if,

$$(\text{for } p, q \in P) \ \exists r \in P \ (r \preceq p \land r \preceq q)$$

that is, r extends both p and q in the usual intuition of extension.

Further, letting $D \subseteq P$ to be dense if

$$\forall p \in P \ \exists d \in D \ (d \preceq p)$$

a set $G \subseteq P$ is defined as P-generic over M if it is consistent and closed upward (i.e., a filter in P) and moreover:

$\forall D \subseteq P$, D is dense and $D \in M$ implies $G \cap D \neq \emptyset$ (G meets every dense set in M)

(see: [4], pp. 155-56).

3. INFINITY PRINCIPLES

whereas by the density of the set $D_{\alpha\beta}$ in M:

$$D_{(\alpha\beta)} = \{p \in P_\kappa;\ \exists n \in \omega (<\alpha, n> \in \mathrm{dom}(p)\ \wedge$$

$$\wedge <\beta, n> \in \mathrm{dom}(p)\ \wedge p(\alpha,n) \neq p(\beta,n)\}$$

(α and β are uncountable cardinals of M and $\alpha \neq \beta$) and the statement $MA(k)$[22] we obtain in $M[G]$ a κ-sequence of distinct functions form ω into 2 such that $(2^\omega \geq |\kappa|)^{M[G]}$, in which case taking $\kappa = \omega_2$ in M this is an obvious refutation of **CH**. Some extra condition, the *Countable Chain Condition* (**c.c.c.**)[23] is needed to make sure that the cardinals in M are preserved in $M[G]$, as cardinals are not absolute, something that is proved to hold for the specific definition of the partial order P_κ ([13], p. 205).

Admittedly, the existence of a P_k-generic set G for any cardinality k greater than $\aleph_1$, which meets the dense set $D_{(\alpha\beta)}$ of all conditions p defined at any (α, n) is guaranteed by the statement $MA(k)$ in the role of an ad hoc actual infinity assumption for cardinals greater than $\aleph_1$. The conventional view is that $MA(k)$ is, in fact, not some kind of actual infinity assumption in establishing the existence of a P_k-generic set G in M for $k > \aleph_1$, for the simple reason that we can talk about uncountable cardinals inside countable models, e.g. one can define (essentially due to the Skolem-Löwenheim Theorem), the first uncountable ordinal ω_1^M within a countable, transitive model M of any finite fragment of axioms of **ZFC**. Therefore, the main restriction should be to check that **c.c.c.** holds for any particular partially ordered of forcing conditions, something that can be intuitively conceived of as securing the possibility of producing dense sets of compatible forcing conditions without bothering about an uncountable number of incompatible conditions. But although this view fully conforms with a formalist's aspect of the theory, it can nevertheless give some ground to my claim as to the need to implicitly turn to some form of (actual) infinity axiom to prove conjectures about continuum. In my approach, this has also to do with the context in which one chooses to talk about countability, that is, either in terms of formal-analytic processes and absoluteness results or in an 'observational-operational' level. I'll return to this discussion as soon as I complete my brief review of forcing procedures.

An equivalent form of $MA(k)$, (i.e., $MA(\aleph_0)$), for the countable cardinal $\aleph_0$ is easily proved to guarantee the existence of a generic set G over the countable model M. But this poses no theoretical doubts; by the countability of the

---

[22] The various statements of *Martin's Axiom* (**MA**) typically incorporate two parts. $MA(k)$ is the assertion that a certain property holds for any infinite cardinal k and **MA** is then the statement that $MA(k)$ holds for every k less than the continuum. A standard form of $MA(\kappa)$ is: Whenever $<\mathbf{P}, \leq>$ is a non-empty **c.c.c.** partial order and $\mathcal{D}$ is a family of $\leq \kappa$ dense subsets of **P**, then there is a filter G in **P** such that $\forall D \in \mathcal{D}\ (G \cap D \neq \emptyset)$. Then **MA** is the statement $\forall \kappa < 2^\omega\ (MA(\kappa))$, ([13], p. 54).

[23] With regard to a partial order $(P, \leq)$, the *Countable Chain Condition* (**c.c.c.**), is the statement that every antichain (any family of pairwise incompatible elements) of the partially ordered P is countable.

ground model M we can straightforwardly produce a countable dense set of forcing conditions $\{p_n\}$ and prove the existence of a generic set G over M.[24]

I focus now closer on two critical stages in P. Cohen's construction of the 'disproof' of **CH**, which in my view provide a clue to the inherent impredicativity of continuum and the need to recourse to other actual infinity principles on questions relevant to its nature and properties.

The first one is the need to rely on the countability of the original model M to prove that there exists a complete sequence of forcing conditions P_n such that for any statement A, there exists a natural number n such that either P_n forces A or P_n forces $\neg A$. In fact completeness of P_n over M guarantees the existence of forcing sets $X[G]$ by means of a generic set G or in Cohen's notation it guarantees the existence of forcing sets in $M[G]$ such as $\bar{a} \subseteq \omega$, where $\bar{a} = \{k;\ \exists n\ (P_n\ \text{forces}\ k \in a)\}$. As already stated the existence of a generic set G within a countable model M is easily proved as an equivalent form of the statement $MA(\kappa)$ for cardinal $\kappa = \aleph_0$.

The second one is that the proof of the consistency of $\neg$ **CH** for a fixed cardinal $\aleph_\tau$, $\tau \geq 2$ is obtained by implicitly applying $MA(\kappa)$ for cardinalities κ less than or equal to $\aleph_\tau$, to obtain a generic set G of such an infinite cardinality; in [2] it is applied to $\aleph_\tau$ elements a_δ belonging to a generic set G of forcing conditions of cardinality $\aleph_\tau$, thus getting a complete sequence P_n to determine by forcing that a_δ and $a_{\delta'}$ are distinct for $\delta \neq \delta'$.

The application of $MA(\kappa)$ is evident too in the 'disproof' of **GCH** by the forcing method in Boolean-valued models V^B. There, a generic set of forcing conditions $C(\omega \times \omega_\kappa, 2)$ over infinite cardinals $\omega \times \omega_\kappa$, adjoins $\aleph_\kappa$ new subsets of ω using finite pieces of information (in the sense of $n \in a$ or $\neg n \in a$) for the members of the $\aleph_\kappa$ new subsets of ω ([1], Ch. 2).

As already mentioned, one could argue that there is no need to turn to a greater than $\aleph_0$ infinity assumption, in the form of $MA(\kappa)$, to secure the existence of generic sets of any infinite cardinality, as all cardinals including uncountable ones should be considered relativized as 'countable' ones within the countable ground model M, due to certain results leading to the Skolem paradox (see: [13], p. 141). Moreover one can always make an uncountable cardinal κ of M to 'collapse' in the extended model $M[G]$ to a countable one by a proper extension technique on the set of forcing conditions $P = \text{Fn}(\omega, \kappa)$[25] and also based on the absoluteness of $\bigcup$ operation in $M[G]$. But then it is questionable whether M will ever be able to provide an enumeration *in rem* of any infinite (in fact, an uncountable one) ordinal κ. It is questionable too, whether the extension techniques used to produce dense sets $D_{(\beta)}$ of forcing conditions p within a countable model M can stand from my particular point of

---

[24] $MA(\aleph_0)$ known also as the *Rasiowa-Sikorski lemma* states that:

Let $(P, \leq)$ be a poset (partially ordered set) and $p \in P$. If D is a countable family of dense subsets of P then there exists a D-generic filter $\mathcal{F}$ in P such that $p \in \mathcal{F}$. (A filter $\mathcal{F}$ is called D-generic if $\mathcal{F} \cap E \neq \emptyset$ for all $E \in D$).

[25] This is the poset of finite partial functions from the countable ordinal ω into an uncountable ordinal κ of M under the ordering $\forall p, q \in \text{Fn}(\omega, \kappa) : p \leq q \leftrightarrow p \supset q$.

3. INFINITY PRINCIPLES

view as proper enumeration techniques when dealing with uncountable ordinals, as it is precisely the case with uncountable $\beta \in$ range(p); for instance, taking as conditions p the functions of $P = \mathrm{Fn}(\omega, \beta)$, $\beta = \omega_1$, then simply adjoin a pair $< n, \beta >$ to a condition p for some n not already in dom(p). The forcing conditions p in the particular example belong to the poset of all finite partial functions from ω into β and thus by extension any set $D_{(\beta)}$ can be made dense for every ordinal $\alpha < \beta$.

In the present example, one might wonder whether it can be properly established, in an 'observational-operational' sense, that after adjoining a countable number of finite subsets of ω to dom(p) and taking their countable intersection, we should define by necessity the same uncountable ordinal β in the range of p as before. This has little to do with **c.c.c.** property too, which nevertheless does not hold in the poset $\mathrm{Fn}(\omega, \beta)$ under the usual ordering, because **c.c.c.** eliminates such irritable situations as, for instance, adjoining finite subsets of ω to dom(p) in a finite number of steps and at the same time producing uncountable incompatibilities, yet my argument is that forcing an extension on a condition p for any uncountable ordinal in its range, is an artificial treatment of the notion of enumeration and certainly not in the sense of a horizon of (discrete) noetic-noematic acts. .

The same argument applies in the proof of the preservation of cardinalities between M and $M[G]$, which is a crucial fact in establishing the consistency of $\neg$ **CH** with the other axioms of **ZF** theory. An extension technique (and also the *Definability Lemma*) helps define a countable set Y_δ in ground model M containing the actual values which the function f^G on an infinite ordinal α in $M[G]$ is forced to take, where the model M itself may have no way to 'tell' these particular values without forcing them by extension ([4], pp. 167-69). In addition and relative to my general argument in this article, the assumption of **AC** is necessary to prove both an important lemma (the delta-system lemma) setting a criterion for proving that the poset $P = \mathrm{Fn}(\kappa \times \omega, 2)$ satisfies **c.c.c.**, and also that under property **c.c.c.** in M the poset P preserves the cardinals between M and $M[G]$ (see for details: [13], pp. 205-207).

Therefore, I think the discussion reasonably reduces to the meaning of uncountability within a countable model and also to the fundamental difference between countability and continuity in general. Either you choose to feel unbothered by the definition of a 'countable' ordinal ω_α^M of any infinite rank within a countable model M which nevertheless the 'inhabitants' of M cannot recognize as such as they lack the means to test its countability (by means of a function inside M from ω onto ω_α^M) or you feel that this is an artificiality in a purely axiomatical mathematical context that downplays the meaning of countability as an 'observational-operational' process within the real world of phenomena. In the former option, you have to rely on a modified version of Skolem-Löwenheim Theorem which provides for the existence of a countable, transitive model M for any finite fragment of axioms of **ZFC** and on certain absoluteness results within transitive models ([13], pp. 136-141). But, as I have already pointed out, the proof of the existence of such a model involves, at a certain stage of the construction (e.g., by fixing a well-order in a certain class), the assumption of the *Axiom of Choice*, which is independent from the rest of **ZF** system and is generally considered as an actual infinity axiom.

If one takes the second option, then he may find that any approach of countability that does not take into account its de facto status as an enumeration process implemented in an ever receding horizon of events that incorporates a participating 'observer', is an artificial construction from a phenomenologically oriented point of view, no matter how solid its axiomatical foundation might be. From this point of view, to come back to the proof of the consistency of $\neg$ **CH** by the forcing method, the existence of a generic set G over a countable model M having a non-empty intersection with any family of dense sets D of an uncountable cardinality κ defined within M, can be established by necessarily applying $MA(\kappa)$ in the sense of an actual infinity assumption.

The application of the statement $MA(k)$ for any cardinal $k > \aleph_1$ (or of proper forcing axiom in the same context) and of **AC** as *ad hoc* infinity principles, seems to do justice to my general argument on the impossibility to carry over the language of a predicative universe referring syntactically to distinct, well-defined objects to a continuous impredicative substratum, without being trapped in some sort of circularity in axiomatical reasoning on infinity or without introducing back-door some infinity principle of an *ad hoc* character. Why do I claim that these infinity principles are of an *ad hoc* character? Because, as it may have been already evident, they are taken as 'leap-of-faith' assumptions 'bridging the gap' between what is expressible in a first-order universe of countably many syntactical means and what ultimately founds the impredicative nature of mathematical continuum.

This might, yet deeper, be explained by the incompatibility between our natural intuition of continuum (including that of mathematical continuum) as an impredicative substratum rooted, in a phenomenologically motivated approach, in the continuous unity of the temporal flux of consciousness and the phenomenological perception of individuals-substrates of analytic statements of any axiomatical theory and of their fundamental categorial properties as *a priori* evidences of intentionally directed 'lowest-level' cognitive experience.

3.3 Remarks

It is 50 years now since P. Cohen's proof of the independence of *Continuum Hypothesis* and there is still an ongoing debate as to the content and meaning of **CH** or of its generalized form **GCH**.[26] Progress is not lacking in new mathe-

---

[26] I call into attention here Gödel's critique of those who oppose Cantor's set theory on the grounds that mathematical objects should be admitted to the extent in which they are interpretable as acts and constructions of our mind or at least completely penetrable by our intuition ([7], p. 518). He commented that if the Cantorian axiomatical system offers a complete description of some well-defined reality then **CH** should be either true or false and its eventual undecidability would mean that the difficulties of the problem 'are perhaps not purely mathematical'. By then, around 1947, he was of course unaware of the 'disproof' of **CH** by P. Cohen published pretty much later (1962); however his conjecture about the probability of a not purely mathematical character of **CH** can only give credit to my claim

3. INFINITY PRINCIPLES

matical approaches to the question and among them is W. Hugh Woodin's claim that **CH** is false ([20]). In W. H. Woodin's view thanks to Cohen's method of forcing no large cardinal hypothesis can settle the *Continuum Hypothesis*, a fact noted independently by Cohen and Levy-Solovay; on this account, he is currently reaching out to settle the **CH** question in terms of a global approach, termed the multiverse approach to the universe of sets, through which it is expected " to mitigate the difficulties associated with the formal unsolvability of fundamental problems such as that of the continuum hypothesis, and the latter feature is the primary motivation for such an approach." ([22], p. 102; see also: [21]).

For an intuitionistic approach to the **CH** question I refer to [8], where an attempt is made at a proof of **CH** at the cost, though, of the assumption of a strong intuitionistic *Continuity* (or *Choice*) *Principle* which by itself entails a kind of *ad hoc* shift to infinity to the extent that it establishes the possibility of the definition of a mapping $\gamma : \alpha \longrightarrow \beta$, where $\alpha \in \omega^\omega$, $\beta \in \omega^\omega$ such that $(\forall n) \ [(\gamma)^n : \alpha \longmapsto \beta(n)]$.

The mapping $(\gamma)^n : \omega^\omega \longrightarrow \omega$ (any sequence α in ω^ω is assumed as a more or less determinate one) can be imagined as being produced by a 'black box' process step by step; therefore one relies on assumptions linked in final count with one's subjective 'observations' extended over an indefinite horizon. These 'observations' are, in effect, intersubjectively the same and such that: $\forall \alpha \ \exists m \ [\gamma(\bar{\alpha}m) \neq 0]$ where $\bar{\alpha}m =< \alpha(0), ..., \alpha(m-1) >$ and $\alpha \in \omega^\omega$, $m \in \omega$ ([8], p. 124).

This conclusion can be derived from the step-by-step construction of γ: At each stage n we look at the finite segment of the sequence coded by n and either determine a natural number p suitable for the infinite sequence-member of ω^ω whose first part is the finite sequence coded by n, in which case we set $\gamma(n) = p + 1$, otherwise we set $\gamma(n) = 0$ (ibid. p. 124).

On a fundamental level, the shift to infinity by intuitionistic continuity principles, naturally including Brouwer's *Continuity Principle for Universal Spreads* and Weyl's *Open Data Principle* (see: [17]), is a prolongation over an indefinite horizon of finite segments of sequences, that is of finite subsets of ω^ω, as complete mathematical objects retaining the essential (as atoms) and $\in$-relational character of their elements.

In this sense, intuitionistic continuity principles can be seen in the same viewpoint as certain extension or prolongation axioms of nonstandard theories e.g. the Prolongation Principle of *Alternative Set Theory* (AST) which extends AST-countable classes of objects over the horizon of countability to the vagueness of Continuum. This last principle preserves elements of countable classes in advancing the horizon of 'hereditary' finiteness in such a way that they retain their fundamental character when restricted to its standard domain (see: [14], p. 131-132).

In general, the passage to the continuum in most nonstandard theories, other

---

on a possible phenomenological dimension of this question.

than A. Robinson's extensional-type formulation, is induced either by means of elementary isomorphic embeddings to 'saturated' domains or by extension (prolongation) principles which are essentially of an *ad hoc* character in the sense that they 'embed' the predicative universe of the standard structure together with any other standard objects into a nonstandard 'continuous' domain.

In my arguments so far, I have tried to show that no formal solution of major continuum-related questions in mathematical foundations (such as the **CH** question) can be expected, without adopting at least some kind of *ad hoc* actual infinity principle or involving another independent infinity axiom. This can possibly motivate a deeper reflection as to whether impredicativity of mathematical continuum stems from that of phenomenological continuum. I certainly note that both L. E. J. Brower and H. Weyl had to a large extent modelized intuitive continuum, which they inherently associated with the continuum of mathematics, after Husserl's description of the flux of temporal consciousness, leaving though the core problematic of the impredicativity (and on a deeper level the transcendence) of the self-constituting continuous flux out of further mathematical discussion.

Perhaps the whole question of the nature of continuum will be in the coming years the object of a holistic approach bringing together such diverse disciplines as Phenomenology, Logic and Foundations, Quantum theory, Neurobiology and Artificial Intelligence.

BIBLIOGRAPHY

[1] Bell, J. L.: (1985), *Boolean-valued Models and Independence Proofs in Set Theory*, Oxford: Clarendon Press.
[2] Cohen, P.: (1966), *Set Theory and the Continuum Hypothesis*, Mass.: W.A. Benjamin.
[3] Diaconescu, R.: (1975), Axiom of Choice and complementation, *Proc. AMS*, V. 51, pp.175-178.
[4] Drake, F., Singh, D.: (1996), *Intermediate Set Theory*, Chichester: J. Wiley & Sons.
[5] Feferman, S.: (1999), Does mathematics need new axioms?, *American Mathematical Monthly*, 106, pp. 99-111.
[6] Gödel, K.: (1940), The consistency of the axiom of choice and of the generalized continuum-hypothesis with the axioms of set theory, *Annals of Mathematical studies*, 3, Princeton: Princeton University Press.
[7] Gödel, K.: (1947), What is Cantor's Continuum Problem, *The American Mathematical Monthly*, 54, 9, pp. 515-525.
[8] Gielen, W., De Swart, H. & Veldman, W.: (1981), The Continuum Hypothesis in Intuitionism, *The Journal of Symbolic Logic*, 46, 1, pp. 121-136.
[9] Hauser, K.: (2002), Is Cantor's Continuum Problem Inherently Vague?, *Philosophia Mathematica*, 10, 3, pp. 257-285.
[10] Husserl E.: (1976), *Ideen zu einer reinen Phänomenologie und phänomenologischen Philosophie, Erstes Buch*, Hua Band III/I, hsgb. K. Schuhman, Den Haag:M. Nijhoff.
[11] Husserl, E.: (1974), *Formale und Transzendentale Logik*, Hua Band XVII, hsgb. P. Janssen, Den Haag: M. Nijhoff.
[12] Husserl, E.: (1966), *Zur Phänomenologie des Inneren Zeitbewusstseins*, Hua Band X, hsgb. R. Boehm, Den Haag: M. Nijhoff.
[13] Kunen, K.: (1982), *Set Theory. An Introduction to Independence Proofs*, Amsterdam: Elsevier Sc. Pub.
[14] Livadas, S.: (2005), The Phenomenological Roots of Nonstandard Mathematics, *Romanian Jour. of Infor. Science and Technology*, (ed. D. Dascalu), 8, 2, pp. 115-136.

[15] Quine, W. v. O.: (1937), New Foundations for Mathematical Logic, *American Mathematical Monthly*, 44, pp. 70-89.
[16] Tieszen, R.: (1984), Mathematical Intuition and Husserl's Phenomenology, *Noŭs*, (3), V. 18, pp. 395-421.
[17] Van Atten, M., Van Dalen, D. & Tieszen, R.: (2002), Brouwer and Weyl: The Phenomenology and Mathematics of the Intuitive Continuum, *Philosophia Mathematica*, 10, 3, pp. 203-226.
[18] Van Dalen, D.: (2004), *Logic and Structure*, Berlin: Springer-Verlag.
[19] Vopěnka, P., Balcar, B.: (1967), On complete models of the set theory, *Bull. de l' Acad. Polon. des Sci.*, 15, pp. 839-841.
[20] Woodin, H. W.: (2001), The Continuum Hypothesis Part I and II, *Notices of the AMS*, 48, resp. 6, 7, pp. resp. 567-576 & 681-690.
[21] Woodin, H. W.: (2011), The continuum hypothesis, the generic-multiverse of sets and the Ω conjecture, in: *Set Theory, Arithmetic and Foundations of Mathematics*, New York: Cambridge University Press.
[22] Woodin, H. W. & Heller M. (eds.): (2011), *Infinity, New Research Frontiers*, New York: Cambridge University Press.

Are Mathematical Theories Reducible to Non-analytic Foundations? [0]

STATHIS LIVADAS

1 Introduction

As it is implied by the title above, I intend to discuss the possibility of a non-analytic foundation of mathematical theories and, in that case, offer a phenomenologically motivated point of view. By the term non-analytic, I refer both to the general connotation of this term as the impossibility to completely analyze a systematic body of knowledge up to its constituent elements through a set of fundamental principles and in a specific mathematical-logical sense to the impossibility in reaching completeness in the description of a formal mathematical object or even of a mathematical theory itself within its own predicative environment; this is, for instance, related with the eventual indescribability of a certain formal object within a first-order theory with the sole expressional means of the theory in question, e.g. in the formal description of an open interval of the real line with first-order means. In my view, inasmuch as a non-analytic foundation of mathematical theories may be ultimately associated with a Husserlian phenomenology of consciousness, it can lead in the first place to the non-analytic character of pre-predicative experience and on a constitutional level to an inherently impredicative[1] character of temporal objectivities taken as such through a phenomenology of temporal consciousness. The present paper is mostly related with a view of mathematical objects (in the sense of objects of formal axiomatical theories) as ultimately temporal objects, that is, as outcomes of a constitutional process associated with the phenomenology of temporal consciousness. As it stands out, my point of view, further defended in the following sections, may be considered as being a controversial perspective even among Husserlian scholars working in the interface of

---

[0]This article has been published originally in electronic form in the journal *Axiomathes*, on Feb. 2, 2012, DOI: 10.1007/s10516-012-9182-3, and is republished with kind permission from Springer Science+Business Media for the book *Contemporary Problems of Epistemology in the Light of Phenomenology*.

[1]Generally, an impredicative notion is one that the *definiens* cannot but be defined in terms of the *definiendum*, in the sense that the definition of an entity (object, concept) somehow involves or presupposes a totality including the entity being defined. This concerns, for example, the definition of an object by a quantified sentence in which the scope of the quantifiers includes the entity being defined; e.g. in case we talk about an open set of a topological space, this is an impredicative notion inasmuch as it cannot be described but in terms of its parts (basic open sets) which are of the same genus as the whole.

phenomenology and logic or the philosophy of mathematics; this concerns, for instance, the foundation of arithmetic on the intuition of numbers as objects or as concepts of numbers. For this reason, I also offer the following bibliography, [6], [9], [10], and [26].

In accordance with this view, one can pose the following questions: Are mathematical objects temporal objects and in what sense can be taken as such? Should individuals - atoms of mathematical-logical formulas, inasmuch as they are taken to be complete abstractions of last substrates of intentionality[2] towards an 'empty something' (*leer Etwas*) be regarded as constituted within temporality and consequently as re-identifying immanences[3] of the constituting flux of consciousness? In such a case can one consistently regard them, in a formal-ontological context as idealized, atemporal and dimensionless singularities, e.g. in the intuitionistic sense of natural numbers taken as timeless points within the continuum of real numbers, in contrast with the notion of real numbers taken as (nested) choice sequences of rational intervals[4] ([31], p. 212)? Moreover, should we regard any finite collection of irreducible individuals and *a fortiori* infinite collections of them as atemporal, ontologically well-defined entities for which a notion of temporality can be dispensed with by viewing them as complete mathematical objects in temporal actuality? Put in other words, should we regard mathematical objects, going so far as to include geometrical figures, as completely disjoint from an underlying notion of temporal process which should rather have to be accounted for, even in taking such objects as purely abstract forms in formal mathematical reasoning?

Let us take, for instance, natural numbers taken in intuitionistic theory as durationless, non-extensive ideal objects of an *a priori* two-ity intuition in the process of registering of a sequence of original impressions, the latter process based on the notion of Husserlian transversal intentionality[5] ([31], pp. 206-208). Insofar this is a process within temporal constitution, it necessarily implies a notion of duration even in reflecting on the instantaneity of a single moment

---

[2] Intentionality is a phenomenological notion which is not to be understood as a relation of a psychological character towards the objects of experience. By intentionality it is meant something fundamentally deeper and *a priori*. To a non-expert in phenomenology it can be roughly described as grounding the *a priori* necessity of orientation of a subject's consciousness towards the object of its orientation.

[3] An immanent object is thought of as a correlate of an intentional consciousness in contrast with a transcendent to the consciousness common physical object whose objectivity is put anyway by phenomenology into brackets.

[4] A detailed discussion of mathematical objects, e.g. of choice sequences meant as temporal objects in intuitionistic theory, in relation with the Husserlian phenomenology can be also found in M. van Atten's *Brouwer meets Husserl: On the Phenomenology of Choice Sequences*. (see, [2]).

[5] By the term transversal intentionality, we usually refer to two *a priori* features of this particular form of intentionality, that is, to the retention and protention; they can be roughly communicated as respectively a kind of spontaneous conservation in memory (retention) and a spontaneous expectation of an original impression (protention). They are key concepts in describing the constitution of a continuously descending (to the past) sequence of immanences of original impressions within the flux of consciousness. For more details, see: [12], resp. §11, §24.

1. INTRODUCTION

associated with an original impression in actual presence which is indeed the phenomenological view of the matter as there is only a specious present *a priori* attached to an 'onward' directed protention and a 'backward' directed retention (primary memory).

In considering the possibility of having a complete fulfillment of intentions towards very large (bordering to countable infinity) natural numbers, I turn to Husserl's earlier ideas in *Logical Investigations* on the static and dynamic fulfillment of acts of knowledge. What is phenomenologically meant with the act of fulfillment is a, by means of this act, two-fold constitution of intentional objects, that is, as intuited objects on the one hand and as reflected upon objects on the other, in the mode of their re-identification within consciousness, ([17], p. 41). For, insofar as objects of mathematical theories can be taken as complete abstractions of objects of phenomenological perception through categorial intuition[6], we can point to an implication of temporal constitution already in *Logical Investigations* inasmuch as in dynamic fulfillment the elements of relation and their associated acts of knowledge are temporally tied in phenomenological fashion and they are unfolding in a certain phenomenological temporal form. On the other hand, in static fulfillment the components of the effect of the aforementioned temporal process remain in an objective temporal and 'thingness' formation. This way, a first-step unfulfilled intention-meaning towards an object finds a more or less satisfactory fulfillment in second-step as intuition-meaning or intuiting (*Anschauung*) of the object within the unity of consciousness, whereas in static relation there is only this fulfilled meaning within temporal unity without having a preceding stage of unfulfilled intention ([17], p. 40). In view of the above, it is highly questionable whether, for instance, the infinite countable cardinal $\aleph_0$, meant in the sense of an upper limit of the ascending sequence of successive natural numbers, can become a fulfilled intention by clinging to the possibility of an indefinitely open horizon of reiterating intentional acts of the form 'I always can do', which is grounded each time on the intentionality towards an original impression in actuality to produce a new $n \cup \{n\}$ ([25], p. 236). In that case, possibly with the help of a counting device, we can have a fulfilled intention of a large natural number only as an original impression in consciousness (let's say, by two-ity intuition) associated with the descending sequence of retentions of preceding natural numbers which has ideally become a vague 'continuous' sequence of retentions of pre-

---

[6]This special kind of intuition is described in Husserlian texts as reaching a purely formal object, e.g. the objects of pure logic (as *mathesis universalis*), by abstracting from a kind of intentionality towards an 'empty form'. This is not akin to a process of complete abstraction through which we can be led by a modification over content to a common invariant part of the object in question, even one that is left with no traits relative to a material content. This way, there may well be certain categorial forms in perceptual statements, e.g. those concerning the forms of quantity and the determinations of a number (for instance, 'something'-'nothing', 'all'-'none') which are meaningful propositional elements but may lack any objective correlates in the sphere of real objects. Generally, the categorial intuition of a mathematical essence, e.g. that of a canonical hexagone, is regarded as independent of the particular physical instantiation of this essence, ([30], pp. 128-129). More on the Husserlian notion of categorial intuition in [16], (pp. 661-665).

ceding retentions and this way as far back as the starting natural number of the enumeration. Therefore, taking a very large natural number in the sense of a formal-ontological object with attached to it categorial objectivities[7] (e.g. relational properties in formal representation), then it can only be the object of a fulfilled intention inasmuch as it can become an original impression in actuality with respect to an intentional consciousness. For that reason even in taking infinitely large natural numbers as ideal objects, this is conditioned on the possibility of their registration as original givennesses in actuality and on their effective procession towards infinity, which is by this token largely ideal, in the sense of a potentially *ad infinitum* performance of intentional acts of a two-ity type. This kind of reasoning should be also relevant with regard to any sequence of discrete, finite objects of a formal theory which can become as such contents of intentional acts directed to them in actuality.

I draw attention here to the fact that in Husserl's transcendental phenomenology, virtually introduced with his elaboration of *Ideas*, ideal mathematical objects and associated truths (in terms of the meaning of judgements referring to them) are omnitemporal and acausal entities, meant though as constituted invariants of acts of cognition ([30], p. 57). In this respect, they may be associated with the subjective unity of consciousness inasmuch as they can eventually become idealizations on the condition of first being fulfilled objects of intentionality in the present now of the temporal flux of consciousness. Moreover, the meaning-fulfillment of a mathematical object as an original givenness in temporal actuality should also lead to its categorial objectivities which are expressible in a formal language by fundamental syntactical relations, e.g. enumerability, the relation of ordering, the relation of transitivity of ordinals, analytic irreducibility in the case of a syntactical individual, etc. For instance, the fundamental properties of being transitive and well-ordered by $\in$ of an ordinal number are ideal meanings which can be taken as idealizations of fulfillments of intention-meaning towards a concrete, finitistic mathematical object carried out in the present now of intentional consciousness.

However, the idealization involved in higher than $\aleph_0$ cardinalities, as we will see in section 3, is of a radically different character as it cannot be derived by abstraction of *ad infinitum* performable present-now (*gegenwärtige*) intentional acts, but it seems to be rooted in the constituting source of temporal unity which conditions the modification of the content of these discrete intentional acts into correlated immanences constituted within the homogenous whole of the unity of consciousness. I will call this kind of idealization a **second-level idealization**, whereas the former one which is associated with the fulfillment, each temporal moment, of the intentionality towards a concrete object or state-of-affairs in the present now of the flux, a **first-level idealization**.

---

[7]These are objectivities, mirrored in syntactical objectivities, which are *a priori* associated with any intentional object upon its reflection. As long as we talk about a predicative reflection upon an object we necessarily associate with it objectivities of a higher degree, e.g. substantivity, relatedness with other objects, plurality of singularities, orderings, etc. ([15], pp. 28-29).

1. INTRODUCTION

In section 3, I will try to show in what sense a well-known infinity statement within a formal-axiomatical system (i.e. the Cantor result, $X \prec \mathcal{P}(X)$, referring to the cardinality of an infinite set X) involves some form of second-level idealization; this kind of idealization can be also seen to underlie the undecidability of certain well-known uncountable infinity statements within Zermelo-Fraenkel (**ZF**) set theory (see, p. 21). In my view, any actual infinity assumption in the sense of acceptance of the existence of an actual infinity in presentational immediacy can be associated with a second-level idealization. In this respect, the generation of continuum in intuitionistic theory, e.g. by L.E.J. Brouwer's continuity principle for universal spreads or by A. Troelstra's principle of open data, can be seen as associated with a second-level idealization inasmuch as lawless sequences, in the sense of objects unfolding in temporal progression, are nevertheless taken as complete formal objects in axiomatization. This is a remark of a special significance, in the notable absence of the Axiom of Choice in intuitionistic theory, ([23], pp. 196-197).

In section 4, it will be shown that some critical steps in the construction of undecidability proofs would be missed out in the absence of second-level idealizations; more specifically, one is referred to those proofs concerning certain non-recursiveness results that lead to the proof of Gödel's First Incompleteness Theorem. I chose to specifically deal with Gödel's famous foundational theorem, as it highlights the eventual indescribability by formal finitary means of abstract mathematical concepts involving at least indirectly a kind of impredicative unity, in contrast with the solid intuition of discrete, finite-time processes associated e.g. with finitistic arithmetical operations.

I will also try to make clear in what sense the application of an actual infinity principle, that is, of the Axiom of Choice (**AC**) as a form of second-level idealization, is critical in the derivation of the well-known Skolem-Löwenheim theorem in mathematical foundations. We must bear in mind that this theorem is about the absoluteness of first-order mathematical formulas between two σ-signature structures within the range of any infinite cardinality and has as a paradoxical by-product the Skolem paradox. Therefore, in view of my general approach, I choose to deal with the Skolem-Löwenheim theorem inasmuch as, except for its wide-range applications in various branches of mathematics, it has a deep foundational impact to the extent that we can talk about the same first-order things in models of various infinite cardinalities. This is, for instance, of a particular importance in defining uncountable cardinals within a countable model in P. Cohen's proof of the consistency of the negation of Continuum Hypothesis (**CH**) with the rest of axioms of **ZFC**. It is notable that the Skolem paradox led Skolem himself to the conclusion that first-order axiomatization in terms of sets cannot be a satisfactory foundation of mathematics, whereas P. Cohen extended this pessimism to the claim that ' it is unreasonable to expect that any reasoning of the type we call rigorous mathematics can hope to resolve all but the tiniest fraction of possible mathematical questions.' ([18], p. 372).

2 Syntactical forms and individuals of formal theories in a phenomenological view

In *Formale und Transzendentale Logik*, [13], Husserl inquired into the deeper meaning and the domain of reference of analytic judgements, turning to what is most fundamental, what is, in fact, irreducible in the built-up of analytic statements of any degree of complexity. Assuming that any analytic statement incorporates registered facts or objects as formal-ontological objects, then these objects, taken in the sense of sensuous objects (*Sinnesobjekte*) and predicate bearers (*Seinsobjekte*) together with any doxical modalities fundamentally reflecting consciousness-based states e.g. doubt, certainty, negation etc., belong to the domain of formal apophantics. Formal apophantics conditions truth within a formal theory and uses categories referring to meanings as supposed such as subject, predicate, proposition and judgement, yet it derives its senses from the domain of objects ([29], p. 274). As Husserl put it, judgements in the sense of apophantic logic which he thought to be close to Aristotelian logic, are states-of-affairs as supposed which may be considered as autonomous unities. All other categorial suppositions within these judgements have the place of 'parts' ([13], p. 132). In contrast to formal apophantics, Husserl defined formal ontology as the *a priori* logical science concerned with the elaboration of formal judgements, relations and operations with respect to objects as (intentionally) registered. The domain of formal ontology, concerning mathematical science in general and the theory of sets and of cardinal numbers in particular, is the domain of facts and objects as registered and further apprehended by categorial intuition as 'empty' somethings in general (*Etwas-überhaupt*) and modifications of an 'empty something'. On this account, all formal mathematical analysis as well as the theory of sets and of cardinal and ordinal numbers can be taken to be an ontology inasmuch as it is an *a priori* doctrine of objects and it is moreover a formal one to the extent that it is bound to the pure modes of 'something' in general ([13], pp. 80-82 & [29], pp. 274-283).

Generally, concerning the analytic principles of apophantic logic, the Husserlian view is that it is on the subjective side that it is to be found the *a priori* structure of evidence and the effectuations associated with this structure, whose 'uncovering' demonstrates the essential subjective situations corresponding to their objective sense. Therefore, fundamental principles of pure logic, e.g. the principles of contradiction, of excluded middle, the laws of modus ponens and modus tollens, etc., may be reduced to the evidences of their subjective correlates, in the sense that all judgements must be led in contact with 'the things themselves' to which they refer and must conform to them either in a positive or negative adequation ([13], p. 201). This way, these analytic principles are subject to a critical review concerning their universal objective validity to the extent that their once for all truth is bound to subjective evidence constraints, which may be de facto associated with a partial adequation corresponding to subjective situations (concerning, for instance, the principle of excluded middle) or conditioned on the principle of intersubjectivity (e.g. in

2. SYNTACTICAL FORMS

the case of certain syntactical formulas of predicate calculus bound to universal or existential quantifiers) in the sense of ideal judgements holding for all beings possibly having the same living experience. Overall, the main part of the Husserlian distinction between the apophantic and the formal-ontological level which largely shapes a phenomenologically motivated view of syntactical formulas in mathematical logic can be summed up as follows: 1) a judgement in a formal-ontological sense is not directed toward the judgement itself but toward its thematic objectivity, 2) the thematic object is identical in all variations of syntactical operations, 3) all typical forms assigned to a determinate objectivity, as categorial forms within the unity of its thematic field, are invariable e.g. relation, state-of-affairs, plurality, individuality, order, rank, etc. 4) the coherence of a judgement is ultimately founded on the unity of its thematized object-substrates and their associated categorial objectivities ([13], pp. 116-123). Concerning the relevance of these statements with the structure of syntactical forms in mathematical logic and in particular with the role of absolute formulas within mathematical models ordered by set inclusion[8], I draw attention to the fact that in the aforementioned Husserlian view, **(i)** the essential part of a judgement's 'turn' towards its thematic object implicates the effectuation of certain identifications with regard to the object in question within the chain of judgements, leading to a cohesive 'global' determination in which the most fundamentally important are the object-substrates of the lowest level, that is the primary thematic objects of a synthetic judgement of a higher degree. These could be taken to be the objects of the domain of a model of an axiomatic mathematical theory (Husserl referred at this point to the objects of the domain of a science in general, [13], p. 118), **(ii)** in the course of forming higher order judgements in relation to certain object-substrates, the cohesion of those judgements should be ultimately traced in the identity of the object-substrates themselves, in the formation of corresponding categorial objectivities as syntactical forms associated with them. This identity, as we will see in next sections, is ultimately one that is founded on a temporal unity which is associated with a phenomenology of temporal consciousness on the part of the subject performing the judgements in question.

In phenomenological view, any attempt at a radical deconstruction of the analytic structure of a sentence of any degree of complexity will inevitably lead to sentences about last object-substrates (or individual-substrates) and to properties related to them. As E. Husserl claimed, these sentences are no more of an analytic character but lead to evidences of intentional experience. In this approach, individual-substrates as intentional evidences can be taken as belonging to the following two categories: the ultimate material substances (or eidetic material singularities) with regard to a content and the formal singularities with regard to a form which are pure individual singularities with

---

[8]It is interesting to note that P. Cohen, in commenting on Gödel's proof of the consistency of **AC** and **CH** with the rest of the axioms of **ZF**, mentions the application of the notion of the absoluteness (of formulas) as an application of a new, essentially philosophical concept ([18], pp. 356-357).

no material content whatsoever. A formal singularity as pure eidos, termed 'Dies-da' by Husserl (close to the meaning of Aristotelian τόδε τι), is called an individuum inasmuch as it can be instantiated as bearing a concrete 'thingness' substance (*sachhaltiges Wesen*), ([15], pp. 33-35). To this last category belong the syntactical individuals of predicate formulas within a formal mathematical theory considered by Husserl in *Ideas I* as corresponding to intentionalities towards 'empty somethings'. The radical reduction which in addition to individual-substrates reaches their predicative environment as well, should include in this respect the 'noematic nucleus'[9] of corresponding intentional acts; in case we talk about a syntactical atom of a formal - logical formula, it should include e.g. the $\in$ predicate as the formal abstraction of the noematic correlate of the corresponding individual-substrate whose horizon has an outer 'layer' that is the boundary between the individual-substrate in question and the rest of Husserlian Life-World.[10] The formal abstractions of individual-substrates, i.e. the syntactical atoms of logical formulas, numerals, as well as aggregates of them in the form of sets or classes of sets and also mathematical objects referring to them such as functions of pure analysis, Euclidean or non-Euclidean domains of such functions etc., were considered by Husserl as fundamentally associated with intentionalities towards an empty 'something' devoid of any material content, in other words as intentionalities towards an 'empty substrate' (*Leersubstrat*) ([15], p. 33).

This type of reduction is meant as the result of the elimination of all possible doxical modalities in the construction of analytic sentences of any level of complexity as, for instance, in general statements expressing doubt (S might be p), corroboration (S is in fact p) or negation (S is not p) and so on, including also categorical forms uniquely defined by their syntactical structure, e.g. when one quantifies over elements satisfying a particular analytic property S, [$\forall p\ (S)$ or $\exists p\ (S)$]. What is left ultimately is a multiplicity of individual-substrates with a non-analytically describable 'inner' content, in the sense of intentionally perceived objects and re-identified as uniquely determined and well-defined noematic objects[11] within temporal consciousness associated moreover with a noematic nucleus (or nucleus-form). Nuclei-forms (*Kernformen*) as noematic

---

[9]The noematic nucleus (*Kernform*), is a phenomenological term referring to the ensemble of syntactical forms assigned to a last object-substrate of a sentence, associated in turn with its categorial objectivities by virtue of being content of an intentional act towards a specific 'something'. In that sense, terms as diverse as man and paper share a common indecomposable substantival nucleus irrespective of the sentences they might be encountered in, ([13], p. 310).

[10]The Life-World in a Husserlian sense can be roughly described to a non-phenomenologist as the physical world in its ever receding 'horizon', including in an intersubjective sense all phenomenological reduction - performing subjects in a special kind of presence in the World. More on this in E. Husserl's *The Crisis of European Sciences and Transcendental Phenomenology*, [11].

[11]A noematic object manifests itself as an immanence within the unity of the flux of a subject's consciousness and it is constituted by certain modes of being as such, i.e. a well-defined temporal object immanent to the unity of the flux, whose origin is founded on the moments of hyletic-noetic perception.

2. SYNTACTICAL FORMS

correlates of intentional individual-substrates, taken, for instance, as syntactical forms of atoms of analytic sentences can be thought to invariably retain their essential character in the subsequent construction of analytic statements of any higher order. In this point of view, the non-logical $\in$ predicate is even more fundamental than the equality predicate, a claim formally founded in that the analytic notion of equality presupposes a notion of mutual inclusion; as it is well-known this is reflected in the adoption of the *Extensionality Axiom* in the axiomatical foundation of standard set theory and of any formal theory treating sets as definite collections of objects.

My view is that this radical reduction to intentional individuals of experience as substrates of analytic statements in the lowest possible level of analytic reduction can put in a new perspective the formal role of urelements (elements which by essence cannot be sets) of transitive classes under $\in$ predication. As it will become clear further, the notion of an intentional individual-substrate constituted as a re-identifying noematic object across time and an invariant (under various predicative situations) predicate bearer, can provide a solid interpretation to formal individuals of absolute formulas within transitive set-theoretical models ordered by set inclusion.

It is notable that evidences of individual-substrates of analytic judgements whose very evidence can only be seized by intentional experience in its 'lowest' possible level were described by Husserl as deprived of any inner structure - even lacking a temporal form - at least not one expressible by any analytic means ([13], p. 211). Such objects, irrespective of being thingness- or empty-substrates, together with their 'attached' noematic correlates in the form of an inherent predicative formation, can be taken to represent on the level of a formal theory indecomposable syntactical individuals appropriating *eo ipso* a relational property with respect to any other. By all accounts, owing to the noetic-noematic constitution[12] and to the retentional forms of the constituting flux of consciousness, it is possible to re-identify an individual-substrate x of intentional experience as the one and same noematic object-substrate x under varying predicative situations in the progression of time flux. Any attempt to pass from these irreducible individuals to a constituted objectivity of a higher order can only entail circularities in description or *a priori* terms. For instance, in *Ideas I* Husserl referred to the multi-ray intentionality of the synthetic consciousness which 'transforms' the perception of a collection of concrete objectivities into the constitution of a single objective whole by what he termed a monothetical act whose essential (*wesensmässig*) characterization implicitly points to a creeping transcendence ([15], p. 276).

---

[12] A brief reference to the meaning of noetic objects, mainly described in E. Husserl's *Ideas I* can be summed up as follows: In contrast to noematic objects, noetic objects described as moments of hyletic-noetic perception can be only thought of as evident 'givennesses' of the *a priori* orientation of intentionality without any reference to a temporal-noematic constitution. For instance the color of a tree trunk, as a noematic object, is the invariably one and the same immanent object of temporal consciousness constituted out of a multiplicity of real hyletic-noetic moments of the concrete experience intentionally directed to the particular tree trunk ([15], p. 226).

Now, I draw attention to syntactical individuals as members of transitive classes to review their proof-theoretic role in the absoluteness of certain predicate formulas within **ZFC**.[13] This may help clarify the implicit semantical content of syntactical individuals within the structure of a formal axiomatical theory, taken as formal-ontological objects in abstraction corresponding to irreducible contents of intentional acts.

It is very important, for instance, to assure absoluteness of certain bounded quantifier set-theoretical formulas in the built-up of hierarchies of transitive classes L_α within Gödel's Constructible Universe **L**, in order to prove that **L** serves as a model of **ZFC** plus **CH**, [**ZFC** plus **CH**: **ZF** theory + **AC** (*Axiom of Choice*) + **CH** (*Continuum Hypothesis*)]. For such formulas the property of absoluteness is basically related to the transitivity property of the corresponding class. As a matter of fact, this has much to do with the invariability of the $\in$ - predicative character of zero-level elements within a transitive model in the recursive definition of classes of any rank inside it.[14] For instance, by transitivity property any bounded quantifier formula φ of the form

$$(\exists u \in x)\, \psi \text{ or } (\forall u \in x)\, \psi$$

is absolute between transitive models M and $N (M \subset N)$ whenever formula ψ is.

The simple proof in [21], (p. 118), is implicitly based on two assumptions. First, that in the inductive definition of absolute formulas, atomic formulas ψ of the form $i \in j$ and $i = j$ are absolute and second, that any bounded variable u of the formula φ in N can be invariably identified with an urelement[15] u_M under $\in$ - predication in 'lower' model M.

Both assumptions may radically reduce to admitting the possibility of existence of intentional individual-substrates, retaining in formal representation their double nature both as distinguishable individuals-as such and as individuals bearers of an invariable predicative nucleus in the subsequent construction by transfinite recursion of classes of a higher rank.

---

[13] In rough terms, an absolute formula φ inside a set-theoretical model X keeps the 'mirror' image of itself in any other set-theoretical model Y ordered by set inclusion $(X \subset Y)$ with respect to the original model X.

[14] A class M is transitive if for any $x, y, z \in M$ whenever $x \in y$ and $y \in z$, $x \in z$. This is equivalent to the statement that whenever $x \in M$ and x is not a zero-level element (i.e., not an urelement under $\in$ predication) then $x \subseteq M$.

[15] P. Cohen dismissed urelements as fictitious objects x_i such that $\forall y\ \neg(y \in x_i)$ yet $x_i \neq x_j$ for $i \neq j$ ([20], p. 202). Yet, it might make sense to talk about such objects in the sense I have proposed, that is of indecomposable syntactical atoms taken as abstractions of irreducible individual-substrates of intentional experience. I note here that irrespective of whether one introduces individuals as urelements dropping the Axiom of Extensionality as Fraenkel and Mostowski did, in constructing appropriate models in which the *Axiom of Choice* fails, or dismisses them altogether reserving this denomination only for null-set ($\emptyset$) while retaining a notion of individuals as zero-level elements in a cumulative type structure, the underlying concept of 'indecomposable' individuals preserving invariably their syntactical and (in appropriate interpretation) semantical character remains essentially the same. Standard Zermelo-Fraenkel theory does not refer explicitly to urelements, yet they are indirectly introduced by the Foundation Axiom.

2. SYNTACTICAL FORMS

There is still an open question of how we could possibly ground the uniqueness (and inherent distinguishability for that reason) of a particular syntactical atom corresponding as aforesaid, even in the absence of a material content, to an empty-something of intentionality. My claim is that its uniqueness may, indeed, be derived by being the content of a unique intentional act directed to it, so that in temporal-constitutional terms it may be defined as the unique noematic object in objective reflection corresponding precisely to the meaning of our distinct act, as meaning and content of intentional acts are implying each other in transcendental phenomenology. It is known, that in Husserl's view the content of an intentional act is thought of as the meaning of the act by virtue of which consciousness refers to an object or state of affairs as its own ([30], p. 53).

The relevance of the above with certain claims by D. Krause & A. Coelho in [20], concerning the distinguishability of the formal elements of a relational mathematical structure, can be appreciated to the extent that the indistinguishability of formal elements of such a structure can be 'lifted' by associating ordinal numbers to any collection of these elements. Taking any finite extensions of ordinal numbers as corresponding to the intuition of natural numbers equipped moreover with a sense of well-ordering, this eventual distinguishability has much to do with the particular sense of natural numbers, associated for both Husserl and Poincaré with the irreducibility of the content of arithmetical propositions. I associate this particular intuition of ordinal numbers with the unique, original evidence of irreducible individual-substrates as intentional objects of experience in the constitutional scheme: original impression-retention-protention.

Therefore urelements of an extended Zermelo-Fraenkel universe (ZFU, $\in$) taken as non-identical yet indistinguishable elements by means of the definition of an $\mathcal{A}$-indistinguishability relation within a relational structure, can be made distinguishable by associating to any collection of them an ordinal number, so that it is possible to talk about a collection σ_0, σ_1, σ_3, ..., σ_{n-1} of such objects. This is a result of the simple proof that any ordinal as a well-ordered structure $\langle A, < \rangle$ is a rigid structure, i.e. the only automorphism within this structure is the identity function ([20], p. 201). In other words, in a rigid structure $\mathcal{A}$ the notion of non-identical elements and of $\mathcal{A}$-distinguishable elements coincide.

Let us note that the question of the individuality of quantum entities in the context of quantum mechanics has provided for much theoretical discussion on the nature of quantum objects as they are regarded by some physicists (notably by Scrödinger) as non-individuals upon which a notion of identity does not make sense, whereas by others as bearing a kind of intrinsic individuality by means of which ' they might be qualitatively the same in all aspects representable in quantum mechanical models yet numerically distinct' ([33], p. 376). It is true that D. Krause & A. Coelho cling to the view that the mathematical structure of quantum mechanics has a non-trivial rigid expansion (i.e., not one obtained by trivially adjoining the ordinal structure) whose physical intuition is that quantum objects are somehow 'intrinsically' distinguishable.[16]

3 Infinity within a formal theory from a phenomenological viewpoint

As it is known, Cantor reached his famous $c = 2^{\aleph_0}$ result about the cardinality of real numbers as an outcome of his earlier (1891) result, that $\aleph_0 < 2^{\aleph_0}$, and the subsequent application of an essential form of the Power Set Axiom, namely that the subsets of a (possibly infinite) set form a set. It is notable that in the earlier proof of $\aleph_0 < 2^{\aleph_0}$, Cantor applied a variation of diagonal method to produce a number which is nowhere in any sequence $u_1, u_2, ..., u_n, ...$ of reals inside an interval (a, b) of real numbers, whereas by essentially the same method he proved that the second number class (ω) which, in Cantor's *Grundlagen* notation, is the set associated with the first infinite ordinal ω (ω is also included as one of its members) has more elements than the set of natural numbers ([22], p. 91). In both proofs the underlying technique in showing that a set has a power greater than that of natural numbers is to exhibit, given a sequence of members of the set, a member of the set which is not in the sequence but which can be nevertheless obtained as a kind of limit of a subsequence. At this point, it seems there is some ground to present some phenomenologically motivated arguments. In the first place, there is a certain vagueness concerning the meaning of the limit of a sequence which cannot be specified as belonging to the collection of the terms of the sequence. Given that we can eventually, through a limiting process, accede to a term of this kind, we can see that there must be at least two conditions to be fulfilled.

First, that we are capable of performing intentional acts in actuality and ideally in infinitum (**first-level idealizations**) and then store them in a kind of descending retaining sequence and, second, that the whole process can be constituted as an immanent objectivity in the present now of temporal consciousness (**second-level idealization**). For, let us suppose the impossibility of a second-level idealization. Then taking, for instance, the second number class (ω), how could we possibly conceive of a least ordinal a^∞ member of (ω) which is greater than all ordinals in the infinite increasing sequence $a, a', a'', ...,$ except by objectifying as a continuous whole in the present now an ideally infinite extension of intentional acts performable each time anew in actuality?

As a matter of fact, in a new proof, in 1891, Cantor sought to overcome the dependence on irrational numbers by proving that for any set L and a fixed pair of distinct elements, the set of functions from L to this pair has a power strictly greater than that of L. As it turns out, Cantor was later led to the famous formula $c = 2^{\aleph_0}$, i.e. that the power of the continuum is that of the set of functions from the natural numbers to the pair $\{0, 1\}$, by admitting to a new set-existence principle equivalent to the Power Set Axiom as we know it today ([22], pp. 94-95). This principle is summed up in that if L is a set, so is the

---

[16]More on the debate over the distinguishability of quantum particles within the formal metatheory of quantum mechanics in [1], [5] and [20].

3. INFINITY

domain of all functions from L to a fixed pair. Taking into account that any such function can be fully determined by the subset of L which is mapped by that function to a fixed element of the pair, one is virtually reduced to the adoption of the Power Set Axiom, namely that the collection of the subsets of any set forms a set. But, on the formal level, this came out at the cost of admitting to the existence of an infinite set which cannot be counted or well-ordered by some definable way, whereas on a deeper subjective level its cardinality might motivate some phenomenologically associated assumptions, similar to the ones noted above in connection with the earlier proof of $\aleph_0 < 2^{\aleph_0}$. It is noteworthy that the Power Set Axiom for cardinalities greater than or equal to $\aleph_0$ has been recognized by some set-theorists to be linked in a somewhat inherent way to the character of uncountable infinity and we may quote here P. Cohen's view of the matter in [4], (p. 151), namely that the set C (the continuum) " is generated by a totally new and more powerful principle, namely the Power Set Axiom. It is unreasonable to expect that any description of a larger cardinal which attempts to build up that cardinal from ideas deriving from the Replacement Axiom can ever reach (*the power of*) C. Thus C is greater than $\aleph_n, \aleph_\omega, \aleph_\alpha, ...$ where $\alpha = \aleph_\omega$, etc. This point of view regards C as an incredibly rich set given to us by one bold new axiom, which can never be approached by any piecemeal process of construction."

A more general result than that of $\aleph_0 < 2^{\aleph_0}$, which can also answer indirectly the question of whether there exist cardinalities greater than that of continuum, consists in the proof of the general assumption that a one-to-one mapping from any non-empty set X into its set of subsets $\mathcal{P}(X)$ cannot be onto. This is a result often referred to as a generalization of Cantor's diagonal argument. The standard proof goes like this:

Let us assume that there is such a mapping f which is a one-to-one mapping from X onto $\mathcal{P}(X)$. We then define a subset A of X in terms of $A = \{x; x \notin f(x)\}$. Since f is assumed to be onto $\mathcal{P}(X)$ there must be $a \in X$ such that $f(a) = A$. Therefore a has two possibilities: to be either in A or in $X \backslash A$. If it is in A then $a \notin f(a) = A$, so we get $a \in A \rightarrow a \notin A$. This is impossible so a must be in $X \backslash A$; then $a \notin A$ so $a \in f(a) = A$. Again we get the contradictory $a \notin A \rightarrow a \in A$, so the mapping f cannot be onto.

However from a phenomenologically motivated point of view, in case we take X as an, at least, countably infinite set, at the stage we have formed the infinite subset $A = \{x; x \notin f(x)\}$ to which the element a may or may not belong, we have to formally abstract it as an objective whole (comprising an indefinite aggregate of elements x 'generated' by the particular predicate formula) from its constituted unity in the present now of temporal consciousness. The question is then, what kind of idealization this unity could be associated with, given that the formal elements x are taken as complete abstractions of intentionalities towards 'empty-somethings'. In case it would be a first-level idealization of a series of intentional acts of the form 'I always can do' performed each time in actuality, we would have a set or rather a class of sets $\mathcal{P}(X)$ which could be counted or well-defined in some way. My claim, however, is that regardless of the rank of cardinalities above $\aleph_0$, what fundamentally conditions the existence of an infinite subset A of X and eventually that of the power-set set $\mathcal{P}(X)$ of X, is the possibility to transform on a formal level an ideally infinite series of intentional acts of the form $a \in A$ or $a \notin A$, represented by the formula $x \notin f(x)$, into an objective whole corresponding to the definition of the set $A = \{x;\ x \notin f(x)\}$. In case the set X is at least countably infinite, the set $\mathcal{P}(X)$ can be conceived of as a complete mathematical object by way of abstraction from an objective, continuous whole in the present now 'generated' in effect, in the present case, out of a series of discrete, temporal, cognitive acts running ideally *ad infinitum*. This objective whole may be further radically reduced to the temporal source of the continuous unity of any objectivity within the immanence of consciousness inasmuch as we may regard mathematical objects as special case perceptual objects fundamentally conditioned on a temporal constitution. On this account, there is a strong reason to regard the existence of the set of all subsets of an at least countably infinite set X as reduced to a second-level idealization regardless of the rank of cardinality of X in the canonical scale above $\aleph_0$.[17]

In the following, I will try to show how an important result, associated with fundamental consistency proofs within **ZF** theory, is conditioned on the implicit application of both kinds of idealizations as referred to on p. 4. I am more focused, however, on the second-level idealization as it provides, in my view, a strong clue towards a non-analytic foundation of mathematical theories.

It is well-known in Model Theory that the Skolem-Löwenheim Theorem is a general case theorem roughly stating that we can talk about the same things (i.e., first order sentences) in models of any infinite cardinality and its importance can be easily seen by its wide range of applications, e.g. every group, field, ordered field, etc. has a countable subsystem of the same type; also one can easily derive by its application that Peano arithmetic has non-standard models ([32], p. 113).

One of its specific instances is the so-called Skolem paradox, namely the derivation of a countable model for **ZF** theory, given that $\mathrm{Mod}(\mathbf{ZF}) \neq \emptyset$. This leads to the paradoxical situation of getting a countable model for a theory in terms of which one can prove the existence of uncountable sets, e.g. those with at least the power of continuum. As a matter of fact, this argument cannot be formalized within **ZF** theory and it is only finitely many statements holding in the model that can be proved within **ZF**. This is related, generally, to Gödel's incompleteness, that is, to whether one can in principle, arguing from **ZFC**, produce a set model for all of **ZFC** which is of course denied by the First Incompleteness Theorem. But this is a situation which we may

---

[17] A similar kind of reasoning may be also applied with regard to certain statements concerning uncountably infinite cardinality. For instance, in a proof of the numerical equivalence between an open interval (a, b) of the real line and the whole set of reals R, we have to construct two *ad hoc* formulas, $y = a + (b-a)x$ and $z = \tan\pi(x - \frac{1}{2})$, as numerical equivalences between uncountably infinite sets. These are founded though, as abstractions of one-to-one correspondences, on finite-time, discrete acts of cognition and yet we regard them as complete mathematical objects in actual immediacy ([28], pp. 37-38).

3. INFINITY

overcome on the grounds that one needs a finite amount of **ZFC** at a time, e.g. certain formulas are proved absolute within a transitive model M owing to sufficiently large finite fragments of **ZF**. For instance, if **ZFC** $\vdash y$ then there is a finite list of axioms of **ZFC**, $\varphi_1, .., \varphi_n$, such that $\varphi_1, .., \varphi_n \vdash y$. But this again is bound to the assumption that finite objects as formal deductions of **ZFC** can only mention a finite number of sentences of **ZFC** even if the latter is infinite. However, this is ultimately conditioned on the measure in which a formal language like that of **ZFC** can catch the often vague boundary of finiteness, e.g. in relation to metatheoretical objects in Gödel's incompleteness proofs as we'll see in section 4.

On the interpretational level, the Skolem paradox is 'lightly' overcome by distinguishing the notion of countability inside and outside a model. The model may lack the means to define countability to those within it, e.g. by means of bijections to the natural numbers, but all the same countability may be definable for those 'outside' the model. Skolem's paradox has also its special place in P. Cohen's construction of the proof of consistency of the negation of *Continuum Hypothesis* with the other **ZFC** axioms by appealing to the existence of greater then $\aleph_0$ cardinals within a countable, transitive model M ([21], p. 205). In what comes next, I will point to an underlying presence of second-level idealizations, in the form of actual infinity assumptions, in reaching the derivation of Skolem-Löwenheim Theorem in two different versions of its proof, that is, in [32] and in [21].

In the version of [32], a major key to the proof is the Model Existence Lemma which tells us that if a set Γ of first-order sentences is consistent then Γ has a model of cardinality at most the cardinality of the corresponding language L. The standard construction of a model $\mathcal{U}$ of Γ is based on the definition by recursion of a Henkin extension T_ω of a theory T[18] which is conservative over T and then on the application of Zorn's lemma for the construction of a maximal extension T_m of T_ω.

As the cardinality of the language L_m of T_m and therefore of L_ω of T_ω (as there is no change of language from T_ω to T_m) is, in fact, the cardinality of its closed terms, it suffices to focus on the cardinality of sentences $\exists x\varphi(x)$. It can be easily seen by recursive definitions and induction on n that the numbers of terms and formulas of the language L_ω of T_ω is the same as the number of constants of original language L plus the witnesses ([32], p. 108-109). Therefore turning our attention to the cardinality of witnesses which coincides with the cardinality of existential formulas $\exists x\varphi(x)$, as in Henkin theory T_m we add a constant-witness for each existential formula, we can see how (countable) counting techniques are substituted by logical equivalents or derivatives of the Axiom of Choice, over a 'pre-existing' infinity.

For, letting the cardinalities of constants c_i and of variable-terms x_j of original language L be respectively κ and $\aleph_0$, we have that the cardinality of existential statements is, by means of the set $A = \{\exists\, x(x_0 = c_i);\ i \in I\}$,

---

[18]A theory T is called a Henkin theory if for each sentence $\exists x\varphi(x)$ there is a constant c such that $\exists x\varphi(x) \to \varphi(c) \in T$; in that case c is called a witness for $\exists x\varphi(x)$ ([32], p. 104).

$\max(\kappa, \aleph_0) = \kappa \cdot \aleph_0 = \kappa + \aleph_0 = \mu$ (by the Axiom of Choice in the form of absorption laws, ibid., p. 108). It is clear that an enumeration of terms-variables $x_j, j \in N$ above $\aleph_0$ is substituted by an *ad infinitum* possibility to choose constants $c_i, i \in I$ of a cardinality κ greater than $\aleph_0$, to 'fill-in' the existential formulas of the form $\exists x(x_0 = c_i)$. By assumption of the Axiom of Choice in essentially the same sense we have that the cardinality of a language L is κ in case L has $\kappa \geq \aleph_0$ constants, a key fact in the proof of both downward and upward Skolem-Löwenheim Theorem as it suggests that the cardinality of the language L' of an extended set $\Gamma' = \Gamma \cup \{c_i \neq c_j;\ i, j \in I\}$ is κ' in case we add κ' new constants $\{c_i;\ i \in I\}$ such that $c_i \neq c_j$ to the language L of Γ (ibid., p. 112). An interesting question *a propos* is what kind of objects the syntactical constants $\{c_i;\ i \in I\}$ should be considered to be. Are they to be thought of as singleton sets (but then which would count as zero-level elements?) or as urelements for which there is a strong objection as to the soundness of the relation $\{c_i \neq c_j;\ i, j \in I\}$ (see footnote 15).

It should be noted that although the Model Existence Lemma (and therefore its inclusive Completeness Theorem for first-order logic) is ultimately based on the Axiom of Choice, it was nonetheless shown by Henkin in 1954 to be equivalent to the Boolean Prime Ideal Theorem which was, in turn, shown to be weaker than **AC** by Halpern and Levy in [8]. However, in view of my motivating approach, even weaker forms of **AC**, such as the principle of Dependent Choice - proved in [7] to be equivalent to Tarski's Lemma which is in turn applied in certain completeness proofs, ([3], pp. 62-64) - presuppose anyway a notion of pre-existing actual infinity.

The indirect recourse to the Axiom of Choice is also necessary in [21] for the proof of the downward Skolem-Löwenheim Theorem, in fixing a well-order inside a set $Z(\beta)$ so that a finite number of formulas $\varphi_1, ..., \varphi_n$ are absolute between a set A, $(A \subset Z(\beta))$, and a class Z ([21], pp. 139-141). It is noteworthy that this approach takes into consideration the impossibility to define a model of **ZFC** for all axioms of **ZFC**, proving the existence of a countable, transitive model M for a finite fragment $\varphi_1, ..., \varphi_n$ of the axioms of **ZFC**.[19] Although, as a consequence, the result above complies with the First Incompleteness Theorem, it nonetheless involves the elusive presence of an actual infinity factor (i.e. of the Axiom of Choice) in choosing successively well-ordered objects within the set $Z(\beta)$, where β is a limit ordinal.

Consequently in view of the above, the conclusion to be made is that the countability of a model M within whose context it is impossible to define e.g. the uncountable second limit ordinal ω_1^M, - even if it becomes 'technically'

---

[19]As a matter of fact, there exists a set model $H(\kappa) = \{x;\ |\mathrm{trcl}(x)| < \kappa\}$ for **ZFC - P** for a regular cardinal $\kappa > \omega$ but the Power Set Axiom (**P**) fails in $H(\kappa)$, unless κ is strongly inaccessible. The problem is that the existence of a strongly inaccessible cardinal cannot be proved within **ZFC** ([21], pp. 133-134). This fact certainly lends a further credibility to the claim on p. 11 that the Power Set Axiom 'sets up' an impredicative infinity factor within the **ZFC** system by admitting to the existence of a set that cannot be counted or well-ordered in some definable way.

4. DEFICIENCY

possible to do so 'from the outside' by Skolem's paradox, - is in fact a 'fake' countability conditioned on the intuition of a pre-existing indefinite, continuous substratum in presentational immediacy on which to possibly induce a well-ordering *ad infinitum*.

A brief discussion of **AC** in the light of my overall approach seems to be worthwhile here. An intuition of the *Axiom of Choice* as an actual infinity principle of a metatheoretical content is that we can, in principle, apply a criterion of choice at any infinity level which could provide us with the possibility to choose a formal individual with an inherent $\in$ predication attached to it (think of it as an urelement of a set-theoretical model) among an infinity of potential choices; put in a phenomenological context, it is equivalent to applying someone's concrete intentionality each time in actual present among other potential intentionalities in an on-going progression.

I argue that a notion of well-ordering may be *a priori* induced on the level of hyletic - noetic perception[20] by the sole virtue of the 'property' of an intentional object to bear an outer horizon, i.e. that part of the Life-World which is not the object or parts of the object. Evidently, this 'property' provides for a complementary domain of 'observation' for a next phenomenological perception which by its very enactment provides for a new complementary domain and so on. This way a notion of well-ordering may be grounded on the level of intentionality with regard to a multiplicity of original givennesses as objects of intentional perception. Now, what is left after discarding all other details of constitution is fundamentally the possibility to intentionally perceive (and immanently retain by retention) individuals ('things-' or 'empty-substrates') through protentions of intentionality within the domain of Life-World experience. This way, it looks possible a fundamental reduction of the *Axiom of Choice* to the notion of a sequence of ideally *ad infinitum* intentional acts of an *a priori* character within an objective continuous unity, inducing on a formal level a well-ordering among any aggregation of formal-ontological objects.

On a still deeper level, an application of the Axiom of Choice should be conditioned on the existence of a constituted temporal unity in whose context to perform, in principle, indefinitely many intentional acts of a well-meant choice. Therefore, from my general point of view, **AC** should be meant as a second-level idealization.

4 The deficiency of the notion of finitistic in Gödel's First Incompleteness result

In mathematical foundations a key step in proving the incompleteness of a recursive and consistent extension **T** of **ZF** theory is to prove that the set of theorems of the extension **T** is not recursive ([21], pp. 38-40). In this approach

---

[20]This kind of perception can be roughly described as the perception associated with intentional consciousness as such, 'prior' to an objective temporal constitution. Thus, the 'sensed' color of a tree is the hyletic-noetic moment of the intentional act by which the noematic or 'objective' color is 'adumbrated' ([15], p. 226).

the notion of a recursive (or decidable) set plays a major role by the following Theorem 4.1, which represents recursive sets such as the set of natural numbers or the set of finite sequences by means of formulas of **ZF**. Recursiveness and calculability of functions and predicates (and consequently of sets as unary predicates) are by Church's thesis equivalent notions and they may be essentially associated with discrete, finite-time cognitive acts on sets of natural numbers in the scope of reaching a conclusion within a finite number of steps.[21] A recursive set might thus be in a certain sense linked to the discrete way an 'observer' applies his intentional 'observation' towards a countable collection of well-defined objects possibly by the intermediary of a digital device. I take as well-defined objects in the particular formal-mathematical context the abstractions of formal-ontological objects registered as unique contents of intentional acts in actual presence.

Generally, based on the definition of the expression number of a designator $\mathcal{U}$ (a name-term for a particular object inside a language L) and also on the definition of a sequence number for an n-tuple $(\alpha_1, ..., \alpha_n)$, it can be shown that a theory T in a first-order language L is decidable iff the set Thm_T of expression numbers of theorems of T is recursive (or calculable by Church's thesis) ([27], p. 116 & pp. 122-123). This result is obtained by taking into account that the expression number $\ulcorner \mathcal{U} \urcorner$ assigned, e.g. to designator $\mathcal{U}$, is defined by induction on the length of $\mathcal{U}$; for instance, following the notation of [27], if by the formation theorem, $\mathcal{U} = vv_1....v_n$, where v is a symbol for the index n and $v_1, ..., v_n$ are lower order designators, then the expression number of $\mathcal{U}$ is:

$$\ulcorner \mathcal{U} \urcorner = < SN(v), \ulcorner v_1 \urcorner, ..., \ulcorner v_n \urcorner >$$

where $SN(v)$ is the number assigned to the symbol v ([27], p. 123). That means, in case the designator $\mathcal{U}$ is an arbitrary-length formula and moreover involves variables bounded to universal quantifiers, the assignment of a number corresponding to the particular designator $\mathcal{U}$ entails a lack of finitistic rigor in the construction of the proof of calculability of Thm_T. Similar concerns may be raised regarding the structure of both Gödel's incompleteness theorems where a form of Theorem 4.3 is applied. This particular theorem, known as the Cantor's Diagonal Lemma or Fixed-Point Lemma, is conditioned after all on the acceptance of representability formulas of the type $\mathbf{ZF} \vdash \forall u \; \exists! w \; \chi(u, w)$ (a Level-2 assertion, see footnote 24) and consequently it associates non-rigorously finitistic metatheoretical objects with formal objects u and w ([21] pp. 40-41). It is well-known that a special case of the Fixed-Point Lemma known as Tarski's Undefinability of Truth Lemma leads to Gödel's First Incompleteness Theorem.

---

[21] For instance, every finite set A with members $m_1, ..., m_n$ is recursive because it has the explicit definition

$$A(\alpha) \leftrightarrow \alpha = m_1 \vee .... \vee \alpha = m_n$$

in the aforementioned sense. Many other functions and sets are proved to be recursive in this sense, e.g. sequence numbers and the set of sequence numbers over sets of n-tuples $(\alpha_1, ..., \alpha_n)$ ([27], pp. 116-117).

4. DEFICIENCY

My main argument next, is that the incompleteness of formal systems with at least the expressive capacity of formal arithmetic is largely due to the non-rigorously finitistic character of metatheoretical objects corresponding to formal objects of the theory,[22] the latter taken as possible outcomes of extensions by definition within a consistent formal theory. As it comes out, a key element in the proof of the first incompleteness result is that the set of theorems of **ZF** or of any consistent set of axioms **T** extending **ZF** is not recursive. The proof of this fact can be obtained either by Theorem 4.2 below, based in turn on aforementioned Theorem 4.3, or by applying Cantor's diagonal argument and the Representability Theorem for the special case of a consistent extension T of the arithmetical theory N ([27], p. 131). The latter proof is, however, bound to the inherent 'vagueness' of Cantor's diagonal argument in assigning a unary predicate Q such that $Q(\alpha) \leftrightarrow \neg P(\alpha, \alpha)$ for any numeral α. This 'vagueness' may be linked to the presupposition of an actual infinity in terms of which it is possible to define a unary predicate Q with $Q(\alpha) \leftrightarrow \neg P(\alpha, \alpha)$ for all numerals α; in other words, for all such α so that Q is distinct from all unary predicates $P_{(a)}$ with $P_{(a)}(\alpha) \leftrightarrow P(\alpha, a)$. As it is also the case with the application of Level-2 assertions in proving the non-recursiveness of the set of theorems of any consistent extension of **ZF** theory, Cantor's diagonal argument entails also indirectly a non-rigorous finitistic character of metaheoretical objects.

Let us now follow the steps of the proof of incompleteness of a recursive, consistent extension **T** of **ZF** in [21] (pp. 38-41).

THEOREM 4.1. *Given any recursive set $\mathcal{N}$ of natural numbers there is a formula $\chi_\mathcal{N}(x)$ which represents $\mathcal{N}$ in the sense that for all n,*

$$n \in \mathcal{N} \longrightarrow (\mathbf{ZF} \vdash \chi_\mathcal{N}(\ulcorner n \urcorner) \text{ and } n \notin N \ (\mathbf{ZF} \vdash \neg \chi_\mathcal{N}(\ulcorner n \urcorner))$$

Recursive sets of finite sequences and recursive predicates in several variables are likewise representable.[23]

Let it be noted here that this theorem is proved in metatheory, that is, in a language referring to finitistic metatheoretical objects by means of natural numbers in the place of symbols introduced in an extension of **ZF** by definition. Now, I prove that the set of theorems deduced from a consistent and recursive set of axioms **T** extending (the recursive set of axioms) **ZF** is not itself recursive.

THEOREM 4.2. *Let **T** be any consistent set of axioms extending **ZF**. Then the set of theorems $\{y;\ \mathbf{T} \vdash y\}$ is not recursive.*

Proof: If it were recursive, then by Theorem 4.1, there would be a set-theoretical formula $\chi(x)$ of **ZF** such that for any $y \in \{y;\ \mathbf{T} \vdash y\}$:

$$(\mathbf{T} \vdash y) \longrightarrow (\mathbf{ZF} \vdash \chi(\ulcorner y \urcorner))$$

---

[22] The term formal object here and elsewhere in the text refers to its sense as an object of a formal-axiomatical theory.

[23] The notation $\ulcorner y \urcorner$ in W.V.O. Quine's convention represents the symbol $\ulcorner y \urcorner$ in an extension of **ZF** by definition, corresponding to a finitistic object y in metatheory.

And for any $y \notin \{y;\ \mathbf{T} \vdash y\}$:

$$(\mathbf{T} \nvdash y) \longrightarrow (\mathbf{ZF} \vdash \neg\chi(\ulcorner y \urcorner))$$

Now we fix ψ (by Theorem 4.3) so that: $\mathbf{ZF} \vdash (\psi \leftrightarrow \neg\chi(\ulcorner\psi\urcorner))$ (**I**). But this means that $\mathbf{T} \nvdash \psi$ (**II**) for obviously ψ would not belong to the set $\{y;\ \mathbf{T} \vdash y\}$ since within $\mathbf{ZF}$ it is logically equivalent to $\neg\chi(\ulcorner\psi\urcorner)$. Also by (**I**): $\mathbf{ZF} \vdash \psi$ since $\mathbf{ZF} \vdash (\psi \leftrightarrow \neg\chi(\ulcorner\psi\urcorner))$. But then $\mathbf{T} \vdash \psi$ (**III**) as $\mathbf{T}$ is taken to be a consistent extension of $\mathbf{ZF}$. By (**II**) and (**III**) we have that $\mathbf{T} \nvdash \psi$ and $\mathbf{T} \vdash \psi$ which means that T is inconsistent, a contradiction ◊

It is straightforward to see how this result fits in the proof of Gödel's First Incompleteness Theorem for $\mathbf{ZF}$, namely that if $\mathbf{T}$ is a recursive consistent extension of $\mathbf{ZF}$ then it is incomplete in the sense that we may find a sentence φ such that $\mathbf{T} \vdash \varphi$ and $\mathbf{T} \nvdash \varphi$. The simple proof in [21] is as follows:

If there were no such φ, then for every φ either $\mathbf{T} \vdash \varphi$ or $\mathbf{T} \vdash \neg\varphi$ and, assuming $\mathbf{T}$ consistent, these cannot both be valid. Then we could decide whether $\mathbf{T} \vdash \varphi$ by programming a computer to start listing all formal deductions from $\mathbf{T}$ and stop when a deduction of φ or $\neg\varphi$ has been found. But this is conditioned on the recursiveness of the set $\{\varphi;\ \mathbf{T} \vdash \varphi\}$ which was proved by 4.2 not to be recursive.

In case we take $\mathbf{T}$ to be $\mathbf{ZF}$, its incompleteness is de facto demonstrated by the undecidability of the *Axiom of Choice* (**AC**) ($\mathbf{ZF} \nvdash \mathbf{AC}$ and $\mathbf{ZF} \nvdash \neg\mathbf{AC}$), whereas in case $\mathbf{T}$ is extended to $\mathbf{ZFC}$ its incompleteness is demonstrated by the undecidability of *Continuum Hypothesis* (**CH**) ($\mathbf{ZFC} \nvdash \mathbf{CH}$ and $\mathbf{ZFC} \nvdash \neg\mathbf{CH}$). Generally, no matter how we extend $\mathbf{ZF}$ to a recursive, consistent set of axioms $\mathbf{T}$, the First Incompleteness Theorem guarantees that there will always be sentences undecidable by $\mathbf{T}$. Now, I turn again to the steps leading to the proof of incompleteness of any recursive and consistent extension $\mathbf{T}$ of $\mathbf{ZF}$ before going on with my arguments on the relevance of a non-analytic and possibly phenomenologically motivated interpretation.

As a matter of fact, Theorem 4.1 proves that any recursive set is formally representable within $\mathbf{ZF}$ by corresponding to any metatheoretical (finitistic) object n a formal object $\ulcorner n \urcorner$ in the place of the free variable of a $\mathbf{ZF}$ formula, added as a constant by definition within $\mathbf{ZF}$. However, by 4.2 it is proved that there can be no recursively enumerable process to check all formal deductions from $\mathbf{ZF}$ (or from any recursive consistent extension of $\mathbf{ZF}$), a result basically due to the non-rigorous definition of the notion of finitistic in Level-2 assertions. This is particularly important from my standpoint, as Level-2 assertions[24] do

---

[24] An example of a Level-2 satisfaction formula within $\mathbf{ZF}$ is:

$$\mathbf{ZF} \vdash \forall x \in \omega,\ \mathcal{X}_{\text{odd}}(x) \vee \mathcal{X}_{\text{odd}}(x + \ulcorner 1 \urcorner)\ (1)$$

where there is no rigorously defined finitistic character of objects x, whereas in a Level-1 formula such as $\mathcal{X}_{\text{odd}}(x) \equiv (\exists y \in \omega)\ (x = 2\ulcorner y\urcorner + 1)$ (**2**), one should be able to check *in rem* whether, for example, $\mathbf{ZF} \vdash \mathcal{X}_{\text{odd}}(\ulcorner 7\urcorner)$ or $\mathbf{ZF} \vdash \neg\mathcal{X}_{\text{odd}}(\ulcorner 12\urcorner)$.

The incompatible character of formulas (1) and (2) with respect to the finitistic or non-finitistic character of the formal objects involved, seems to be a reflexion of the asymmetry

4. DEFICIENCY

not implicate rigorously defined finitistic objects and consequently do not fall within the range of strictly acceptable formulas in the sense of Theorem 4.1. The application of such a satisfaction formula, i.e. of **ZF** $\vdash \forall u\ \exists!w\ \chi(u,w)$, which is a key step in the proof of the following well-known theorem below, by virtue of which it is partly due 4.2 also stands behind the Second Incompleteness Theorem and Tarski's Undefinability of Truth Lemma.

THEOREM 4.3. *If $\varphi(x)$ is any formula in one free variable x, then there is a sentence ψ such that* **ZF** $\vdash \psi \leftrightarrow \varphi(\ulcorner\psi\urcorner)$.

It seems that there is some meta-proof-theoretic 'effect' of the non-rigorously finitistic character of metatheoretical objects, e.g. those represented in the satisfaction formula **ZF** $\vdash \forall u\ \exists!w\ \chi(u,w)$, in getting the result of the theorem above and consequently of 4.2. I remind that 4.2 is applied straightforward to prove the First Incompleteness Theorem, i.e. that there exists a sentence φ within a recursive, consistent extension **T** of **ZF** such that **T** $\vdash \varphi$ and **T** $\nvdash \varphi$.

It is also true that in S.C. Kleene's *Introduction to Metamathematics*, [19], the constraint of finitistic with regard to any formal object is also in place to be able to talk about a decision procedure or, in other words, about a meta-mathematical effectively decidable predicate $\mathcal{R}(x, Y)$, where Y is a proof of the formal object $A(\mathbf{x})$, $\mathbf{x}$ being the numeral corresponding to the natural number x. This would make possible by Gödel numbering to correlate the effectively decidable predicate $\mathcal{R}(x, Y)$ that corresponds to the metamathematical statement 'Y is a proof of $A(\mathbf{x})$' with the effectively decidable number-theoretic predicate (function)

$$R(x, y) \equiv \{y \text{ is the natural number correlated to formal object } Y, \text{ such that } \mathcal{R}(x, Y)\}$$

This way, and also by Church's thesis that every effectively calculable function (every effectively decidable predicate) is general recursive, we are led to an equivalence of the notions of a general recursive and an effectively decidable predicate. This leads, however, to an unsolvability of the decision problem in a formal system **S**, that is, to the non-existence of a decision procedure for determining the provability of any formula in **S** ([19], pp. 309 & 313). It turns out that determining a formula of the system **S** as provable, by effectively representing a corresponding formula $B(\mathbf{x})$ for any natural number x, implicitly involves a non-rigorous notion of finitistic for the formal object involved, just as it was the case with the derivation of 4.2 which resulted in the non-recursiveness of the set of theorems deduced from a recursive, consistent extension of **ZF**.

Conclusively, in the context of the discussion above, each formal object should represent a finitistic metatheoretical object, otherwise it would make no properly meant sense e.g. to talk about a decision procedure regarding the

---

between the universal and the existential quantifiers of the respective formulas. We can possibly draw a parallel here with the notions of *Verifizierbarkeit* (verifiability) and *Falsifizierbarkeit* (falsifiability) in relation to the validity of universal logical sentences in the Popperian theory of knowledge (see: Popper K.: *Logik der Forschung*, Wien: Springer, 1934).

metamathematical predicate $\mathcal{R}(x,Y)$, where Y is a formal object telling us that it is a proof of $A(\mathbf{x})$ for any particular natural number x corresponding to the numeral $\mathbf{x}$. This means that each Y should be generated from a finite number of initial objects by a finite number of applications of recognized operations e.g. those of arithmetical theory. In that case, the initial objects should be either conceivable as generated themselves from some other finitely many initial objects by a finite number of recognized operations or as irreducibly finitistic objects themselves, conceivable (in a phenomenological sense) as associated with finite-time cognitive acts on the part of an intentional subject. In case we take the formal object Y as merely a multiple sign-configuration constituted out of a finite number of occurrences of symbols from a preassigned countable list, we could possibly reach as far as taking these sign-configurations as abstractions of intentionalities towards a concrete (possibly empty) 'something', that is, as contents of intentional-type enactments in actual present akin to L.E.J. Brouwer's two-ity intuition contents.

In such a view, finitistic formal objects possibly generated by a finite number of arithmetical-kind operations, may be associated with a **first-level idealization**, whereas the generation of infinite objects by means of Level-2 formulas may be associated with a **second-level idealization** (see, p. 180), inasmuch as Level-2 formulas presuppose an implicit assumption of an impredicative, continuous substratum on which to generate formal objects throughout ideally *ad infinitum* extendible finite-time knowing acts. The impredicative substratum assumption, in turn, can be further grounded on an underlying notion of temporal constitution reaching as far back as the constitutive factor of the continuous objective unity of temporal consciousness. It is noteworthy that, back on the formal level, the richness of the expressional means and the formula-engendering capacity of formal theories, such as **ZF**, transcends that of recursively enumerable processes which may be thought of as reducible to finite-time, discrete intentional acts. This is something that evidently seeks an interpretation beyond a strictly analytic point of view.

The vaguely finitistic character of metatheoretical objects in establishing incompleteness results can be also noted in the original form of Gödel's First Incompleteness Theorem, presented for instance, in [19] (pp. 207-208). In that original version we can produce, relying on a Gödel numbering, an undecidable formula $Ap(\mathbf{p})$, substituting by G. Cantor's diagonal method the numeral $\mathbf{p}$ for the free variable α in $Ap(\alpha) \equiv \forall b \, \neg A(\alpha, b)$ where p is the Gödel number of the formula $Ap(\alpha)$, in a free variable α, and b is the the Gödel number of the proof of this formula. Therefore, the formula $Ap(\mathbf{p}) \equiv \forall b \, \neg A(\mathbf{p}, b)$ asserts its own unprovability but on the (dubious) implicit assumption that Cantor's diagonal method preserves the finitistic character of metamathematical objects in an *ad infinitum* process of progressing enumeration. Regarding, in particular, the proof of incompleteness theorems for arithmetic, it is questionable whether one can diagonalize outside a formal system even in diagonalizing outside what is knowable to be true of natural numbers, in the formation of each new Gödel formula. This is an argument evidently related with Gödel's abstract notion of

4. DEFICIENCY

proof where 'provable' is meant as equivalent to 'knowable to be true' ([30], p. 116).[25]

As it happened, Gödel in his phenomenologically motivated quest to provide an interpretation to incompleteness results, was strongly preoccupied with the notion of meaning clarification (that is, essentially, with categorial intuition) in such thought structures or thought contents as proofs, meaningful propositions, etc. In this sense, he found out that proofs tied to incompleteness results, for instance, the proof of **CON(PA)** (consistency of Peano Arithmetic), must involve objects or concepts which are not completely representable in space-time as meaningless, finite, discrete sign-configurations accessible to concrete intuition in Hilbert's finitistic sense ([30], p. 133). As it was the case with the stages of the proof of the first incompleteness theorem discussed above, one has ultimately to appeal to the metamathematical content of sign-configurations and deal with abstract objects and concepts that are in a certain (metatheoretical) sense non-finitistic.

Even if Gödel had in mind some kind of better clarification or deeper intuition of abstract concepts brought upon by acquiring a more thorough categorial intuition of mathematical essences, I still hold to the view that what fundamentally conditions, on the phenomenological level, the process of meaning attribution to abstract concepts is the possibility to constitute them in the first place as re-identifying, noematic objects within temporal unity, this kind of unity being understood as the objectified unity of the transcendental subjectivity of temporal consciousness.[26] For that reason, we might better consider this transcendence as the ultimate root of the evident incompatibility produced on the formal level between the concrete, sensible intuition of finite sign-configurations reducible to concrete fulfillments of intentionality towards a specific 'something' and the vagueness of uncountable infinity stemming from the transcendental and therefore impredicative character of the unity of (constituting) temporal consciousness in terms of which the intentional contents in question are perceived as temporal instantaneities.

So far undecidable statements of **ZF** have to do in an explicit or implicit sense with some kind of uncountable infinity, e.g. **CH**, **AC**, **SH** (Suslin's Hypothesis), **KH** (Kurepa's Hypothesis), and they are moreover proved to be in one or the other way interconnected; for instance, **Con(ZFC)** ⊢ **Con(ZFC+ CH)** and **Con(ZFC)** ⊢ **Con(ZFC+ ¬ CH)**. **SH** follows from **MA** + ¬**CH** but it also holds: ◊ → ¬**SH** and ◊ is consistent with **GCH** ([21], pp. 80-81); **MA**, the well-known Martin's Axiom, is also an independent statement making claims about uncountable infinities.

As **CH** is a statement directly associated with mathematical Continuum, it

---

[25] There is a certain controversy around Cantor's diagonal method, known as *Diagonalverfahren*, as it is thought to use self-referential or non-predicative concepts like 'the set of all sets'. In my view, this method may be deeper related with the dubious finitistic character of metamathematical objects in an *ad infinitum* process of enumeration conditioned on the existence of an actual infinity (not a natural, causal one) in presentational immediacy.

[26] A brief description of the relation between object constitution and meaning attribution in the Husserlian approach is offered in the Appendix at the end of this section.

is worth referring to P. Cohen's conclusion in *Set Theory and the Continuum Hypothesis* that ' the problem of **CH** is not one which can be avoided by not going up in type to sets of real numbers. A similar undecidable problem can be stated using only the concept of real numbers.' ([4], pp. 151-152). Cohen went on to state that even in postulating as a vague article of faith that any statement in arithmetic is decidable in a higher order system such as the **ZF** Set Theory by adding perhaps some extra appropriate infinity axiom, there will still remain set-theoretical questions which cannot be expressed as statements about integers alone. It is remarkable, that W.H. Woodin's older progress in deciding **CH** by partly relying on the principle of projective determinacy and on certain stronger versions of Martin's Axiom and a recent one by placing it in a new generic-multiverse context having to do with generic extensions of universes of sets that can accommodate large cardinal axioms, does not seem exempt from actual infinity assumptions such as the Axiom of Choice (see respectively, [34] and [35]).

Now keep in mind that on pages 197–198, I referred to the indirect effect a non-rigorous definition of finitistic in metatheoretical objects might have on proving the non-recursiveness of the set of theorems deduced from any consistent extension of ZF. We may say that a loose notion of finitistic in metatheory (as reflected in Level-2 assertions) 'plants a bug' in the structure of the proof of Theorem 4.3 whose application thereafter in Theorem 4.2 leads to the proof of the non-recursiveness of the set of theorems of any consistent extension of **ZF**. As this result essentially means that the expressional depth of set-theoretical statements exceeds that of statements involving integers alone, it can motivate a two-fold claim: 1) insofar as finitistic metatheoretical objects are perceived by some form of concrete intuition as well-defined, discrete, finitely generated objects and in phenomenological view as ultimately reduced to thingness- (or empty)-substrates of finitely many intentional acts carried out in actual present (**first-level idealizations**), they formally help define recursive sets such as those of Theorem 4.1 and can be represented by means of set-theoretical formulas as 'lawful' formal objects of any consistent **ZF** extension. 2) in the case, though, they are not rigorously finitistic but display a 'shade' of inherent (uncountable) infinity induced by their temporal constitution as objective wholes in a sense contrary to the above (**second-level idealizations**), they let their metatheoretical non-finitary content 'slip' through the syntactical structure of relevant proofs (e.g. that of Theorem 4.3) to finally produce results such as the non-recursiveness of set-theoretical deductions and lead to undecidability results on a formal-theoretical level.

In conclusion, as it was also shown in previous sections in connection with the phenomenologically motivated notions of **first-level** and **second-level idealization**, there seem to be strong clues towards a non-analytic foundation of mathematical theories especially in view of undecidable statements evoking some kind of impredicative, actual infinity. In the bottom line, we lack a theory which can, on the syntactical level, describe individual-substrates otherwise than as already objectified irreducibilities. At the same time, there is no theory which can describe the continuum (generally, any greater than $\aleph_0$ cardinality) by any other means except by implicitly or explicitly endorsing a notion of infinity that reflects a temporally constituted, continuous substratum in presentational immediacy.

5 Appendix

We can raise the possibility of forming an object of knowledge roughly based on the following conditions referred to in Husserl's *Logical Investigations*: a) the *a priori* character of the noetic form of intentionality independently of any concrete empirical act conditioned on psychological constraints and b) the purely logical character of the ideal conditions of an object's knowledge grounded on the content of the acts of knowledge. On account of the first condition a thinking subject should be, in principle, capable to implement all sorts of acts to ground theoretically his knowledge and on account of the second condition we should consider theoretical meaning, associated with truthfulness of judgements in descending order and with logical laws reducible to fundamental logical principles, as expressions of conditions grounded on the content of acts of knowledge. Although these laws as *a priori* conditions of knowledge can be taken as such independently of a possible relation to a subjectivity, yet they were considered by Husserl as somehow 'susceptible to a reversal' by means of which they acquire as expressive experiences (*ausdrückliche Erlebnisse*) a relation to a knowing subject.

This is also a claim brought upon in the supplementary volume to the *Logical Investigations* completed in 1913, ([17]), where the expressibility of lived experiences is explicitly conditioned on the acts of judgement of a subject who can form by a judgemental act, irrespective of whether an object of judgement is transcendental or immanent to his consciousness, an expression referring, e.g. to an experienced feeling of desire or generally any lived-in experience nonexpressible as such, in a way that: directs to it a reflective phenomenological perception (*Wahrnehmung*), puts it under the general meaning of 'desire' and through this meaning and the particularity of the content of the specific desire gives it its definite meaning ([17], p. 63).

With regard to the meaning of linguistic forms, Husserl implicated anyway at this stage an intentional subjectivity by evoking his well-known thematic from *Ideas I* and the *Phenomenology of Inner Time-Consciousness* on intentionally constituted objects of consciousness, which refers to an object as supposed in the sense that it is the reflective expression of the 'empty significative intention' corresponding to it ([17], p. 74). Further, a common foundation of object and meaning was envisaged by Husserl as the double-sided content of knowing acts in terms of which the possibility of a theoretical knowledge can have no other sense than the meaningfully thought objects; in reverse, as we can turn back from objects to meanings the possibility of a theory can " mean nothing else than the 'validity' or better the substantivity (*Wesenhaftigkeit*) of the related meaning." ([14] p. 242).

In this sense, talking about the meaning of an object and the fulfillment of a meaning-oriented intention essentially express the same thing inasmuch as objects are thought of as contents of intentional acts and their intuiting (*Anschauung*) as fulfilled through a meaning-oriented intention in a dynamical relation unfolded within phenomenological temporality ([17], pp. 39-40). In what proves to be a fundamental difference between the constituting and the constituted level Husserl considered the temporally constituted objects of an intentional act of cognition to be in a statical relation, whereas the realization of any intentional act towards its content, inasmuch it is a fulfillment within temporal consciousness, to 'be' in a dynamical relation.

Overall, the solid foundation of meaningfully thought objects, irrespective of whether they are taken as fundamentally registered by intentionality (formal-ontological objects) or as supposed (objects of an apophantic domain), can be traced to their possibility of existence as fulfillments of intentional acts of a temporal consciousness. This possibility establishes the theoretical ground to consider registered-in, lowest-level intentional objects, including, as formal-ontological objects, the objects of logical-mathematical theories, as re-identifying immanences within constituted temporality; this latter temporality being, in turn, ultimately conditioned on the transcendental subjectivity of the unity of temporal consciousness. As it has been undertaken to show elsewhere ([24]), this kind of transcendence within immanent temporality, referred to by Husserl as the absolute ego of consciousness or the absolute subjectivity of the flux of consciousness in [12], stands also as a metaphysical 'hole' in the epistemological foundations of formally representable physical theories such as quantum mechanics. This might, of course, be true of formal mathematical theories as such and the case of the incompleteness result among others, as reviewed above, helps to provide some clues to this claim.

BIBLIOGRAPHY

[1] Adams, R. (1979), Primitive Thisness and Primitive Identity, *Journal of Philosophy*, 76, 1, 5-26.
[2] Atten, v, M.: (2006), *Brouwer meets Husserl: On the Phenomenology of Choice Sequences*, Synthese Library, V. 335, Dordrecht: Springer.
[3] Bell, L. J. & Slomson, B. A.: (2006), *Models and Ultraproducts*, Dover Publications.
[4] Cohen P.: (1966), *Set Theory and the Continuum Hypothesis*, Mass.: W.A. Benjamin.
[5] French, S.: (1989), Identity and Individuality in Classical and Quantum Physics, *Australasian Journal of Philosophy*, 67, 4, 432-446.
[6] Føllesdal, D.: (1969), Husserl's Notion of Noema, *Journal of Philosophy*, 66, pp. 680-687.
[7] Goldblatt, R.: (1985), On the role of the Baire Category Theorem and Dependent Choice in the foundation of logic, *The Journal of Symbolic Logic*, 50, 2, pp. 412-422.
[8] Halpern, D.J. & Levy, A. (1971), The Boolean prime ideal theorem does not imply the axiom of choice, in: *Axiomatic Set Theory*, AMS Proc., pp. 83-134.
[9] Hill, C.O.: (2010), Husserl on Axiomatization and Arithmetic, in: *Phenomenology and Mathematics*, (ed. M. Hartimo), pp. 47-69, Springer Science+Business Media B.V. 2010.
[10] Hill, C.O. & Rosado Haddock, G.E.: (2000), *Husserl or Frege? Meaning, Objectivity, and Mathematics*, La Salle, Open Court.
[11] Husserl, E. (1962), *Die Krisis der Europäischen Wissenschaften und die Transzendentale Phänomenologie*, Hua, Band VI, hgb. W. Biemel, Den Haag: M. Nijhoff.
[12] Husserl, E. (1966), *Zur Phänomenologie des Inneren Zeibewusstseins*, Hua, Band X, hgb. R. Boehm, Den Haag: M. Nijhoff.

5. APPENDIX

[13] Husserl, E. (1974), *Formale und Transzendentale Logik*, Hua, Band XVII, hgb. P. Janssen, Den Haag: M. Nijhoff.
[14] Husserl, E.: (1975), *Logische Untersuchungen*, (Prolegomena zur Reinen Logik), Hua, Band XVIII, hgb. E. Holenstein, Den Haag: M. Nijhoff.
[15] Husserl, E. (1976), *Ideen zu einer reinen Phänomenologie und phänomenologischen Philosophie*, Erstes Buch, Hua, Band III/I, hgb. K. Schuhmann, Den Haag: M. Nijhoff.
[16] Husserl, E.: (1984), *Logische Untersuchungen*, Hua, Band XIX1, (zweiter Band, erster Teil), hgb. U. Panzer, Den Haag: M. Nijhoff.
[17] Husserl, E.: (2002), *Logische Untersuchungen, Ergänzungsband, Erster Teil*, Hua, Band XX/I, hgb. U. Melle, Dordrect: Kluwer Acad. Pub.
[18] Kanamori, A.: (2008), Cohen and Set Theory, *The Bulletin of Symbolic Logic*, 14,3, pp. 351-378.
[19] Kleene, S.C.: (1980), *Introduction to Metamathematics*, New York: North-Holland Pub.Co, .
[20] Krause, D. & Coelho, A.M.N.: (2005), Identity, Indiscernibility, and Philosophical Claims, *Axiomathes*, 15, 191-210.
[21] Kunen K.: (1982), *Set Theory. An Introduction to Independence Proofs*, Amsterdam: Elsevier Sc. Pub.
[22] Lavine, S. (1994), *Understanding the Infinite*, Cambridge, Mass.: Harvard University Press.
[23] Livadas, S.: (2010), Impredicativity of Continuum in Phenomenology and in Non-Cantorian Theories, in: *Causality, Meaningful Complexity and Embodied Cognition*, (ed. A. Carsetti), pp. 185-199, Springer Science+Business Media B.V. 2010.
[24] Livadas, S.: (2011), The Expressional Limits of Formal Language in the Notion of Quantum Observation, *Axiomathes Online ISSN 1122-1151*, DOI 10.1007/s10516-011-9168-6, pp. 1-25.
[25] Lohmar D.: (2002), Elements of a Phenomenological Justification of Logical Principles, including an Appendix [...] on the Transfiniteness of the Set of Real Numbers, *Philosophia Mathematica*, 10, 3, pp. 227-250.
[26] Rosado Haddock, G.E.: (1987), Husserl's Epistemology of Mathematics and the Foundation of Platonism in Mathematics, *Husserl Studies*, 4, 2, pp. 81-102.
[27] Schoenfield, J.: (1967), *Mathematical Logic*, Reading, Mass: Addison Wesley Pub.
[28] Simmons, F.G.: (1963), *Introduction to Topology and Modern Analysis*, Tokyo: McGraw-Hill Kogakusha, Ltd.
[29] Sokolowski, R.: (1974), *Husserlian Meditations*, Evanston: Northwestern University Press.
[30] Tieszen, R. (2005), *Phenomenology, Logic, and the Philosophy of Mathematics*, Cambridge: Cambridge University Press.
[31] van Atten, M., Van Dalen, D., & Tieszen, R. (2002), Brouwer and Weyl: The Phenomenology and Mathematics of the Intuitive Continuum, *Philosophia Mathematica*, 10, 3, 203-226.
[32] van Dalen, D. (2004), *Logic and Structure*, Berlin: Springer-Verlag.
[33] van Fraasen, B. (1991), *Quantum Mechanics: An Empiricist View*, Oxford: Clarendon Press.
[34] Woodin, H. W. (2001), The Continuum Hypothesis I & II, *Not. Amer. Math.Soc.*, 48-6, resp. 567-576 & 681-690.
[35] Woodin, H. W. (2011), The Realm of the Infinite, in: *Infinity: New Research Frontiers*, (ed. M. Heller & W.H. Woodin), Cambridge University Press.

The Notion of Process in Nonstandard Theory and in Whiteheadian Metaphysics[0]

STATHIS LIVADAS

1 Introduction

This work is an original attempt to provide a connection, on the interpretational level, between A.N. Whitehead's philosophy of organism mainly exposed in his opus *Process and Reality*, [29], and the underlying roots of the axiomatical foundation of nonstandard mathematical analysis taken as such and also as a supportive metatheory in certain nonstandard alternatives of quantum mechanical theory. It should be noted that the relation between Whitehead's philosophy of organism and quantum mechanics in general has already been the object of research with various claims as to their mutual relevance in [5], [8] and [23]; M. Epperson's work in [5] will be a major reference source in this respect.

My guiding motivation will be the key notion of the Whiteheadian philosophy of organism which is that of process, in the Category of the Ultimate, described as the becoming of actual entities (termed also actual occasions). In M. Epperson's interpretation of quantum mechanics, this is characterized as a clear ontological principle, in the sense that " every fact is a determinant in the becoming of every new fact, such that the evolution of any fact entails both temporally prior facts and logically prior potentia as data, and an integration of these data that is unique to that evolution." ([5], p. 120). To the extent that the Whiteheadian process entails a metaphysical character inasmuch as it is associated with an actual entity as the outcome of a real concrescence of a multiplicity of potentia, which is otherwise indescribable but only in its outcome (or in terms of the coordinate division of 'satisfaction'), it will be associated on the interpretational level with the underlying assumptions in axiomatizing the existence of nonstandard entities.

In doing so, except for a brief but (hopefully) meaningful reference to some basic principles of the Whiteheadian cosmological scheme below, there will be also a brief reference to the theoretical context of nonstandard mathematical analysis in its two main ramifications, the extensional part (A. Robinson, E. Zakon) and the intensional part (mainly E. Nelson's Internal Set Theory)

---

[0]This article appears originally in the book *Contemporary problems of Epistemology in the Light of Phenomenology.*

in sections 3 and 4. Further in section 5, I will employ certain notions of the Whiteheadian cosmological scheme in providing an interpretation of two versions of nonstandard quantum mechanics such as those presented in the pioneering work of M. O. Farrukh in [6] and also in A. Raab's work in [19]. As a matter of fact, sections 3, 4 and 5 contain some nonstandard formalism and terminology, considered vital in grounding my overall arguments, which is nevertheless not absolutely necessary for a reader with no sufficient relevant knowledge in comprehending the ensuing discussion. In the built-up of my arguments I will make some parallel references to corresponding notions of the Husserlian phenomenology, whereas in section 2, I will associate A.N. Whitehead's theory of extension, an organic part of his overall doctrine, with the question of incommensurability of events in quantum mechanics, based on Y. Tanaka's work in [25].

I will mainly rely on the following principles of A.N. Whitehead's philosophy of organism inasmuch as they can be linked with the 'underlying semantics' of nonstandard mathematical theory as such and also in its merit as a formal metatheory of quantum mechanics. A greater emphasis will be given to his theory of extension, commonly referred to as Whitehead's epochal theory of time, as leading to an inexplicability of the genetic division in the process of becoming of an actual entity within the world (in the sense of its becoming concrete) as opposed to the 'phase' of its having become concrete (coordinate division).

These principles form part of the categorial scheme of Whitehead's philosophy of organism which branches into four distinct categories: (**I**) The Category of the Ultimate, (**II**) The Categories of Existence, (**III**) The Categories of Explanation, and (**IV**) The Categoreal Obligations. It is useful to keep in mind that the guiding motivation behind the Whiteheadian categorial scheme is that philosophy should be explanatory of abstraction and not of concreteness. As Whitehead himself put it, " Each fact is more than its forms, and each form 'participates' throughout the world of facts [..] but the individual fact is a creature, and creativity is the ultimate behind all forms, inexplicable by forms, and conditioned by its creatures" ([29], p. 20).

From the Category of the Ultimate, I rely on the notion of creativity, akin in its fundamentality to the Aristotelian category of 'primary substance', which is the ultimate principle by which the 'many' conceived of as the universe taken in disjunction, become each time an actual occasion, thereby constituting the universe taken in conjunction; in a sense, this is the underlying principle abridging plurality to unity.

From the eight Categories of Existence and the Categories of Explanation, I mostly rely on the following:

(**i**) The actual entities (also termed actual occasions) which are the last irreducible constituent 'things' of which the world is constituted and which are associated with the primary notion of process (or creativity) inasmuch the latter is the becoming of actual entities, (**ii**) The prehensions, or concrete facts of relatedness which are thought of by Whitehead as being a generalization

1. INTRODUCTION

of Descartes' 'mental cogitations' and Locke's 'ideas' and are associated with a fundamental analysis of an actual entity into its most concrete elements. Prehensions are defined as relational properties associated with a process of becoming (concrescence) and point to a subjective factor in which a concrete element is the prehension in question. This kind of analysis discloses the actual entity to be a concrescence of prehensions originating in the process of its becoming. Analysis in terms of prehensions is termed in the Whiteheadian scheme 'division' and is subsequently analyzed to the complementary notions of genetic and coordinate division. Every prehension consists of three factors: (a) the 'subject' that prehends, that is, the actual entity in which that prehension is a concrete element; (b) the 'datum' which is prehended; (c) the 'subjective form' which is the mode by which the subject prehends that datum, (iii) The nexūs (plural of nexus) which are sets of actual entities in the unity of the relatedness constituted by their prehensions of each other, that is, constituted in the objectifications of each other and (iv) The eternal objects or pure potentialities 'applied' for the specific determination of facts, which are thought of as pure potentialities realized in the becoming of an actual entity and contributing to its definiteness. It should be noted here that prehensions of actual entities are termed 'physical prehensions', whereas prehensions of eternal objects are termed 'conceptual prehensions'.

I also retain the fundamental notion of concrescence (from the Category of the Ultimate) which may be associated with the process of becoming of an actual entity in which the potential unity of many entities (actual and non-actual) in disjunctive diversity acquires the real unity of one actual entity in its having become. Here lies a metaphysical foundation of Whitehead's categorial scheme in that " the potentiality for being an element in a real concrescence of many entities into one actuality is the one general metaphysical character attaching to all entities, actual and non-actual" ([29], p. 22). In Whitehead's ontological notion of the world of actuality, the Category of the Ultimate is the most fundamental inasmuch as it is based on the notion of process which is meant as an 'advancing progress' (or concrescence) of actual entities by which they acquire their real unity from a plurality of potentia in disjunctive diversity. In this categorial scheme the mode an actual entity becomes constitutes what the actual entity is; its 'being' is constituted by its 'becoming'. This conditions Whitehead's Ontological Principle, termed also the 'principle of efficient and final causation', to the extent that the process of becoming has its reason either in the character of some actual entity in the actual world of that concrescence or in the character of the subject which is in the process of concrescence ([29], p. 24).

Dealing with the notion of extensive continuum Whitehead regarded extension in abstraction, inasmuch as it is defined as a relational scheme grounding the possibility of integrating a plurality of objects within the real unity of experience, as a given 'substratum' susceptible of contemporary actualisations of multiplicities of definite actual or non-actual entities. In that sense it is divisible but not divided and through its real division by each occurrence of actual entities, the notions associated with the epochal theory of time and also that of the spatialisation of corresponding actual entities come into play. Actual entities in the sense of real objectifications are evident presentations (cf. with the Husserlian *Gegenwärtigungen*) to the experience of a prehending subject in which case " they are only directly relevant to the subject in their character of arising from a datum which is an extensive continuum. They do, in fact, atomize this continuum." ([29], p. 62). The extensive continuum is, in this regard, a unique relational complex in which all potential objectifications find their actualisations and in which there are always actual entities beyond actual entities as non-entities necessarily imply absence of relations (prehensions). Whitehead considered this continuum in its proper generality as independent of any historicity and also as not implying any shapes, dimensions or measurability which are thought of " as additional determinations of real potentiality arising from our cosmic epoch." (ibid. p. 66).

It seems reasonable, at this point, to call attention to an implicit impredicative notion of process in the axiomatical foundation of non-standard theory as such (and in its reformulation as a quantum-mechanics supportive theory) and to the content of Whitehead's notion of process in *Process and Reality*. In both approaches we can clearly see an underlying subjective (and non-objectifiable) factor in shaping respectively standard mathematical objects and concrete actualities in objective reality. It may be helpful here to cite A.N. Whitehead's view of the interrelation of coordinate analysis vs. genetic analysis in describing the passage from real potentiality to actuality.

" Physical time makes its appearance in the 'coordinate' analysis of the 'satisfaction'. The actual entity is the enjoyment of a certain quantum of physical time. But the genetic process is not the temporal succession: such a view is exactly what is denied by the epochal theory of time. Each phase in the genetic process presupposes the entire quantum, and so does each feeling in each phase. The subjective unity dominating the process forbids the division of that extensive continuum which originates with the primary phase of the subjective aim. The problem dominating the concrescence is the actualization of the quantum *in solido*.[...] There is a spatial element in the quantum as well as a temporal element. Thus the quantum is an extensive region. This region is the determinate basis which the concrescence presupposes.[...] The concrescence presupposes its basic region, and not the region its concrescence. Thus the subjective unity of the concrescence is irrelevant to the divisibility of the region. In dividing the region we are ignoring the subjective unity which is inconsistent with such division." ([29], pp. 283-284).

Further, the subjective form of the coordinate division is associated with the emergence of conceptual feelings which are related to the totality of the region (of an actual entity) and are not restricted to the divided subregion but only as merely potential coordinate subdivisions which is equivalent to saying that conceptual feelings are related to the actual entity in its entireness and not to its 'coordinate subdivisions' ([29], pp. 286-287). We should point here to the fact that A.N. Whitehead, in evident divergence from the Husserlian

1. INTRODUCTION

subjectivist approach, is led to an assumption of an extensive connection serving as the foundational ground for consecutive actualisations, those running e.g. from an antecedent actual entity A through to a next actual entity B. Thus, a fundamental scheme of extensive connection is assumed to articulate on a uniform plan: 1) the general conditions corresponding to the bonds that unite the atomic actualisations in a unique nexus; 2) the general conditions corresponding to the bonds that unite the infinite number of coordinate subdivisions of the satisfaction of an actual entity ([29], p. 286). In short, common extensiveness provides for the possibility to treat an atomic actuality as it were a multiplicity of coordinate actualities and, in reverse, to treat a nexus of many actualities as it were one actuality. There are no meaningful physical relations out of the extensiveness scheme in the sense that any actual occasion in the physical world cannot but be a correlate of a concrescence within this extensive connection scheme. Taken in a restricted sense, common extensiveness may be linked with the classical ontological question of whole and parts inasmuch as this may be taken equivalent to the notion of an extensive whole and extensive parts.

On this account, even in adopting T. de Laguna's more general notion of extensive connection (ibid., p. 287), a major deficiency of the corresponding Whiteheadian approach, which initially led to a confusing notion of 'point' defined in terms of a theory of durations, may be found out in suspending the question of a subjectivity that underlies extensive connection, the latter being merely thought of as an objectified state of things. In this respect, Whitehead admitted in his earlier work, *The Principles of Natural Knowledge*, [30] and *The Concept of Nature*, [31], to a certain inaptitude of the extensive abstraction method to define a 'point' without entering a theory of duration, whereas his ambiguous re-evaluation of the notion of point further in *Process and Reality* does not seem to much clarify things ([29], pp. 297-301). He also seems to lapse into circularity with respect to the problem of time as he was further driven to admit that space and time are aspects of nature that presuppose the extensiveness scheme, whereas extensiveness as such cannot at all determine by itself the special processes that relate to the physical time and space ([29], p. 68-69).

Of course, Whitehead admitted in the Categories of Explanation, the autonomous internal real constitution of an actual entity within the process of creative advance. In such an interpretation, the actual entity is the 'subject' of its own 'immediacy', in the sense of the completion of a process of transformation from a decoherence (state) within concrescence to a unique coherence (state) upon satisfaction. However, there is a certain deficiency of the descriptive means to account for the constitutional capacities of an actual entity in the process of its own self-creation which may seem all the more evident taking into account the constitution of time as an objective process within actual world and even deeper, taken as a reflection of its ever in-act self-constituting subjectivity. In response, A.N. Whitehead applied certain principles of his categorial scheme, e.g. the Ontological Principle, the Relativity Principle, the notions of process and prehension, etc. to account for, which to one or the other extent may be ultimately taken to imply a constituting subjectivity associated with concrescent processes within actual world.

It should be noted that in a Whiteheadian sense, the term extensiveness refers to something more fundamental than (at least) epistemic spatio-temporality and can be thought of as the general scheme of relations that permit to a plurality of objects to 'fuse' into the real unity of a unique experience. However, the act of becoming, though it may concern anything having a temporal extension, it is nonetheless not extensive itself, in the sense that it may be divisible in anterior and posterior acts of becoming corresponding to the extensive divisibility of what has become ([29], pp. 67, 69).

In conclusion, Whitehead's suspension of the role of constituting subjectivity led him in the first place to a reduction of the relational extensiveness to the classical question of extensive whole and extensive parts, whereas his eventual attempt in achieving a satisfactory treatment of a resulting circularity by defining a spatial point through the notion of an abstractive ensemble hurt to the problem of an infinitely regressing sequence of connecting regions ([29], pp. 297-300). In this respect, I refer marginally to Husserl's notion of intentionality and its *a priori* directedness towards an (intentional) object by which we can reduce the notion of a spatial point-individual to the abstract form of an empty-something (*Leersubstrat*) without any material content, even without an inner analytically describable one ([14], [15], resp. pp. 33-34 & p. 211). Moreover, on a constitutional level associated with the phenomenology of temporal consciousness, Husserl reduced the notion of a spatiotemporal point to that of a specious present conceived of as a non-point-like temporal unit within the immanence of consciousness in the *a priori* connection: protention - original impression - retention ([16], pp. 76-83).

Generally, in a formal-mathematical context, points in the sense of irreducible individuals of standard mathematical theories are associated with zero-level elements within a general cumulative structure (mainly by means of the Foundation Axiom of **ZFC** Theory), whereas in the version of non-standard theories by ultrapower construction they are associated with a definition of infinitesimals of various orders in which the infinitesimals of a given order appear to be atoms without inner structure to the immediately higher order until we unravel their own structure in a kind of Russian doll game and reveal a class of elements of a lower order playing provisionally the part of indecomposable atoms-points.[1]

---

[1] In nonstandard analysis this leads to a view of points, e.g. of the nonstandard extension R^* of the set of real numbers R, as having an inner structure to the extent that they are formally defined as equivalence classes of infinite sequences modulo an ultrafilter $\mathcal{F}$ over the set of natural numbers. In this context, the standard real numbers of R are represented as the constant equivalence classes of R^*.

2 Some prompts from questions of quantum measurement

As already stated in section 1, there have been various approaches as to the mutual relevance of Whitehead's cosmological scheme with quantum mechanics in general, either in the so-called 'old' version associated with the early work of Planck and Einstein and applied to Bohr's 1913 atomic model or the 'new' version associated with the work of Heisenberg, Schrödinger, Bohr et al, commonly referred to as the Copenhagen Interpretation. Here are some correlated features of quantum theory taken in its 'historical entirety', as referred to in [5] (pp. 129-132), and of the Whiteheadian philosophy of organism, beyond the most common correlation which is that of the quantum state evolution in the former and the concept of concrescence in the latter. These are:

(i) The presupposition of a world of existing, mutually interrelated facts. This presupposition grounds the logical necessity of nonlocal correlations of physical objects taken as serial historical routes of quantum actual occasions such as those encountered in EPR-type experiments; it grounds, as well, the possibility of an actual infinity as a presentational immediacy in forming in abstraction infinite extensions of finitistic in scope predicate formulas, as we'll see in next section, (ii) The inclusion of some of these facts in the state specification or in the act of measurement and the exclusion of the rest of facts with their potentia. The exclusions relate to a process of negative selection productive of the decoherence effect, (iii) The evolution of a system of a multiplicity of facts to the unity of a novel fact, (iv) The requirement that this evolution proceed relative to a particular fact, belonging to a subsystem of facts, referred to in quantum mechanics respectively as 'indexical eventuality' and the 'measuring apparatus'; Whitehead's equivalent term, is the prehending subject as given in his Ontological Principle and the Category of Subjective Unity, (v) The measurement or state specification that entails the actualization (or concrescence) of one novel fact/actual entity from a multiplicity of valuated potential facts/entities which themselves arise from antecedent facts (data); in quantum mechanical description this non-unitary evolution terminates in a matrix of probability valuations, anticipative of a final unitary reduction to a single actuality/quantum state. Ultimately then, concrescence/state evolution is a unitary evolution from multiplicities of actualities to a unique actuality. In a yet alternative quantum mechanical description, there is a vector projection of the actual, evolving multiplicity of facts onto a vector (or subspace) representing a potential 'formally integrated' eigenstate. The Whiteheadian analog of the vector projection onto a potential integration is the ingression - where a potential formal (in the sense of applying a form to the facts) integration arises from the ingression of a specific 'potentiality of definiteness' via a 'conceptual prehension' of that specific potentiality (the term 'potentiality of definiteness' is used as equivalent to that of eternal object, see p. 3). Though Whiteheadian 'ingression' and the quantum mechanical vector 'projection' are thought of as conceptually equivalent, a certain divergence is pointed out as to the 'primacy' of each one of the two in the process of actualization ([5], p. 131).

Further, there are two characteristics, shared by both the quantum mechanical and Whiteheadian notions of potentia. First, there is a sense of pure potentia, meaning that an eternal object, in Whiteheadian approach, 'is a pure potential in the universe' which, conceptually felt, is itself neutral as to the fact of its physical ingression in any particular actual entity of the temporal world. In quantum mechanics, this pure potentiality is reflected in that the state vector $|\Psi>$ can be expressed as the infinite sum of vectors belonging to an infinite number of subspaces of infinite dimension, representing an infinite number of potential states or 'potentialities of definiteness' referent to no specific actual occasions and potentially referent to all. Second, as quantum mechanical projections are 'inherited' from the facts constituting the initial state of the system, similarly, in the Whiteheadian scheme antecedent facts, when prehended, are typically 'objectified' by one of their own historical 'potential forms of definiteness' ([5], pp. 131-132).

Next, I will point to a possibility of interpretation of the incommensurability condition in quantum measurement in terms of Whitehead's epochal theory of time, which leaves aside the question of the divisibility of a complex quantum event into atomic component events. As it stands, the adoption of the indeterminacy principle in the Copenhagen interpretation of quantum mechanics is linked with the necessity of a statistical treatment as one cannot predict the future behavior of an individual quantum entity due to the indivisibility of the relation of the observer and the observed. In an attempt to provide a common interpretational framework for N. Bohr's complementarity and Whitehead's epochal theory of time, Y. Tanaka's approach in [25] can be essentially summed up in that the incommensurability condition[2] of two quantum events a and b, and the characterization of the individuality of a quantum event a in terms of the formal definition of the indivisibility of a by a certain event x:

The event a has the character of 'individuality' $\Leftrightarrow_{def} (\exists x) (\sim aDx)$

is a way of disconnecting the individuality of a quantum event from a notion of atomism in the sense of the divisibility of a complex event into atomic component events. Instead, what comes up here is a notion of the 'individuality' of an actual occasion (or entity) in the process of concrescence, insofar this is associated with the genetic division of the actual occasion in question taken in its entirety, as it is described in Whitehead's epochal theory of time ([25], p. 3). In a certain sense, the character of the 'individuality' of a quantum event a is associated with its indivisibility in relation to any event b, which may be further reduced to Whitehead's metaphysical distinction between the coordinate and genetic analysis of an actual occasion inasmuch as genetic analysis entails also the principle of causality within the 'internal' development of an actual

---

[2]The incommensurability condition is defined as the indivisibility in both directions $\sim aDb$ and $\sim bDa$ of two quantum events a and b. The formal definition of the divisibility of a by b is: $aDb \Leftrightarrow_{def} a = (a \cap b) \cup (a \cap \neg b)$. Therefore $\sim aDb \Leftrightarrow a \neq (a \cap b) \cup (a \cap \neg b)$ & $\sim bDa \Leftrightarrow b \neq (b \cap a) \cup (b \cap \neg a)$.

2. SOME PROMPTS

occasion; moreover, it is not associated with physical time as each 'phase' of the genetic process presupposes the entire quantum (actual entity) ([25], p. 8). In contrast with the atomistic view of events implicitly presupposed in classical physics, 'indivisibility'(or 'individuality') of an event in quantum mechanics is associated with an irreducible contingency in the respective context of measurement. This special character of quantum 'individuality' is shown to formally result in the breakdown of Bell's inequality ([25], pp. 14-15). In relation to this sort of quantum 'individuality', I note that in Whitehead's view each instance of concrescence " is itself the novel individual 'thing' (*clar. of the author*: actual entity) in question. There are not 'the concrescence' and 'the novel thing': when we analyze the novel thing we find nothing but the concrescence." ([29], p. 211).

There is a deeper question here, inasmuch as Whitehead's genetic division may be ultimately rooted on a kind of 'internal' temporal transcendence in the shaping of a quantum measurement along the triangle quantum object - measuring apparatus - conscious observer and it is going to be touched again in the final conclusions of this paper. As a matter of fact, Heisenberg, (in *The Physical Principles of the Quantum Theory*, [13]), had notably refrained to talk about the objective reality of the intermediate state of a quantum system between the experimental preparation and measurement in the sense of a transition from the 'possible' to the 'actual', as he believed that the description of the intermediate development between two objectively measured or measurable states did not correspond to a physical reality. This non-objectifiability is echoed in Whitehead's Principle of Relativity according to which every actuality is a potential determinant in the becoming of every new actuality, in a way that the potentiality of being an element of a real concrescence of many entities into a unique actuality ' is the one general metaphysical character attaching to all entities, actual and non-actual', ([29], p. 22). This allegedly metaphysical characteristic within each real concrescence implies the implicit presence of a transcendental factor underlying the process of becoming as such of a real entity in actuality, which is 'self-annulled' upon actualization (in terms of being) of the real entity in question.

In any case and on a metatheoretical level, the jump of truth values in the process of measurement which is the formal result of the absence of an isomorphism between Boolean and non-Boolean structures - assuming that a quantum object, considered as an objective existence, is the non-distributive lattice (i.e., non-Boolean) of its properties - forces for a Boolean observer the need of the existence of an objective time in which he must 'move' ([12], p. 2396). It is notable that the question of formally 'filling-in' the existing gap in the process of quantum measurement is associated with J. von Neumann's projection postulate (or 'the reduction of the wave function' postulate) which assignes to the mathematical translation $\tau(s(t))$ of the physical state $s(t)$ of a quantum quantity Q_i upon a first-kind measurement at time t the same eigenvector ψ_κ as to the translation $\tau(s(t_1))$ of the state $s(t_1)$ of the quantity Q_i at time t_1 soon after the measurement ([4], p. 334). As a matter of fact, even if we assume Von Neumann's projection postulate or Van Fraassen's modal interpretation of quantum mechanics as 'external' metatheoretical conditions in a purely logical way, we cannot be led by any analytical linguistic means to a complete description of the 'change of states' that takes place during the measurement process in the compound system 'quantum system + measuring apparatus'.

3 Nonstandardness in formal-mathematical theory

In case we characterize the predicate standard in non-standard mathematical analysis as referring to a notion of 'fixedness' in informal mathematical discourse, then we can see in the following how this formal notion acquires in E. Nelson's *Internal Set Theory*, ([18]), by its axiomatical underpinning, a meaning that can be taken under certain assumptions as analogous to the meaning of an actual entity in the Whiteheadian sense. Moreover, it will be made clear the extent to which the axiomatical foundation of non-standard numbers is conditioned on an implicit assumption of a standard universe meant as the outcome of 'fixed horizon' processes concerning well-meant mathematical objects. In present context by the designation, well-meant mathematical objects, I characterize those formal objects which may be taken as finitistic outcomes of complete, reproducible, finite-time, discrete mental processes. It is notable that historically the development of the theory of infinitesimal and infinite entities within classical mathematics was always facing questions concerning their objective existence as they entered as shadowy entities in definite applied mathematical problems (e.g. the area of curved surfaces, the instantaneous velocity of a moving body, etc.); nevertheless their approximative status in calculations was leading to empirically sound results. As a matter of fact, even in discarding the infinitesimal quantities of the type $\frac{d}{ds}$ of the 17th century calculus and adopting the famous Weierstrass $\delta - \epsilon$ criterion for the definition of a function (or a sequence) limit no one could still give an articulate description of the sort of infinitesimal numbers involved, much more to provide a recursive process to produce, for instance, each time a number $\frac{1}{n}$ such that $\frac{1}{n} < \epsilon$ for any (standard) number $\epsilon > 0$. In the following, we will see that non-standard theories, though they may qualify as axiomatically consistent theories in generating non-standard entities, they nevertheless cannot define them in terms, for instance, of a recursively enumerable process over sets and functions explicitly defined over natural numbers, but must instead employ principles that are conditioned on the assumption of an impredicative (i.e., one that the *definiens* cannot be defined but in terms of the *definiendum*) actual infinity.

A standard application of the (upward) Skolem-Löwenheim Theorem over the class $\mathcal{P}$ of Peano structures is that there exist non-standard models of Peano arithmetic **PA** for every cardinality $\kappa > \aleph_0$ which are not isomorphic to the standard model $\mathcal{N} =< N, +, \cdot, s, 0 >$. It is critical to see, though, that this is a result basically due to mathematical statements conditioned on the assumption of an impredicative infinity. For one thing, the Skolem-Löwenheim Theorem is not only conditioned on the Model Existence Lemma but also on

3. NONSTANDARDNESS IN FORMAL-MATHEMATICAL THEORY   215

the Compactness Theorem whose well-known formulation is that an arbitrary set of sentences Γ has a model iff each finite subset of Γ has a model.

Let us consider, in the context of Henkin theories,[3] a standard proof of the Compactness Theorem that consists in proving the equivalent assertion, namely, that Γ has no model iff some finite subset of it has no model ([26], p. 111). The non-trivial part of the proof is getting that whenever Γ has no model then some finite subset of it has no model too. By Model Existence Lemma, Γ is inconsistent, that is $\Gamma \vdash \bot$, therefore there exists a finite collection of sentences $\tau_1, ..., \tau_n \in \Gamma$ such that $\tau_1, ..., \tau_n \vdash \bot$. By the same lemma, the collection $G = \{\tau_1, ..., \tau_n\}$ has no model which proves Compactness Theorem. But working with Henkin theories in which for each sentence $\exists x\ \varphi(x)$ one has to provide a closed term t making $\varphi(t)$ true within the corresponding model, one must admittedly pass from an indefinite totality of closed terms t_i making the arbitrary set Γ of sentences τ_i inconsistent to a finite collection $\{t_1, ..., t_n\}$ making inconsistent the finite set of sentences $\{\tau_1, ..., \tau_n\}$. What is noteworthy, is that we have to conceive of a process by which we essentially reduce the intuition of an impredicative substratum incorporating an indefinite aggregation of objects in an ever expanding 'horizon' to an intuition associated with the perception of finitely many well-defined objects.

It is noteworthy that in proving the Compactness Theorem one has to rely also on the Model Existence Lemma and consequently on the assumption of the Axiom of Choice or alternatively on certain weaker logical forms (e.g. the Boolean prime ideal theorem). The common denominator in all logical variants of the Axiom of Choice is that they are not derivable from the Zermelo-Fraenkel Set Theory and that on a cognitive level they involve the possibility of an extension of a well-meant process of choice over an unbounded infinity. In the immediately following, I will be more specific with the underlying role of the Axiom of Choice in proving the Skolem-Löwenheim Theorem in [26]; as a matter of fact, the application of this actual infinity axiom or of some logically equivalent form of it is necessary in all known proofs of the Skolem-Löwenheim Theorem.

A major key to the proof of Skolem-Löwenheim Theorem is the lemma that if a set Γ of sentences in a language L is consistent then Γ has a model of cardinality at most the cardinality of language L. In the first place, the construction of a model $\mathcal{U}$ of Γ is based on the definition by recursion of a Henkin extension T_ω of a theory T which is conservative over T and then on the application of Zorn's lemma for the construction of a maximal extension T_m of T_ω. As it is well-known, Zorn's lemma is proved to be logically equivalent to the Axiom of Choice.

As the cardinality of the language L_m of T_m is, in fact, the cardinality of its closed terms, it suffices to focus on the cardinality of the set of sentences $\exists x \varphi(x)$.[4] Therefore turning our attention to the cardinality of witnesses c_i,

---
[3]A theory T is called a Henkin theory if for each sentence $\exists x \varphi(x)$ there is a constant c such that $\exists x \varphi(x) \rightarrow \varphi(c) \in T$; in that case c is called a witness for $\exists x \varphi(x)$ ([26], p. 104).

[4]It can be easily seen by recursive definitions and induction on $n \in N$ that the numbers

which coincides with the cardinality of existential formulas $\exists x \varphi(x)$, - as in a Henkin theory we add a constant-witness for each new existential formula -, we can see how counting techniques are substituted by assumptions of a well-ordering over a 'pre-existing' infinity (i.e. of the Axiom of Choice).

For, letting the cardinalities of constants c_i and of variable-terms x_j of original language L be respectively κ and $\aleph_0$ we have that the cardinality of the set of existential statements $A = \{\exists\, x(x_0 = c_i);\ i \in I\}$ is $\max(\kappa, \aleph_0) = \kappa \cdot \aleph_0 = \kappa + \aleph_0 = \mu$ (by the application of the Axiom of Choice in the form of absorption laws, ibid., p. 108). It is clear that an enumeration of terms-variables $x_j, j \in N$ above the countability threshold $\aleph_0$ is substituted by an *ad infinitum* possibility to choose constants $c_i, i \in I$ of cardinality κ greater than $\aleph_0$ that 'fill'-in each time anew an existential formula of the type $\exists x(x_0 = c_i)$. By assumption of the Axiom of Choice in essentially the same sense we get that the cardinality of a language L is κ in case L has $\kappa \geq \aleph_0$ constants, a key fact in the proof of both downward and upward Skolem-Löwenheim Theorem as it suggests that the cardinality of the language $L^{'}$ of an extended set of sentences $\Gamma^{'} = \Gamma \cup \{c_i \neq c_j;\ i,j \in I\}$ is $\kappa^{'}$, in case we add $\kappa^{'}$ new constants $\{c_i;\ i \in I\}$ such that $c_i \neq c_j$ to the language L of the original set Γ (ibid., p. 112).

Next, I will try to show how non-standard mathematical theories are built as consistent extensions of standard theories provided with an extra axiomatical formulation that essentially 'projects' the universe of standard processes (these meant in a non-rigorous fashion as distinct, finite-time operations carried out within objective world) over an unbounded, indefinite horizon. Taking into account that in Whiteheadian approach the ultimate acts of immediate actual experience are actual entities, prehensions and nex$\overline{u}$s and all the rest are (with regard to our experience) derived abstractions then we can see in the following how a particular branch of non-standard analysis, the Internal Set Theory (**IST**), formalizes, by three extra *ad hoc* axioms added to the corpus of axioms of Zermelo-Fraenkel theory, the possibility of forming indefinite collections of formal objects taken in the sense of actual entities, in a way that may be associated on the one hand with a concrescence of prehensions associated with the subjective unity of a performing subject and on the other hand with their actualization in the co-ordinate division of 'satisfaction'.

The Internal Set Theory is generally considered, if properly interpreted, as an intensional part of nonstandard analysis along with other nonstandard and non-Cantorian theories such as Alternative Set Theory (AST) ([27]), ultrafinitist theories (J. Hjelmslev, S. Lavine, A. S. Yessenin-Volpin) and more recently Nonstandard Class Theory [2] and the Theory of Hyperfinite Sets [3].

In a non-Cantorian sense infinitesimals and infinitely large numbers do not exist in an objective way as in the extensional part of nonstandard mathematics (e.g. Robinsons' nonstandard analysis) but their meaning is indirectly related to the subjective limitations of an 'observer' performing his 'observations' in a local and non-Cantorian way (roughly meant, not over a pre-established actual

---

of terms and formulas of the language L_m of T_m is that of the number of constants of the original language L plus the witnesses ([26], p. 108-109).

3. NONSTANDARDNESS IN FORMAL-MATHEMATICAL THEORY

infinity) in his witnessed universe.

From a syntactical point of view, E. Nelson introduced in the classical ZFC theory a new unary undefined predicate *standard* together with three axioms, the Transfer (T), the Idealization (I) and the standardization (S) axioms. The axiomatical equipment of the new predicate *standard* consists of the three axioms below, where by the term internal formula is meant a formula of ordinary mathematics which does not involve the predicate *standard* even indirectly; otherwise it is called external. Evidently, in spite of their syntactical role in the theory these axioms induce a nonstandard extension in the domain of 'fixed' objects, where the term 'fixed' (or in a broad sense finitistic) can be used as the intuition of the new predicate *standard* in informal mathematical discourse.

- The Transfer Principle (T):

  $\forall^{st} t_1 .. \forall^{st} t_n [\forall^{st} x \ A \longleftrightarrow \forall x \ A]$ where A is an internal formula whose only free variables are $x, t_1, ..t_n$.

  The intuition behind (T) is that if something is true for a fixed but arbitrary x then it is true for all x.

- The Idealization Principle (I):

  $\forall^{stfin} x' \exists y \forall x \in x' \ A \longleftrightarrow \exists y \forall^{st} x \ A$ where A is again an internal formula.

  That is, to say that there is a y such that for all fixed x we have A is the same as saying that for any fixed finite set of x's there is a y such that A holds for all of them.

- The Standardization Principle (S):

  $\forall^{st} X \exists^{st} Y \forall^{st} z \ [z \in Y \longleftrightarrow z \in X \text{ and } A]$ where A is any formula external or internal.

  Intuitively, we can say that if we have a fixed set, then we can specify a fixed subset of it by giving a membership criterion for each fixed element (see [18], pp. 3-11).

One of the simple consequences of the Idealization Principle (I) is the very existence of nonstandard elements, in particular that every infinite set contains a non-standard element, a result which de facto invalidates the induction theorem of standard arithmetic.[5] But this result, is conditioned on the assumption 'encoded' in the Idealization Principle, that predicating a property formalized by an existential internal formula A for any standard element x (of an indefinite collection of such elements) is equivalent to predicating the same property for any element x of any standard finite set of such x's. This is again,

---

[5] The simple proof goes like this: let us take the internal formula A to be $y \neq x$ for any x, y where x is a standard element. Then, by (I) for any standard finite set x' and for all $x \in x'$ we have that there is a y such that $y \neq x$, which means that y is non-standard. Taking this argument in the case where x and y range over any infinite set, we have that every infinite set contains a non-standard element; in particular there is (at least) a non-standard natural number.

as in the proof of the Compactness Theorem on p. 215, about the possibility of 'projection' of an indefinite togetherness of formal objects, conditioned on the existence of an impredicative continuous substratum in presentational immediacy, onto a 'tangible' finite ensemble of such objects associated with the concrete intuition of discrete finite-time acts. In a sense, both the Transfer Principle and the Idealization Principle may be viewed as essentially an axiomatical means to formalize the passage from an indefiniteness associated with concrescent processes to the fixedness associated with actual entities upon actualization.

Concerning Robinson's introduction of nonstandard elements by the construction of B-enlargements of standard models in [20] or Zakon's introduction of nonstandard numbers by the set-theoretical non-constructive version of a quotient space of equivalence classes of infinite sequences modulo an ultrafilter over the set of natural numbers in [21], one has to eventually apply some form of the Axiom of Choice or its logical equivalent Zorn's lemma. In Zakon's version, Zorn's lemma is applied to guarantee the existence of an ultrafilter extending the Fréchet filters of all cofinal subsets of natural numbers, whereas in Robinson's nonstandard analysis the Axiom of Choice and the Zorn's lemma are both applied through the Compactness Theorem in the construction of an appropriate ultraproduct as a model for a set K of sentences ([20], pp. 13-19). Although A. Robinson was admittedly careful to note that non-standard models are constructed within the framework of classical mathematics and ' thus affirm the existence of all sorts of infinitary entities', nonstandard theorists generally claim to banish or at least circumvent the platonistic character of Cantorian mathematics in reaching non-standard definitions for infinitary and infinitesimal quantities.

However, the application of the Axiom of Choice or of its various logically equivalent versions, by the very assumption of a Cantorian infinity in presentational immediacy conditioning this principle (which may be ultimately thought to be reducible to an impredicative subjectively constituted substratum), attests to the fact that no matter the formal ways to represent a nonstandard mathematical entity there is no possibility to suppress the redundancy of a 'midway' non-predicative process in reaching the non-standard entity in question. It is self-evident that in such case a non-standard entity should be taken as the final phase towards the actualization, or 'satisfaction' of a concrescent process in Whiteheadian sense. A clue from standard mathematics may help to better comprehend the place of the Whiteheadean notion of concrescence in formal mathematical discourse: taking a mathematical entity in its 'entirety', e.g. the open unit interval $(0,1)$, as an actual entity in the sense of a fact associated with an immediate subjective experience, then a divisibility up to exhaustion to its constituent elements may be founded on the genetic division in the process of 'satisfaction' of the actuality in question. The actualization of this actual entity is, in fact, tied up with the emergence of prehensions referring to the totality of the corresponding region which are not confinable to any of its subregions, these latter ones meant as already completed actualizations.

The open unit interval is not conceivable in a Whiteheadian sense but as an actualization of an otherwise impredicative concrescence of prehensions. As it is well-known, an open real interval (a, b), in a kind of circularity in definition, cannot be defined but in terms of subintervals of the same genus as the original interval (a, b).

4 A Whiteheadian view of a non-standard topological construction

In the following to strengthen my arguments on the relevance of the Whiteheadian philosophy of organism with the underlying conceptual basis of non-standard analysis, I will consider, with some hopefully limited use of mathematical terminology and formalism, the construction of a unique standard topology on the set $2^{*\omega}$ of finite and infinite binary sequences under prefix ordering $\leq$.[6] This topology based on the notion of topological proximity and the definition of topological halos of standard points x of a standard topological space X is essentially due to T. Sari in [22]. By this construction I want to show that standard entities are associated, at least on the axiomatical level, with distinct, finitistic-mode 'actions' with respect to well-defined objects which are extended indefinitely in the field of their actualization to produce external formulas. These formulas expressible through the syntactically undefined predicate standard ultimately generate nonstandard objects.

Let's consider the space $2^{*\omega}$ as a standard space by the Transfer Principle[7] and construct for the internal formula $x \leq y$ referring to the elements x, y of $2^{*\omega}$ the following sentence: $\exists^{st} x\, \forall y,\ x \leq y$ (**1**). By the dual form of the Idealization Principle (**I**) this is equivalent to the sentence $\exists^{stfin} x'\, \forall y\, \exists x \in x',\ x \leq y$.

By (**1**) and the specialization preorder $\leq$ in $2^{*\omega}$ we can define the relation of topological proximity $y \cong x$ (a reflexive and transitive relation on a space X) for any standard element x of $2^{*\omega}$ as follows:

$$x^{st}\ \&\ y \cong x \Leftrightarrow \forall^{st} U \in \mathcal{O}\,(x \in U \to y \in U)\ (\mathbf{2})$$

where the class $\mathcal{O}$ of opens is the standard (Scott) topology of $2^{*\omega}$.[8] Due to the definition of the topological proximity, one has the notion of the topological

---

[6] In general, prefix ordering is a partial order which orders sequences of elements based on an initial common finite segment. Concerning the space $2^{*\omega}$, taken either with Alexandroff or Scott topology, this definition is extended to a specialization pre-order, to include both finite and infinite sequences of binary digits: $l \leq m$ iff for every open (upper set) O of $2^{*\omega}$, $l \in O \to m \in O$ ([28], p. 25).

[7] The Transfer Principle enables us to transfer sets and formulas from a standard to a nonstandard environment so long as the formulas in question do not involve the new predicate standard.

[8] The Scott topology is a topology with remarkable computational significance and can be roughly said to guarantee that: (i) if information x 'passes' a test (open set) $\mathcal{O}$ then any greater information 'passes' it *a fortiori* and (ii) if the limit of a special sequence of better and better approximations 'passes' a test $\mathcal{O}$ then some of the approximants already pass; more details on [24], pp. 646-647.

halo of a point $x \in X$ by the external subset of X, $\operatorname{hal}(x) = \{y \in X;\ y \cong x\}$. Formally within Internal Set Theory, this is an ambiguously defined set whose elements are those elements of X which are infinitely close to x.

As a matter of fact, a unique standard topology is proved to be generated for any standard space X and any standard point x, such that

$$\forall^{st} x \in X\ \operatorname{hal}(x) = p(x)$$

where $\operatorname{hal}(x)$ is the topological halo of x and $p(x)$ its $\mathcal{P}$-halo, ([22], pp. 117-118).

The main point is that we can construct a unique topology on the standard space $2^{*\omega}$, based on the halos of its standard points, which is a construction essentially reduced to the bounded formula (**1**): $\exists^{st} x\ \forall y,\ x \leq y$. But this formula is equivalent by dual (**I**) to the formula $\exists^{stfin} x'\ \forall y\ \exists x \in x',\ x \leq y$ which reduces the existential formula bounded to a standard element x of an otherwise indefinite collection to a formula bounded to a standard and finite (and therefore well-defined) element x among an existent well-defined (standard and finite) collection x' of such elements.[9] A similar kind of finiteness-standardness can be also remarked in the proof of the uniqueness of the standard topology generated by the topological halos of standard points in [22] (pp. 119-121).

On the other hand, the topological halos of standard points x are defined through the external formula (**2**)

$$x^{st}\ \&\ y \cong x\ \Leftrightarrow\ \forall^{st} U \in \mathcal{O}\ (x \in U \to y \in U)$$

which means that they can be hardly taken as sets at least in the standard sense since they are by-products of an illegal subset formation (i.e., one that applies the undefined predicate standard in forming subsets by the Comprehension Axiom). Consequently, by the very structure of the topological proximity relation a 'nonstandard' inner structure of halos is generated which is consistent with the natural intuition of open sets, to the extent that they are generated by the topological halos of standard points, as involving a notion of impredicative continuity. It is important here to note the topological sense of the infinitely near in the definition of topological halos, meant as an *ad infinitum* process of generating standard mathematical objects in the form of standard open sets U.

To the extent that this process is abstracted from an ideally *ad infinitum* extended temporal series of discrete acts of forming 'fixed' (standard) mathematical objects taken as actualisations in 'satisfaction', the external set $\operatorname{hal}(x)$ can be approached, in the Whiteheadian sense of an actual entity, as involving the subjective form of coordinate division associated with conceptual feelings related to the totality of the region of the actual entity in question (see, p. 4). In this approach, the subjective unity dominating the genetic process 'forbids' the coordinate division of the extensive continuum (the nonstandard 'inner'

---

[9] In [17], it has been proved that the opens $A = {}^{S}\{E \subset 2^{*\omega};\ \forall^{st} x \in E,\ \operatorname{hal}(x) \subset E\}$ of space $2^{*\omega}$ induced by the topological halos of its standard points x by means of the topological proximity $\cong$, are indeed its Scott opens.

content of topological halos) which originates with the primary phase of the subjective aim. Of course, in the present case the genetic division in the concrescent process of 'satisfaction' is carried through a subjective form of both physical and conceptual prehensions of the particular actual entity (i.e., of the topological halo of a standard point x), as it is a formal object reducible to certain temporally founded mathematical acts.

5 A Whiteheadian approach of the construction of a nonstandard quantum mechanics

There is a pioneering research activity in the last decades to connect nonstandard mathematical theory with the formal metatheory of quantum mechanics. On account of this, it is hoped that nonstandard mathematics will play an important role in the interpretation of a number of results in number theory, in quantum physics and also in their relation ([7], p. 2). As we will see below, an important methodological tool in applying nonstandard mathematical methods is the hyperfinite[10] (or more generally hyperdiscrete) extension of a standard space together with the Transfer Principle. As a matter of fact, a major question of quantum mechanical theory is to construct an appropriate mathematical tool to handle on the same footing both the discrete and continuous spectrum of a self-adjoint linear operator, such as the Hamiltonian of a quantum system. More specifically, while eigenvectors of the Hamiltonian can be identified to bound states of the system in the discrete case, the representation of continuum states by appropriate vectors is problematic and is treated in the conventional Hilbert space framework only approximately.

There have been several approaches to this problem in conventional formalism (e.g. via the rigged-Hilbert-space formalism or the partial-inner-product spaces) but with limited success mainly due to a difficulty in the definition of the scalar product. However, hyperfinite constructions seem to well correspond to the need for a combination of both the discrete and continuous properties of hyperfinite objects; for example, hyperfinite objects are ideally suited to describe the peculiarity of wave-particle behavior in quantum physics through shadow images of nonstandard objects ([7], p. 8). Moreover, several 'exotic' objects of mathematical metatheory, e.g. divergent integrals common in field theories (Dirac's delta function in particular), viewed as hypercomplex unlimited numbers can well have a nonstandard interpretation. Some works in this orientation are [1], [9], [10] and [32].

In the following, I will take into consideration two major nonstandard approaches to quantum mechanics, those of M.O. Farrukh in [6] and of A. Raab in [19], which are mainly motivated by the aforementioned problematic, to discuss the conceptual connection between the nonstandard approach in quantum mechanical theory and Whitehead's notions of genetic and coordinate division

---

[10]Roughly talking, the notion of a hyperfinite set (or space) is an extension of the corresponding standard notion of finiteness in a nonstandard environment. For details on the definition and properties of hyperfinite sets by ultrapower construction see: [11], p. 188.

in his theory of extension. In [6], the nonstandard construction of ultra eigenvectors corresponding to all spectral points of internal self-adjoint operators makes it possible to set up a formalism valid for both the discrete and continuous spectrum, whereas in [19], the introduction of nonstandard hulls in the calculus of nonstandard extensions of self-adjoint operators is motivated by the assumption of the indistinguishability of infinitesimally different states in performing a measurement ([19], p. 5). In the following, a certain amount of nonstandard quantum theory formalism is deemed necessary which the reader may wish to skip to enter the conclusions on pages 225–227.

Concerning the mathematical formalism in [19], it is proved that the spectrum of a self-adjoint operator A is well approximated by the eigenvalues of its nonstandard extension B, i.e. given the eigenvalue λ of standard operator A, then there exists an eigenvalue λ' of B such that $\lambda' \approx \lambda$; this nonstandard proximity relation $\approx$ between any two elements x, y is roughly defined as equivalent to the statement that their normed difference $\| x - y \|$ is infinitesimal. Then, as the nonstandard operator B has a complete set of normed eigenvectors, there exists a vector x belonging to the hyperfinite-dimensional Hilbert space H (externally containing the standard Hilbert space $\mathcal{H}$ by a certain nonstandard extension) such that $Bx = \lambda' x$. However as stated above, the nonstandard proximity relation $\approx$ between the standard eigenvalues λ and the nonstandard ones λ', is based on the existence of infinitesimals and on their definition by an external syntactical formula equivalent, for a norm-generated topology, to the formula (**2**) (p. 219), i.e.

$$x \text{ is infinitesimal in case } \forall^{st}\epsilon > 0, \text{ we have } \| x \| < \epsilon \quad (\mathbf{3})$$

In this respect, it is straightforward to see that formula (**3**) implies formula (**2**) (the reverse is obvious) as:

$$x \text{ is infinitesimal in case } \forall^{st}\epsilon > 0, \| x \| < \epsilon$$

$$\Leftrightarrow x \text{ is infinitesimal in case } \forall^{st}\epsilon > 0, \| x - 0 \| < \epsilon$$

$$\Leftrightarrow x \text{ is infinitesimal in case } \forall^{st}\epsilon > 0, -\epsilon < \| x - 0 \| < \epsilon$$

Then, by the norm-generated metric $d(x, y) = \| x - y \|$ which implies that $d(x, o) = \| x - 0 \|$ and the metric-induced standard open sphere $\mathcal{B}(o, \epsilon) = \{x; \, d(x, 0) < \epsilon\}$ we easily have, taking also into account that 0 is a standard number, that

$$\forall^{st}\mathcal{B}(o, \epsilon), \quad o \in \mathcal{B}(o, \epsilon) \rightarrow x \in \mathcal{B}(o, \epsilon) \Leftrightarrow x \approx 0 \quad \diamond$$

Further, the possibility to deduce a well-defined Loeb measure $°E_\Omega$[11] associated with the probability function $\mu_L^{(x,y)} = <x, °E_\Omega y>$, for vectors x, y

---
[11] As with hyperfinite spaces (sets) encountered already and taking account of the scope of this paper, I prefer to inclusively describe all variations of Loeb measure as referring to a σ-additive probability measure specifically defined for a nonstandard environment; for details, see: [1]

5. A WHITEHEADIAN APPROACH

belonging to the nonstandard hull $°H^{12}$ of the Hilbert space H, is ultimately reduced to the nonstandard proximity relation $\approx$, by setting $\mu_L^{(x)} = \mu_L^{(y)}$ whenever $x \approx y$.

A remark also to be made regarding nonstandard extensions of standard self-adjoint operators is that the set of Borel functions contains all functions we need to retrieve standard results by the relation $g(A)(x) = °(f(B)^*x) = °f(B)x$ (where $*x$ is the nonstandard copy of x, A is a standard self-adjoint operator and B its nonstandard extension, g(A) a real-valued Borel function and f(B) its nonstandard extension; [19], p. 15). In this respect, it is noteworthy that Borel functions inasmuch as they refer to σ-algebras of opens of the respective topology essentially incorporate all that can be said, on the formal level, relative to the underlying continuous spatiotemporal configuration and for that reason they can be taken to 'encode' all that can be standardized in this respect. These open (or respectively closed) sets can be taken as formally representing the possibility of existence of a field of genetic division with regard to a Whiteheadian-type concrescence in the actual world.

Concerning the nonstandard approach in [6], there is, at first, a review of P. Dirac's efforts to extend the principles of quantum measurement for an observable whose corresponding operator has a discrete spectrum, to those for an observable whose operator is of a continuous spectrum. In those equations, Dirac had to invoke the δ-Dirac function $\delta(\xi - \xi')$ for all ξ, ξ' in the continuous spectrum of the corresponding operator, which, as it is well-known, fails to be a function in the conventional sense of a unique-valued mapping for each element of its domain. One of the remedies to this awkward situation is the introduction by Gelfand of an extension of the standard Hilbert space $\mathcal{K}$, which is the rigged Hilbert space $(\Phi, \mathcal{K}, \Phi')$, where $\Phi \subset \mathcal{K}$ is a dense subset endowed with a finer topology than $\mathcal{K}$ and Φ' is the dual space of Φ (the space of continuous linear forms on Φ) equipped with the strong dual topology ([6], p. 178).

Yet, the difficulty with this formal approach lies in the fact that there is no possibility to enlarge the Hilbert space $\mathcal{K}$ of physical states to include eigenstates of the continuous spectrum, that is, to include transition eigenstates induced by the measuring process itself. As a matter of fact, the space Φ' fails to be a true enlargement of $\mathcal{K}$ in the sense of giving an admissible result for any eigenvalue of a measured observable because it lacks the definition of a scalar product ([6], p. 178-179). On this account, M.O. Farrukh's nonstandard approach envisages a nonstandard extension $\mathcal{K}^*$ of a Hilbert space $\mathcal{K}$ possessing by the Transfer Axiom all the standard properties of $\mathcal{K}$. The extension $\mathcal{K}^*$ can moreover give a definite meaning to a well-known property of standard Hilbert spaces, namely that if an eigenvalue λ belongs to the continuous spectrum of a self-adjoint operator A densely defined on $\mathcal{K}$, then for any $\epsilon > 0$ there exists a vector $f \in \mathcal{K}$ (corresponding to a state of the system) with $\| f \| = 1$ such that

---

[12] The nonstandard hull $°H$ of the hyperfinite-dimensional Hilbert space H is defined as the quotient space $°H = \frac{\text{fin}(H)}{H_0}$ of the set of finite hyperreals, fin$H$, by the equivalence relation $\approx$ which defines two vectors as equivalent iff their difference has infinitesimal norm. This equivalence relation defines the set H_0 by: $H_0 = \{x \in H; \| x \| \approx 0\}$, ([19], p. 5).

$\| Af - \lambda f \| < \epsilon$ ([6], p. 178). Due to the absence of infinitesimal quantities in standard theory, this property cannot determine a unique eigenvalue λ for a given eigenvector f even in taking an upper bound of the errors $\| Af - \lambda f \|$.

On the contrary, by postulating ϵ as infinitesimal we can guarantee the existence of at least one ultra eigenvector f (associated with an ultra eigenstate) corresponding to a unique standard value of λ, irrespective of whether λ belongs to the discrete or continuous spectrum of an operator, in a way that no distinction between the discrete and continuous spectra is warranted. Therefore, we may have a sound definition of Dirac's 'exotic' δ-function in terms of $\text{st}(<f_\lambda, f'_\lambda>) = \delta^{\lambda'}_\lambda$, for any λ, λ' in the standard part of the spectrum of a self-adjoint operator A whose family $\{f_\lambda\}$ of ultra eigenvectors normalized to unity satisfies: $\| Af_\lambda - \lambda f_\lambda \| \approx 0$ ([6], p. 184). Moreover, in a nonstandard Hilbert space $^*\mathcal{K}$, the necessity of definition of a standard probability function, so as to have a proper physical interpretation within nonstandard quantum theory, implies the explicit acceptance of only the standard values of the inner product $<f, E_\lambda(A)f>$.[13]

To sum up Farrukh's nonstandard construction: a nonstandard formulation of quantum mechanics defines the set of physical states of a quantum system as the quotient space $S(^*\mathcal{K}) = U(^*\mathcal{K})/ \leftrightarrow_{^*\mathcal{K}}$, where $U(^*\mathcal{K})$ is the set of unit vectors of nonstandard Hilbert space $^*\mathcal{K}$ and $\leftrightarrow_{^*\mathcal{K}}$ is an equivalence relation on $U(^*\mathcal{K})$ putting in the same equivalence class all unit eigenvectors of the form $e^{i\varphi} \cdot f, g$ ($\varphi \in {}^*R$) that have an infinitesimal difference, i.e. $\| e^{i\varphi} \cdot f - g \| \approx 0$. Accordingly, it is proved that those eigenvectors $f, g \in {}^*\mathcal{K}$ for which $f \leftrightarrow_{^*\mathcal{K}} g$, i.e. those representing the same physical state and therefore corresponding to the same standard self-adjoint operator, generate the same probability function $\nu_{f,A} = \nu_{g,A}$ ([6], p. 191).

It is also important, in view of my scope, to take into account one of the axioms of Farrukh's nonstandard formulation of quantum mechanics, namely that, " The result of any measurement of an observable can only be one of the **standard** spectral values of the corresponding operator. As a result of the measurement, the physical system finds itself in a state represented by an ultra eigenvector of the operator representing the measured observable, corresponding to the measured spectral value". This axiom points, with another axiom stating that: If a system makes a transition between the state represented by the vector f_1 and the state represented by the vector f_2, then the transition probability is given by:

$$\text{tran prob}(f_1 \to f_2) = \text{st} |<f_2, f_1>|^2$$

---

[13] In such a case, the definition of a proper probability measure $\mu_{f,A}$ for ultra eigenvectors f of the nonstandard space in question, is founded on the possibility of assigning a standardized form to the inner product associated with a function $\varphi_{f,A}$ such that:

$$\varphi_{f,A}(\lambda') = \text{st} <f, E_{\lambda'}(A)f> = \begin{cases} 0 & \text{if } \lambda' < \lambda \\ 1 & \text{if } \lambda' > \lambda \end{cases}$$

5. A WHITEHEADIAN APPROACH

to a standardized form of the deduction of probability of getting the value λ as a result of a measurement on a quantum system in a state represented by f and subject also to the condition that the system may undergo a transition to one of a countable subclass of states $\{g_i : i \in J\}$, ([6], Axioms 3 & 5, pp. 191-192).

In the bottom line, the existence of a nonstandard Hilbert space in the nonconstructive version of [6] (akin to Zakon's nonconstructive definition of the nonstandard extension of the set of real numbers, p. 13) rests upon the acceptance of the Axiom of Choice by relying on the existence of a free ultrafilter $\mathcal{F}$ on the set of natural numbers N. In this way, one can induce an equivalence relation of nonstandard proximity $\approx$ (not directly associated with the notion of infinitesimals as before) on the set $\mathcal{G}$ of all sequences of natural numbers by:

$$\text{for } a, b \in \mathcal{G},\ a \approx b \text{ iff } \{n;\ n \in N\ \&\ a_n = b_n\} \in \mathcal{F}$$

and thus define a nonstandard structure, based on the Transfer Axiom and the definition of relations holding for almost every $n \in N$, that is, for any element of N belonging to the ultrafilter $\mathcal{F}$.

At this point one might rightfully wonder why there is a need to go that far into the formalism of nonstandard mathematical theory as such and also as a metatheory of quantum mechanics to see a possible connection with the core of the Whiteheadian cosmological scheme in general and his theory of extension in particular. My view is that, as long as we consider mathematical operations as abstract forms of subjective acts carried out within the objective domain of spatiotemporality, then we can interpret the formal axiomatical means applied in the construction of nonstandard mathematical structures as simply 'filling-in' a gap in the description 'generated' by the genetic division corresponding to a concrescence within the actual world, which evidently cannot be a description in terms of the coordinate division of an already carried out process. Then, irrespective of whether one is based on the intensional part of nonstandard analysis or on the extensional part, the way to formalize the genetic division as referent to a concrescent immediacy where the primary fact is the dative phase of the actual occasion in question, is either by applying an actual infinity principle in an abstraction of the real-world infinity given in presentational immediacy or by applying standardized norms to the formal-axiomatical description of that concrescent process.[14] In the extensional nonstandard approach this is essentially done by applying the Axiom of Choice or its logical equivalents and in E. Nelson's intensional approach mainly by axiomatically representing a concrescent process in abstraction, by the standardized form of a bounded by universal quantification internal formula (Transfer Axiom) and also by an internal formula whose bounded variables are reducible to a standard finite ensemble.

---

[14] Here the term standardized is used in the informal sense of fixedness but it nevertheless retains a deep underlying sense of 'finite' expressibility in relation to the fulfilled phase of satisfaction in the becoming of an actual entity.

Of course, it may seem as going too far in drawing a parallel between the Whiteheadian notions of genetic and coordinate division in the process of becoming of an actual entity with even a vague notion of fixedness in the context of a formal theory. Yet, there is a possibility to examine such a connection, under the sole assumption that we regard mathematical objects, especially objects of formal-axiomatical theories, as special-kind abstractions of perceptual objects implying a subjectivity of certain constitutive modes. In any case, the role of subjective unity in the completeness of the phases of a process of concrescence is put explicitly forth in Whitehead's categorial scheme, specifically in the Category of Subjective Unity and that of Freedom and Determination, among his nine Categoreal Obligations. Concerning the Category of Freedom and Determination, he stated that, " This category can be condensed into the formula, that in each concrescence whatever is determinable is determined, but that there is always a remainder for the decision of the subject-superject of that concrescence" ([29], pp. 26-28).

At this point, it seems worthy to turn to Whitehead's limited reference to infinitesimals in the chapter referring to measurement in *Process and Reality*. There, in dealing with the problem of measurement in a classical sense, Whitehead argued that measurement depends ' upon counting and upon permanence'. For instance, inches can be counted on a metal rod taken as a yard-measure but on the condition that the rod is permanent in both its internal relations and with respect to some of its extensive relations to the geometry of the world. In the first place, counting depends on its straightness and straightness, in turn, on its place in the space-time geometry of the world. Whitehead's answer to those who could argue that the measurement reduces to a comparison of infinitesimals or to an approximation of infinitesimals is simply negative for, in his view, there are no infinitesimals ([29], p. 328). Consequently, his next statement seems quite interesting in that, " In mathematics, all phraseology about infinitesimals is merely a disguised statement about a class of finites", inasmuch as it is related with the problem of measurement, e.g. taking the yard-measure as a reference unit then any measurement entails an approximation as to its straightness. This in turn, may be further reduced to purely subjective factors that guarantee the invariability of relevant circumstances independently of the exactitude reached by a constant betterment of the physical conditions in the set-up of measurement. In Whitehead's view there is a final dependence upon direct intuitions in such a way that relevant circumstances remain unchanged in the sense that there is an appearance of invariability of relevant circumstances which is ' always a perception in the mode of presentational immediacy' ([29], p. 329). Moreover, this presentational mode of perception which reminds us of the Husserlian notion of *Gegenwärtigung* (presentification) can be in no sense private as it would then be valid only for a particular observer, a claim which also indirectly points to the Husserlian notion of intersubjectivity.

In final count, although Whitehead explicitly denied the existence of infinitesimals as a theoretical interpretation of the question of approximation in the measurement of magnitudes, he nevertheless alluded to an associated finitistic content and, most important, reduced the question of minute approximation and indirectly that of infinitesimals to constitutional processes associated with a subjectivity whose presentational perception is intersubjectively the same within the world. Moreover, he seems to go further towards a convergence with the Husserlian notion of a unity-constituting ego by reducing the feelings (or rather quasi feelings in his statement) introduced by the coordinate division of actual entities, ' to subjective forms which are only explicable by categoreal demands arising from the unity of the subject'. Whitehead concluded that the coordinate division of an actual entity produces feelings whose subjective forms are partially eliminated and partially inexplicable ([29], p. 292).

In view of the above, we can reach a two-fold conclusion: first, that insofar the question of infinitesimals and therefore of nonstandard magnitudes is linked to a process of ever better approximations in measurement, the 'existence' of nonstandard magnitudes is ultimately associated with subjective forms of feelings which may reduce to the unity of the subject. It seems that a vagueness of the notion of the unity of a subject (leading to an a-temporal subjectivity in Husserl's phenomenology of temporal consciousness) lies behind Whitehead's claim, namely, that the coordinate division of an actual entity produces feelings whose subjective forms are partially eliminated and partially inexplicable. Second, insofar the subjective forms of feelings are associated with the unity of the subject, then objects/actual occasions must be always a perception in the mode of presentational immediacy and therefore at the stage of 'satisfaction' they should be registered as actual occasions in the character of concrete objects (or state-of-affairs) which entails their 'fixedness' or, in other words, their 'finitistic' objectification.

6 Conclusion

As it stands out, actual entities to the extent that, taken as ultimate facts of immediate actual experience, are associated with coordinate division, they are presented as complete, finitistic objects at the stage of 'satisfaction' and for this reason they acquire a 'fixedness' as temporal forms, in contrast with the genetic division associated with potentia of actual occasions as multiplicities of real world concrescences. In the latter case, we face the persistent question of the impossibility 'of penetrating' into the stage of concrescence as such by any formal linguistic means including those of a nonstandard theory, which means that the genetic division is exempt, in terms of a process, of any kind of objectification. This may help to better assess from Whitehead's own viewpoint his claim that ' in mathematics all phraseology about infinitesimals is merely a disguised statement about a class of finites'.

The whole approach seems to be leading to a kind of transcendence at the stage of a real concrescence towards the conjunctive unity of a new actual entity out of a disjunctive multiplicity of potentialities which may be further reduced, in a phenomenologically motivated view, to the immanent transcendental character of an absolute subjectivity conceived of as a constituting factor beyond the objectivity of A.N. Whitehead's advancing process. A further discussion could touch on the possibility of laying a common foundation, especially on an immanent transcendental level, between the Whiteheadian philosophy of organism and certain aspects of the Husserlian phenomenology.

BIBLIOGRAPHY

[1] Albeverio, S., Fenstad, J.E., Hoegh-Krohn, R., Lindstom, T.: (1986), *Nonstandard Methods in Stochastic Analysis and Mathematical Physics*, Orlando: Academic Press.
[2] Andreev P., Gordon E. (2001), An Axiomatics for Nonstandard Set Theory, Based on Von Neumann-Bernays-Gödel Theory, *The Journal of Symbolic Logic*, 66, 3, pp. 1321-1341.
[3] Andreev, P., Gordon, E.: (2006), A Theory of Hyperfinite Sets, *Annals of Pure and Applied Logic*, 143, 1-3, pp. 3-19.
[4] dalla Chiara, M.L. (1977), Logical Self Reference, Set Theoretical Paradoxes and the Measurement Problem in Quantum Mechanics, *Journal of Philosophical Logic*, 6, pp. 331-347.
[5] Epperson, M.: (2004), *Quantum Mechanics and the Philosophy of A.N. Whitehead*, New York: Fordham University Press.
[6] Farrukh, O.M.: (1975), Application of nonstandard analysis to quantum mechanics, *Journal of Mathematical Physics*, 16, 2, pp. 177-200.
[7] Fesenko, I.: (2006), Several nonstandard remarks, *AMS/IP Advances in the Mathematical Sciences*, AMS Transl. Series 2, 217, pp. 37-50.
[8] Folse, H.: (1974), The Copenhagen Interpretation of Quantum Theory and Whitehead's Philosophy of Organism, *Tulane Studies in Philosophy*, 23, 33.
[9] Francis, E.C: (1981), Application of non-standard analysis to relativistic quantum mechanics, *Journal of Physics A: Mathematical and General*, 14, 10, pp. 2539-2551.
[10] Friedman, A.: (1994), Nonstandard extension of quantum logic and Dirac's bra-ket formalism of quantum mechanics, *International Journal of Theoretical Physics*, 33, 2, pp. 307-38.
[11] Goldblatt, R.: (1998), *Lectures on the Hyperreals: An Introduction to Nonstandard Analysis*, New York: Springer-Verlag.
[12] Grib, A.A.: (1993), Quantum Logical Interpretation of Quantum Mechanics: The Role of Time, *Int. Jour. of Theoretical Physics*, 32, 12, pp. 2389-2400.
[13] Heisenberg, W.: (1930), *The Physical Principles of the Quantum Theory*, Chicago: The University of Chicago Press.
[14] Husserl, E. (1995), *Ideen zu einer reinen Phänomenologie und phänomenologischen Philosophie, Erstes Buch*, Hua Band III/I, Dordrecht: Kluwer Acad. Pub.
[15] Husserl, E. (1974), *Formale und Transzendentale Logik*, Hua Band XVII, hsgb. Paul Janssen, Den Haag: M. Nijhoff.
[16] Husserl, E. (1966), *Zur Phanomenologie des Inneren Zeibewusstseins*, Hua Band X, hsgb. Rudolf Boehm, Den Haag: M. Nijhoff.
[17] Livadas, S.: (2007), Indiscernibility in topologies of finitely observable properties, *Journal of Multi-valued Logic and Soft Computing*, 13, pp. 127-143.
[18] Nelson, E.: (1986), *Predicative Arithmetic. Mathematical notes*, Princeton: Princeton Univ. Press.
[19] Raab, A.: (2004), An approach to nonstandard quantum mechanics, *Journal of Mathematical Physics*, 45, 12, pp. 4791-4809 .
[20] Robinson, A.: (1966), *Non-standard Analysis*, Amsterdam: North-Holland Pub.
[21] Robinson, A. & Zakon, E.: (1969), A set-theoretical characterization of enlargements, in: *Applications of Model Theory to Algebra, Analysis and Probability*, (ed. W.A.J. Luxembourg), pp. 109-122, New York: Holt, Rinehart & Winston.
[22] Sari, T.: (1995), General topology, in: *Nonstandard analysis in practice*, (eds. F. Diener & M. Diener), pp. 109-144, Berlin: Springer Verlag.
[23] Shimony, A.: (1965), Quantum Physics and the Philosophy of Whitehead, in: *Boston Studies in the Philosophy of Science*, (eds. R. Cohen & M. Wartofsky), 2:308, New York: Humanities Press.
[24] Smyth, B. M.: (1992), Topology, in: *Handbook of Logic in Computer Science*, (eds. S. Abramsky, D. Gabbay, T. Maibaum), pp. 641-761, Oxford: Clarendon Press.

6. CONCLUSION

[25] Tanaka, Y.: (2004), The Individuality of a Quantum Event: Whitehead's Epochal Theory of Time and Bohr's Framework of Complementarity in: *Physics and Whitehead: Quantum, Process and Experience*, (eds. Timothy Eastman & Hank Keeton), pp. 164-179, New York: State University of New York Press.
[26] van Dalen, D.: (2004), *Logic and Structure*, Berlin: Springer-Verlag.
[27] Vopěnka P.: (1979), *Mathematics in the Alternative Set Theory*, Teubner-Texte zur Mathematik, Leipzig: Teubner Verlag.
[28] Vickers, S.: (1989), *Topology via Logic*, Cambridge: Cambridge University Press.
[29] Whitehead, N.A.: (1978), *Process and Reality. An Essay in Cosmology*, New York: The Free Press.
[30] Whitehead, N.A.: (2007), *An Enquiry Concerning the Principles of Natural Knowledge*, (originally published in 1919), New York: Cosimo, Inc.
[31] Whitehead, N.A.: (2007), *The Concept of Nature*, (originally published in 1920), New York: Cosimo, Inc.
[32] Yamashita, H.: (2002), Nonstandard methods in quantum field theory I: a hyperfinite formalism of scalar fields, *Intern. J. Theor. Physics*, 41, pp. 511-527.

Is there a Link Between the Continental Ego and the Temporality of the Epistemic Domain? [0]

STATHIS LIVADAS

1 Introduction

The present article undertakes a meaningful discussion involving two seemingly diverse notions: On the one hand, there is the notion of the continental ego that could be said to trace its origin in the Cartesian *cogito*, nurtured subsequently during the evolution of various branches of German subjective idealism (I. Kant, J. Fichte, F. W. Schelling) and fully blossomed in the emergence of Husserlian phenomenology and its existentialist offshoots (J. P. Sartre, M. Heidegger, E. Levinas) in the 20th century. On the other hand, there is the notion of the temporality of epistemic universe, the latter term meant here as the domain of epistemology (in the sense of a philosophy of science) in a holistic approach that refers to the objects of epistemic domain as those registered-in by an intentional-type experience, expressible and formalized within the descriptive limits of a formal theory.[1] This means that the objects of physical experience, formalized as objects of a formal metatheory corresponding to the physicalistic description, can be considered as formal-ontological objects on an equal footing with the objects of a formal axiomatical theory as such. In what I shall develop next, the notion of temporality in a most profound sense will prove to be the cornerstone upon which to demonstrate the relevance of the continental ego as a temporality-constituting ego with the origin of temporality of the epistemic universe. Obviously this discussion is based on a presupposition of epistemic objects, in general, as temporally constituted even in taking them in complete abstraction as objects of the domain of a formal theory.[2] On this account, my main objective is to point to a persisting 'residuum' re-

---

[0] This article is especially written for the book *Contemporary problems of Epistemology in the Light of Phenomenology.*

[1] In fairness, the attempt to establish an underlying connection between the transcendence of temporal ego and the root of the objective temporality of epistemic domain may be seen as a radically new approach and, probably, a controversial one. The reader is referred, for instance, to T. Adorno's critique (in *Against Epistemology: A Metacritique*) of Husserl's intention, in line with the Bergsonian and Gestalt theory, to restore "metaphysics 'scientifically', that is with anti-metaphysical armature" ([1], p. 115).

[2] A phenomenologically motivated view of objects of a formal axiomatical theory as temporally constituted is offered in [25].

garding the possibility of completeness of the formal description of epistemic objects/state-of-affairs, in the sense of objects of systematic knowledge communicable either within a loose natural linguistic environment or within a formal axiomatical one. It should be made clear that in referring to this 'residuum' in the context of epistemology, we must have principally in mind the axiomatical means by which, for instance, the notion of a process in the sense of a continuous transformation of well-defined objects of discourse is made expressible in analytic terms. This is mainly dealt with in sections 5, 6, 7 and 8, where I try to show that the 'residuum' I talk about, can be fundamentally reduced to the original source of a constituted temporality, by which we can have the intuition of the unity of a whole, conditioning *eo ipso* the apprehension of concrete objects as constituted beings. The unity of a whole in the sense of an actual infinity in presentational immediacy, should be taken as a kind of infinity freely generated through our mental faculties, where any possible imaginable bound can be automatically annulled by further extending it through imagination. This infinity is obviously not akin to physical spatiotemporal infinity bound to natural laws and conditioned by causality. At this point, I should make clear what seems to be a fundamental difference between actual infinity in presentational immediacy and natural-physical infinity subject to the laws of causation which can be meant as presupposing the possibility of being extended beyond any hitherto 'observed' spatiotemporal boundary. Husserl was very careful in clarifying this difference in *Logical Investigations*, ([15], pp. 299-300), where he explicitly stated that: 'The fact that we freely extend spatial and temporal stretches in imagination, that we can put ourselves in imagination at each fancied boundary of space or time while ever new spaces and times emerge before our inward gaze - all this does not prove the relative 'foundedness' of bits of space and time, and so does not prove space and time to be really infinite, nor even that they can really be so. This can only be proved by a law of causation which presupposes, and so requires, the possibility of being extended beyond any given boundary.' ([20], p. 45).

In this context, one can establish a holistic approach, on the one hand, towards epistemic objects of physical 'observation', e.g. the objects of the subatomic realm and generally the objects of quantum mechanical theory, and on the other, towards their respective formal abstractions, inasmuch as they are taken as registered-in objects of intentional experience, more precisely in the Husserlian sense of objects of a formal-ontological domain.[3] The primary foundation of this holistic approach should be, as it will be further developed in next

---

[3] Husserl defined formal ontology as the *a priori* logical science concerned with the elaboration of formal judgements, relations and operations with respect to objects as intentionally registered. The domain of formal ontology can be taken as the domain of science in general and, concerning the mathematical theory of sets and cardinal numbers in particular, it is the domain of facts and objects as intentionally registered and fundamentally apprehended by categorial intuition as 'empty somethings' in general (*Etwas-überhaupt*) and modifications of 'empty somethings'. On this account, all formal mathematical analysis including the theory of sets and of cardinal and ordinal numbers can be taken to be an ontology inasmuch as it is an *a priori* doctrine of objects and moreover a formal one to the extent that it is bound to the pure modes of 'something' in general, see: [14], (pp. 80-82) & [25].

1. INTRODUCTION

sections and taking into account my general approach, the noematic constitution of both kinds of objects as well-defined, immanent to the consciousness and temporal ones.

In sections 2, 3, 4, I attempt a rather extensive look to the temporal content of the continental ego concerning respectively the Husserlian, Heideggerian and Sartrean approaches, trying at the same time to bring out their underlying convergences mainly with regard to the transcendent, a-temporal character of the constituting 'self' of objective temporality. This is taken as the ever in-act subjective root of the absolute flux of consciousness in Husserlian analysis, as the subjective root of the ecstatic character of Heideggerian Da-sein and, by the same token, of the Sartrean 'Being-for-itself'. Taking also into account the Heideggerean view of time consciousness, which stands close to the corresponding Husserlian approach by virtue of Heidegger's introduction of the transcendental principle of the ekstatic unity of the temporality of Da-sein, I look deeper into the nature of the existentialist ego (including the Sartrean *Pour-soi*) as a subjective temporal ego which seems to be the root of certain contradictory conclusions reached on the subjective level, e.g. the illusory intuition of our finiteness or our illusory apprehension of nothingness. In this respect, I particularly refer, at some length, to the Sartrean idea of temporal ego in *L' être et le néant* ([30]), where one is led to the impredicative character of moments of actuality and the necessity to turn to some kind of non-temporal subjectivity.

There exists an evident similarity in these respective approaches, in that they are irreducibly rooted to a kind of absolute subjectivity, non-describable in terms of ontological being in temporal objectivity without alienating itself from its mode of 'being' as a subjectivity. For instance, Heidegger's ekstatic temporality as a form of existence of Da-sein is termed so as it is defined to be an impetus which 'throws away' everything that exists (in terms of being in ontological sense) inasmuch as it is conceived as a movement without any pause or rest. What the different forms of this élan vital of temporality have in common, is that they assemble the diverse moments each of which is already a 'throw away' of itself into a unity that is at once rejection, opening, alienation ([2], pp. 202-03). From this point of view, the phenomenological analysis of time consciousness and the temporality of existentialist ego can possibly lend themselves as a common theoretical underpinning to a deeper understanding of the impredicative character of the continuous unity of time consciousness, to the extent that they both lead to an inherent impossibility of an ontological definition of the absolute subjectivity of consciousness except by its 'auto-alienation' in objective reflection.

At the stage we have come to talk about an absolute subjectivity, inaccessible to any description carried out in terms of ontological being, even eluding its apprehension in terms of reflecting-reflected, being apprehensible only in objectified self-projection, we may realize that we have come across the aforesaid 'residuum', only this time it is encountered as an immanence within an embodied consciousness. It is remarkable that Husserl had thought of the absolute subjectivity of consciousness as the residuum left after an annihilation of the world of physical things, in the sense that "no real being, no being which is presented and legitimated in consciousness by appearances, is necessary to the being of consciousness itself (in the broadest sense, the stream of mental processes)." ([17], p. 110). That is, while the being of consciousness as an absolute immanental being is, by essential necessity, not brought out by any existing thing of the physical world (*nulla 're' indiget ad existendum*), a transcendent object of physical reality is entirely referred to the evidence of presence of an actual consciousness. On this account, consciousness in its 'purity' 'is' a self-contained absolute being to which nothing is spatiotemporally external and, yet, it cannot be contained within any spatiotemporality, for in that case it would a temporally objectified being subject to the laws of causation. It follows, that in taking the whole spatiotemporal world, which includes the human ego as a subordinate reality, as a 'secondary' being posited by an intentional consciousness, we can reach in extremis the conclusion that the world is constituted by consciousness as something identical arising from motivated multiplicities of experiences, beyond which there is nothing: "*Es ist ein Sein, das das Bewusstsein in seinen Erfahrungen setzt, das prinzipiell nur als Identisches von motivierten Erscheinungsmannigfaltigkeiten anschaubar und bestimmbar - darüber hinaus aber ein Nichts ist.*" ([16], p. 106).

In closing this section and referring to the notion of temporality of the continental ego, I point to the fundamental distinction between the phenomenological time as the unitary form of all mental processes within the stream of temporal consciousness emanating from the pure ego and the objective or scientific time, that is, the time of spatiotemporality. Obviously, in talking about the temporality of the continental ego and taking into account certain variations with regard to its conception in the respective approaches above, I leave aside the latter sense of objective spatiotemporality. The reason is that this kind of (scientific) temporality is conditioned on the 'existence' of a subjective factor preceding its objectification within the real world. And as Husserl stated in his late texts on temporality the primary phenomenon (*Urphänomen*) of the stream (of consciousness) is the phenomenon of all phenomena, of all what is given to us in whatever sense as being, inasmuch as all that exists is given as such in the primary-phenomenal stream, and further in the mode of the stream as identically the same durating unity ([21], pp. 1-2).

2 The transcendence of the ego of Continental Philosophy

In the following three sections I'll try to bring out some fundamental similarities with regard to the creeping transcendence of the temporal ego in the Sartrean, Heideggerian and Husserlian theoretical approaches. In the present section, I will start putting the emphasis on some key notions in the Sartrean approach to the temporality of ego, and then I will compare them to the corresponding notions in Husserl's and Heidegger's description of temporal ego.

In comparing the notion of the ecstatic rapport of the 'Being-for-itself'

2. THE TRANSCENDENCE OF THE EGO... 235

($Pour$-soi)[4] to the past and future and the Husserlian notion of the self-constitution of the temporal flux of consciousness, there is found in both approaches, a transcendental factor which in the case of Sartrean temporality seems to be the annihilation ($néantisation$), not described as something real, of the 'Being-in-itself' (En-soi) - the source of appearance of 'Being-for-itself' in the world - and the peculiar 'ontological' nature of the 'Being-for-itself' ([30], p. 173). Sartre was led to the introduction of these *a priori* notions of a rather transcendental character as he tried to provide a consistent interpretation for the temporal conservation of the identity of personal ego, a problem often reduced in later continental philosophy to interpreting the unity of temporal forms (e.g. anteriority-posteriority) of consciousness. In fact, his approach was partly motivated by an attempt to refute R. Descartes' assumption of the existence of a non-temporal entity, such as God, and of the continuing creation and also I. Kant's notion of the synthetic unity of *cogito*, consequently to provide a temporal unity on which to ground the synthetic relation of before/afterwards and more generally the interconnection of events in the world.

Therefore, we can talk about a transcendence in the Sartrean temporality, inasmuch as this temporality is thought as not existing in terms of being but as merely the mode of 'being' of a purely subjective consciousness - J.P. Sartre's 'Being-for-itself' - which is always ecstatically in advance of itself; it exists in a certain sense ontologically as we can name it or predicate unto it certain characteristics but in virtue of its ontological 'being', it is actually never what it is predicated to be. In this respect, it is already behind it, in present actuality, and the temporality of 'Being-for-itself' cannot be conceived but as a passing annihilation that implies by necessity a past.

As a matter of fact, the ecstatic dimension of temporality of the 'Being-for-itself' is described as the distance to itself and this distance is nothing real, nothing that can be predicated as being in itself. It is simply a 'null', an evanescence which 'is been' as a separation and it is taken to define in ecstatic unity the rapport of the 'Being-for-itself' with its past, grounding this way in an endless regression the appearance of any consciousness as 'being already born'.[5] It should be noted that whatever might be, in J. P. Sartre's view, the way the 'Being-for-itself' appears in the world, it nonetheless comes in ecstatic unity with its past, which on the one hand excludes an absolute beginning in the presence of the 'Being-for-itself' in the world and on the other hand grounds temporality as the ecstatic mode of being of the 'Being-for-itself'.

---

[4]The content of the original Sartrean term *Pour-soi*, in distinction to the *En-soi* (Being-in-itself), can be roughly taken as implying a kind of transcendent subjectivity of consciousness.

[5]The last consequence may lend itself as a well-meant answer to the existentialist question of life and death. Assuming that my consciousness is, as any other subject's, a temporal one, then it comes out that the finiteness of my existence is not the finiteness of myself that I experience, but it is always the finiteness of others; I can never experience my own first moment (birth) and last moment (death) but only as ecstatic moments (or in Husserlian terms as intentional moments of the absolute flux of consciousness), that is, in P. Merlan's words: "*in the modus of having already forgotten birth and still expecting death...Always I have already had time, and always shall I still have time.*" ([28], pp. 36-37).

"There is no temporality, but the 'Being-for-itself' is temporalised as it exists" ([30], *translation of the author*, p. 172). The past as something not posed in front of the 'Being-for-itself' is ecstatically already behind and out of its thematic field to the extent that it is no more expecting to be 'clarified'. Evidently, these core notions seem to be close to the Husserlian notions of retention and protention and generallly to the constitution of time consciousness, which I'll comment next, along with the general Husserlian approach.

But let us insist a little more on the Sartrean approach to temporal subjectivity. Reflecting, for instance, on my self now that I draw a line in a piece of paper, is in a full and complete sense already a past in terms of a state-of-affairs: I draw a line in a piece of paper, whereupon as this state-of-affairs is coming over me at present now, it is already deflected to the state of already-not being (which is a deficiency of its full sense as 'Being-in-itself') by the annihilating property of the 'Being-for-itself'. This way the 'Being-for-itself' is at once before and after of the 'Being-in-itself', it is, in fact, never 'Being-in-itself', it is always the ecstatic tendency towards past and future which is its mode of 'being' temporal. By this Sartrean definition of past and future as ecstatic limits of the temporality of 'Being-for-itself' one is led to an a-temporality in absolute coincidence of the 'Being-for-itself' with itself (*ibid.*, p. 177).[6]

The Sartrean a-temporality in the case of absolute coincidence with 'Being-for-itself', seems to be close to the Husserlian notion of the non-existence of a point-like, absolutely self-standing temporal present, as anything intentionally perceived as original impression in present actuality is tied up intentionally to a just-passed-by in retention and a yet-to come in protention (see, [18]). I also regard Sartre's ecstatic unity underlying the third ecstatic dimension[7] as close enough to the Husserlian notion of the absolute ego of temporal consciousness, objectified as a temporal unity of its immanent objects which is moreover a homogenous temporal unity in itself, in the form of an objective continuous whole. Then naturally raises the question on the subjectivity behind this objective unity of temporal consciousness and consequently of any form of constituted unity, and this kind of subjectivity seems to lie in the root of any conceivable form of temporal ego; to this inquiry Husserl offered, as I shall give a clue below, the supposition of a non-temporal transcendental ego ([18], § 36).

As it turns out, we may be led by Husserl's longitudinal intentionality (*Längstintentionalität*), as an intentional form of the flux of consciousness, to

---

[6] Although J.P. Sartre was recognizing that none of the ecstatic forms towards present, past or future bears an ontological priority over the others, he nevertheless put the emphasis on the ecstasy of the present in contrast with M. Heidegger's emphasis on the ecstasy of the future. In his view, this is due to the fact that the 'Being-for-itself' becomes a past by virtue of a revelation of itself in present actuality; moreover by virtue of the revelation of a 'deficiency' of itself becomes a not yet-present (*ibid.*, p. 177).

[7] A temporal transcendence also underlies the third ecstatic dimension where the 'Being-for-itself' in a constant interplay of 'reflecting-reflected' eludes itself in an all-encompassing ecstatic unity in which it is grounded as the ecstatic tendency towards any 'Being-in-itself' inside its ever receding thematic field.

2. THE TRANSCENDENCE OF THE EGO... 237

a yet deeper constituting factor of a transcendental kind, termed the absolute ego, which ought to 'be' a pre-reflective, non-objectifiable and thus impredicative subjectivity, the ever in-act subjectivity of the continuous unity of temporal consciousness. There is no parallel corresponding notion to this kind of absolute subjectivity in Heidegger's analysis of the temporality of the 'Being-in-the World', (Da-sein), for Heidegger reduced the original ecstatic temporality to quite perplexing ecstatic forms of proper existence of the 'Being-in the World'; nevertheless they were both deeply concerned with the phenomenological-subjective origins of objective (or scientific) time, ([2], p. 210). What is of importance from my point of view, is that they both reduced the temporal unity of immanent objects within consciousness and finally the self-constituting unity of temporal consciousness itself to one or the other kind of transcendence. Heidegger described it as the ecstatic unity of a presentifying Da-sein which *a priori* retains and anticipates (in the sense of tending towards), whereas Husserl, except for the supplemental reduction to the time-constituting absolute ego, introduced, on the level of objectivity, the *a-priori* intentional forms of retention and protention of the flux of consciousness to provide a foundation for the temporal identity of its immanent objects and the longitudinal intentionality for the constitution of the passing flux of consciousness in itself as an objective whole.[8] By all accounts, the transcendence in Heidegger's description of the temporality of Da-sein lies precisely in the description of its ecstatic temporality as an impetus alienating the being-in-itself of Da-sein from its ontological substance and transforming it into ceaseless motion; in other words it is the ever in-act transcendence that assembles the temporal states of Da-sein into a unity in the scheme presentifying (*Gegenwärtigen*), retaining (*Behalten*), anticipating (*Gewärtigen*). This way temporality is for Heidegger the ecstatic unity of the ecstatic moments of Da-sein ([2], p. 203).

As it comes out, also on account of the following two sections, Heidegger's notion of ecstatic temporality is close to the Sartrean view of subjective temporality, concerning in particular the transcendental character of the ecstatic temporality of the 'Being-for-itself', something not quite strange given the influence that phenomenology had on Sartre's philosophical formation. Whatever may be the divergences between Sartre and Heidegger in the description of the temporality of 'Being-for-itself' and of Dasein, or between them and Husserl concerning the character of the deeper subjective source of the unity of temporal consciousness, I consider as most important in reaching my conclusions a common underlying factor of their respective approaches. This is a 'residual' transcendental subjectivity, not describable in ontological terms, impredicative as an objectivity and therefore of a non-analytic character, which is a constituting (and not constituted) factor of the continuous unity of each subject's consciousness and also in intersubjective sense of all subjectivities by virtue of

---

[8] For an original presentation of the transversal and longitudinal forms of intentionality, the reader is referred to Husserl's *Zur Phänomenologie des Inneren Zeibewusstseins*, ([18], resp. § 11, § 24 & § 39).

being-in-the world.

3   A comparative look into the Husserlian ego and the Heideggerian Da-sein

In *Sein und Zeit*, ([12]), Heidegger raised the question of the eventuality of a circular description of the ontology of being, concluding that the whole attitude of ἀπορεῖν in connection with the meaning of being renders this question 'legitimate'. Moreover Da-sein as the field where every being - including each one's self - and also every possible inquiry about its being belongs, is considered as the site of the understanding of being ([12], p. 7). In Heideggerian sense, Da-sein is not an instance of being for the representational abstraction of being; rather, it is the site of the understanding of being. Further, Da-sein is described as 'being' ahead of itself, that is, as projecting itself upon its potentiality-of-being before going on to any mere consideration of itself ([12], p. 373). 'It is thrown in the world' and in 'taking care of it', that is, in existing in the unity of an entangled thrown project, Da-sein is disclosed as a 'There'. While being-in-the-world has always already expressed itself, being-together-with-others means that it keeps itself in average interpretedness that is articulated in discourse and expressed in language.[9] As it stands out, the circumspect taking care of common sense is grounded in temporality, in the mode of making present that awaits and retains. As far as Da-sein enters into discussion as the ultimate bastion of the question of being, we may see some fundamental similarities and also some divergences with the Husserlian ego, taken as the ultimate transcendental source of the objective unity of being in the Life-World.[10] We can point to a sense of advancement ahead of itself of Da-sein in establishing itself as a caring self within the world which, though obviously not identical, bears a common pre-predicative origin with the Husserlian intentional ego inasmuch as the latter is a self-founded 'moment' establishing itself in performing the phenomenological reduction that divides the world into a pre-constitutional (pre-phenomenological) and post-constitutional one. To the extent that the most primitive intentional moment of experience of even a

---

[9]Discourse is in itself temporal since, all speaking about.., of.., or to.., is grounded in the ecstatic unity of temporality. The kinds of action associated with discourse are rooted in the primordial temporality of taking care of things, irrespective of whether it is related to things within time or not. In this sense, inasmuch as discourse is always talking about beings, predominantly not in the sense of theoretical statements, the temporal constitution of discourse and the temporal characteristics of language patterns can be faced only if the problem of the fundamental connection between being and truth has been unfolded in terms of the problematic of temporality. Further, taking account that the ontological meaning of 'is' cannot be defined in the sense of a superficial theory of propositions and judgements, the 'origination' of its significance can be clarified and moreover the formulation of concepts can be made ontologically possible only in terms of the temporality of discourse, that is, of Da-sein in general ([12], pp. 320-21).

[10]The Life-World in Husserlian terminology can be roughly described to a non-phenomenologist as the physical world with its ever receding horizon including in inter-subjective sense all knowing subjects in a special kind of presence in the World. More on this in E. Husserl's *The Crisis of European Sciences and Transcendental Phenomenology*, [13].

3. A COMPARATIVE LOOK

sole intentional consciousness in the world is irreducibly self-founded, even in the complete annulment of the objective world, put anyway within brackets, already discloses an at least implicit affinity with the sense attributed to Da-sein by virtue of the *a priori* 'moment' of the latter to project itself ahead of its potentiality-of-being-in-the world. Another fundamental similarity may be clearly seen to lie in the possibility of grounding both Da-sein and the Husserlian ego upon temporality. In *Sein und Zeit*, the circumspect taking care of common sense is grounded on temporality inasmuch as it makes possible the constitution of a present that awaits and retains. This is the way through which the advancement of Da-sein ahead of itself is making itself 'explicit' within the world, that is, in the mode of presentifying (*Gegenwärtigen*) retaining (*Behalten*) and awaiting (*Gewärtigen*). In comparison, the Husserlian ego established as the absolute subjectivity of each one's stream of temporal consciousnness is making itself objectively present in self-constituting its temporal self as a reflexion of its ever in-act transcendent subjectivity. The particular modes of Da-sein in making itself 'explicit' in actual present, through 'now, - not yet' and 'now, - no longer' associated with the 'then' and 'on that former occasion', are founded in presentifying, and are close to the corresponding Husserlian modes, e.g. of anterior-simultaneous (*Vor-zugleich*) which is grounded on a presentifying instant as its 'nearest realization' and it is *a priori* bound with it through transversal intentionality.

Further, Heidegger established temporality as a way of Da-sein of making itself expressible in addressing what it takes care of; as it stands, this addressing and discussing that also interprets itself is grounded in a making present and it is only possible through this, ([12], p. 374). Although temporality as ecstatically open and horizontally constitutive of the clearedness of the 'There' is in these terms recognizable in the interpretedness that takes care of, this does not, however preclude the possibility that primordial temporality as such, as well as the origin (temporalizing itself in it) of expressed time may remain unknown and unconceived (*ibid.*, p. 375). My point is that we have on the one hand, a temporality constitutive of the clearedness of the 'There' as the means of making Da-sein expressible in taking care of and by being-together-with-things at hand, and on the other hand, the origin of temporality, which can only be expressible by temporalizing itself in expressed time, 'being' in itself virtually unknown and unconceivable. Moreover, the ecstatic unity of temporality - that is, the unity of the 'outside-itself' in the raptures of the future, the having-been, and the present - is the condition of the possibility that there can be a being that exists as its 'There'. Taking the whole constitution of being of Da-sein as the the unified ground of its existential possibility, then ecstatic temporality clears the 'There' primordially and it is the primary regulator of the possible unity of all essential existential structures of Da-sein (*ibid.*, p. 321). Further, it is only in terms of the rootedness of Da-sein in temporality that we gain insight in the existential possibility of the phenomenon grounding the fundamental constitution of being-in-the-world. The corresponding Husserlian notion of the absolute ego of consciousness, is about a transcendental ego constitutive of temporality and consequently of spatiality (in terms of an objective temporal whole) that is temporalized in objectifying itself within the objective unity of each one's temporal consciousness. Inasmuch as the absolute ego can be known in objective temporality only as a mirror reflexion of its transcendental self, it is bound to remain a-temporal, unobjectifiable and for that reason absolutely impredicative, since (objective) time is the condition of the attribution of any predicates, even those of existence and individuality, to any objectivity ([29], p. 168). A divergence, in respective approaches, that can be noted here, is that the Heideggerian Da-sein is attributed with an ecstatic moment that projects its presence in the world as caring about its 'being' in being-with-other-beings, whereas the Husserlian absolute ego is completely 'impersonalized' and obscure and remains as such in spite of Husserl's painstaking efforts in Bernau manuscripts and later to elucidate its 'ontic' character, while trying at the same time not to get trapped in a maze of circularities.

Even though the 'being' of Da-sein is founded in the pre-ontological terms of care, its ontological meaning is, according to Heidegger, grounded in temporality as constituting the disclosedness of the 'There' and also of the World disclosed in the disclosedness of the 'There'. In this sense, the ontological constitution of the world must then also be grounded in temporality, more specifically the existential and temporal condition of the possibility of the world lies in the fact that temporality, as an ecstatic unity, has something like a horizon ([12], p. 333). Further, insofar, as Da-sein temporalizes itself, a world is also founded to exist, since the world is neither objectively present, nor at hand, but temporalizes itself in that temporality; Da-sein 'is' there, together with the outside-itself of the ecstasies (ibid., p. 334). In other words, the world is transcendent but it is grounded in the horizontal unity of ecstatic temporality. It is due to the ecstatically and horizontally founded transcendence of the world that it is made ontologically possible for beings to be encountered within the world and objectified as encountered beings. In view of the above, the subjectivity of the world is the subjectivity of Da-sein which is, in ontological terms, the existing Da-sein whose being is properly grounded in temporality (ibid., p. 335). To come back to Heidegger's characterization of the temporality of Da-sein and recognize the convergence with Husserl's views on the origin of temporality, I note that it is in the ecstatic unity of temporality understood along with the unthematic and unrecognizable as such datability (the self-evident relational structure of the 'then, when..', 'on that former occasion when..', 'now that..'), that Da-sein has always already been disclosed to itself as being-in-the-world and inner-worldly beings have been discovered along with it (ibid., p. 375).

It is remarkable that the problematic about the source of temporality of Da-sein, led Heidegger to note that the time the Da-sein 'allows' itself has gaps in it, claiming also that it would be wrong to think that the lapses of time that Da-sein 'allows' itself may be represented by a continuous stream of nows; it would be rather conceived of as primarily determined in terms of how it 'has' its time in a manner corresponding to its actual existence (ibid., p. 377). It is here evident that Heidegger draws a line between temporality disclosed in the

3. A COMPARATIVE LOOK

ecstatic being-in-the-world-with-other-beings which could be paralleled with Husserl's objectively constituted temporality that is intersubjectively unique, and the temporality appropriate to Da-sein itself in a manner corresponding to its actual existence. This latter temporality could be paralleled with the self-constituting temporality whose subjective origin is the absolute ego of the flux of consciousness, meant as a homogenous temporal flux generating all temporal divergences within its self-constituting immanence (e.g. immediate past-present-athematic future) ([18], § 36).

In what regards the 'meanwhile', e.g. in the 'then...until then', which the 'taking care' of Da-sein can articulate by making each time anew a present in awaiting by giving further 'thens', Heidegger points to a duration as 'the time revealed in the self-interpretation of temporality, a time that is actually but unthematically understood in taking care of as a span' ([12], p. 376). In this sense the making present that awaits and retains interprets a 'during' with a span because in so doing it is disclosed to itself as ecstatically stretched along temporality in a way that is due to the ecstatic temporality of factual Da-sein in being-in-the-world. In comparison, Husserl described the time elapsed in the 'then..until then', in terms of the notions of transversal and longitudinal intentionality: he generated each 'now, not yet' through the protention of transversal intentionality, then immanentized each present now based on original impression and *a priori* associated with a descending tail of retentions and finally produced the duration of 'in-between' by introducing the notion of longitudinal intentionality which makes the descending tail of retentions appear in the continuous mode of a whole retrievable by secondary memory in the present now of intentional consciousness. It is remarkable that, in Heidegger, temporalizing does not mean a 'succession' of the ecstasies, in the sense that the future is not later than the having-been and the having-been not earlier than the present. The unity of the horizontal schemata of future, having-been and present is grounded on the ecstatic unity of temporality. Consequently, the horizon of the whole of temporality determines whereupon a being factically existing is essentially disclosed. As Heidegger put it, it is on the basis of the horizontal constitution of the ecstatic unity of temporality, that something like a disclosed world belongs to the being that is always its 'There' (*ibid.*, p. 334). This means, temporality temporalizes itself as a future that makes present in the process of having been, which is evidently reminiscent of the double form of the intentionality of consciousness in Husserlian terms: On the one hand, there 'is' the transversal intentionality as *a priori* binding an original impression to the attached protentions and retentions, that is, by retaining what is registered in the present now while having been already 'anticipated', and on the other hand, the longitudinal intentionality by which a stored memory can be retrieved by secondary memory in the present now of consciousness by having been retained as a continuously descending sequence of retentions constituted as a whole within the objective unity of the stream of consciousness. These given, and notwithstanding the divergences in the description of the Husserlian ego and the Heideggerian Da-sein, it is of primary importance to note that in both approaches the capital issue of the original source of temporality is left in relative obscurity, in part because of the fear to fall into circularities taking into account the extreme difficulty of shaping a meaningful discourse on this notion. This difficulty is evidently seen, for instance, in the Husserlian designation of the a-temporal absolute ego as a *nunc stans*, which is apparently a contradiction in terms, and also in the characterization of consciousness as intentionally directed experience, something that points to pre-predicative intentionality structures termed so to the extent that they 'anticipate'- without, by essential necessity, having temporally constituted - actual predicated instances. In this sense intentionality of consciousness defines a domain of real possibility, anterior to actuality ([11] p. 12). It is also seen in the Heideggerian description of Da-sein in the pre-ontological terms of 'taking care' or of 'being thrown into existence' for the sake of a potentiality-of-being-of itself, or yet, in terms of the 'outside-of-itself' of the ecstatic unity of temporality. This is the reason, by all accounts, that both Husserl and Heidegger talked about temporality only in the context respectively, of constituted objectivity and of being-in-the-world, considering the description of temporal duration or of temporal unity as only a being-in-the-world discourse, where any '*ante*' situation is virtually left in a circularities-generating, 'non-ontological' and therefore impredicative context.

4 The Temporality of the 'Being-for-itself' in J.P. Sartre

The question of temporality in relation to an underlying subjectivity is a vital part of the problematic in J.P. Sartre's analysis of the 'ontology' of *Pour-soi* developed in his well-known work, *L' être et le néant*. In fact, he was led by a consistent critique of the views of philosophers of the likes of R. Descartes and H. Bergson to the question of temporality as inherently linked to a unifying act. It is in terms of this unifying act that temporality is conceived as a quasi-multiplicity, a dissociation in terms of a unity, that is, in fact, an irreversible succession (of moments) through temporal unity. In this sense, we cannot conceive it as a content bearer whose being would be given as an objectivity, for in that case there would be no answer to the question of how this being in-itself can be fragmented into multiplicities or of how the temporal minima as contents in themselves can be associated within the unity of a unique temporality ([30], p. 71). Consequently, temporality does not exist in terms of a (static) being, it can rather be described as the mode of 'being' which 'is' itself in advance of itself so that the temporal conjunctions in advance of and after of can be intelligible for it as reciprocally defined. Inasmuch as there is an advancement (essentially an alienation) of being with regard to itself, it becomes meaningful to talk about in advance and after of itself, in general, to talk about in advance of and after of. It follows that there can be no conceivable temporality but as an 'internal' structure of the 'Being-for-itself', in the sense that there is no ontological priority of the 'Being-for-itself' over temporality, but rather that temporality is the mode of being of the 'Being-for-itself', to the extent that the latter 'exists' ecstatically with regard to itself. In Sartre's concise expression, temporality does not exist (in terms of ontological being),

4. THE TEMPORALITY OF THE 'BEING-FOR-ITSELF' 243

yet the 'Being-for-itself' temporalizes itself in existing and moreover, taking into account a phenomenologically related approach of the past, present and future, it cannot exist otherwise than in a temporal form ([30], p. 172).

Further, in grounding conceptually the ecstatic nature of the 'Being-for-itself', Sartre talked about the surge of a being, that is, of the 'Being-for-itself' which, in annihilating the 'Being-in-itself' and in making present all dimensions corresponding to the various correlations that it bears with its 'Being-in-itself', makes apparent through human reality, a quasi-multiplicity associated also with the appearance of numbers in the world. J.P.Sartre, distinguished three ecstatic dimensions of the 'Being-for-itself', with the understanding that the sense of the ecstasy is taken as the distance of the 'Being-for-itself' from itself which is not to be considered as something real, not even something conceivable as being in itself. In this sense, each ecstatic dimension is a mode through which the 'Being-for-itself' is projected in relation to itself, a declination with regard to its being-in-itself 'separated' by a null (*néant*) that makes the 'Being-for-itself' a shift of its 'being'. By virtue of this property, the 'Being-for-itself' can never be conceived of as being what it 'is', for what it 'is' is already behind it, in the sense of a perpetual past and by this factual state the past should be considered as a necessary structure of the 'Being-for-itself', to the extent that the 'Being-for-itself' cannot 'exist' but as an annihilating passing implicating 'something' overtaken ([30], p. 173). This kind of ecstatic unity of the 'Being-for-itself' with its past, as an original and annihilating relation of the 'Being-for-itself' with 'Being-in-itself', seems close in meaning with the corresponding Heideggerian conception of the alienation of Da-sein in projecting itself towards past or future, at least in that it establishes a transcendental and *a priori* foundation of temporal constitution. It is remarkable, though, that J. P. Sartre put the emphasis on the ecstasy of the present, in contrast to the Heideggerian emphasis on the ecstacy of the future, for it is in revelation to itself that the 'Being-for-itself' is its own past as it is also in revelation to itself that it is a 'deficiency' with regard to its own future. In dispersing itself in the three dimensions past-present-future, none of which has an ontological priority over the others and none of which can exist without the other two, and due, at least, to the single fact that the 'Being-for-itself' annihilates itself in projecting itself along these ecstacies, it is temporal ([30], p. 177). On this account, the 'Being-for-itself' is ever either in advance or in retard of itself and it 'is' never in 'the state of rest' with itself.

In resting on itself, the 'Being-for-itself' should 'be' in the a-temporal phase of absolute coincidence with itself, which is something that is strongly reminiscent in a first reading, of the Husserlian notion of specious present within the immanence of consciousness, meant as an *a priori* articulation at once of original impression, protention and retention. On a deeper level, it can be seen as posing from another angle the question of the transcendental and a-temporal character of the origin of temporality identified with the origin of the absolute ego in Husserlian view, for in the eternal interplay of reflecting-reflected what the 'Being-for-itself' is determined as 'being' is already its past, while what is also determined as its 'being' projects its already 'not-yet-self', thereby generating the objectified unity of temporality. Moreover to the question whether this constant change of present to a past at once generating a new present, implies an internal change of the 'Being-for-itself', the answer is that it is the temporality of the 'Being-for-itself' that is the foundation of change and not the change that is the foundation of temporality ([30], p. 179).

As it stands, in admitting to an ecstatic nature of the 'Being-for-itself' by virtue of its spontaneity, it is clearly by a presupposition of temporality that it becomes meaningful a 'self-refutation' of spontaneity as thematically given (for otherwise it would be perpetually its being-in-itself) and then also a 'refutation' of the 'self-refutation', this latter taken as being-in-itself a concrete state of affairs. In that sense, what is valid for the 'Being-for-itself' as a presence in the world is also valid for temporalization in its totality. It is then, a whole never completed, a totality 'self-refuting' and self-evading, meant as an extraction of its being-in-itself in the unity of a same emergence, in other words, an elusive whole which, at the instant of its self-givenness, 'is' already beyond ([30], pp. 184-85). In this Sartrean view, temporal consciousness is conceived as the human reality temporalizing itself as a totality that cannot be described as existing but in terms of its own overpassing, which means that it can never 'exist' as being-in-itself within the limits of an instant, for in that case the 'Being-for-itself' would be affirmed as being-in-itself which would contradict its character as never 'existing' in terms of being. In contrast, temporality as an actual totality temporalizes itself in rescinding the instant.

It is clear that the nature of the Sartrean 'Being-for-itself' and of its inherent temporality are very close to the corresponding notion of the Husserlian absolute ego of consciousness, inasmuch as both are by essence referred to a temporality as a necessary condition of their objectification and by the same measure as themselves a-temporal and origins of temporality by which they can be only conceived of as their 'replicas' in the ever restrictive relation reflecting-reflected. In establishing themselves as being-in-the-world, they become the ultimate reason of the emergence of temporality as fulfillment of a continuous objective whole, ever refuting its 'being-in-instantaneity' and thereby laying the foundation for a new deeper context of discussion with regard to the inherent temporality of intuitive continuum.

On this account, a subjective foundation of intuitive continuum that involves in an essential way a notion of quasi-multiplicity in the Sartrean sense described above, can lead, as a kind of transcendental subjectivism, that is not a solipsism, to a deeper comprehension of continuum within a formal mathematical theory in terms of which a generation, e.g. of the objects of arithmetic, becomes meaningful. Moreover, concerning the transcendence of a self-constituting subjectivity, which is essentially the nature of the 'Being-for-itself', there seems to be a common interpretational content with the respective Husserlian and Heideggerian approaches, to the extent that this kind of subjectivity establishes temporality in constantly alienating itself from its ontic 'being'. Moreover, it 'is' the ultimate subjective origin of a continuous temporal unity which is the *sine qua non* condition for the immanentization of multiplicities of discrete objects of registered-in perception (including the ones of a formal theory), associated as such with a sense of temporal duration founded upon the objectified form of a homogenous inner temporality. A temporal duration ever conceived as fulfilling an immanent continuous whole may, in turn, 'generate' a sense of actual infinity meant as a boundless, immanent to the consciousness, infinity in presentational immediacy.

5 Quantum objects as temporal objects

In what comes next, I will try to outline an approach in which a broad class of epistemic objects, in the general sense of objects of human knowledge, can be taken as temporal objects associated further with a temporality originating in the constituting consciousness of an 'interacting' observer. On this account, it will be useful to refer to P. Heelan's classification of objects in [11], (p. 6). There, he distinguishes the following kinds of objects taken in the sense of unities, identities, wholes, and stable subjects of properties: the phenomenal objects, that is, those objects given primordially in perception and manifest in consciousness, and the constructed objects given to us indirectly in perception through sensible signs, e.g. a bunch of electrons in a bubble chamber, which are characterized by him as transcendent correlates of phenomenal objects and are further divided into: (i) those conceived as having determined spatial coordinates at each instant, for instance a classical particle, even though they are not directly perceptible but only through some sign of their presence and (ii) the fields through which those objects above yield a sign of their presence, in the sense of infinitely extended media for three-dimensional wave motions, provided that they also yield a sensible sign of their presence. To the extent, that these are affirmed as unconditioned objects on the basis of evidence, they are called objects in the strict or formal sense, or simply strict objects. In what follows, I shall give a special emphasis to those objects that are shaped as well-defined objects of perception through some kind of direct or indirect interaction with a conscious observer, an interaction which by its very enactment underscores the subjective foundation of temporality in shaping their objectification.

For this purpose, I will make a special reference to the process of quantum measurement as a special case of quantum process in which (**i**) a conscious observer within a macroscopic environment can, by a macroscopic instrument (the measuring apparatus), infer the state of an observed microscopic system (e.g., a quantum state-of-affairs) and (**ii**) it can do so only after the measurement process is over, which means that he cannot infer anything about the observed quantum system in the time interval Δt during the interaction, so long as it is in a 'non-objectifiable' state. Of course, there is an open question as to where one can locate the 'cut' between the quantum and the classical level in performing a quantum experiment. Let's take for example, von Neumann's mathematical treatment of an experiment involving the intermediate level of a second classical-level apparatus measuring the combined system of a first apparatus plus the observed quantum system which is to be treated quantum mechanically, ([35]). In pursuing my argument, I will rely on some formalism describing the state of the combined system before and after the interaction. Let O be the operator representing a quantum state to be measured, let O_n be its eigenvalues and $\psi_n(x)$ the corresponding eigenfunctions in the x-representation. Let the initial wave function of the quantum observable to be measured be

$$\Psi = \Sigma_n C_n \psi_n(x)$$

and let the measuring apparatus be in a well-defined state represented by a wave packet $\varphi_0(y)$. Then the combined system has an initial wave function

$$\Psi_0 = \varphi_0(y)\Sigma_n C_n \psi_n(x)$$

Assuming a strong enough interaction between the observed system and the observing apparatus on the quantum level so that all other disturbances may be neglected, we obtain for the wave function of the combined system after the time Δt of interaction the equation:

$$\Psi = \Sigma_n C_n \psi_n(x) \varphi_0(y - \lambda O_n \Delta t)$$

Letting ΔO_n represent the change of the eigenvalues O_n for successive values of n and then letting the quantity $\lambda \Delta t \Delta O_n \gg 1$, it follows that the wave packets multiplying different $\psi_n(x)$ will not overlap; that is, to each wave packet $\varphi_0(y - \lambda O_n \Delta t)$ after the interaction will correspond a definite wave function $C_n \psi_n(x)$. If we then observe this combined quantum system with a second apparatus, then it will register a value of y corresponding to a particular wave packet $\varphi_0(y - \lambda O_n \Delta t)$ associated in turn with a definite eigenfunction $\psi_n(x)$ of the post-interaction state of the original quantum system. In effect, there is a collapse of the original linear combination of products to a definite product $\psi_m(x)\varphi_0(y - \lambda O_m \Delta t)$ whose probability is shown to be $|C_n|^2$ just as it would be if there would be only one measuring apparatus. As a matter of fact, von Neumann's approach leads to an infinite chain of classical-level observers where in each case one may put the 'cut' between the classical and the quantum level, 'somewhere' between the last combined quantum system and the next measuring apparatus. This is because, ontologically speaking, it is quite ambiguous to say that that there is a real transition in a macrosystem (original quantum system & first apparatus) when there is a collapse from the wave function

$$\Psi = \Sigma_n C_n \psi_n(x) \varphi_0(y - \lambda O_n \Delta t)$$

to a definite state $\psi_m(x)\varphi_0(y - \lambda O_m \Delta t)$ ([3], pp. 21-24). In D. Bohm's ontological interpretation of quantum mechanics, the difficulty in von Neumann's approach is essentially due to the fact that he regards a quantum state represented by a wave function as standing on its own, albeit in interaction with the classical level. In contrast, Bohr's view can be considered as more consistent in regarding the notion of a quantum object/state as meaningless, except in taking the whole experimental process (observed system & observing apparatus)

5. QUANTUM OBJECTS AS TEMPORAL OBJECTS

as an irreducible whole, therefore abolishing the need of interaction between the quantum and the classical level.

The whole discussion bears testimony to the inherent difficulties in determining the ontology of a quantum object/state, if such an ontology in conventional terms really exists. All the more so, when there is the 'hidden' parameter of time that should be taken into account in talking about an interaction between the quantum and classical level or even in Bohr's view in talking about the performance of a quantum experiment as an unanalysable whole. In the present case, one could pose the question of the meaning of the strong inequality $\lambda \Delta t \Delta O_n \gg 1$, in securing the non-overlapping of the wave packets $\varphi_0(y - \lambda O_n \Delta t)$ of the pointer associated with corresponding eigenfunctions $\psi_n(x)$ of the observed object. In a first mathematical reading, this means that the quantities ΔO_n and Δt cannot be nonstandard (infinitesimal) numbers, for in that case their product could never exceed unity due to the non-validity of the Archimedean principle with regard to nonstandard numbers. Then, what about the corresponding quantum state for nonstandard values of ΔO_n and Δt, that is, for those such that $\lambda \Delta t \Delta O_n \ll 1$. In formal interpretation, in the time interval during the period of interaction the various components of the wave function of the combined system

$$\Psi(x, y, t) = \Sigma_n C_n \psi_n(x) \varphi_0(y - \lambda O_n t)$$

will overlap and interfere and the amplitude of the wave function above will become a rapidly fluctuating function of x, y and of time t.

But then, we might raise the question, could we perform, in principle, some advanced form of measurement on the system (quantum object & first apparatus) that would produce a 'collapse' of the wave function within a curtailed time dt of interaction such that $\lambda dt \, dO_n \ll 1$, and perform in chain this measurement in trimming each time anew the time length of interaction to ever smaller infinitesimalities? Could that be run ideally ad infinitum? It seems, this is a reasonable argument, to the extent that we formally define the time t of interaction as the argument of a (rapidly fluctuating) function, which means that it is conditioned, as a continuously varying extensional variable, on its pre-determination as a constituted objectivity. This argumentation, which obviously leads to a circular conception of time in performing a quantum experiment, is another way of generating the ontological impasse demonstrated by the von Neumann's infinite chain of observers experiment. In naively ontological terms, one could then pose the question of whether, in obtaining the same eigenfunction $\psi_\kappa(x)$ for an 'observed' quantum object between two successive measurements performed in so short a time interval, we can neglect the phase factor, the corresponding quantum state of the observable remaining in-between the almost simultaneous measurements with the same eigenfunction $\psi_\kappa(x)$.

Evidently, this is a question that presupposes the acceptance of an independent quantum reality that can 'stand on its own', that is, independently of being observed, in other words as a constituted objectivity within a homogenous objective temporality. As a matter of fact this is a question which, in general terms, brought about a long historical discussion on the ontological meaning of quantum 'observations', with N. Bohr strongly opposing any meaningful talk of a quantum state except in the context of an experimental preparation and its measurement result conceived as an irreducible whole. In his view, both Heisenberg's approach with regard to the theory of potentialities and von Neumann's idea of classical and quantum level and the 'cut' between them, were considered as confusing inasmuch as they conceded, even indirectly, to the existence of a quantum state, represented by a wave function, 'standing on its own'. Concerning von Neumann's thesis this is true to the extent that, even in generating a classical-level observing apparatus which, through an endless regression of joint quantum-level observable plus apparatus systems, comes finally to be identified with a non-physical terminus, there is a 'residuum' of independent ontological being of the quantum observable.

It it to be noted here that in von Neumann's view, the need to resort to a non-physical terminus in the theoretically infinite chain of measuring apparatuses comes as a result of three factors: first, that any joint system of a quantum observable & measuring apparatus is subject, as long as it is considered a quantum system, to processes of the second kind, that is, to processes which are continuous, causal, and, reversible and also described by the equations of motion[11]; second, any new physical system brought into interaction with the previously joint system quantum observable & measuring apparatus, will act as a quantum system thus being also subject to processes of the second kind; and third, inasmuch as a measurement is a finite process yielding a definite (finitistic, in effect) result, then it should be terminated in a non-physical entity, presumably the mind or consciousness of an observer ([9], pp. 468-69).

Although on the formal level, the 'vacuum' in the quantum state that shows up in collapsing the wave superpositions at the instant of classical-level measurement is 'patched' up by the adoption of the projection postulate, the philosophical (or rather, ontological) side of the question of measurement was left almost untreated in spite of the fact that von Neumann's approach alluded to the existence of a non-physical consciousness to the point of being often described as dualistic. However, he did not specifically deal with the role of consciousness in 'breaking' up the chain of superpositions, much less did he enter a deeper discussion on the nature of the ego of consciousness in shaping up a definite measurement by objectifying a hitherto entangled quantum state. It was, in fact, F. London's and E. Bauer's original work back in 1939, that explicitly claimed the primary role of the conscious activity of the human mind in reducing the wave packet of joint quantum systems, even though S. French claims in [9] that their account of the role of consciousness was not to effect a reduction of the wave packet. Undoubtedly, the London-Bauer approach was historically most of all others close enough to a phenomenologically-motivated

---

[11] In contrast, processes of the first kind involved in the quantum level of measurement, are described as discontinuous, non-causal, and irreversible.

5. QUANTUM OBJECTS AS TEMPORAL OBJECTS

one and it is, indeed, susceptible to a clear phenomenological reading, especially with regard to the act of reflection of the ego of consciousness in setting up a new objectivity in the process of measurement by cutting the chain of statistical relations summarized in the expression of the wave function of joint quantum systems ([27]). In S. French's reading, the separation of the ego (in accepting its 'participation' within the quantum domain) from the measured statistical ensemble is not to be thought of as a physical means of provoking the collapse of the wave function of the ensemble, but rather as generated by the immanent faculty of introspection of the ego in question, by which it unfolds a mutual separation of both an ego-pole and an object-pole through a characteristic act of reflection ([9], pp. 484-85).

What is still missing, though, in the aforementioned approaches is a deeper study of the temporal character of the 'observing' ego, in the sense of an objectivity-constituting ego. In doing so, one can deny the attribution to a quantum observable of an independent ontological being while at the same time avoiding the solipsistic pitfall of transposing in an absolute sense its 'existence' to the existence of a constituting ego. By taking into account the temporality-constituting character of the ego of consciousness (or conscious mind, in the sense of the non-physical terminus of a quantum experiment), one can concede to an 'existence' of a quantum observable (e.g. of an entangled quantum state) on a pre-constitutional level, that is, at a stage prior to its objectification by an intentional consciousness which is by itself time-constituting. To the extent that a quantum observable finds itself in the time of interaction in a pre-objectification state it is meaningless to refer to its ontological being, as its being is by essential necessity bracketed by the impossibility to 'penetrate' into anything that precedes its reflection as a temporal objectivity, implying by this token a mutual separation of an ego-pole and an object-pole. Inasmuch as the ego of consciousness objectifies itself by reflecting on itself one is shifted, in a yet more radical reduction, to a pure transcendence beyond any objective temporality, this time within the immanence of each one's consciousness in which being and being-in-constituting are essentially identical. This way, the 'residuum' left in establishing a infinite chain of observing apparatuses in v. Neumann's approach, or in arbitrarily abridging the elapsed time between the time of quantum interaction and its classical-level registration is made a question of forging a well-meant objectivity by a consciousness whose temporal ego objectifies by objectifying itself. This means, that the question of an ontology of a quantum state in itself is a question of an ontology of an absolute ego of consciousness as a temporal constituting factor inaccessible to objectivity except in its own auto-reflexion, which is evidently a circular impasse. At least, one is left with a motivation for focusing the discussion on the origin of the 'ontological vacuum' (concerning the in-between state) generated by the collapse of the wave packet in a quantum experiment that includes the participation of a classical-level observer, in the transcendental, time-constituting ego of consciousness. Unfortunately, though, a circular impasse is generated then within the immanence of consciousness, to the extent that the temporality constituting ego cannot be apprehended but in reflecting on itself which means that it is already an objectified replica of itself which obviously is not itself. Evidently, this is not a matter of abridging ideally infinitely the 'time' elapsed between the reflecting act of absolute ego and its reflected objectification, just as this is not a matter of abridging ideally infinitely the 'time' elapsed between an interaction at the quantum level and its classical-level registration.

This approach of a constituting temporal ego within a quantum context, can come to terms with the defining essence of the Sartrean 'Being-for-itself' in the sense of being nowhere within objective time, while at the same time establishing the ecstatic character of temporality which, moreover, to the extent that it always tends towards its ontological being but it never 'is' as presently been and also to the extent that it 'is' an ever ecstatically extending leap towards its 'shall immediately be' objectified as 'already having been', it shares also the transcendent self-alienating nature of Heideggerian Da-sein. One could reasonably claim that 'being-in-objectifying' a hitherto entangled state of a joint quantum system and 'being-in-ecstatically-projecting' itself towards being-in-the world, are essential properties that may be attributed to one and the same 'always-in-act' subjectivity that can ontologically exist only in self-alienation, in accepting its constituting (or at least participating) presence in the physical world. Besides, in considering the *a priori* retentional and protentional forms of the absolute flux of consciousness and in supplementary radical reduction the essential character of its absolute ego, as never being in objectivity but always 'being in constituting', it also bears a close affinity to the transcendental characteristics of the Husserlian absolute ego, in a way that may do justice to the alleged claim of this article, namely to the possibility of a relatedness of the temporality of continental ego with the temporality of epistemical objects, these latter taken as objects-correlates of a temporal ego.

It may be noted here that in Husserlian view, perceptual objects in general, bracketing their objective ontological being, are not defined but by identification, within the continuous unity of the temporal flux of consciousness, of multiplicities of non-identical, adumbrating profiles in their immanent duration ([16], p. 231). Moreover, their spatial extension in the sense of a time-fulfillment is transposed to each one's consciousness as an immanent moment through which we continuously come across spatial or qualitative discontinuities ([19], p. 70).

6 The underlying temporality in certain foundational questions

In the following, I will discuss mainly questions arising from contemporary research in mathematical foundations, related in particular with the character of the well-known, independent from standard **ZF** Set Theory, axioms which are the *Axiom of Choice* (**AC**) and the *Continuum Hypothesis* (**CH**). As a matter of fact, it is known that both axioms have been proved to be independent from the rest of **ZF** due to the breakthrough results of Gödel (1938) and P. Cohen (1962). The obvious and deeply running influence of these two axioms

6. THE UNDERLYING TEMPORALITY

within foundational mathematics has been proved quite enduring to the effect that their broader appeal to the logical-mathematical community is also due to their controversial character insofar as they are believed by some set-theorists to be reducible to a non-analytical content. Gödel himself had already claimed in *What is Cantor's Continuum Problem* (1947), that if the current standard axiomatical system was well-defined then the *Continuum Hypothesis* should be either true or false, which means that in the opposite case this question could not be taken as being of a purely analytical character; as it is well-known P. Cohen proved in 1962 the consistency of the negation of *Continuum Hypothesis* with the rest of the axioms of **ZFC** and consequently its independence from **ZFC**, thus lending further credibility to Gödel's provision. It is remarkable that the inspiring influence of the aforementioned questions has helped foster further research within mathematical foundations, associated mainly with the work of W. H. Woodin, M. Magidor, K. Kunen and others.

What is so important about these two axioms can be respectively summed up in the following: concerning **CH**, we inquire about the possibility of the existence of an intermediate level of infinity between the countable infinity of natural numbers ($\aleph_0$) and the uncountable infinity of reals ($\aleph_1$), in view of the proposed well-known Cantor formula $2^{\aleph_0} = \aleph_1$; as it is also known, this intermediate existence question is generalized, in terms of the formula $2^{\aleph_\alpha} = \aleph_{\alpha+1}$ where α is any infinite cardinal, to the general question whether there is an intermediate level of infinity between any two successive infinite cardinals in the canonical scale above $\aleph_0$. In spite of the landmark theorems of Gödel (1938) and P. Cohen (1962) establishing the independence of **CH** from the axioms of **ZFC** theory, one has the feeling that, first, this is a question not necessarily of an analytic character, given the inherent vagueness of the notion of non-finitistic within a a first-order formal language (see, [7]), and, second, that this is a question not yet settled once for all. Concerning the second view, I will draw attention, in the following, to H.W. Woodin's latest results on the matter, as they are presented in [37].

On account of the *Axiom of Choice*, there is, first, a persisting belief among set-theorists that without it it is extraordinarily difficult to prove anything non-trivial about sets and, second, there is a sense in which its application is fundamentally associated with the following two mental faculties: the ability to constitute an actual infinity in the present now of consciousness, in the sense of freely extending spatial and temporal stretches in imagination while ever new spatiotemporal wholes emerge in front of our inward gaze (something that is obviously not related with the real possibility of an indefinitely extending spatiotemporality which is bound to causal-natural laws), and the ability to perform acts uniquely defined by their content, in the specific case, choosing each time a unique element among an infinite collection of aggregates of such elements. In a certain sense, it can be said that these acts, implying *in rem* the presence of a subjective factor, essentially constitute much of what is implicitly presupposed in formally constructing anything beyond finitistic bounds within a mathematical theory: the notion of an indefinite extension of the domain of an axiomatical system and the possibility of applying each time a subjective criterion to generate uniquely defined meaningful acts associated with concrete object-contents.

I am not going to deal with the philosophical discussion and the controversy generated by the deep impact of the aforementioned independence results and those further generated by them, for there exists already an extensive bibliography. Instead, I shall focus on W.H. Woodin's recent revisiting of the *Continuum Hypothesis* as well as of other large cardinal axioms within a far broader context which is that of a generic multiverse of sets,[12] and indicate the unavoidable application of the two fundamental intuitions referred to above in a kind of implicit circular reasoning. As a matter of fact, and entering into some technical details, an early problem regarding the notion of a generic multiverse V_M, generated in the universe of sets V by a countable transitive set M such that $M \models$ **ZFC**, is that in accepting the Ω Conjecture[13] as true (and also that there exists a proper class of Woodin cardinals which is a large cardinal axiom not provable within **ZFC** theory), then the generic-multiverse position "is a brand of formalism that denies the transfinite by reducing truth about the universe of sets to truth about a simple fragment such as that of the integers, or [..], the sets of real numbers" ([37], p. 103). Indeed, by the de facto violation of two critical multiverse laws, one faces the problem of reducing multiverse truth about the collection of possible universes of sets to truth about the reduced multiverse of fragments of that 'global' universe, e.g. to the fragmented universe V_{δ_0+1} of the original multiverse, consequently denying a transfinite 'extension' beyond $\delta_0 + 1$, δ_0 being the least Woodin cardinal, ([37], pp. 102-105).

It is to be noted, though, that in accepting Ω Conjecture, which within Ω-logic is strongly associated with W.H. Woodin's argument against the *Continuum Hypothesis*, one has to previously endorse notions of logical validity and of provability of a sentence ϕ within a countable theory T in set-theoretical language, that are respectively constrained on universal quantification over the class of all ordinals α (and also over all complete Boolean algebras), and in the case of provability on the topological characteristics of universally Baire subsets of the set of real numbers. Regarding universally Baire subsets, it is important to see that the Baire property of these sets, implicitly introduces a notion of actual infinity to the extent that the definition of the Baire property of a subset A of a topological space X, implies that A differs from an open

---

[12]Taken that a multiverse of sets refers to the collection of possible universes of sets, then a generic multiverse of sets is generated from each universe of the collection by closing under generic extensions (enlargements) in Cohen's forcing sense and under generic refinements (inner models of a universe of which the given universe is a generic extension; for details and formal definition, see [37], pp. 102-103.

[13]The Ω Conjecture can be regarded as simply the conjecture that the Gödel completeness theorem holds for Ω-logic, that is, supposing there exists a proper class of Woodin cardinals, then:

$$\text{For all sentences } \phi, \; \emptyset \models_\Omega \phi \text{ if and only if } \emptyset \vdash_\Omega \phi$$

For details, see [36].

6. THE UNDERLYING TEMPORALITY

set U by a meager set;[14] that is, there is an open set U such that $A \triangle U$ is meager (where $\triangle$ denotes the symmetric difference). Obviously, the content of topological notions, in general, is such that it is indescribable solely by first-order linguistic means, something that is reflected in the impredicative sense of topological openness, and this formal impredicativity seems precisely due to an underlying actual infinity conditioning the apprehension of topological forms as objective wholes transcending the expressional capacity of a first-order theory. In a sense broadly outlined in this article, this actual infinity is meant as engendered by mental reflection in the present now of actuality, where we can freely extend it to ever new boundaries while all the same possibly reflecting on it as an objectified whole.

In seeking a way out of the difficulty posed by the violation of both first and second multiverse laws in accepting the Ω Conjecture and the existence of a proper class of Woodin cardinals, W.H. Woodin has focused, in terms of the construction of inner models, on the possibility of constructing transitive enlargements of Gödel's constructible universe L that preserve the ordinals and are compatible with large cardinal axioms, an approach largely based on a fundamental level on the particular structure of L as logically definable from the parameters of a set $(X, \in)$. This possibility is also based on properties of objects and relations of L conditioned on the absoluteness of formulas involving ordinal numbers within L, e.g. for any set a, there exists an ordinal α such that $a \in L_\alpha$, and further on the transitivity of the enlargements N of L.[15] It is remarkable, that the definition of the constructible universe L does not require the Axiom of Choice, therefore ensuring that if the system **ZF** is consistent, so is **ZFC**; yet the proof of certain absolute sentences, like the one stating that for all ordinals $\alpha \geq \omega$, $\mid L(\alpha) \mid = \mid \alpha \mid$ (for cardinals $\mid L(\alpha) \mid$, $\mid \alpha \mid$), need the Axiom of Choice. As it turns out, this particular sentence is a necessary step for the proof of the consistency of *Continuum Hypothesis* within the constructible universe L.

For one thing, the whole conception of the Inner Model Program is to provide a model in which the Axiom of Choice does not fail, that is, it should be consistent with the Axiom of Choice, and yet there could be constructed generalizations of the constructive universe L which are compatible with large cardinal axioms. Knowing that large cardinal axioms are unprovable within **ZFC**, a pragmatist's argument on this account (or a skeptic's argument, in Woodin's formulation), would be that any large cardinal axiom within **ZFC** theory is either consistent with the axioms of this theory, or there is an elementary proof that the axiom cannot hold ([37], p. 97). The Inner Model Program seeks a built-up of inner models which by their inductive nature may solve

---

[14] A meager set E (or a set of first category) is a set that, considered as a subset of a (usually larger) topological space, is in a precise topological sense small or negligible; i.e. if $\forall \epsilon > 0$ there exists a finite or countable collection $I_1, I_2, \ldots$ of (possibly overlapping) intervals such that $E \subset \bigcup_\kappa I_\kappa$ and $\sum_\kappa \mid I_\kappa \mid < \epsilon$.

[15] For a deeper discussion of the metatheoretical content of the notion of ordinals, of the absoluteness of formulas and that of transitive sets, see [25].

the problem of the whole hierarchy of large cardinal axioms by revealing their layer-by-layer structure, starting with the constructible universe L as a ground model; only it seems to emerge a problem due to this very conception. One may have to justify the refutation of the existence of a large cardinal axiom generated by a counterexample, in line with the skeptic's view, while taking into account that by constructing the hierarchy of all lower-level inner models one has solved *in rem* the problem of existence of all smaller large cardinals. In other words, in acceding to still stronger large cardinal assumptions, e.g. in extending the Inner Model Program to the level of one supercompact cardinal ('ultimate L'), this 'ultimate' extension cannot serve any longer as the basis for the formal justification of the consistency of this large cardinal axiom or of any new one. In that case, we cannot hope to provide the formal consistency of any new large cardinal axiom in ignoring previous large cardinal axioms and for that reason ignoring structural considerations of 'ultimate L' ([37], pp. 115-117). Nevertheless, the 'ultimate' extension of the Inner Model Program (where no single formal axiom has been derived to this day) leads to the proof of the inconsistency of such axioms as that of the existence of a weak Reinhardt cardinal, (posing a serious challenge to the conception of the universe of sets by its problematic results), through a very detailed analysis. It looks impossible, though, that the structural characteristics of inner models in the upward scale of their hierarchical construction would not contain some sort of actual infinity assumption[16] and consequently an implicit acceptance of an infinity in presentational immediacy that would be originally constituted as a temporal whole within the immanence of consciousness.

An actual infinity in this sense, which is clearly not a spatiotemporally extensible natural infinity conditioned on the physical laws of causation, taken in presentational immediacy as a boundless mental horizon in terms of which one can perform discrete cognitive acts ideally *ad infinitum*, may be thought of as the objectification in reflection of an ever in-act subjectivity that 'sheds' its 'being' into 'being'-in temporally constituting. It is in terms of this approach, that we can have a reasonable connection of the character of the (founded in temporality) continental ego with the temporality of mathematical objects taken as registered-in formal-ontological objects that may be further thought of, on a temporal-constitutional level, as abstractions of temporal re-identifications of multiplicities of specific intentional cognitive acts.

7 Can mathematical continuum be reduced to a phenomenological continuum?

At this point the reader might rightfully wonder what all this talk about the temporal ego of the phenomenological school or that of the phenomenologically motivated existentialist school, taken as an 'in-act' subjectivity of consciousness, has to do with the notion of continuum in a formal mathematical theory

---

[16]I refer, in particular, to the definition of suitable extenders and of 'fantom' extenders, ([37], p. 115)

7. CAN MATHEMATICAL CONTINUUM BE REDUCED?

or in any case with any sort of mathematical activity. My answer to this reasonable objection is that it depends, in principle, on the general philosophical stance of someone doing mathematics and especially foundational mathematics. If he finds mathematics as a formal abstraction of some (possibly *a priori*) kind of relation we bear with mathematical objects in general, as presented upon us and further associated with certain functions of the human mind, he might then come to accept my discussion as meaningful indeed and my clues as making some headway towards a deeper understanding of mathematical continuum.

As a matter of fact, E. Husserl saw no essential difference, in terms of intentional orientation, between the intuition of physical and of mathematical objects. Even though, he considered the latter, especially in their standing as objects of a formal mathematical theory, as associated with a special kind of intuition (categorial intuition). A counterargument to this Husserlian view is put up by those who insist on an essential difference between mathematical and perceptual intuition on the grounds that while in perception objects of intuition are determinate and individually identifiable, this seems to be what is missing in the case of mathematical objects, e. g. in the mathematical intuition of the symbol $\emptyset$ standing for the empty set ([32], pp. 399-400). This particular counterargument can be overcome, in the first place, on the grounds that it may be taken to refer to a mere convention of formal language as much as the term absolute vacuum in the theory of physics seems to be. But there is more to it and goes deeper into the difference between physical and mathematical objects on the level of intentionality.

On this account, Husserl made a distinction on the intentional level between 'thingness'-substrates, (*sachhaltige Substraten*), referring generally to objects as bearers of a 'thingness' content and empty-substrates, (*Leersubstraten*), referring to 'empty somethings' together with their corresponding syntactical objectivities. The latter class of intentional objects as 'state-of-things' (*Sachverhalte*) with all categorial objectivities associated with them belong to a particular class of objects of pure logic as *mathesis universalis*; e.g. syntactical elements of set-theoretical formulas, numerals, functions and their well-defined Euclidean or non-Euclidean domains, belong to this class ([16], p. 33). For example, taking the reading of a pointer registering the measurement of a quantum experiment as a material sign, this sign regardless of its particular material content has a mode of being a sign-as such, and therefore as an intentional object (of hyletic-noetic perception)[17] it can be regarded as a 'state-of-things', in other words an 'empty something' which in noematic[18] constitution can be assigned, as a

---

[17]The 'objects' that are described as moments of hyletic-noetic perception can be only thought of as evident givennesses of intentionality without necessarily referring to a temporal-noematic constitution. For instance the color of a tree trunk, as a noematic object, is the invariably one and the same immanent object of temporal consciousness constituted through a multiplicity of real hyletic-noetic moments of the concrete experience intentionally directed to the particular tree trunk ([16], p. 226).

[18]A noematic object manifests itself as an immanence within the unity of the flux of a subject's consciousness and it is constituted by certain modes of being as such, i.e. a well-defined temporal object immanent to the unity of the flux. In contrast, a noetic object as a

well-defined object, a definite mathematical specification.[19] This subtle distinction between physical and mathematical objects can nevertheless be taken, on the phenomenological-intentional level, as motivating a unitary approach to put both objects under the same interpretational vantage point.

It is noteworthy, that K. Gödel in a supplement to his paper *"What is Cantor's Continuum problem?"* figured out that there is something more than just through sensations or combinations of sensations that physical objects are given to us, "e.g., the idea of object itself [...] Evidently, the 'given' underlying mathematics is closely related to the abstract elements contained in our empirical ideas." ([8], p. 398). His point was that, contrary to Kant's assertions, if these abstract constituents do not follow by some kind of action of things upon our sense organs they are nevertheless not purely subjective but they must represent some other kind of relationship between ourselves and reality. D. Føllesdal takes these abstract features and primarily Gödel's emphasis on the idea of the object itself as linked to a notion of individuation of objects that leads to the notions of identity and distinctness, and consequently to the process of counting, which makes them representable as principal mathematical elements ([8], p. 399). Given the aforementioned interpretation of syntactical objects of formal-mathematical logic as fundamentally intentional objects, this kind of individuation of objects can be taken as referring to their 'lowest-level' perception in the sense of irreducible individuals of intentionality.

At this stage, I have presumably given some clues to a possible unifying approach towards perceptual and mathematical objects, to consider specific mathematical objects, such as the choice sequences of intuitionistic mathematics,[20] as generated by applying both the so-called two-ity intuition and also the primordial intuition of intuitionistic mathematics. The intuitionistic approach to the continuum is not only to a large extent modelized, at least in the Brouwerian writings, after the phenomenology of time consciousness but also because it is exactly this approach that puts under a new point of view the fundamental difference between the two-ity intuition and the primordial intuition of mathematics, the latter being essentially the notion of intuitive continuum. L.E.J Brouwer in his early formation (Ph.D thesis, 1907) and later, made several comments on the intuitive continuum that can be said to be pretty much

---

multiplicity of real moments of hyletic-noetic perception, may be described solely in terms of its original givenness to the intentionality of consciousness.

[19] To come back to the instance of null set (∅) in mathematical theory, which presumably formalizes 'ontological' nothingness, we can say that since it presents itself as an original givenness of the intentionality of consciousness it will be absurd to call it nothingness in phenomenological sense; for, as an original givenness it is already a concrete fulfillment in time.

[20] Choice sequences as sequences unfolding in time progression were originally taken as a means to represent real points of continuum, and are generally divided to lawlike and lawless ones. What basically distinguishes a lawlike choice sequence from a lawless one is that the former even if not given by a prescribed formula, it is a determinate one and thus has a fixed horizon whereas the latter is fully or partially indeterminate one, whose horizon is not fixed in advance and where except for the obvious specification of the uniqueness of each value of the sequence anything can occur in its progression.

7. CAN MATHEMATICAL CONTINUUM BE REDUCED?

based on Husserl's description of temporal consciousness. This is also the case with H. Weyl, working independently, concerning his ideas on the matter in the well-known monograph *Das Kontinuum*.

I do not intend to enter into great details in describing Brouwer's or Weyl's approach of intuitive and further of mathematical continuum put up in accordance with phenomenological principles; van Atten *et al* offer a fine exposition on the matter in [33]. I'll rather draw attention to the radical difference between the 'first act of intuitionism' (two-ity intuition) and the 'primordial intuition of mathematics' (the foundation of intuitive continuum) and also to a phenomenological dimension of the graph-extensional version of the Weak Continuity Principle presented in [34].

The relevance of Brouwer's approach to the intuitive continuum with the phenomenological notion of the absolute flux of consciousness or even deeper with its subjective ego can be traced, in the first place, in his discussion of the intuitive continuum as the primordial intuition of mathematics: it is described as the "the substratum, divested of all quality, of any perception of change, a unity of continuity and discreteness, a possibility of thinking together several entities, connected by a 'between', which is never exhausted by the insertion of new entities", in which continuity and discreteness occur as inseparable complements and where it is impossible to construe one of them as a primitive entity without implicating the other in the same primitive sense ([33], p. 205).

The intuition of discreteness, called the two-ity intuition, is the empty form of all intuitions and provides the basis of the discrete aspect of the intuition of mathematics; by means of the two-ity intuition we can generate natural number sequences and also any finite combinatorial objects generated from natural numbers ([33], p. 206). As a matter of fact, Brouwer's two-ity intuition can be largely interpreted by means of the transversal intentionality of the flux of consciousness (*Querintentionalität*), in the scheme original impression-retention-protention, the two latter terms meant as *a priori* intentionalities towards respectively past and future (see: [18], §§ 11, 24). To the extent, though, that the two-ity intuition is abstracted as the empty form of the common substratum of all two-ities, it is conditioned on its free extensibility ideally *ad infinitum*, which points directly to the assumption of an underlying substratum in the sense of the primordial intuition of mathematics as referred to above. This is why, the two-ity intuition is associated with the discrete aspect of the primordial intuition of mathematics, later termed by Brouwer the 'first act of intuitionism'. It is clear, though, that the intuitive continuum in the aforementioned sense is a kind of impredicative infinity freely generated by human mind and, in view of my general approach, may be taken as founded on a temporal unity constituting subjective origin whose 'being' and 'being-in-constituting' can be conceived of as identical. As I have pointed out elsewhere in the text (p. 2), this infinity is not identifiable with the physical, theoretically *ad infinitum* extensible spatiotemporality, which is bound to the laws of causality and generally to mathematically representable empirical laws. It is a boundless infinity in presentational immediacy, in no other way apprehensible but as an objectified temporal whole within the immanence of consciousness, leading by essential necessity to an underlying subjectivity in the general sense of a temporality-constituting ego.[21]

In the intuitionistic approach, natural numbers are taken in abstraction as durationless points, whereas the same cannot be claimed about real numbers considered as incomplete objects. Yet, in the flow of inner time we are not aware of any durationless now-point, as there is no 'autonomous' present in original impression but rather a specious present composed *a priori* of original impression together with retention and protention. We could try, though, to approach a real point in the intuitive continuum by an infinite sequence of nested rational intervals the lengths of which converge to 0. This possibility, called the 'second act of intuitionism', allowed a modelization of intuitive continuum based on the generation of freely proceeding convergent sequences in which each real number as an ideally durationless point is characterized as the species of such non-lawlike sequences. To be close to his view of real numbers as incomplete objects, L.E.J. Brouwer regarded lawless sequences in the sense of indefinitely proceedable sequences as better representing intuitive continuum, e.g. a point P (representing a real number) to which a freely proceeding sequence of rational nested λ-intervals $\lambda_{\nu_1}, \lambda_{\nu_2}, .., \lambda_{\nu_n}, ..$ of the general form $[\frac{\alpha}{2^{\nu-1}}, \frac{\alpha+1}{2^{\nu-1}}]$ converges, is defined as the sequence itself and not something as a limiting point of the sequence ([33], p. 212).

It is noteworthy that both Brouwer and Weyl handled choice sequences in the logical formulas of Continuity Principles as complete and determinate objects, in spite of their infinite extensibility, to provide an intuitionistic foundation for real analysis. In this sense, intuitionistic continuity principles such as the Weak Continuity Principle (**WC-N**) are, in principle, black box principles extending *ad infinitum*, at least in the unrestricted case, the horizon of finitely many intentional acts of a generating subject to the vagueness of infinity; the latter idea presupposes the existence of an impredicative continuous substratum in the sense of the primordial intuition of mathematics.

In [34], the main motivation of Van Dalen *et al* for providing a a graph-extensional version (**GWC-N**) of the Weak Continuity Principle was to extend Brouwer's Weak Continuity Principle (**WC-N**)[22] to all kinds of choice sequences (lawlike and lawless alike), taking into account that any kind of restriction on the unfolding generation of the terms of a sequence stems from the noetic-noematic correlation of the intentional acts of a freely generating subject with the intensional properties of the sequence in question. Such restrictions accepting anyway the existing initial segment of the choice sequence could be definitive 'From now on restriction P_j^i holds and will not be revised any more' or provisional 'for an unspecified number of stages restriction P_j^i holds' ([34],

---

[21]Obviously, the presentation in previous sections of the versions of a general, purely subjective, time-constituting ego acquires its epistemological relevance in the context of this kind of discourse.

[22]This fundamental continuity principle has as a direct consequence the well-known intuitionistic theorem that all full functions are continuous and thus the continuum is unsplittable.

pp. 335-36).

Actually there is no difference between Van Dalen *et al* and L.E.J Brouwer, except for one, in the Continuity Principle for numbers below:

$$\forall \alpha \, \exists x \, A(\alpha, x) \implies \forall \alpha \, \exists m \exists x \forall \beta \, [\bar{\beta}m = \bar{\alpha}m \longrightarrow A(\beta, x)]$$

where α, β range over sequences of natural numbers, m, x over natural numbers and $\bar{\alpha}m$ stands for $< \alpha(0), ..., \alpha(m-1) >$, that is, the initial segment of sequence α of length m. The difference, in question, is that in **GWC-N** the predicate $A(\alpha, x)$ is stronger than extensional, in the classical definition of the term; it is graph-extensional which means that the choice sequence α enters $A(\alpha, x)$ only through its values. This given, what might be the role of the graph-extensionality of $A(\alpha, x)$ in **GWC-N**, in view of its capacity to cover the widest possible range of choice sequences and what does it mean from a deeper phenomenologically oriented view?

I propose to give the following interpretation in accordance with my general approach: any two-ity intuition can be conceived of as realized in terms of a noetic-noematic type generation of a sequence of natural numbers, where these numbers enter only as such, that is, by their values as 'general somethings', in the sense of distinct, irreducible *Etwas-überhaupt* in Husserlian sense (see, p. 262). Therefore, **GWC-N** Principle is, by this measure, a valid continuity principle as any restrictions on the part of a generating subject acting by phenomenological perception (*Wahrnehmung*) should be 'first-order' restrictions and restrictions of such a type in the context of discussion, might be considered the phenomenological perception of each new term of a choice sequence as an original impression, its immediate retention in consciousness and also the retention of the collection of the terms generated thus far, that is, of the initial segment of the sequence. The latter retention may be seen to refer to Husserl's longitudinal intentionality, which already bears the creeping transcendence of continuum in constituting the descending sequence of retentions as the continuous unity of a whole.

Consequently in this view, **GWC-N** may be taken as a proper continuity principle for choice sequences, as it eliminates by the graph-extensionality of the predicate $A(\alpha, x)$ any higher order restrictions on the generation of the terms of a sequence. Such restrictions, e.g. a provisional restriction of the type 'from now on, the choice sequence α is constant' cannot be taken of an intentional character. It is important to note that Van Dalen *et al* prove in [34], along with an alternative proof by A. Visser, that the original version of the Continuity Principle **WC-N** does not hold in general for extensional predicates, precisely by producing a higher order restriction in the process of a strictly numerical unfolding of the terms of the choice sequence (pp. 340-41).

8 The impredicativity of phenomenological continuum as reflected in formal theory

8.1 The place of actual infinity in the independence of CH

We saw that in intuitionistic theory, continuity of real analysis is basically founded on continuity principles such as those already referred to or on alternative versions of them (e.g. Brouwer's Universal Spread Law). On a deeper level, these principles are essentially conditioned on phenomenologically motivated assumptions such as the primordial intuition of mathematics and the first act of intuitionism.

In what concerns the Cantorian **ZF** theory, the formal introduction of mathematical continuum is primarily based on the application of three axioms: the Infinity Axiom, the Replacement Axiom and, most important, the Power Set Axiom. There is a fundamental difference between the latter two: The first one helps to define step-by step a new set by means of a functional predicate, whereas the second is a completely different axiomatical tool 'straightforwardly' generating a new richer set $\mathcal{P}(X)$ whose cardinality is greater than that of its base set X; it is well-known that in the case of a countably infinite collection it gives rise to the extremely rich set C whose cardinality is the cardinality of continuum. As P. Cohen put it, "it is unreasonable to expect that any description of a larger cardinal which attempts to build up that cardinal from ideas deriving from the Replacement Axiom can ever reach C". He was referring of course to the cardinality $\aleph_1$ of the set of all countable ordinals but also to cardinals such as $\aleph_2,...,\aleph_\omega, .., \aleph_\alpha, ...$ where $\alpha = \aleph_\omega$, etc., produced by a piecemeal process of construction starting from $\aleph_0$ and applying at each stage the Replacement Axiom. In that case C would be greater than each of these cardinals and the *Continuum Hypothesis* would be obvious false, something left to future generations to decide perhaps by seeing more clearly the problem ([4], p. 151).

In my view, the 'asymmetric' character of the Power Set Axiom with respect to the other axioms of **ZF** owes much to to the radical difference between two fundamental intuitions. The intuition of an *ad infinitum* enumeration of an aggregate of distinct objects, which can be thought of as the performance of a series of intentional acts close to the meaning of the two-ity intuition in intuitionistic analysis, and the act of forming subsets of (ideally) infinitely-run enumerations as objective wholes including their elements all at once in present actuality. The latter mental act should be by necessity a temporal constitution to ground the passing from the level of phenomenological perception of multiplicities of irreducible individuals and their passive association as retentional aggregates, to the collections or subcollections forming 'instantly' from them as objectivities in temporal unity. Phenomenologically speaking, we have to turn to inherently homogenous and consequently impredicative and non-analytic forms of the temporal flux to ground the objective unity of the multiplicities of immanent objects in consciousness constituted as temporal wholes. In the context of a formal mathematical theory, as instances of the immanent objects we are talking about, can be thought of objects-substrates of mathematical

8. IMPREDICATIVITY OF PHENOMENOLOGICAL CONTINUUM

theories in the sense of 'thingness-somethings' or rather 'empty-somethings' endowed with an *a priori* 'nucleus' of categorial objectivities (*Kernform*). As already pointed out, in a more fundamental level we can be led to a purely a-temporal transcendence which 'is' the absolute subjectivity behind the constituted continuous unity.

It is notable that there are already numerous mathematicians, mostly working in mathematical foundations, who have doubts about the possibility of defining continuum as a set or those who admit at least of a non-analytic character of the question of the cardinality of continuum. Among them, is S. Feferman who insists that **CH** is an inherently vague statement which cannot be settled by any new axioms added to **ZFC** theory, [7]. As far as **CH** is generally considered more than any other relevant conjecture linked to the nature of mathematical continuum and as its independence is proved to underlie the independence of other infinity statements within **ZFC** (e.g., Suslin's Hypothesis, the question of the conservation of c.c.c. property of the product of any two c.c.c. spaces), it is my intention in the next to stress the need of assuming the *Axiom of Choice* as an actual infinity axiom in the proof of the consistency of both **CH** and ¬ **CH** with the axioms of **ZFC**.

It is well-known that one of the common forms of the *Axiom of Choice* (**AC**), states that given a non-empty class of non-empty sets $\{X_i\}$, $i \in I$, we can choose exactly one element from each set in the class to form the non-empty product $\prod_{i \in I} X_i$. It is also known that this axiom, characterized as an actual infinity axiom by certain non-standard set-theorists, in the sense of being conditioned on an actual infinity mentally constituted in presentational immediacy, is applied to produce the independence of *Continuum Hypothesis*. As a matter of fact, it is at least indirectly presupposed in Gödel's proof of the consistency of **CH** with the axioms of **ZF** and in P. Cohen's proof (by the forcing method) of the consistency of ¬ **CH** with the rest of the axioms of **ZF**.

In the rest of this subsection I will attempt to sketch a phenomenologically oriented interpretation of **AC** and then bring out its implicit role in the proof of the consistency of ¬ **CH** with the rest of axioms of **ZFC**[23] as it gives a strong clue to the assertion that no matter what model we are working in (e.g. a countable transitive base model M in the theory of forcing) we have to assume some actual infinity principle to prove any conjecture about uncountable infinity. Before dealing with this, I will try to bring out the fundamental metatheoretical importance of the notion of absoluteness of mathematical objects (or formulas) and also that of the transitivity of sets (or structures) in establishing crucial foundational results, for instance, independence results by the forcing method.

To be more specific, the metatheoretical (in fact, phenomenologically motivated) meaning possibly given to the notion of absoluteness, e.g. of atomic formulas, is the invariable conservation of the possibility to be intentionally oriented towards a 'general something' in the sense of an irreducible *Etwas-*

---

[23]The role of **AC** in proving **CH** can be also seen, in working within Gödel's constructible universe L, insofar as the Axiom of Constructibility **V**=**L** implies **AC**, (see: [23], p. 175).

überhaupt, irrespective of a 'thingness' (*sachhaltiges Substrat*) or absolutely 'empty' content (*Leer-etwas*), in the unfolding of arbitrary extensions within the formal-ontological domain of formal (transitive) structures. In general, these extensions are meant to be associated with a notion of actual infinity in presentational immediacy, for instance, in acceding to the metatheoretical content of the infinity statement $MA(\kappa)$ for any cardinal $\kappa > \omega$ in the forcing method, or yet to be associated with the notion of impredicatively specified sets required in the proof of the consistency of **CH** with the axioms of **ZFC**.

A key question in trying to establish independence results by forcing techniques, is to ensure that people 'living' within a countable transitive model M can force any axiom of set theory to be true in extended forcing model $M[G]$ without even having an intuition of what a generic set G really is, which means without acceding to the generic nature of G consequently without acceding to its metatheoretical meaning. As it comes out, the generic character of G is proved in taking account of the countability of the base model M and the absoluteness of notions such as 'partial order' or 'dense' for M, otherwise as generally the generic set G may not belong to M it would then be needed the extra countable chain condition (c.c.c.) of the partial order P, a fact that points to a higher than countable infinity statement and moreover indirectly leads to an independence result since the question of whether the product of any two c.c.c. spaces is c.c.c., is independent of **ZFC** theory ([23], p. 50).

To come back to the question of possibly ensuring that the forcing relation $p \models y$ can be decided within a countable transitive model M of **ZFC**, K. Kunen established, in [23], the equivalence of the formula $p \Vdash \phi(\tau_1, .., \tau_n)$, generally defined in universal set V, with the relativized to M formula $p \Vdash^* \phi(\tau_1, .., \tau_n)$. The most difficult part in establishing this equivalence, is in taking the formula $\phi(\tau_1, \tau_2)$ to be the atomic formula $\tau_1 = \tau_2$.

My reference to this particular example is intended to demonstrate the relevance of the concept of absoluteness in securing that the forcing formula $p \Vdash y$ can be decided within a countable model M. As a matter of fact, absoluteness of ordinals will also prove to be of critical importance in reaching the seemingly paradoxical 'collapse' of uncountable cardinals within the countable base model M in the proof of independence of the *Continuum Hypothesis*, ([23], pp. 205-208). At the moment, I note that the question of whether $p \Vdash^* \tau_1 = \tau_2$ must depend on whether $q \Vdash^* \pi_1 = \pi_2$ for various q in the forcing partially ordered set P, and for $\pi_1 \in \text{dom}(\tau_1)$, $\pi_2 \in \text{dom}(\tau_2)$. As it stands out, due to the definition by recursion of a characteristic function $\mathbf{H}(P, \tau)$ of a P-name[24] τ, one can prove the absoluteness of $\mathbf{H}$ and consequently of a P-name τ for

---

[24]In forcing theory, a P-name τ is the definition by transfinite recursion of a 'label' corresponding to an object τ_G in extended forcing model $M[G]$. A P-name τ is defined as the binary relation τ where

$$\forall <\sigma, p> \in \tau \, [\sigma \text{ is a } P\text{-name} \wedge p \in P]$$

'Inhabitants' of the countable model M can, in principle, comprehend the P-name τ, while they will possibly not comprehend its corresponding object τ_G as it requires knowledge of forcing set G that is generally not a subset of M, (see:: [23], pp. 186-89).

8. IMPREDICATIVITY OF PHENOMENOLOGICAL CONTINUUM 263

transitive models of **ZF**, by going back to absoluteness of more fundamental set-theoretic relations, e.g. of the $\in$ or $\cup$ relations, within transitive models of **ZF** (minus the power-set axiom).[25] Further, based on the recursive definition of a P-name $\hat{x}$ in terms of $\hat{x} = \{<\hat{y}, 1_P>;\ y \in x\}$, where 1_P is the largest element of partial order P, and the absoluteness of this definition essentially due to the absoluteness of atomic formula $y \in x$ for transitive models of **ZFC**, it is also proved that the P-name $\hat{x}$ corresponding to an object x of M is identified with that object x, which means that that the forcing model $M[G]$ is indeed an extension of M, that is, $M \subset M[G]$.

Turning to the underlying intuition of **AC**, it can be summed up as extending, in principle, over an indefinite horizon the right to uniquely 'observe' and treat individuals as such and at least in $\in$-inclusion relation with any aggregate of them.

On a level of constitution, we may say that as a particular individual-substrate is in original givenness the object of intentionality at the 'lowest level' of phenomenological perception, there exists a notion of ordering by the sole virtue of the intentional 'property' of the object in question to bear an outer horizon, i.e. that part of the Life-World which is not the object or part of the object, thereby defining in complementary sense the field of next potential 'observations'. Consequently a notion of well-ordering is immanently induced by representing an intentional individual as a noematic individual possibly belonging to a multiplicity of other such objects in the constituting flux of consciousness. Now, what is left after discarding all other details of constitution is the possibility to intentionally 'observe' in re-iterating cognitive acts individuals-substrates as protentions of intentionality in the domain of 'observation'. Moreover, the *Axiom of Choice* presupposes a notion of actual infinity in presentational immediacy in the sense of an objective and invariably existing continuous substratum on which to 'embed' intentional individuals as well-defined, distinct objects in continuous unity.

In summing up this phenomenologically motivated interpretation, **AC** can be interpreted as founded first on the existence of a subject performing cognitive acts of an intentional character theoretically *ad infinitum* and second, on the evidence of a constituting flux of consciousness in the continuous unity of which any intentionally apprehended object can be constituted as a temporal, well-defined and uniquely determined (in varying predicative situations) noematic object. Any such object can be defined both as an objectivity in-itself and in some kind of relation (e.g. of order) to any other. Grounded then as a well-defined noematic object in its *a priori* categorial environment, it can be attributed with proper sense mathematical properties e.g. extensionality, a

---

[25] As a matter of fact, these set-theoretical formulas are reducible to Δ_0 formulas, which are easily proved to be absolute for any transitive model M, ([23], pp. 118-19). It is notable, in turn, the the inductive definition of Δ_0 formulas can lead to a metatheoretical reduction of their absoluteness, within transitive models, to the possibility of invariably projecting the individuality of syntactical atoms (as syntactically indecomposable individuals) and their associated nonlogical predicate $\in$ throughout any extension of their base model under set-inclusion.

notion of order in formal mathematical sense, etc.

I do not intend to enter into a detailed exposition of P. Cohen's theory of forcing in view of a metatheoretical assessment of the role of **AC** in the proof of the consistency of ¬ **CH** with **ZFC**.[26] Instead, I'll try to be as clear as possible in the presentation of my arguments.

Generally, in forcing techniques we rely on global properties forced to objects such as to functions f_G of a forcing model $M[G]$ by means of a P-generic set G over a countable transitive base model M, where P is a poset of forcing conditions $(P, \leq)$ in M. The P-generic set $G \in M[G]$ can be roughly said to have the property of a special filter to force compatible extensions of any condition p over M and it is moreover very generic in the sense of having non-empty intersection with any dense set of conditions in M.

Now we are going to see that the generic properties of G can lead to contradictions in case the poset $(P, \leq)$ of conditions is not c.c.c..[27] The c.c.c condition is a necessary constraint to be satisfied by a set of conditions P of M in the process of the proof of consistency of ¬ **CH** as it preserves cardinalities between the base model M and the extended model $M[G]$ ([23], p. 207). As a matter of fact in the classical proof of consistency of ¬ **CH** with **ZFC**, we can, based on the Δ-system Lemma,[28] define a proper set of conditions, namely the set of finite partial functions $\mathrm{Fn}(\kappa \times \omega, \mathbf{2})$ from $\kappa \times \omega$ into $\mathbf{2}$ (κ an uncountable cardinal of M), satisfying c.c.c..[29] It turns out, though, that the proof of Δ-system Lemma for $\mathrm{Fn}(\kappa \times \omega, \mathbf{2})$ needs the **AC**.

It may now have become clear the necessity of the c.c.c. constraint for the partially ordered set $\mathrm{Fn}(\kappa \times \omega, \mathbf{2})$, as it reduces uncountably infinite possibilities in the domain of conditions $\mathrm{Fn}(\kappa \times \omega, \mathbf{2})$ to countably many compatible extensions of these conditions. Let us keep in mind that forcing a compatible extension g for any condition p in M and this way *ad infinitum* is a definite cognitive act in actual presence and by virtue of this it can be abstracted as a discrete act of a performing subject in time progression. In the mathematical context we discuss, these acts should correspond to an open-ended class of countably many compatible extensions. Indeed, this is ensured by the c.c.c. condition which, in the case of the proof of consistency of ¬ **CH**, is based on

---

[26] For a detailed exposition of forcing theory the reader may consult P. Cohen's original *Set Theory and the Continuum Hypothesis* [4], K. Kunen's *Set Theory. An Introduction to Independence Proofs* [23] or F. Drake's & D. Singh's *Intermediate Set Theory* [5].

[27] A partial order $(P, \leq)$ has the *Countable Chain Condition* (c.c.c.) iff every antichain (any family of pairwise incompatible elements) of the poset P is countable. Letting $P \neq \emptyset$, the elements $p, q \in P$ are defined as compatible if,

$$(\text{for } p, q \in P)\ \exists r \in P\ (r \preceq p \wedge r \preceq q)$$

that is, r extends both p and q in the usual intuition of extension. For example, if p, q are finite partial functions from ω to $\mathbf{2}$ and $p \leq q$ iff $q \subset p$, then p and q are compatible iff they agree on $\mathrm{dom}(p) \cap \mathrm{dom}(q)$ in which case $p \cup q$ is a common extension of p and q.

[28] A family $\mathcal{C}$ of sets is called a Δ-system iff there is a fixed (finite) set r, called the root of the Δ-system, such that $a \cap b = r$ whenever a, b are distinct members of $\mathcal{C}$.

[29] The same approach essentially applies for the proof of θ-chain condition for a set of partial functions of a larger then ω cardinality $\mathrm{Fn}(I, J, \lambda)$ (see: [23], pp. 212-213).

8. IMPREDICATIVITY OF PHENOMENOLOGICAL CONTINUUM

the application of Δ-system Lemma mentioned above.[30]

This is, in fact, what the c.c.c. condition is all about: it eliminates an uncountable number of incompatible conditions p, meaning that even in the case of uncountable numbers in the domain or range of such conditions we can nevertheless proceed with countably many compatible extensions of them and on this account apply the statement $MA(\kappa)$ and define a fairly generic set G. In a more intuitive nuance, the c.c.c. property opens up the possibility of 'suppressing' a uncountable infinity factor underlying the domain of definition of forcing conditions p_α, in view of forming (in countably many steps) compatible and consistent extensions of p_α something that could, in principle, be linked to discrete noetic-noematic acts of a performing subject.

As the c.c.c. condition, which is satisfied, in general, by finite partial functions $\text{Fn}(I, J)$ of a countable range J, is mostly based on the Δ-system property of $\text{Fn}(I, J)$ (and the countability of J), and since in turn the Δ-system Lemma depends on the application of the *Axiom of Choice*, I think that I have somehow managed to bring out the implicit need to turn to some form of actual infinity principle to prove, in an essentially discrete 'operational' context, a statement involving uncountable cardinalities.

8.2 How to interpret the undecidability of infinity statements inside ZF theory?

A major step in proving the incompleteness of a recursive consistent extension T of **ZF** is to prove that the set of theorems of T is not recursive ([23], pp. 38-41). In this proof the notion of a recursive (or decidable) set, which may be intuitively linked to the discrete way an 'observer' applies his intentional 'observation' with regard to an enumerable collection of distinct elements possibly by the intermediary of a digital device, is playing a key role by the application of the following theorem. This theorem represents recursive sets such as the set of natural numbers or the set of finite sequences by formulas of **ZF**.

THEOREM 8.1. *Given any recursive set R of natural numbers there is a formula $\chi_R(x)$ which represents R in the sense that for all n,*

$$n \in R \longrightarrow (\mathbf{ZF} \vdash \chi_R(\ulcorner n \urcorner) \text{ and } n \notin R \, (\mathbf{ZF} \vdash \neg \chi_R(\ulcorner n \urcorner))$$

Recursive sets of finite sequences and recursive predicates in several variables are likewise representable.

I note that this theorem is proved in metatheory that is, in a language referring to finitistic metatheoretical objects by means of natural numbers in the place of symbols introduced in an extension of **ZF** by definitions. It is easy to prove the following very important outcome, namely that the set of theorems of a consistent and recursive set of axioms T, is itself not recursive ([24], pp. 345-346).

---

[30]The mathematically motivated reader is referred to an example offered in [23], (p. 55), showing how the non-existence of the c.c.c. property of $(P, \leq)$ can lead to inconsistencies.

THEOREM 8.2. *Let T be any consistent set of axioms extending* **ZF**. *Then the set of theorems $\{y;\ T \vdash y\}$ is not recursive.*

Based on 8.2, we can proceed straightforward to the proof of Gödel's *First Incompleteness Theorem*, namely that if T is a recursive consistent extension of **ZF** then it is incomplete in the sense that there is a sentence φ such that $T \nvdash \varphi$ and $T \nvdash \neg \phi$ ([23], p. 38). Considering T to be **ZF**, its incompleteness is de facto demonstrated by the undecidability of the *Axiom of Choice* (**AC**) (**ZF** $\nvdash$ **AC** and **ZF** $\nvdash$ ¬**AC**) and in case T is extended to **ZFC** by the undecidability of *Continuum Hypothesis* (**CH**) (**ZFC** $\nvdash$ **CH** and **ZFC** $\nvdash$ ¬**CH**).[31] It turns out, though, that the whole proof-theoretical machinery in constructing incompleteness results involves the so-called Level-2 assertions, e.g. those of the type

$$\mathbf{ZF} \vdash \forall x \in \omega,\ \mathcal{X}_{\mathrm{odd}}(x) \vee \mathcal{X}_{\mathrm{odd}}(x + \ulcorner 1 \urcorner) \quad (1)$$

where there is no rigorously defined finitistic character of objects x in metatheoretical sense. On this account, there is room for some discussion concerning a loose sense of finitistic, in other words, a 'shade' of actual infinity in the level of metatheory, leading, in effect, to the incompleteness results ([24], pp. 349-351).

As a matter of fact, there have been expressed serious doubts concerning the truth or falsity of **CH**, that is, as to whether any new axioms will settle the matter, alluding to an inherent vagueness of the statement that seems to point to some kind of non-analytic character. It is noteworthy that around 1947 in *What is Cantor's Continuum Problem*, ([10]), K. Gödel claimed that if Cantorian theory completely describes some well-defined reality then it should ultimately decide **CH** as either true or false and its eventual undecidability would mean that the difficulties of the problem "are perhaps not purely mathematical". It was well after his views at the time, that P. Cohen (1962) proved the independence of **CH** from the rest of axioms of **ZFC** (along with that of **AC** from **ZF**), thus leaving the discussion open till now as to their fundamental character inside Cantorian set theory.

My view is that there should be some inherent reason for these particular sentences to be proved independent from the existing **ZF-(C)** theory. In one or the other way, these and any other statements making claims about the nature and properties of actual infinity touch on what is by its very nature non-analytic, that is essentially, on what ultimately underlies continuous unity as an objective whole; for instance, on what is making possible to conceive the m first terms $(< \alpha(0), ..., \alpha(m-1) >)$ of an unfolding choice sequence all at once in actuality, in the assumption of a continuity principle in intuitionistic analysis. Or, in yet another instance, on the possibility to assume the Power-Set Axiom and determine the set $\mathcal{P}(\omega)$ of all subsets of ω (the first countable limit ordinal) as an actually existing collection of finitistic objects.

To turn the discussion on a fundamental level, talking about the possibility of reflecting on a continuous whole as an objectivity, is a way of introducing a

---

[31] Generally, no matter how we extend **ZF** to a recursive consistent T the First Incompleteness Theorem guarantees that there will always be sentences undecidable by T.

8. IMPREDICATIVITY OF PHENOMENOLOGICAL CONTINUUM

subjectivity upon which it should be rooted this possibility and this subjectivity should not be reducible to any kind of objectivity for then it would belong to the universe of all possible objectivities. In a yet deeper leap of thought it should be a non-temporal subjectivity which in an essential and not incidental way can only constitute and not be constituted and on this account it cannot be predicated even by the predicates of existence and individuality for it should then be an objectivity in constituted temporality. Then we are left with no analytic means to describe it and the only ontologically meaningful way to talk about it, is to take its objective 'mirror'-reflexion as an ever-instantiated continuous whole which by necessity reflects its inherent impredicativity on the formal-mathematical level; for instance, in the special inclusion relation part/whole in which the part belongs to the same lowest genus as the undivided whole. Or, in another instance, in inducing circularities in those definitions where the *definiens* cannot be defined but in terms of the *definiendum* (e.g., in the definition of an open interval of the real line).

In this way we are led to two fundamentally distinct levels of perception. The constituted one on which to 'embed' the known predicative universe of any analytic theory naturally including any formal - mathematical discipline and the constituting one which seems to be a pure impredicative substratum. This way inquiring on whether the cardinality of $\mathcal{P}(\omega)$ should be equal or greater to the next cardinality of countable ω in the canonical scale (in general, whether *Generalized Continuum Hypothesis* (**GCH**) holds: $2^{\aleph_\alpha} = \aleph_{\alpha+1}$, for any ordinal α) seems to reduce on a fundamental level and irrespectively of any particular cardinalities on the canonical scale involved, to the fundamentally distinct character between what belongs to the constituted level of reality, that is, what is predicable and analytically expressible by first-order means in a countable number of steps and what constitutes this very level, objectified as a continuous unity whose analytic description necessarily engenders some kind of circularity. To cite an example, producing a sequence of finitistic objects as subsets of ω by some digital device is a recursively enumerable process and it belongs to the constituted level. But this is done against the backdrop of the constituting level which makes possible to conceive the collection $\mathcal{P}(\omega)$ of all subsets of ω as a constituted objective whole in presentational immediacy.

The discussion above can lead to a two-fold claim: 1) insofar as finitistic metatheoretical objects are taken by some form of intuition as unique and well-defined objects and in phenomenological approach by a noetic-noematic constitution as well-defined objects of finitely many intentional acts in the open-ended horizon of experience, they may define a recursive set in the well-meant sense of 8.1, and they can therefore be represented by means of set-theoretical formulas as 'lawful' formal objects in any consistent extension of **ZF**, 2) in the case, though, they are not rigorously finitistic and let a shade of actual infinity (in presentational immediacy) in their metatheoretical content, in a sense contrary to the above, 'slip' through the syntactical structure of respective theorems, they eventually produce non-recursiveness of set-theoretical deductions and subsequently undecidability results on a formal-theoretical level.

9 Conclusion

In this article I have attempted to provide a meaningful approach to a possible connection between the transcendent character of the continental ego as fundamentally a temporality-founded ego and the temporality associated with certain objects of the epistemic domain, in the present work mainly with quantum observables and mathematical objects as syntactical objects of formal-axiomatical theories bearing though a specific metatheoretical content. In doing so, I mostly referred to particular creeds of the so-called continental philosophy, namely to the existentialist approaches towards mental ego of J.P. Sartre and M. Heidegger and to the phenomenological analysis of the pure ego of consciousness of E. Husserl. There was of no less importance my scope of bringing about a common holistic base in dealing with epistemic objects, seemingly as completely diverse in a first reading as, e.g. quantum objects/state-of-affairs and their formal-mathematical counterparts, which may be founded in their view as (i) registered-in objects of some kind of *a priori* motivated mental act and (ii) as temporally constituted objects referred to an original time-constituting subjectivity. At first sight the question of such a connection might strike someone as being rather arbitrary, almost bizzare. Certainly it is not the kind of stuff that would make a naive platonist or an unrepenting formalist eager to applause. Yet, there is an approach some decades now towards a view of mathematical activity and mathematical objects as intimately linked to mental processes and consequently to concrete modes of functioning of the brain or even deeper to subjective states of consciousness. That there would be possibly an association of a yet largely unexplored content between the modes of constitution of consciousness and pending interpretational questions concerning unconventional quantum effects such as quantum entanglement states or the collapse of superposition states and also, on the formal level, of undecidability results about continuum seems grounded, in principle, on the general assumption that quantum objects/state-of-affairs are by essential necessity constituted as objectivities in the presence of at least one classical-level observer and that mathematical objects are special cases of perceptual objects. The latter argument about mathematical objects taken, though, in the sense that these objects involve some kind of noematic-temporal constitution and as lowest-level syntactical objects of formal theories imply, on the metatheoretical level, a phenomenologically described *a priori* orientation (call it intentionality) on the part of a knowing subject.

A relevant question here seems to be the kind of influence on the analytic level of theory that a reduction of non-local quantum results or of mathematical higher infinity statements as fundamentally referring to a problem of temporal constitution on the part of corresponding subject might have. It is hard to tell in view of the ontological (not kinematic) character of the analytic tools of any formal theory but it could possibly offer a whole new approach to these questions and perhaps an interconnection with other epistemological disciplines (e.g. microphysics of the brain, neurobiology, philosophy of mind, etc.).

9. CONCLUSION

In my view, the pending question at the core of this discussion is whether there is something transcendental, almost bordering to the 'mystical', in the self-constitution and the 'ever-in-act' character of the temporal ego, in general, as the ultimate source of the temporal unity of the World and its objects (including mathematical ones). Or whether, e.g. the elusive 'inner' state of an entangled quantum system in performing a quantum measurement or yet the impredicative character of mathematical continuum or of any actual infinity statement, rather stems from the fact that one may not be entitled to a consistent and complete description of the objects of a domain - be it a physical or a mathematical one - that contains among its objects the domain itself and moreover the questioning subject.

In any case, the fact that a reduction to some kind of original temporality-constituting subjectivity can be established *in rem* seems almost undeniable.

BIBLIOGRAPHY

[1] Adorno, T.: (1982), *Against Epistemology: A Metacritique*, Oxford: B. Blackwell Publisher Ltd.
[2] Bernet, R.: (1994), *La vie du sujet*, Paris: ed. PUF.
[3] Bohm, D & Hiley, J. B.: (1995), *The undivided universe*, New York: Routledge.
[4] Cohen, P.: (1966), *Set Theory and the Continuum Hypothesis*, Mass.: W.A. Benjamin.
[5] Drake, F., Singh, D.: (1996), *Intermediate Set Theory*, Chichester: J. Wiley & Sons.
[6] Enderton, H.: (1972), *A Mathematical Introduction to Logic*, New York: Academic Press.
[7] Feferman, S.: (1999), Does mathematics need new axioms?, *American Mathematical Monthly*, 106, 99-111.
[8] Føllesdal, D.: (1999), Gödel and Husserl, *Naturalizing Phenomenology*, Ch. 13, pp. 385-400, Stanford Ca: Stanford Univ. Press.
[9] French, S. (2002). A Phenomenological Solution to the Measurement Problem? Husserl and the Foundations of Quantum Mechanics, *Studies in History and Philosophy of Modern Physics*, 33, 467-491.
[10] Gödel, K.: (1947), What is Cantor's Continuum Problem, *The American Mathematical Monthly*, 54, 9, pp. 515-25.
[11] Heelan, P.: (1988), *Space-Perception and the Philosophy of Science*, University of California Press.
[12] Heidegger, M.: (1996), *Being and Time. A Translation of Sein und Zeit*, transl. J. Stambaugh, Albany: State University of New York Press.
[13] Husserl, E. (1962), *Die Krisis der Europäischen Wissenschaften und die Transzendentale Phänomenologie*, Hua Band VI, hsgb. W. Biemel, Den Haag: M. Nijhoff.
[14] Husserl, E.: (1974), *Formale und Transzendentale Logik*, Hua Band XVII, hsgb. P. Janssen, Den Haag: M. Nijhoff.
[15] Husserl, E.: (1984), *Logische Untersuchungen*, Hua Band XIX1, (zweiter Band, erster Teil), hsgb. U. Panzer, Den Haag: M. Nijhoff.
[16] Husserl, E.: (1976), *Ideen zu einer reinen Phänomenologie und phänomenologischen Philosophie, Erstes Buch*, Hua Band III/I, hsgb. Karl Schuhmann, Den Haag: M. Nijhoff.
[17] Husserl, E.: (1983), *Ideas pertaining to a pure phenomenology and to a phenomenological philosophy*, First Book, transl. F. Kersten, The Hague: M. Nijhoff.
[18] Husserl, E.: (1966), *Vorlesungen zur Phänomenologie des inneren Zeibewusstseins*, Hua Band X, hsgb. R. Boehm, Den Haag: M. Nijhoff.
[19] Husserl, E.: (1973), *Ding und Raum*, Hua Band XVI, hsgb. U. Claesges, Den Haag: M. Nijhoff.
[20] Husserl, E.: (2001), *Logical Investigations*, transl. J. N. Findlay, (ed. D. Moran), London & New York: Routledge.

[21] Husserl, E.: (2001), *Späte Texte über Zeitkonstitution, Die C-Manuscripte*, Hua Materialien Band VIII, hsgb. D. Lohmar, Dordrecht: Springer.
[22] Kleene, S.C.: (1980), *Introduction to Metamathematics*, New-York: North-Holland Pub. Co.
[23] Kunen, K.: (1982), *Set Theory. An Introduction to Independence Proofs*, Amsterdam: Elsevier Sc. Pub.
[24] Livadas, S.: (2009), The Leap from the Ego of Temporal Consciousness to the Phenomenology of Mathematical Continuum, *Manuscrito* (Revista Internacional de Filosofia), 32, 2, pp. 321-356.
[25] Livadas, S.: (2012), Are mathematical theories reducible to non-analytic foundations?, *Axiomathes Online*, DOI 10.1007/s10516-012-9182-3.
[26] Lohmar, D.: (2002), Elements of a Phenomenological Justification of Logical Principles, including an Appendix [...] on the Transfiniteness of the Set of Real Numbers, *Philosophia Mathematica*, 10, 3, pp. 227-250.
[27] London, F., Bauer, E. (1983). The theory of Observation in Quantum Mechanics, in: J.A. Wheeler & W.H. Zurek (Eds.), *Quantum Theory and Measurement*, (pp. 217-259). Princeton: Princeton University Press.
[28] Merlan, P.: (1947), Time Consciousness in Husserl and Heidegger, *Philosophy and Phenomenological Research*, 8, 1, pp. 23-54.
[29] Patočka, J.: (1992), *Introduction à la phénoménologie de Husserl*, Grenoble: Ed. Millon.
[30] Sartre, J.P.: (1943), *L' être et le néant*, Paris: Ed. Gallimard.
[31] Shoenfield, J: (1967), *Mathematical Logic*, Addison Wesley Pub.
[32] Tieszen, R.: (1984), Mathematical Intuition and Husserl's Phenomenology, *Noŭs*, 18, 3, pp. 395-421.
[33] van Atten, M., van Dalen, D. & Tieszen, R.: (2002), Brouwer and Weyl: The Phenomenology and Mathematics of the Intuitive Continuum, *Philosophia Mathematica*, 10, 3, pp. 203-226.
[34] van Atten, M., van Dalen, D.: (2002), Arguments for the Continuity Principle, *The Bulletin of Symbolic Logic*, 8, 3, pp. 309-347.
[35] von Neumann, J.: (1955), *Mathematical Foundations of Quantum Mechanics*, Princeton: Princeton University Press.
[36] Woodin, H. W.: (2011), The continuum hypothesis, the generic-multiverse of sets and the Ω conjecture, in: *Set Theory, Arithmetic and Foundations of Mathematics*, New York: Cambridge University Press.
[37] Woodin, H. W. & Heller M. (eds.): (2011), *Infinity, New Research Frontiers*, New York: Cambridge University Press.

www.ingramcontent.com/pod-product-compliance
Lightning Source LLC
Chambersburg PA
CBHW050132170426
43197CB00011B/1810